AQA Psychology B

AS

Exclusively endorsed by AQA

Mark Billingham
Sarah Ladbrook
Sue Standring
Regina Teahan

Nelson Thornes

Published in 2008 by:
Nelson Thornes Ltd
Delta Place
27 Bath Road
CHELTENHAM
GL53 7TH
United Kingdom

11 12 / 10 9 8 7 6 5

A catalogue record for this book is available from the British Library

ISBN 978 0 7487 9826 1

Cover photograph by Photolibrary

Illustrations include artwork drawn by Angela Knowles, Peters and Zabransky UK Ltd, Harry
Venning (concept by Don Stubbs) and Wearset Ltd

Page make-up by Wearset Ltd

Printed in China by 1010 Printing International Ltd

The authors and publisher would like to thank the following for permission to reproduce
material:
p3: Science Photo Library / Simon Fraser; p7: (top to bottom) Getty Images / Time &
Life Pictures; Getty Images / Yvonne Hemsey; p16: Getty Images / Imagno; p19: Natalie
Rogers; p28: Getty Images / Dan McCoy – Rainbow; p29: (top to bottom) Alamy / Medical-
on-Line; Getty Images / UHB Trust; p34: Getty Images / Dave M. Benett; p43: Alamy /
Andrew Paterson; p44: Getty Images / Kurt Vinion / Stringer; p46: (top to bottom) Rex
Features / Mike Daines; Rex Features / Huw Evans; p50: National Anthropological Archives,
Smithsonian Institution, 02440800 / 85-8666; p52: Image courtesy of the Advertising
Archives; p64: Getty Images / Katja Zimmermann; p65: Getty Images / Altrendo Images;
p75: (top to bottom) Alamy / Digital Vision; Getty Images / Pam Francis; p83: Alamy
/ Neil McAllister; p127: Alamy / © JUPITERIMAGES / BananaStock; p138: From the
film Obedience (© 1968) by Stanley Milgram, © renewed by Alexandra Milgram, and
distributed by Penn State Media Sales; p195: Science Photo Library / Tony Craddock;
p217: Psychology Archives – The University of Akron; p213: Alamy / Andrew Paterson;
p215: Getty / Davies and Starr; P235: Alamy / Corbis Premium RF; p246: PECS products,
Pyramid Educational Consultants UK Ltd.

p27: Fig. 7, 'The Response of a Simple Cell', Introduction to Psychology 14th ed., Atkins,
Hilgard, Smith, Hoeksema, Fredrick, © 2003 Wadsworth, part of Cengage Learning Inc, Figs
5–12, p163. Reproduced with permission; p129: Fig. 1, Yerkes Dodson law, 'The Relation of
Strength of Stimulus to Rapidity of Habit-Formation', Robert M. Yerkes and John D. Dodson,
Journal of Comparative Neurology & Psychology, 18, 459–489, 1908. Published by John
Wiley Inc.; p133: Fig. 3, The Psychology of Social Norms by Muzafer Sherif, 1936; p160:
Figs 2, 3, Flow diagram (Fig. 3.1) and Relationship between attitude, object attitude and
the three aspects (after Eagly and Chaiken 1993) (Fig. 4.1), Essential Social Psychology by
D. C. Pennington, Edward Arnold 1986. Reprinted with permission of Hodder Educational;
p241: Fig. 7, example of an embedded figure, A Manual for the Embedded Figures Test,
Witkin, Oltman, Raskin and Karp. Reprinted with permission of Mind Garden Inc; p241:
Fig. 8, The Ebbinghaus illusion, Hermann Ebbinghaus 1850–1909; p243: Fig. 9, example
of the Wisconsin Card Sorting Task. Reproduced by special permission of the publisher,
Psychological Assessment Resources, Inc., 16204 North Florida Avenue, Lutz, Florida
33549, from the Wisconsin Card Sorting Test by David A. Grant, PhD and Esta A. Berg,
PhD, copyright 1981, 1993 by Psychological Assessment Resources, Inc. (PAR). Further
reproduction is prohibited without permission of PAR.

Contents

AQA introduction   iv

Introduction for students   vi

Unit 1
Introducing psychology

Biopsychology and other key
approaches: introduction   2

1   Key approaches   4

2   Biopsychology   21

     Examination-style questions for
     Biopsychology and other key approaches   40

Gender development: introduction   42

3   Gender development   44

     Examination-style questions for
     Gender development   79

Research methods: introduction   82

4   Research methods   84

     Examination-style questions for
     Research methods   123

Unit 2
Social psychology, Cognitive psychology and Individual differences

Social psychology: introduction   126

5   Social influence   128

     Examination-style questions for
     Social influence   147

6   Social cognition   148

     Examination-style questions for
     Social cognition   167

Cognitive psychology: introduction   168

7   Remembering and forgetting   170

     Examination-style questions for
     Remembering and forgetting   190

8   Perceptual processes   191

     Examination-style questions for
     Perceptual processes   211

Individual differences: introduction   212

9   Anxiety disorders   214

     Examination-style questions for
     Anxiety disorders   230

10   Autism   231

     Examination-style questions for
     Autism   249

     References   250

     Index   258

AQA introduction

Nelson Thornes has worked in partnership with AQA to ensure this book and the accompanying online resources offer you the best support for your A level course.

All resources have been approved by senior AQA examiners so you can feel assured that they closely match the specification for this subject and provide you with everything you need to prepare successfully for your exams.

These print and online resources together **unlock blended learning**; this means that the links between the activities in the book and the activities online blend together to maximise your understanding of a topic and help you achieve your potential.

These online resources are available on **kerboodle!** which can be accessed via the internet at http://www.kerboodle.com/live, anytime, anywhere. If your school or college subscribes to this service you will be provided with your own personal login details. Once logged in, access your course and locate the required activity.

For more information and help visit
http://www.kerboodle.com

Icons in this book indicate where there is material online related to that topic. The following icons are used:

🔆 Learning activity

These resources include a variety of interactive and non-interactive activities to support your learning.

✅ Progress tracking

These resources include a variety of tests that you can use to check your knowledge on particular topics (Test yourself) and a range of resources that enable you to analyse and understand examination questions (On your marks …).

📝 Research support

These resources include WebQuests, in which you are assigned a task and provided with a range of web links to use as source material for research.

▉ How to use this book

This book covers the specification for your course and is arranged in a sequence approved by AQA.

The book content is divided into two units – Unit 1 and Unit 2 – which match the two units of the AQA Psychology B AS specification. It is then divided into sections matched to the six sections of the specification – Biopsychology and other key approaches; Gender development; Research methods; Social psychology; Cognitive psychology; Individual differences. Each section introduction contains a table mapping the section content to the specification so you can see at a glance where to find the information you need. Sections are then further divided into chapters, and then topics, making them clear and easy to use.

The content of the book is designed to meet the requirements of How science works by giving you the necessary skills and information to plan your own psychological investigations.

The features in this book include:

Learning objectives

At the beginning of each topic you will find a list of learning objectives that contain targets linked to the requirements of the specification.

Key terms

Terms that you will need to be able to define and understand.

Hint

Hints to aid your understanding of the content.

Links

This highlights any key areas where sections relate to one another.

Research study

Summaries of important psychological research studies to enhance your knowledge and understanding of a section.

End-of-chapter activity

Suggestions for practical investigations you can carry out.

Summary questions

Short questions that test your understanding of the subject and allow you to apply the skills you develop to different scenarios. The final question in each set is designed to be a stretch-and-challenge question and to require more thought. Answers are supplied free at www.nelsonthornes.com/psychology_answers.

Nelson Thornes is responsible for the solution(s) given and they may not constitute the only possible solution(s).

AQA Examiner's tip

Hints from AQA examiners to help you with your study and to prepare for your exam.

AQA Examination-style questions

Questions in the style that you can expect in your exam.

AQA examination questions are reproduced by permission of the Assessment and Qualifications Alliance.

Key points

A bulleted list at the end of each topic summarising the content in an easy-to-follow way.

Web links in the book

As Nelson Thornes is not responsible for third party content online, there may be some changes to this material that are beyond our control. In order for us to ensure that the links referred to in the book are as up-to-date and stable as possible, the websites are usually homepages with supporting instructions on how to reach the relevant pages if necessary.

Please let us know at **kerboodle@nelsonthornes.com** if you find a link that doesn't work and we will do our best to redirect the link, or to find an alternative site.

Introduction for students

Welcome to a new and exciting subject – psychology, the scientific study of mind and behaviour. I say 'new' because the authors, all of whom are experienced teachers, have found that most AS students in choosing psychology are selecting a subject they have never studied before. In writing this text, therefore, the authors assume no prior knowledge whatsoever. If you have already studied some psychology, for example at GCSE, we hope that you will continue to be engaged and stimulated by the new content areas and the added depth covered by this book.

There are many textbooks in psychology but what distinguishes this one is that it was planned with a specific student in mind; one taking the subject for the first time and following AQA Specification B (Spec B). The book consists of chapters written by a number of authors all of whom are not just teachers of psychology but also experienced examiners. The reason for having several authors is deliberate; psychology is a vast subject and you will soon appreciate the scope of the subject. In our view, it is best that each topic is covered by an expert in that area. This is rather like being taught by different teachers, each having their distinct preferences and expertise.

Approaches and methods

There are two main themes of the specification at AS (and A2) which feature in this book. These are **approaches in psychology** and **methods**. In the first chapter of Unit 1 you are introduced to the major approaches: biological, behaviourist, social learning theory, etc. It is essential that you get to grips with these. Not only is this a requirement laid down by the Qualifications and Curriculum Authority (QCA) and thus compulsory in the examination, but the approaches also serve as a foundation for topics both at AS and at A2. It is possible to study these topic areas before covering the approaches, for example your teacher may decide to cover Unit 2 before Unit 1, but your understanding will be strengthened and you will gain a more rounded appreciation of psychology when covering the approaches.

In Unit 1 of this book you will also come across a range of research methods used by psychologists. Again, it is absolutely essential that you study these carefully. However, remember that psychology is a 'scientific' discipline and an awareness of scientific methodology cannot be confined to one area of the specification or textbook. You need to be aware of scientific methods in all

areas of the subject. The methods used by psychologists are like the 'toolkit' used by any professional. Just as a plumber or a dentist needs to know and understand their tools before applying them to the task in hand, so a psychologist needs to know and understand the tools when applying them to the study of mind and behaviour. This emphasis on methods is reflected by the numerous research studies included in the book. When considering these studies, you may think about the method of research used, for example experiment, observation, case study, etc.

Core areas and key assessment objectives

Each specification in psychology must include **core areas**. These are social psychology, cognitive psychology, developmental psychology, biological psychology and individual differences. The methods and approaches mentioned above are illustrated through various topic areas representing the core areas. The topic areas chosen for Spec B are those considered to be important and popular within the core area. 'Social influence' is one example of a topic representing social psychology and 'Anxiety disorders' is an example of a topic representing individual differences. Topics within the core areas are easily identified in the book by titles within the units. Developmental psychology is covered by the topic of 'Gender development'.

The AS examination is designed so that you will achieve certain aims and **objectives**. First and foremost, you will be required to demonstrate your knowledge of the subject. This includes facts, specialist vocabulary, concepts, theories and studies. The book contains all the information you need. Key terms (concepts and specialist vocabulary) are clearly identified and defined for you. Theories are presented in an accessible manner and are both comprehensive and sufficiently detailed. Research studies are highlighted. Other studies and references to research in the main text serve to add weight to a theory or to challenge it. You do not need to know all of these studies, but you must familiarise yourself with those mentioned by name in the specification. However, it is useful to remember some of the other studies and references to research because you can use them in an exam as a discussion point.

Secondly, you will be expected to analyse, apply and evaluate psychological knowledge. You will find considerable evaluation of both theory and research in the book. You will also be stimulated into considering applications of theories and psychological research to real world settings. For example, knowledge from memory research can be applied in helping people to study for exams. Examination questions in Unit 2 in particular will test psychological knowledge by requiring you to apply psychological theories and research to scenarios of everyday situations.

Thirdly, in reading this book you will acquire an appreciation of the kinds of question psychologists ask and the ways in which they try to answer these questions. 'How science works' is a regular theme throughout the specification and a key assessment objective. This means that at AS you will be tested in both units on your knowledge and understanding of methodology including evaluation of the different methods. You will notice that, throughout the book, studies are frequently evaluated and you will recognise some common features, for example that studies based on the experimental method have the advantage of tighter control in comparison with other methods. Furthermore, when studying the research carried out by psychologists, and in particular the detailed studies, consider how **you** might investigate aspects of the theory under study. Your knowledge of research skills will be assessed in both units and in Unit 2 questions on 'How science works' will be integrated into topic content. For example, you may get a memory question with sub-sections on aspects of experimental research.

Organisation and structure of the book

The organisation of the book follows that of AQA Spec B. Thus 'Key approaches' is the first chapter with all the approaches laid out in the same order as in the specification; biological first and humanistic last. Similarly in Unit 2, the first topic is 'Social influence' with all the other topics mirroring the order in the specification. We hope that this will make it easier for you to follow the specification and find information when needed, but do not worry if your teachers decide to teach the subject in a different order. They will have their reasons for doing so. Moreover, you do not need to cover all of the material in the book. In Unit 2 you will have to answer one question from each core area, that is one from social psychology, one from cognitive psychology and one from individual differences. However, as there are two topics for each core area, this means that there will be a choice, for example 'Individual differences' includes the topics of 'Anxiety disorders' and 'Autism'. Hence your teachers may decide to only cover one topic for each core area. All the material for Unit 1 has to be studied. This makes sense, as Unit 1 is an introduction to psychology and any division into separate 'topics' would be artificial.

Using the features

You can use some of the features of this book to prepare for the examination. Use the learning objectives to help focus your reading. After reading the section, reflect on what you have read. Can you fulfil the objective? If not, return to the section. When you have been through all the sections of the topic, review it by reading the key points and attempt the summary questions. These should serve as a reminder of what you should know. If there is something you are not sure about, look it up in the chapter or the online glossary. Finally, re-read the whole topic at least once concentrating on the important theories, concepts and studies.

The nature of science

One of the comments that students of psychology sometimes make is that psychology leaves many unanswered questions; that there is still much that is not known and understood and that different studies investigating the same phenomena produce different, even contradictory findings. However this is the nature of scientific inquiry. Science does not consist of established and unchanging facts; rather it is a way of answering questions systematically and objectively. The questions change and give rise to new ones. This happens in all sciences and not just psychology. Whatever your impressions at the end of the course of psychology as a scientific discipline, we hope you will find the book helpful and enjoyable. Good luck!

Regina Teahan

Biopsychology and other key approaches

Introduction

Key terms

Subjective: influenced by personal views/opinions and assumptions, or referring to the internal world of the mind.

Objective: unbiased, detached or impartial, based on facts, not influenced by personal feelings, interpretations or prejudice.

Psychology is defined as the scientific study of mental processes and behaviour. In a sense, we already consider ourselves as psychologists, what Heider (1944) termed naïve scientists, because we all show an interest in other people's thoughts, feelings and the motivations that underlie behaviour. If we say to our friends that we are interested in studying psychology, a common reaction might be 'Psychology? That's just common sense, isn't it?' Psychology is much more than just common sense. Common sense refers to collective wisdom – personal assumptions that are made based on proverbs such as 'Absence makes the heart grow fonder'. These assumptions are **subjective** whereas psychology aims to be an **objective**, scientific discipline.

Modern psychologists are interested in addressing questions such as:

- How can the courts ensure that eyewitness testimonies are reliable?
- How can we ease the effect of parental divorce on children?
- Can we teach animals to use sign language?
- Which drugs are the most effective in reducing the symptoms of schizophrenia?

In addressing these questions, and others, psychologists look to study the mind and behaviour. But exactly how do psychologists study the human mind? We cannot see someone thinking, nor can we observe their memory, their perceptions or their dreams. To address this problem, psychologists adopt a similar approach to other natural sciences such as physics and chemistry. Both natural scientists and psychologists use the scientific method in order to be able to predict, to devise experiments in order to test these predictions, and to analyse the findings statistically in order to establish whether these predictions are supported or refuted.

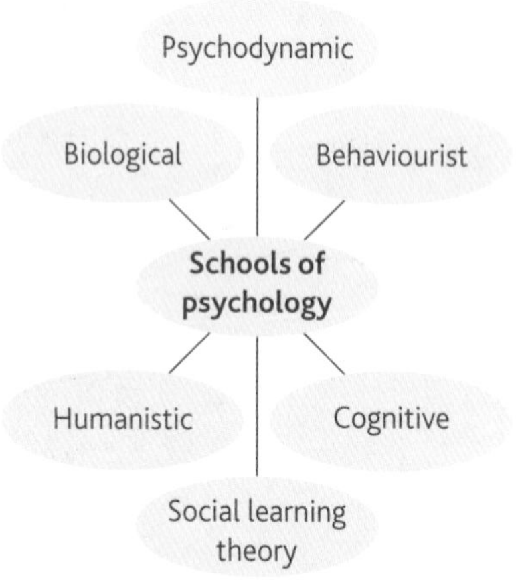

Fig. 1 *Schools of psychology*

Schools of psychology

Within mainstream psychology, there are various schools of thought which each argue for their particular model, or approach, to be used as the theory by which the majority of human behaviour can be explained. For example, behaviourist psychologists (see Chapter 1 Key approaches) argue that the environment and experiences determine and shape all of our behaviours. Biopsychologists, on the other hand (see Chapter 2 Biopsychology), tend to argue towards a genetic basis for behaviour, that is how differences in our chromosomal make-up can have a significant effect on not only our physiology, but also our behaviour. Some psychologists adhere to just one particular school of thought, whilst others appreciate that each school of thought has a different approach to explaining the mind and behaviour and should not be viewed as mutually exclusive. The major schools of thought, or approaches to psychology, are shown in Figure 1.

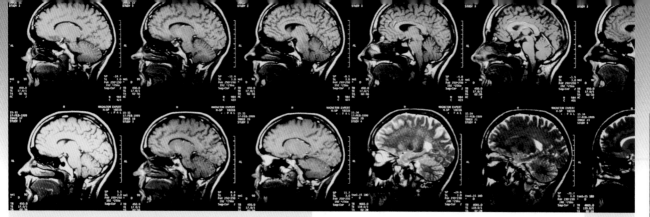

Specification	Topic content	Page
Key approaches		4
The basic assumptions of the following approaches: biological; behaviourist; social learning theory; cognitive; psychodynamic and humanistic		
The distinguishing features of each approach, including research methods used		
The strengths and limitations of each approach, including research methods used		
Biological: the influence of genes; biological structures; the evolution of behaviour	The biological approach	4
Behaviourist: classical conditioning; operant conditioning	The behaviourist approach	6
Social learning theory: modelling; mediating cognitive factors	Social learning theory	10
Cognitive: the study of internal mental processes and the use of models to explain these processes	The cognitive approach	12
Psychodynamic: the role of the unconscious; psychosexual stages; the structure of personality; defence mechanisms	The psychodynamic approach	14
Humanistic: free will; concepts of self and self-actualisation; conditions of worth	The humanistic approach	18
Biopsychology		21
Physiological psychology		
Basic understanding of the structure and function of neurons and synaptic transmission	The structure and function of neurons	21
The divisions of the nervous system		
Localisation of function in the brain (cortical specialisation) including motor, somatosensory, visual, auditory and 'language' centres	Localisation of cortical function	24
Methods used to identify areas of cortical specialisation, including neurosurgery, post-mortem examinations; EEGs, electrical stimulation, scanning techniques, including PET	Methods of studying cortical specialisation	27
Actions of the sympathetic and parasympathetic divisions of the autonomic nervous system, including the adrenal glands, adrenalin and fight or flight response	The autonomic nervous system	31
The genetic basis of behaviour		
Difference between genotype and phenotype	Genotype and phenotype	33
Types of twins: monozygotic (MZ) and dizygotic (DZ)	Monozygotic and dizygotic twins	34
Use of twin studies, and family and adoption studies to investigate the genetic basis of behaviour	Investigating the genetic basis of behaviour	36

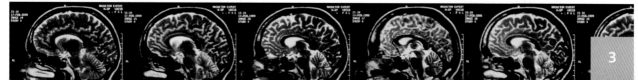

1 Key approaches

The biological approach

Learning objectives:

- Understand what is meant by biological psychology.
- Explain the influence of genes on behaviour.
- Suggest how evolutionary theory can be used to explain human and non-human behaviour.
- Evaluate the biological approach.

Hint

The basic assumptions of the biological approach are:

- Behaviour and thought processes have an innate, biological basis.
- The mind and brain are the same.
- Human genes have evolved to adapt behaviour to the environment.
- Human characteristics, e.g. intelligence are due to our genetic make-up.

Key terms

Chromosomes: the part of a cell that contains genetic information.

Selective breeding: the artificial selection of male and female animals for a particular trait. These animals are then put together to breed and produce offspring. The offspring are then observed to see whether the trait continues over successive generations.

Biology is defined as the study of life (from the Greek *bios* meaning 'life' and *logos* meaning 'study'). A biological perspective is relevant to the field of psychology in three ways:

- physiology – investigating how the brain, nervous system and hormones operate; how changes in the structure and function of organs and chemicals can affect our behaviour
- investigation of heritability – understanding the role that genes might have on our behaviour, for example is intelligence inherited?
- comparative method – different species of animal are studied and compared to humans; this way we can learn and understand more about human behaviour.

Biological psychologists apply the principles of biology to the study of mental processes and behaviour. To appreciate the complexities of human behaviour, however, we must start by first understanding one of the smallest features of our biological make-up: genes.

Influence of genes

Within most cells in the human body, with the exception of red blood cells, is a structure called the nucleus. The nucleus of every cell (apart from sex cells) contains 46 structures called **chromosomes**. Chromosomes are made up of a complex chemical called deoxyribonucleic acid (DNA). The DNA on each chromosome carries units of information called genes. From the moment that we are conceived until our death, our genes interact with the environment to influence every aspect of bodily structure and function. So, what influence do genes have on our behaviour?

Research on the genetic influence of behaviour has often been conducted on non-human species such as rats and mice as they have a shorter gestation period. Psychologists are able to manipulate certain genes in order to measure the effects on behaviour. Genetic mapping, genetic engineering and **selective breeding** programmes have contributed enormously to our understanding of the genetic basis of behaviour.

Bock and Goode (1996), for example, found that when mice were reared alone, they showed a strong tendency to attack other male mice when first exposed to other animals. These mice were not taught to be aggressive, that is from their parents; they just exhibited the behaviour. This research therefore implies a natural, or genetic, tendency in relation to biological aggression.

Aggression is thought to be one of a number of primitive behaviours that both human and non-human species display. Its origins can be traced back over thousands of years. The process of evolution is able to explain why some genes survived and others did not.

i Evolution of behaviour

In 1859, Darwin published *The Origin of Species* in which he proposed that all species of living things have evolved over time from common ancestors through the process of natural selection. Darwin provided scientific evidence to show how random physical and behavioural changes to a species either enable it to adapt to its environment and hence survive, or to become maladaptive and die out. The principle of natural selection therefore explains how the strongest genes survive and are passed onto the next generation, whilst 'weaker genes' die out.

We can observe many examples of evolutionary behaviour in both human and non-human species, for example sexual selection. In the animal kingdom, male species display traits such as mating calls, brightly coloured plumage, in order to attract a mate and successfully reproduce. These traits are then passed on to its offspring thus making them 'attractive' to females. In humans, we can observe evolutionary behaviours such as the rooting reflex. In newborn babies, this reflex is present at birth. Babies will turn their heads towards anything that strokes or touches their cheek or mouth and so this reflex aids breastfeeding and hence survival.

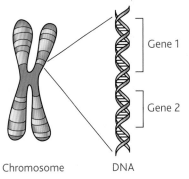

Fig. 1 *According to the Human Genome Project, humans have around 100,000 genes*

■ Link

For more information on experimental methods and ethical issues, see Chapter 4, Research methods.

▨ Evaluation of the biological approach

Table 1 *Evaluation of the biological approach*

Strengths	Limitations
The biological approach uses scientific, experimental procedures in its investigations.	The biological approach is reductionist. It explains all thoughts and behaviours in terms of the actions of nerves or chemicals.
It provides strong arguments for the nature side of the nature–nurture debate.	The approach is over-simplistic. It fails to fully appreciate the influence that environmental factors can have on behaviour.
The biological approach has had many useful applications, for example drugs that alleviate disorders such as bipolar depression.	The approach raises ethical issues, for example genetic mapping. Is it right to artifically manipulate our genetic make-up?

Key points:

- The biological approach stresses the importance of nature in the nature–nurture debate.
- The principles of biology are applied to psychology in order to understand behaviours such as imprinting.
- We are able to manipulate a species' genetic make-up in order to investigate the genetic basis of behaviour.
- Darwin's theory of evolution shows how strongest genes survive and are passed onto the next generation, whilst maladaptive genes die out.
- We can observe many examples of evolutionary behaviour in non-human species, for example sexual selection and, in humans, for example the rooting reflex.

■ Summary questions

1. Outline one assumption of the biological approach in psychology.

2. Explain one strength and one limitation of the biological approach.

3. Suggest how sexual selection in humans may be explained in terms of evolutionary processes.

The behaviourist approach

Biopsychology

Learning objectives:

- Know and understand the basic assumptions of the behaviourist approach.

- Explain some of the evidence in support of the behaviourist approach.

- Evaluate the behaviourist approach.

Hint

The basic assumptions of the behaviourist approach are:

- Behaviour is learned from the environment.
- Behaviour is determined by reinforcement or punishment of past learning experiences.
- Observable behaviour, not minds should be studied.
- Psychology should investigate the laws of learning.

Key terms

Law of Effect: events in the environment produce rewards for some behaviours and not others. Behaviours that produce rewards are repeated whereas behaviours that result in punishment are not.

Operant conditioning: learning due to the consequences of voluntary behaviour, through positive and negative reinforcement and punishment.

Link

For more on experimental methods, see Chapter 4, Research methods.

The philosopher John Locke (1690) described the mind as a *tabula rasa*. By this, Locke meant that all people are born as 'blank slates' and that our behaviour is learnt and dependent upon our interactions and experiences with the environment.

John Broadus Watson (1878–1958) revolutionised psychology and established behaviourism. Watson was heavily critical of the use of introspection adopted by Wundt, and the study of consciousness advocated by Freud. He stated that 'consciousness' could not be seen or meaningfully defined and therefore should not be studied. For Watson, psychology should be the objective study of observable behaviour and responses. He claimed that human behaviour is determined by the environment and that behaviour could be shaped or manipulated. In 1930, he famously said, 'Give me a dozen healthy infants … and I'll guarantee to take any one at random and train him to become … a doctor, lawyer, artist, merchant-chief and, yes, even beggar-man and thief.' After conducting research on animal behaviour, Watson stated that the laws of learning in animals could be applied to humans.

One psychologist who, like Watson, studied animal behaviour was the American Edward Thorndike (1874–1949). Thorndike's **Law of Effect** stated that if behaviour is followed by satisfying consequences, for example pleasure, then that behaviour is 'stamped in' and is more likely to be repeated in the future. If, however, behaviour is followed by unsatisfying consequences, for example punishment, then the behaviour is less likely to be repeated.

Thorndike's Law of Effect was based on his observations of cats trying to escape from puzzle boxes. The cats were placed in the box and the only means of escape was to operate a latch that would allow the door to open. When first placed in the box, the cats took a long time to escape. With experience, these ineffective behaviours (or responses) occurred less frequently and the positive behaviours, that is escape, occurred more frequently, enabling the cats to escape in less time over a number of trials. Thorndike concluded that the cats had learned to escape from the puzzle boxes through trial and error learning. Thorndike's Law of Effect influenced B.F. Skinner to produce his theory of **operant conditioning**.

Operant conditioning

Burrhus Frederic Skinner (1904–90) was an American psychologist. He developed radical behaviourism claiming that feelings and sensations, central to introspection, cannot be measured reliably. Instead, psychology should focus on using scientific methods to make observations of behaviour and its consequences. Skinner claimed that all behaviour is learnt as a result of consequences in our environment, that is operant conditioning. Operant conditioning is concerned with the use of consequences, such as gaining rewards or receiving punishments, in order to modify and shape behaviour.

In the famous 'Skinner box' experiments (Figure 2), he would introduce a hungry rat into the box. Inside the box was a lever which, when pressed, would deliver a pellet of food. When the rat pressed the lever, a pellet of food was dropped onto the tray. The rat soon learned that pressing the lever would result in food (a reward). Skinner observed that, as a consequence of its actions (receiving a pellet of food), the rat continued to display this new learned behaviour – the rat's behaviour had been positively reinforced.

There are two types of reinforcement:

- Positive reinforcement provides a feeling of satisfaction that increases the likelihood of the desired response being repeated in the future, for example a teacher praises you for an excellent piece of work.
- Negative reinforcement involves the removal of an unpleasant experience in order to increase the likelihood of a desired response being repeated, for example you help with the washing-up so that your mother will stop moaning at you. Punishment is the presence of a negative stimulus in order to decrease the likelihood of the response occurring again, for example a child receives a smack from its parent for being naughty.

Skinner's principles of operant conditioning have been applied to many areas of psychology, for example education, prisons and psychiatric institutions. Operant conditioning is also used to modify speech in autistic children. Here, therapists will use a behaviour-shaping technique in autistic children with under-developed speech. When the autistic child begins to imitate the therapist's speech or behaviour, the therapist rewards the child with praise, which acts as a positive reinforcer. The therapist will then continue with this reward system until the child can use words independently and without any prompting from the therapist.

Classical conditioning

Ivan Petrovich Pavlov (1849–1936) was a Russian physiologist. In the 1890s, whilst researching the digestive system of dogs, he observed that whenever a dog was presented with food it would automatically salivate. This led Pavlov to change the focus of his research and predict that if another stimulus was presented to the dog at the same time as the food, then this stimulus would become associated with the food and cause the dog to salivate.

In his experiment, Pavlov rang a bell (a conditioned, or neutral, stimulus) at the same time that food was presented to the dog. The dog continued to salivate as an involuntary reflex response. After a number of trials, Pavlov discovered that he no longer needed to present the food to the dog; the dog salivated just to the sound of the bell. Pavlov referred to this paired association as a conditional reflex. Figure 4 shows a diagrammatic representation of Pavlov's experiment.

We can use the principles of classical conditioning (see Figure 4) to explain many human behaviours, for example a fear of the dentist. Imagine you are lying in a dentist's chair. Suddenly, the dentist touches a nerve with his drill (UCS) which causes you a lot of pain (UCR). You associate the sound of his drill (CS) with the drill touching the nerve (UCS) that caused you pain (UCR). The next time you visit the dentist, you become very anxious, as you have learned to associate the sound of the dentist's drill (CS) with pain (CR).

Fig. 2 *A Skinner box*

Fig. 3 *B.F. Skinner: the Simpsons' character, Principal Seymour Skinner, is named after B.F. Skinner!*

Key term

Classical conditioning: learning due to the association of a neutral stimulus with an unconditioned, reflex response.

Link

For more on experimental methods, see Chapter 4, Research methods.

Biopsychology

■ Hint

In classical conditioning, the animal already possesses the behaviour, for example salivation. Operant conditioning views learning as a much more active process. Skinner was interested in exactly how an animal operates in its environment and how its behaviour leads to certain consequences.

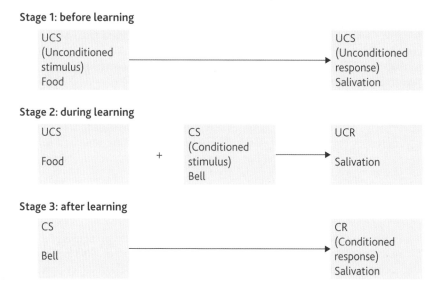

Stage 1: before learning

UCS (Unconditioned stimulus) Food ⟶ UCS (Unconditioned response) Salivation

Stage 2: during learning

UCS Food + CS (Conditioned stimulus) Bell ⟶ UCR Salivation

Stage 3: after learning

CS Bell ⟶ CR (Conditioned response) Salivation

Fig. 4 *Pavlov's classical conditioning experiment*

■ Research study: Watson and Rayner (1920): the study of Little Albert

Aim: To investigate whether an emotional response such as fear could be conditioned in a human being.

Method: Albert was 11 months old when the experiment was conducted. In the experiment, Watson presented a white rat directly in front of Albert. When he reached for the rat, Watson would simultaneously strike a metal bar with a hammer, thus creating a loud noise. This pairing of stimuli occurred several times during a number of weeks.

Results: Watson found that when the rat alone was presented to Albert, he immediately became frightened and showed an attempt to move away from the rat.

Conclusion: Watson and Rayner successfully demonstrated that behaviour is learnt and that a phobia of rats could be conditioned in a baby.

Evaluation: This experiment raised enormous ethical implications. Even after five days, Little Albert still showed evidence of a phobia of rats, although it must be stressed that the conditioned phobia was less evident after a month. There are also methodological issues to consider in this study. Should we generalise the findings of just one case study to use as an explanation for how we acquire phobias?

■ Links

For more on case studies and experimental methods, see Chapter 4, Research methods.

For more on ethical issues in psychological research, see Chapter 4, Research methods.

For more on the Little Albert research study, see p217.

Watson and Rayner further discovered how little Albert's phobia of white rats transferred onto other objects such as a white rabbit, cotton-wool and even Santa Claus's beard!

The principles of classical conditioning have been applied to many areas of psychology, for example in the treatment of atypical behaviour. Aversion therapy can be used in the treatment of alcoholism. At the same time that alcohol is presented, the person is given a drug that induces an unpleasant response such as nausea and vomiting. After repeated pairings, the person begins to associate the alcohol with nausea and vomiting and hence, over time, can cure their addiction.

▥ Evaluation of the behaviourist approach

Table 2 *Evaluation of the behaviourist approach*

Strengths	Limitations
Behaviourists' use of rigorous, experimental methods of research enhances the credibility of psychology as a scientific discipline.	The behaviourist approach ignores the mental processes that are involved in learning unlike the cognitive approach, which views these processes as important.
The approach provides strong arguments for the nurture side of the nature–nurture debate in psychology.	The approach rejects the possible role of biological factors, that is nature, in human behaviour.
The approach has provided a number of practical applications and techniques to shape behaviour, for example the use of rewards in education.	Behaviourists view humans as passive learners at the mercy of the environment unlike humanistic psychologists, who view humans as active agents – being able to control and determine their own development.
	The principles of operant and classical conditioning do not account for spontaneous behaviour in humans.
	The use of animals in applying laws of learning to humans has been criticised. Surely we are more complex than animals?

Key points:

- Psychology should focus on observable behaviour, not minds, if it is to be regarded as a scientific discipline.

- All behaviour is learnt, or determined by, interactions and experiences in our environment.

- Operant conditioning is concerned with the use of consequences or reinforcements to modify and shape behaviour.

- Classical conditioning demonstrates how a new association can be made between a neutral stimulus and an already existing response.

- There are many practical applications of the behaviourist approach, for example the modification of speech in autistic children.

▣ Summary questions

4 Describe one assumption of the behaviourist approach in psychology.

5 What is meant by the Law of Effect?

6 Explain one way in which the behaviourist approach has been applied in psychology.

7 Explain two limitations of the behaviourist approach in psychology.

8 Jack is addicted to gambling. He visits his local betting shop every day. Although Jack knows that his gambling is destroying his marriage, he cannot stop himself because he regularly wins money. Use your knowledge of behaviourism to explain why Jack continues to gamble.

Biopsychology

Social learning theory

Hint

The basic assumptions of social learning theory are:

- Mediational processes, which lie between stimulus and response, influence our behaviour.

- Observational learning has four conditions: attention, retention, motor reproduction, motivation.

- Learning can occur by observing role models in the environment.

- Learning can be a result of direct reinforcement and indirect, or vicarious reinforcement.

AQA Examiner's tip

Make sure you understand the difference between observational learning and operant conditioning. In observational learning, the child observes a model being punished and **acquires** memory of this behaviour. In operant conditioning, punishment **extinguishes** the behaviour.

Key term

Vicarious reinforcement: learning is not a result of direct reinforcement or experience, but rather an individual's observation of another person's experience.

Social learning theory (SLT) can be viewed as a bridge between behaviourism and cognitive learning theories. One of the most influential figures, among others, in social learning theory is Albert Bandura. Bandura claimed that the application of consequences, central to operant conditioning, was not essential for learning to take place. Instead, learning could occur simply by observing others, that is models, in the environment. Central to Bandura's belief was that the mind, behaviour and the environment all play an important role in learning. Social learning theory therefore moved away from radical behaviourism in taking into account the importance of cognitive processes involved in learning.

Bandura's theory of observational learning is based on four conditions that he said were essential for effective modelling to occur:

- attention – the individual notices someone in their environment
- retention – the individual remembers what they observed
- motor reproduction – the individual replicates the behaviour shown by the model
- motivation – the individual seeks to demonstrate the behaviour that they have observed.

To understand the conditions that are necessary for effective modelling to occur, consider the following example. Shelby is five years old and is watching her favourite cartoon on the television. The cartoon shows a young girl helping her mother with the housework. The mother in the cartoon praises the young girl for helping her. After the cartoon ends, Shelby asks her own mother if she can help her with the housework.

Why is Shelby motivated to replicate the behaviour she observed in the cartoon? Shelby has received no direct reinforcement herself, so why would she want to behave in the same way as the little girl in the cartoon? Social learning theorists would state that Shelby has learnt through **vicarious reinforcement**. She has observed the little girl in the cartoon being praised for her behaviour and is now motivated to replicate this behaviour herself in order to gain similar praise.

According to social learning theorists, there are two types of model: live models, who are physically present in our environment, for example mother, teacher, pop star; and symbolic models, for example people who are present in films, books and cartoons (like the scenario above). Symbolic modelling may be considered to have a greater impact in cultures where different forms of media, such as television, are widely available. It is important to note, however, that not all of the behaviours we observe can be directly reproduced. For example, you may be a fan of David Beckham and watch with awe how he takes free kicks. The problem here is that most of us would be unable to reproduce his level of skill!

Social learning theory has been applied to many areas of psychology, for example gender development. In his famous 'Bobo doll' experiment in the 1960s, Bandura showed three- to six-year-old boys and girls a video in which children of a similar age were shown to behave aggressively towards a 'Bobo doll'. At the end of the video, there were three endings:

- The adult in the film commented positively on the behaviour.
- The adult commented negatively on the behaviour.
- The adult made no comment at all.

After the video, the children were then placed in a room with a 'Bobo doll' and their behaviour towards the doll was observed. Bandura found that boys tended to show greater levels of aggression towards the doll compared to girls, even though they had all been exposed to the same behaviour. The girls appeared to be more influenced by the negative comments made by the adult in the video. This led Bandura to conclude that children learn by observing models in their environment and, in conjunction with other **mediating cognitive factors**, imitate their behaviour.

Key term

Mediating cognitive factors: the mental processes that occur in-between a stimulus and response that influence our behaviour.

■ Evaluation of social learning theory

Table 3 *Evaluation of social learning theory*

Strengths	Limitations
Social learning theory takes into account the cognitive processes that are involved in learning.	Social learning theory does not fully explain individual differences, that is to say what may be perceived to be reinforcement for one person, may not be for another.
Social learning theorists use both experimental and non-experimental methods of research, for example Bandura's use of the experimental and observational method when investigating gender differences in aggression.	Social learning theory does not account for all behaviour. For example, if we learn by observing others, how is it that a person becomes a criminal when he or she has not associated with criminals and/or observed criminal behaviour?
Social learning theory has been applied to many areas of psychology and has provided effective explanations of behaviour, for example acquisition of gender roles.	

Key points:

- Social learning theory takes into account the cognitive processes involved in learning.
- We learn by observing others (role models) in our environment.
- There are four conditions necessary for effective modelling to occur: attention, retention, motor reproduction and motivation.
- Social learning theory has been applied to many areas of psychology, for example gender development.

Links

- For more about social learning theory and gender development, see Chapter 3, Gender development.
- For more about observational studies and experimental methods, see Chapter 4, Research methods.

Summary questions

9 What do social learning theorists mean by the term modelling?

10 Using an example, explain what is meant by vicarious reinforcement.

11 What are the four conditions Bandura said were necessary for effective modelling to occur?

12 Explain one strength and one limitation of social learning theory.

13 Greg is playing a game of football in the park with his friends. One of his friends, Jason, notices that a little girl, who is walking nearby, has dropped her teddy bear without noticing. Jason picks up the teddy bear and gives it back to the little girl. The little girl's mother is so thankful that she gives Jason some money. Greg observes all of Jason's behaviours. Use your knowledge of social learning theory to answer the following question: Explain why it is likely that when faced with a similar situation, Greg would help a little girl in the same way as Jason?

Biopsychology

The cognitive approach

Learning objectives:

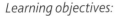 Know and understand the basic assumptions of the cognitive approach.

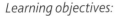 Know models that can be used to explain internal mental processes.

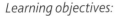 Suggest some applications of the cognitive approach.

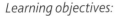 Evaluate the cognitive approach.

Hint

The basic assumptions of the cognitive approach are:

- Mental processes lie between stimulus and response.
- Humans are information-processors.
- Humans actively organise and manipulate information from the environment.
- The mind operates in the same way as a computer – both encode, store and output data.

Key terms

Cognition: comes from the Latin *cognoscere* meaning 'to know'.

Artificial intelligence: the development of computer systems, or programs, to mimic human cognitive functioning.

Link

For more about experimental methods, see Chapter 4, Research methods.

The cognitive approach in psychology primarily focuses on the internal mental processes of an individual. According to Ulric Neisser, **cognition** refers to '[the] processes by which the sensory input is transformed, reduced, elaborated, stored, recovered and used'.

The approach became a dominant force in psychology from the 1950s onwards. According to Anderson (1995), the emergence of modern cognitive psychology was due to research on human performance and attention during the Second World War, developments in computer science, **artificial intelligence**, and the growing interest in linguistics.

The cognitive approach to psychology is radically different from previous approaches in two ways:

- The cognitive approach adopts the use of scientific, experimental methods to measure mental processes thereby rejecting the psychodynamic use of introspection.
- The cognitive approach advocates the importance of mental processes such as beliefs, desires and motivation in determining behaviour unlike the behaviourist approach.

Cognitive psychologists focus on internal mental processes such as memory. They are interested in how individuals can learn to solve problems and the mental processes that exist between stimulus and response. One model that has been used to explain these mental processes is the information-processing approach.

Information-processing approach

The information-processing approach can be compared to a computer in terms of the mind being the software and the brain being the hardware. Just like a computer, we as individuals encode information, store or transform information, and provide an output, or behaviour. This can be easily summarised in a flow chart (Figure 5).

We can use the information-processing model to explain many everyday behaviours, for example, playing a game of badminton: Alicia perceives the shuttlecock coming towards her right-hand side (encoding). She decides to play a forehand shot (decision-making). Alicia hits the shuttlecock over the net and wins the point (output).

The information-processing approach was dominant until the 1980s. Since then, there has been growing interest in both computational and connectionist models to explain human mental processing.

Fig. 5 *The information-processing model which represents our internal mental processes*

▉ Computational and connectionist models

The computational model still uses the computer analogy to explain mental processes. However, the emphasis now is largely to do with the use of simulations to study how human intelligence is structured, that is **what** is involved when information is processed rather then when and how much information is processed. The computational model seeks to explain how our cognitive system operates in terms of the goals, plans and actions that are involved when we perform tasks. The connectionist model, on the other hand, uses a neural analogy – the idea that the mind is made up of a huge array of neurons, or nodes, and that the connections between these nodes form an activating pattern which represents a meaningful, or learnt, association between two or more environmental stimuli.

The cognitive approach has had many practical applications, for example in eyewitness testimony. Cognitive psychologists have helped the police to understand the different ways in which individuals process and recall information. The development of the cognitive interview technique has enabled eyewitnesses to provide a more reliable account of the crime scene.

▉ Evaluation of the cognitive approach

Table 4 *Evaluation of the cognitive approach*

Strengths	Limitations
The cognitive approach focuses on internal mental processes, unlike behaviourism.	Cognitive models have been criticised as over-simplistic – ignoring the complexities of the mind.
The approach uses scientific, experimental methods, unlike humanistic psychologists.	Humans are viewed as machines with the crude comparison of the mind to a computer (software and hardware).
Models such as the information-processing approach have been effectively used to explain mental processes.	Many cognitive theories are based on perfomance of artifical laboratory tasks therefore unrepresentative of everyday behaviours.

Key points:

- ▉ Cognitive psychologists focus on internal mental processes that lie between stimulus and response.

- ▉ Humans are like computers in the way in which both encode, store and retrieve information.

- ▉ Many models, for example connectionist, have been used to explain internal mental processes.

- ▉ The approach has provided many useful applications, for example improving reliability of eyewitness accounts.

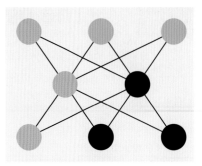

Fig. 6 *When highlighted nodes in the network are activated together, the network may represent the activation of a learned concept*

AQA Examiner's tip

You may find it easier to use diagrams to show your understanding of the models used to represent mental processes.

▉ Summary questions

14 Outline one assumption of the cognitive approach in psychology.

15 Name two models that have been used to explain internal mental processes.

16 Explain one strength and one limitation of the cognitive approach.

17 Holly is playing a game of chess with her friend Dan. She sees Dan move his king one square forward. Holly considers her next chess move. She moves her queen one diagonal square, places Dan in checkmate and wins the game. With reference to this scenario, explain what is meant by the information-processing approach.

The psychodynamic approach

Hint

The basic assumptions of the psychodynamic approach are:

■ Unconscious processes, of which we are unaware, determine our behaviour.

■ Instincts, or drives, motivate our behaviour and energise the mind.

■ Childhood experiences determine adult personality.

■ Personality has three parts: the id, ego and superego.

Key term

Free association: a method used whereby patients are encouraged to talk freely about their concerns and dreams so that the therapist can analyse any unconscious conflict.

Sigmund Freud (1856–1939) was an Austrian neurologist and psychiatrist who was renowned for establishing the psychoanalytic school of psychology where he developed the idea that neuroses (some types of paranoia and phobias) were a result of deeply traumatic experiences in a person's life but which were forgotten or hidden from consciousness. Using a technique whereby the patient was encouraged to talk freely, Freud observed how these traumatic past experiences could be brought to consciousness and confronted both emotionally and intellectually. Freud stated that this 'talking cure' or **free association** allowed the patient to remove the underlying causes of their neurotic symptoms.

The role of the unconscious mind

Freud stated that whenever we make a choice or decision in our lives, hidden mental processes, of which we are unaware and have no control over, determine these choices or decisions. Freud suggested that free will is therefore a delusion; we are not entirely aware of what we are thinking and we often act in ways that have little to do with our conscious thoughts.

The iceberg analogy is often used to explain Freud's theory of human consciousness (see Figure 7). At the surface lies the conscious mind. Here we are directly aware of our thoughts and experiences. For example, if we feel hungry, then we get something to eat. Just below the surface lies the preconscious mind. Here lie our thoughts, feelings and experiences that we are not directly aware of, but that can be easily accessed. For example, a person may be asked what date their birthday is. Finally, deep below the surface lies the unconscious mind. Freud stated that this is where significant psychic events take place. Freud interpreted these events as having symbolic significance. For Freud, the unconscious mind was a place for such things as traumatic memories that were actively pushed into the unconscious by a psychological defence mechanism known as repression.

There are fundamental disagreements regarding the nature of the unconscious mind, in particular, the concept of the existence of the unconscious mind in relation to its scientific validity and whether the unconscious mind exists at all. One of Freud's most notable opponents was Karl Popper. Popper argued that Freud's theory of the unconscious mind was not falsifiable (testable) and therefore unscientific. Popper objected not so much to the idea that things happen in our minds that we are unaware of, but to the investigations of the mind that were not falsifiable.

Psychosexual stages of development

Associated with the view of the unconscious mind was Freud's idea of instincts, or drives. Freud stated that these instincts are the motivating forces that underlie most of our behaviours and 'energise' the mind in all of its functions. Freud proposed that there were a large number of instincts that he grouped into two broad categories:

- ▦ Eros (or life instinct) which accounts for erotic and self-preserving instincts.
- ▦ Thanatos (or death instinct) which accounts for aggression and self-destruction.

Freud's theory of instincts or drives is used to explain how the human being is energised from birth to adult life by the desire to enhance and gain bodily pleasure.

Freud proposed that each individual progresses through five psychosexual stages of development from birth to adulthood. For Freud, early childhood experiences determine the adult personality. These five psychosexual stages are known as oral, anal, phallic, latent and genital (see Table 5). According to Freud, if a child experienced trauma, for example, in any one of these stages, then this may result in fixation, that is the child becomes 'stuck' in that stage and is unable to fully move on to the next stage. These fixations become evident in the adult personality, for example if a child is fixated at the oral stage because of difficulties with breastfeeding, then the person may be over-dependent on others as an adult.

Freud's theory of psychosexual development has been met with criticism most notably from feminists who argue that Freud's theories were particularly male-oriented. Freud himself admitted that he had difficulty understanding and incorporating female desire into his theories, and it was only later in his career that he proposed his theory for female psychosexual development.

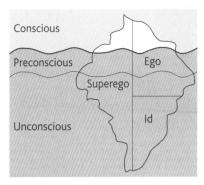

Fig. 7 *The iceberg analogy: the mind is like an iceberg with much of it – the unconscious mind – lying below the surface, exerting a dynamic influence on the conscious mind*

▦ Link

For more about the phallic stage in the psychodynamic approach to gender development, see Chapter 3, Gender development.

Table 5 *Freud's psychosexual stages of development*

Stage	Age	Key features
Oral	0–18 months	An infant's pleasure centres around the mouth. The mother's breast becomes the object of desire since feeding reduces the infant's negative experience of hunger.
Anal	18–36 months	The child gains pleasure from retention and expulsion of faeces. During toilet training, the child can either please parents by using the toilet, or defy parents by witholding faeces, for example.
Phallic	3–6 years	The sexual instinct is focused on the genital area. Boys experience the Oedipus complex and girls, the Electra complex. Resolution of these complexes forms their gender identity.
Latent	6 years to puberty	The sexual drive is present, albeit dormant. Freud stated that the sexual energy is focused (or sublimated) towards peer friendships, school.
Genital	Puberty and beyond	Sexual interests mature and are directed to gaining heterosexual pleasure through intercourse.

▦ Structure of the personality

One of the main features of the psychosexual stages of development is the individual focus on gaining pleasure, based on biological instincts. These instincts, or impulses, derive from the id and form part of Freud's tripartite theory of personality. The theory is termed 'tripartite' as Freud distinguished between three elements within the mind that form the personality:

- ▦ The id, according to Freud, is also known as the pleasure principle. This is the selfish part of our personality where we desire instant gratification of our needs and desires.
- ▦ The superego forms during the phallic stage of psychosexual development. Here we learn to internalise our parental values and social standards. It is also known as the morality principle as we learn and store information about what is considered 'right' and 'wrong'.

AQA Examiner's tip

A common error is to describe, in depth, each of the five psychosexual stages of development. Remember the importance of being concise in describing the key features of the approach.

Biopsychology

The ego, or reality principle, acts as the mediator between the id and the superego. The primary role of the ego is to reduce conflicts that arise from the demands of the id and the moralistic views of the superego. For example, consider a person who desires to have sex with a stranger. The id impulses (desire to have sex) conflict with the superego (the belief that it is socially unacceptable to have sex with an unknown person). Conflict then arises from the two parts of the personality. One way in which the ego deals with the anxiety experienced as a result of this conflict is to use defence mechanisms.

Defence mechanisms

Defence mechanisms are an unconscious resource used when the ego is in conflict with the id and the superego. More accurately, they are referred to as ego-defence mechanisms (see Table 6).

Table 6 *Defence mechanisms*

Term	Explanation	Applied example
Denial	Reducing anxiety by refusing to see the unpleasant aspects of reality.	A student sees that he has a poor grade in his school report but then tells himself that grades do not matter.
Displacement	The mind redirects emotions from a dangerous object to a safe object, that is redirecting emotions to a safer outlet.	An employee is really angry with their boss. Rather than punching their boss, they punch a pillow instead.
Rationalisation	Constructing a logical justification for a decision that was originally arrived at through a different mental process.	Eric is an alcoholic and drinks red wine. However, he tells himself that he drinks it as it has health benefits, in order to avoid facing his alcoholism.
Sublimation	The refocusing or channelling of impulses to socially accepted behaviours.	An aggressive person may join the army as a cover for their violent behaviour.

Fig. 8 *Sigmund Freud*

Link

For more about case studies, see Chapter 4, Research methods.

Research study: Freud (1909): the study of the 'Rat Man'

Aim: To investigate the underlying cause of Ernst Lanzer's (pseudonym: 'Rat Man') obsessive-compulsive neurosis.

Method: Freud saw the Rat Man for about a year. The Rat Man stated that he had obsessive and fearful thoughts about rats and that these thoughts resulted in obsessive behaviours. The origins of these obsessive thoughts of rats seemed to come from his military training. He had heard of a particularly nasty torture where rats were placed in a bucket which was then tied to the buttocks of a person. The rats would then eat their way into the person through the anus. The Rat Man was so fearful that this would happen to his father or a woman that he admired, that he engaged in obsessive-compulsive behaviours.

Results: Freud stated that these behaviours resulted from the love and unconscious hate the Rat Man felt for his father whom he wished to torture with rats.

Conclusion: Freud stated that the obsessive-compulsive behaviours helped the Rat Man to overcome his feelings of guilt and so reduce his anxieties.

Evaluation: In his case study, Freud only focused on the Rat Man's father and made no reference to his mother, who was a particularly domineering figure in his life. These feelings of abandonment as a child might be a more plausible explanation for the Rat Man's obsessive-compulsive behaviours as an adult. In addition, as this is a case study of just one individual, the findings must be treated with caution as they lack generalisability.

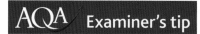

Examiner's tip

It is tempting to focus solely on the criticisms of Freud in examination answers. Consider also the significant contributions that Freud made to the development of psychology and major applications of the approach, for example atypical behaviour.

■ Evaluation of the psychodynamic approach

Table 7 *Evaluation of the psychodynamic approach*

Strengths	Limitations
Freud acknowledged the importance of childhood experiences in determining adult personality	Freud's theories are considered to be unfalsifiable and therefore unscientific
Freud's theories offer causal explanations for underlying atypical psychological conditions	Freud's use of the case study method lacks generalisability
Freud's methods of psychoanalysis are still used in psychiatry today	Freud's controversial idea that infants display sexual urges has received enormous criticism
	The effectiveness of psychoanalysis as a therapy is questioned in comparison to the proportion of patients who recover spontaneously from atypical disorders

Key points:

■ The unconscious mind contains instinctive drives, needs and psychic actions of which we are unaware.

■ The way in which we progress through the five psychosexual stages of development as a child will determine our adult behaviour.

■ Our personality is structured by the interactions of the id, ego and superego.

■ The ego employs defence mechanisms, such as denial, to protect us from feelings of guilt and anxiety.

Summary questions

18 Describe one feature of the psychodynamic approach in psychology.

19 What are the key features of the oral stage of psychosexual development?

20 What is meant by a defence mechanism? Use an example to illustrate your answer.

21 Explain one strength and one limitation of the psychodynamic approach.

22 Explain one way in which the psychodynamic approach differs from the behaviourist approach in psychology.

The humanistic approach

Learning objectives:

- Describe the basic assumptions of the humanistic approach.

- Explain some of the contributions of the humanistic approach.

- Evaluate the humanistic approach.

Hint

The basic assumptions of the humanistic approach are:

- Humans should be viewed as a whole and not reduced to component parts.

- Humans are active agents – able to control and determine their own development.

- Humans strive towards achieving self-actualisation.

- To be psychologically healthy, the real self and ideal self must be congruent.

AQA Examiner's tip

The humanistic approach can be used effectively in examination answers – comparison with the behaviourist approach in terms of its methodology, and comparison to the psychodynamic approach in terms of differing approaches to therapy.

Key term

Congruence: a state of agreement or consistency.

Carl Rogers (1902–87) was an American psychologist who founded humanistic psychology in the 1950s. The approach formed largely due to concerns from therapists regarding the limitations of psychoanalysis. Rogers believed that psychoanalysis failed to fully appreciate and deal with the nature of healthy growth in an individual. In addition, humanistic psychologists were dissatisfied with the deterministic nature and scientific approach of the behaviourists. The humanistic approach was therefore seen as the third force in psychology.

The humanistic approach can be summarised into five core features:

- Human beings must be viewed as a whole and not be reduced to component parts.

- Human beings are unique and must be valued as such.

- Human consciousness includes an awareness of oneself in the context of other people.

- Human beings have free will, that is the ability to choose and determine their own paths in life.

- Human beings are intentional. They seek meaning, value and creativity.

Carl Rogers was concerned with creating a more holistic form of psychology, that is the focus on positive growth within individuals rather than their pathology. Rogers was committed to forming an establishment dedicated to individual, unique issues such as self-actualisation, growth, love and creativity.

Person-centred therapy

Carl Rogers developed person-centred therapy (PCT) in the 1940s and 1950s. Rogers's new therapy, which he termed counselling, was to revolutionise therapy as a whole and, in particular, the relationship between the therapist and client.

For Rogers, an important aspect of therapy was to focus on the client's immediate situation rather than their past (unlike psychoanalysis). By having a more personal relationship with the client, Rogers believed that the client could be brought to a state of realisation in which they can help themselves and use the therapy as a way to achieve a more ideal sense of self rather than remaining in an irrational world.

Person-centred therapy is a non-directive, talking therapy. The therapist encourages the client to express their inner feelings and perceptions. Rather than suggesting how the client might wish to change, the therapist becomes a 'mirror' – listening and reflecting back the client's thoughts and feelings. This way, the client then has free will to decide what changes they would like in order for them to achieve personal growth.

Concept of self

Rogers stated that in order for an individual to achieve personal growth, they must become **congruent** with their sense of self.

Rogers thought that there were three 'selves':

■ the self-concept – the way in which a person sees him/herself

■ the ideal self – the person whom we would like to be

■ the real self – the person we actually are.

The aim of person-centred therapy is to increase the client's level of congruence – to close the 'perceived' gap between the ideal and real self. While no individual ever achieves a perfect state of congruence, Rogers stated that the relative degree of congruence is a good indicator of psychological health.

Rogers believed that an effective therapist should provide the client with three essential elements in order to achieve personal growth and positive self-worth:

■ empathy with the client's emotions

■ genuineness

■ unconditional positive regard.

Rogers stated that many of the psychological problems experienced as adults, for example worthlessness, low self-esteem, were due to a lack of positive regard from our mothers as children. Children who are raised in such environments will only feel worthy if they adhere to certain conditions, that is do what they are told. Rogers describes this as **conditions of worth**. However, children that receive unconditional positive regard, or unconditional love, from their mothers, have the opportunity to fulfil their potential. Rogers said that it is essential that the therapist shows the client unconditional positive regard as a counteracting remedy for the client's earlier childhood experiences. This way, the therapist provides the right environment for the client to work towards achieving their full potential, or what Maslow termed, self-actualisation.

Maslow's hierarchy of needs

In 1943, Abraham Maslow proposed that all human beings have certain needs, which must be met in order to achieve our full potential or **self-actualisation**.

Maslow's hierarchy of needs is often portrayed as a pyramid consisting of five levels, as shown in Figure 10.

Maslow stated that the four lower levels in the hierarchy – esteem, love/belongingness, safety, physiological needs – are referred to as deficiency needs. The top level in the hierarchy – self-actualisation – is referred to as a growth need. Maslow stated that in order to achieve self-actualisation, that is to become a fully functioning, psychologically healthy individual, all deficiency needs must be met first. Only when an individual has satisfied their physiological needs, for example, can they then move up the hierarchy – their physiological needs are now no longer a priority for the individual. However, Maslow stated that if a lower set of needs in the hierarchy is continually unsatisfied, the individual could re-prioritise, that is return to the lower level in the hierarchy, until those needs are reasonably satisfied again. Only when all deficiency needs are met can the individual work towards achieving self-actualisation.

Maslow's hierarchy of needs has had enormous impact and practical application within the workplace, for example. Employers understand that for individual satisfaction and efficiency, it is essential they discover

Fig. 9 *Carl Rogers*

■ Key terms

Conditions of worth: a child will only receive praise, love, etc. from its parents if it behaves in ways that are considered by them to be socially acceptable.

Self-actualisation: the motive to realise one's full potential.

Self-actualisation
(Achieving individual potential)

Esteem
(Self-esteem and respect from others)

Love/Belonging
(Affection, being a part of groups)

Safety
(Our home environment)

Physiological
(Sex, food, sleep)

Fig. 10 *Maslow's hierarchy of needs*

AQA Examiner's tip

It is not necessary to describe each of the needs in Maslow's hierarchy in depth. This can waste time in an examination. Instead, focus on the essential features of the theory: the need for individuals to become self-actualised.

how their employees perceive their jobs in terms of need satisfaction. This then allows employers to match people to jobs that they are not only qualified for, but which would give their employees the most satisfaction as well.

Evaluation of the humanistic approach

Table 8 *Evaluation of the humanistic approach*

Strengths	Limitations
Humanistic psychologists view the person as an active agent, able to control and determine their own development, unlike behaviourism.	Humanistic theories are hard to falsify. They lack predictive power and are therefore unscientific.
Humanistic psychologists promote the idea of personal responsibility – free will as opposed to determinism.	In rejecting the use of the scientific method, humanistic theories lack empirical support.
The subjective experience of a person is of value and importance.	Humanistic psychologists over-emphasise the person's ability to change and develop, for example they ignore cultural constraints.
Person-centred therapy is used by psychologists and counsellors in therapy today.	Individual emotions and consciousness are difficult to study objectively.

Key points:

- Human beings are active agents who have free will to control and determine their own development.
- Rogers stated that to be psychologically healthy, a person's ideal self and real self must be congruent.
- Maslow stated that all individuals strive towards self-actualisation – the ability to realise one's potential.
- Person-centred therapy is still used in counselling today as an effective tool to achieve personal growth and psychological health.

Summary questions

23 Outline one assumption of the humanistic approach in psychology.

24 Describe what Rogers meant by unconditional positive regard.

25 Briefly describe one contribution that Rogers made to the development of psychology.

26 Explain one strength and one limitation of the humanistic approach.

27 Explain one way in which the humanistic approach differs from the behaviourist approach in psychology.

End-of-chapter activity

You can investigate the principle of classical conditioning using the 'eye-blink' response. Using a drinking straw, blow a puff of air into your participants' eyes (UCS). You will notice that this causes your participants to blink (UCR). Next, introduce a noise, such as a buzzer (CS), immediately before you blow a puff of air into your participants' eyes. Repeat this procedure a number of times. You should find that, after a number of repeated associations, your participants should blink to the sound of the buzzer alone (CR). You will need to think about any extraneous variables that you will need to control to help the demonstration of this principle work well. It is always important to consider ethical issues such as gaining consent from your participants before involving them in research.

2 Biopsychology

The structure and function of neurons

- Describe the structure and function of a motor neuron, a sensory neuron and an interconnecting neuron.
- Know and understand how electrical messages are transmitted from one neuron to another.

The divisions of the nervous system

Humans, like other living organisms, have two control systems in order to respond to the environment:

- the nervous system
- the endocrine system.

The organisation of the human nervous system is shown in Figure 1.

The human nervous system is divided into two main sub-systems:

- the central nervous system (CNS) which consists of the brain and spinal cord
- the peripheral nervous system (PNS) which consists of millions of neurons that carry messages to and from the central nervous system. These neurons are known as motor, sensory and interconnecting (or relay) neurons.

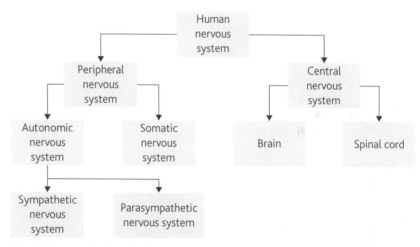

Fig. 1 *The organisation of the human nervous system*

Motor neurons

Motor neurons (or efferent neurons) carry messages away from the brain and spinal cord (CNS) to the organs and muscles in the body.

A motor neuron (see Figure 2) has a cell body with many dendrites (from the Greek word *dendron* meaning 'tree') branching off it. These dendrites have a large surface area in order to connect with other neurons and carry nerve impulses towards the cell body. The axon then carries the nerve impulse away from the cell body. The length of axons vary, for example a neuron in the spinal cord may have an axon 1.2 metres long, whereas a neuron in the brain may only be a few millimetres. Surrounding the axon are special cells known as Schwann cells that wrap around

Fig. 2 *A motor neuron carries messages from the central nervous system to the muscles and organs*

Cell body
Nucleus
Dendrite
Direction of impulse
Myelin sheath
Node of Ranvier
Axon
Synaptic terminals

Biopsychology

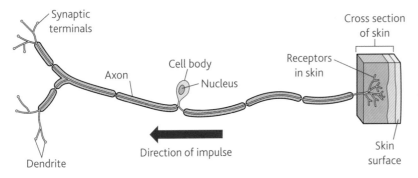

Synaptic
terminals

Cross section
of skin

Axon

Cell body

Receptors
in skin

Nucleus

Dendrite

Direction of impulse

Skin
surface

Fig. 3 *A sensory neuron: carries messages from the peripheral nervous system to the brain and spinal cord*

the axon to form an insulating layer called a myelin sheath. At its end, the axon divides into a number of branches known as synaptic terminals. These synaptic terminals do not actually touch the next neuron; there is a small gap between the synaptic terminals and the dendrites of the receiving neuron. This gap is known as a synapse.

Sensory neurons

Sensory neurons (or afferent neurons) carry messages from the receptors in the body (PNS) to the brain and spinal cord. Receptors such as our sense organs, muscles, skin or joints, detect physical and chemical changes in the body and relay these messages via sensory neurons to the brain or spinal cord (see Figure 3).

Interconnecting neurons

Interconnecting (or relay) neurons are found only in our visual system, brain and spinal cord. These neurons receive messages from the sensory neurons and pass these messages either to other interconnecting neurons or to motor neurons. The interaction of these three types of neuron can be seen in a simple diagram of a reflex arc (see Figure 4).

In a reflex arc, like the knee-jerk reflex below, a stimulus, such as a hammer hitting the knee, is detected by receptor cells in the PNS, which then conveys a message along a sensory neuron. The message reaches the CNS (brain or spinal cord) where it connects with an interconnecting, or relay, neuron. The interconnecting neuron then transfers this message to a motor neuron. The motor neuron then carries the message to an effector, such as a muscle, which causes the muscle to contract and, hence, the knee to move or jerk.

AQA Examiner's tip

Make sure you are able to explain some of the differences between motor, sensory and interconnecting neurons.

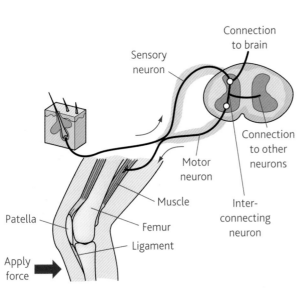

Fig. 4 *An interconnecting neuron: transmits information from sensory neurons to motor neurons as shown in the 'knee-jerk' reflex*

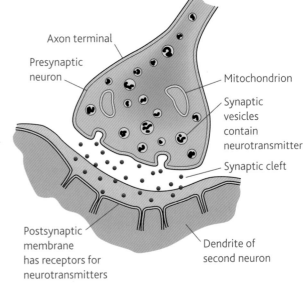

Fig. 5 *A synapse: is the gap that allows electrical impulses to transfer from one neuron to another*

Table 1 *Structural and functional differences between motor, sensory and interconnecting neurons*

	Motor neuron	Interconnecting neuron	Sensory neuron
Function	Carries messages from the CNS to effectors such as muscles and glands.	Transfers messages from sensory neurons to other interconnecting neurons, or motor neurons.	Carries messages from the PNS to the brain and spinal cord.
Length of fibres	Short dendrites and long axons.	Short dendrites and short or long axons.	Long dendrites and short axons.

▨ Synaptic transmission

It is estimated that the human brain contains around one billion neurons and even more synapses. A **synapse** is a specialised gap that allows electrical messages from one neuron to transfer to an adjacent neuron (see Figure 5 on page 22). This is known as synaptic transmission.

When the nerve impulse travels down an axon, it arrives at pre-synaptic terminals. This arrival triggers the release of **neurotransmitters** – chemicals that diffuse across the synaptic cleft (or gap) to the adjacent, post-synaptic neuron. When released, the neurotransmitter must be taken up immediately by the post-synaptic neuron otherwise it will either be reabsorbed by the synaptic terminals from which it was released, or be chemically broken down by enzymes in the synaptic cleft thereby making the neurotransmitter inactive. If successfully transmitted, the nerve impulse is then carried along the post-synaptic neuron until it reaches the next synaptic terminal where the message will continue to pass on via electrical impulses.

Neurotransmitters such as dopamine, acetylcholine or serotonin can either influence the post-synaptic neuron to respond in an inhibitory way (decreases the firing of a cell) or an excitatory way (increases the firing of a cell). Schizophrenia, for example, is a mental disorder thought to be the result of excessive activity of the neurotransmitter dopamine. Here, neurons that respond to dopamine fire too often, that is they are too excitatory, and transfer too many messages throughout the brain as a result. When this occurs, the symptoms of schizophrenia begin to appear. These symptoms can nevertheless be controlled with anti-psychotic drugs such as chlorpromazine, which are designed to block the receptor sites for dopamine.

Key points:

- Motor neurons carry messages from the CNS to the muscles and organs.
- Sensory neurons carry messages from the PNS to the brain and spinal cord.
- Interconnecting neurons transfer messages between sensory and motor neurons.
- A synapse is the gap between one neuron and the dendrites of an adjacent neuron.

▨ Key terms

Synapse: the gap between the end of one neuron and the dendrites of the next neuron.

Neurotransmitter: a chemical substance released from a synaptic vesicle that affects the transfer of an impulse to another nerve or muscle.

▨ Summary questions

1 What is the function of a sensory neuron?

2 Give two differences between a motor neuron and a sensory neuron.

3 What is meant by a synapse?

4 Name four features of a motor neuron.

5 Jemima is visiting her doctor for a routine medical examination. During the consultation, the doctor taps Jemima just below her knee with a hammer. Immediately, her lower leg jerks forward. Use your knowledge of the reflex response to explain why Jemima reacted in this way.

Localisation of cortical function

Learning objectives:

▨ Understand what is meant by localisation of cortical function.

▨ Suggest some examples of localisation of cortical function.

▨ Explain how split-brain research contributed to our understanding of lateralisation of cortical function.

Link

For more about case studies, see Chapter 4, Research methods.

Key terms

Localisation: specific areas of the cerebral cortex are associated with particular physical and psychological functions.

Lateralisation: the dominance of one hemisphere of the brain for particular physical and psychological functions.

Hemisphere: means 'half'; the brain has both a left and right hemisphere.

The human brain is undoubtedly one of the most remarkable structures within our human body. It is estimated to contain more than 100,000 kilometres of axons which receive around 3×10^{14} synapses. The cerebral cortex has the appearance of a scrunched-up piece of paper but these convolutions allow for a total surface area of 75 cm^2 when flattened out. The adult brain typically weighs around 1.4 kilograms and has an average volume of 1.6 litres.

Research study: The study of Phineas Gage (1848)

Aim: To explain the cause of Phineas Gage's change in personality.

Method: Whilst working for the Rutland and Burlington Railroad in New England, 25-year-old Gage was preparing to blast a section of rock using explosives in order to create a new railway line. Unfortunately, Gage accidentally dropped his tamping iron onto the rock which caused the explosive to ignite. The explosion hurled the metre-length iron pole through Gage's left cheek, passed behind his left eye, and exited his skull and brain from the top of his head. The pole was found some metres away covered in bits of Gage's brain.

Results: Miraculously, Gage survived and after months of rest and recovery, looked to regain his old railway job. However, no one would employ him as his personality had changed from someone who was kind and reserved, to someone who was now boisterous, rude and grossly blasphemous.

Conclusion:: As Damasio *et al.* (1994) state, although Phineas Gage's accident was horrific, it has taught us a great deal about the complexity of psychological processes that occur in the human brain.

Evaluation: We must be careful in generalising the findings of this study to explain human behaviour as the findings are based on one very rare case of an unfortunate individual.

During the 19th century, scientists such as Paul Broca and Karl Wernicke discovered that certain areas of the brain held particular functions – known as **localisation** of cortical function. They also discovered that some functions, such as speech and language, were controlled by a particular **hemisphere** (or side of the brain) – known as **lateralisation** of cortical function. Because of these research findings, we have been able to explore, using advances in medical technology, numerous areas of the brain in order to gain a deeper understanding of human behaviour.

The human brain can be viewed as being formed of three concentric layers:

▨ the central core which regulates our most primitive and involuntary behaviours

▨ the limbic system which controls our emotions

▨ the cerebrum which regulates our higher intellectual processes.

The central core

The central core is also known as the brain stem and controls our most primitive behaviours such as sleeping, breathing or sexual behaviour, as well as our involuntary behaviours, such as sneezing. The central core includes structures such as the hypothalamus. The hypothalamus is located in the midbrain and regulates our eating, drinking and sexual behaviour, as well as regulating the endocrine system in order to maintain **homeostasis**.

▨ Key term

Homeostasis: the process by which the body maintains a constant physiological state.

The limbic system

Around the central core of the brain, and closely interconnected with the hypothalamus, is the limbic system which contains structures such as the hippocampus. The hippocampus is thought to play a key role in memory. This was discovered in the 1950s when patients such as HM (see p181) had their hippocampus surgically removed in order to treat severe forms of epilepsy. Upon recovery, HM suffered from a severe form of anterograde amnesia.

The cerebrum

The cerebrum has an outermost layer known as the cerebral cortex. The cortex appears grey because of the location of cell bodies – which is why it is known as grey matter. Beneath the cortex lie myelinated axons which appear as white – hence it is known as white matter. Each of our sensory systems sends messages to and from this cerebral cortex.

The cerebrum is composed of the right and left hemispheres which are connected by a bundle of fibres called the corpus callosum. The corpus callosum enables messages that enter the right hemisphere to be conveyed to the left hemisphere and vice versa. Each hemisphere is further divided into four lobes:

- the frontal lobe – the location for awareness of what we are doing within our environment (our consciousness)
- the parietal lobe – location for sensory and motor movements
- the temporal lobe – location for auditory ability and memory acquisition
- the occipital lobe – location for vision.

The motor area

The motor area is located in the parietal lobe and is responsible for controlling our voluntary movements. Movements on the right side of the body are controlled by the left hemisphere and vice versa. Therefore, damage to the motor cortex results in impaired movements.

The somatosensory area

Also located in the parietal lobe, and separated from the motor area by the central sulcus, lies the somatosensory area which responds to heat, cold, touch, pain and our sense of body movement. The amount of somatosensory area associated with a particular part of the body is related to

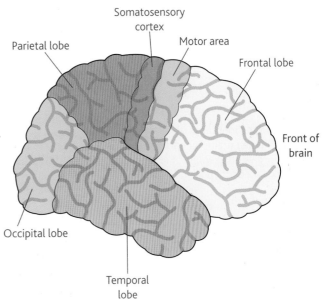

Fig. 6 *Lateral view of the human brain showing some of the major structures and divisions*

its use and sensitivity. For example rats, which move around their environment using their highly sensitive whiskers, have a separate cortical area for each whisker! In humans, our face and hands comprise more than half of our sensory cortex.

The visual area

At the back of the brain lies the occipital lobe whose primary function is vision. Predominately, nerve fibres from the inner half of the retina of each eye cross at the **optic chiasm** and travel to opposite sides of the brain. As a result, damage to the left hemisphere can produce a loss of vision to the right side of our environment. Nerve fibres from the outer edge of each retina do not cross at the optic chiasm, and so damage to the left optic nerve can affect the left eye.

The auditory area

The auditory area is located in the temporal lobe and is responsible for the analysis of speech-based information. Within this lobe is an area known as Wernicke's area, named after Karl Wernicke, who discovered that damage to the left temporal lobe resulted in linguistic deficits. Individuals who experience difficulties in language comprehension suffer from what is known as Wernicke's aphasia.

Split-brain research

Split-brain patients are patients that have undergone a corpus callosotomy, that is a large part of the corpus callosum is lesioned (cut). This procedure was mainly used in the 1950s to treat severe forms of epilepsy. As a result of this surgery, the two hemispheres of the brain are not able to communicate as effectively. In the 1960s, Roger Sperry and Michael Gazzaniga conducted a vast amount of research on split-brain patients by testing various cognitive and perceptual processes. They administered tasks known to be associated with each hemisphere of the brain to the patients. They discovered that the two halves of the brain were able to function quite independently.

Key points:

- Localisation of cortical function refers to specific areas of the brain being responsible for a particular behaviour or action.
- The human brain can be divided into three layers: the central core, the limbic system and the cerebrum.
- The brain is divided into two halves (hemispheres).
- The four lobes of the brain are: frontal, parietal, temporal and occipital; each with particular functions.
- Split-brain research has shown how each half of the brain is able to function quite independently.

Key term

Optic chiasm: the point at which the nerve fibres from both eyes converge.

AQA Examiner's tip

Make sure you are able to explain some examples of localisation of cortical function in examination questions.

Summary questions

6 What is meant by the terms localisation and lateralisation?

7 Name the three concentric layers of the human brain.

8 Name the four lobes of the human brain. For each lobe, give an example of an associated function.

Methods of studying cortical specialisation

Learning objectives:

- Know and understand some of the invasive and non-invasive methods used to study cortical specialisation.

- Explain evidence in support or criticism of these methods.

- Evaluate the use of these methods.

💡 Psychologists have developed many methods of studying cortical specialisation in the brain in order to be able to predict, control and explain human and non-human behaviour. One of the very earliest methods of studying the brain was proposed by Franz Joseph Gall (1758–1828), who developed a technique called phrenology. Gall would feel for 'bumps' on the heads of patients and attribute these to a number of behavioural characteristics, for example a 'tendency to murder'. Phrenology was extremely popular in the 19th century; it was not unusual for people to hire a phrenologist in order to assist in selecting a suitable partner for marriage! However, phrenology was discredited for its lack of scientific evidence. Nevertheless, Gall theorised that different areas of the brain were responsible for a particular function. Today, we use various invasive and non-invasive methods in order to explore and develop our understanding of areas of cortical specialisation.

Invasive methods

Neurosurgery

Neurosurgery is considered to be an invasive method of investigating cortical specialisation as it involves manipulating structures within the brain. There are two main ways in which neurosurgery is performed: **ablations** and **lesions**.

In the late 1950s and early 1960s, David Hubel and Torsten Wiesel conducted a series of experiments on sensory processing. In one experiment, they inserted a microelectrode into the visual cortex of an anaesthetised cat. They then projected patterns of dark and light onto a screen in front of the cat. They found that some neurons within the cat's brain fired quickly when the lines were presented at a certain angle compared to other angles. Hubel and Wiesel called these neurons 'simple cells'. They also discovered that 'complex cells' respond best to lines of a certain angle that move in one direction. Hubel and Wiesel therefore showed how the visual system in the brain builds up an image from a simple to a more complex representation.

Electrical and chemical stimulation

An important technique used for studying cortical specialisation involves electrical stimulation of specified areas of the brain. In 1954, James Olds and Peter Milner were testing the effects of the **reticular formation** in rats when they accidentally placed an electrode in the septal area. They found that this part of the limbic system was associated with pleasure as the rats, who soon learned that they could control the electrical stimulation, would press the lever that initiated the pleasure repeatedly.

The Wada test, also known as the intracarotid sodium amobarbital procedure (ISAP), is a chemical test used to establish which cortical functions are located to which hemisphere of the brain. The procedure is often used on patients prior to surgery in order to establish which side of the brain is responsible for speech and memory so that damage to

Key terms

Ablation: a surgical procedure used to remove areas of the brain.

Lesioning: a surgical procedure used to cut neural connections in the brain.

Reticular formation: a complex network of fibres, extending from the core of the brainstem to the thalamus, involved in maintaining functions vital to life.

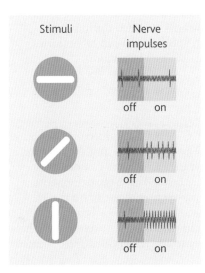

Fig. 7 *Complex cells are the most common type of cell in the visual cortex*

these structures can be minimised during the surgery itself. During the Wada test, the patient is kept awake and an anaesthetic – usually sodium amobarbital – is injected into one hemisphere at a time in order to 'shut down' any language or memory functions in that hemisphere so that a thorough evaluation can be made of the other hemisphere. Recovery from the anaesthesia is quite rapid and an EEG is used to record when all the medication has worn off.

Post-mortem studies

Post-mortem studies are a research method in which the brain of a patient, who has usually been the subject of a longitudinal study because of some rare affliction, such as the inability to speak, is examined after death. The area of the brain that is damaged is then attributed to the affliction suffered by the person during their life. Post-mortem studies have been used for centuries. Before the introduction of contemporary scanning methods and X-rays, it was one of the few ways to study the relationship between the brain and behaviour. Paul Broca (1824–80) was a French physician and anatomist who famously used post-mortem studies to investigate the location of speech production in the brain. One of his first patients was nicknamed 'Tan' because of his inability to clearly speak any words other than 'tan'. In 1861, through an autopsy, Broca discovered that Tan had a lesion in the left cerebral hemisphere caused by syphilis. This area of the brain became known as Broca's area and damage to this section of the brain can lead to Broca's aphasia.

Non-invasive methods

Electroencephalogram (EEG)

Electroencephalogram, or EEG, is a non-invasive measurement of electrical activity of the brain by recording from electrodes placed on the individual's scalp. The EEG represents an electrical signal from a large number of neurons within the brain and the voltage differences between different parts of the brain are recorded. The filtered signal is then displayed on a computer screen which clinicians then use to monitor situations such as the categorisation of different types of epileptic seizures. Neuroscientists and psychiatrists use EEGs to study brain function by recording brain activity in humans and non-humans during various laboratory experiments. EEG patterns recorded during sleep sessions, which are usually conducted in specialised sleep laboratories, have contributed significantly to theories of sleep behaviour.

Scanning

Computerised axial tomography (CAT)

Computerised axial tomography (a CAT/CT scan) is a procedure whereby a narrow X-ray beam is sent through the patient's head and the amount of radiation absorbed is measured. These measurements can be made on hundreds of different axes through the head. These measurements are then fed into a computer where a cross-section of the brain can be photographed or displayed on a screen (see Figure 8). CAT scans are useful for evaluating the amount of swelling due to tissue damage in the brain, or assessment of the size of the ventricles (fluid-filled gaps) located deep within the brain.

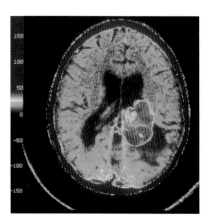

Fig. 8 *CAT scans produce 3D images which can be used to detect tumours and damaged parts of the brain*

Positron emission tomography (PET)

Positron emission tomography (a PET scan) is a procedure whereby different levels of neural activity, in various locations of the brain, are assessed whilst the brain is active. A small amount of radioactive glucose is injected into the person's bloodstream and, after a few minutes, the brain begins to use the radioactive glucose in the same way as it uses glucose which provides the brain with energy. The PET scan then detects and measures the amount of radioactivity emitted when individuals are asked to perform tasks such as solving problems (see Figure 9).

Magnetic resonance imaging (MRI)

Magnetic resonance imaging (an MRI scan) is a powerful technique where scanners use strong magnetic fields and radio waves to produce a high quality image of an individual's brain (see Figure 10). During the procedure, the individual lies in a tunnel surrounded by a large magnet which produces a strong magnetic field. When a certain area of the body is exposed to a radio-frequency pulse, the tissues in the body give out a signal that is then measured. Like the CAT scan, hundreds of measurements can be made to produce precise images of the brain. MRI scans have been particularly useful in diagnosing diseases of the brain and spinal cord, for example multiple sclerosis, which is not detectable with a CAT scan.

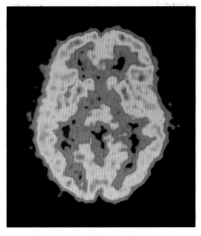

Fig. 9 *PET scans are useful as they enable us to see the human brain in action*

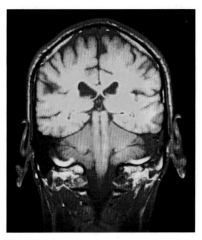

Fig. 10 *MRI scans are able to produce very precise images of the brain*

▦ Evaluation of methods to study cortical specialisation

Table 2 *Strengths and limitations of methods used to investigate cortical specialisation*

Method	Strengths	Limitations
Neurosurgery	Allows for a great deal of specificity and control in the location of damage.	Problem of cause and effect – does lesioning one area of the brain cause damage to other areas?
Electrical and chemical stimulation	Stimulating the brain is a less harmful procedure than surgery and therefore more ethical.	Problems in extrapolating research conducted on animals to explaining human cortical function.
Post-mortem studies	Provides a greater understanding of rare afflictions in individuals.	Obtaining a person's brain, even if they have been the subject of a longitudinal study, can be very difficult.
EEG	No intervention is necessary and therefore allows for natural measurements of brain activity.	Electrodes are not sensitive enough to pick out individual action potentials of single neurons.
Scans	Provides detailed knowledge of areas of the brain that are active whilst completing tasks such as problem solving.	Some scans are time consuming, so therefore unable to record spontaneous behaviour. Ethical issues surrounding the injection of radioactive glucose (PET scan).

Key points:

■ Invasive techniques such as neurosurgery allow for a great deal of precision and control.

■ Post-mortem studies enable scientists to observe rare afflictions in individuals.

■ EEGs have contributed a great deal to theories of sleep behaviour.

■ CAT, PET and MRI scans allow for the study of the brain in action.

Summary questions

9 Give one strength and one limitation of using neurosurgery to investigate areas of cortical specialisation.

10 What does the Wada test involve?

11 Name three methods of scanning.

12 Outline one strength and one limitation of using scans to investigate areas of cortical specialisation.

13 Explain one advantage of using PET scans to investigate cortical specialisation.

The autonomic nervous system

- Describe the role of the autonomic nervous system.
- Know and understand some actions of the sympathetic and parasympathetic nervous systems.
- Understand what is meant by the fight or flight response.

The peripheral nervous system has two divisions:

- the somatic nervous system, which controls skeletal muscles and receives information to and from sensory receptors
- the autonomic nervous system, which maintains homeostasis (see p25) by controlling glands and vital muscles such as the heart, stomach, blood vessels etc. It is known as 'autonomic' because the system operates involuntarily.

The two main divisions of the autonomic nervous system are:

- the sympathetic nervous system
- the parasympathetic nervous system.

Their actions are mostly antagonistic, that is they usually work in opposition to each other (see Table 3), apart from during sexual intercourse, for example, where the male's erection is due to parasympathetic action followed by ejaculation, which is a sympathetic action.

Typically, the sympathetic nervous system functions when quick action is required, for example during a threatening situation, whereas the parasympathetic nervous system does not require immediate action. The sympathetic nervous system can therefore be considered as the 'fight or flight' system and the parasympathetic nervous system as the 'rest and digest' system.

Table 3 *Actions of the sympathetic and parasympathetic divisions of the autonomic nervous system*

Organ	Sympathetic nervous system	Parasympathetic nervous system
Eye	Dilates pupils	Constricts pupils
Salivary glands	Inhibits saliva production	Stimulates saliva production
Lungs	Dilates bronchi	Constricts bronchi
Heart	Speeds up heart rate	Slows down heart rate
Gut	Inhibits digestion	Stimulates digestion
Liver	Stimulates glucose production	Stimulates bile production
Bladder	Inhibits urination	Stimulates urination

AQA Examiner's tip

Make sure you can explain some of the actions of the sympathetic and parasympathetic nervous systems.

In general, the sympathetic nervous system stimulates the fight or flight response to threatening situations, while the parasympathetic nervous system restores the body to its normal state. For example, imagine you are walking home alone late at night. Suddenly, you hear a loud noise behind you. Immediately, your body diverts blood away from your stomach to your muscles in order for you to stay and confront the potential attacker (fight), or run away (flight). Your heart rate increases and other sympathetic responses (as shown in Table 3) are activated. After a short while, you realise that the loud noise was in fact a prowling cat. You feel a sense of relief and notice that your breathing starts to

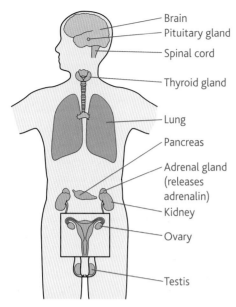

Brain
Pituitary gland
Spinal cord
Thyroid gland
Lung
Pancreas
Adrenal gland (releases adrenalin)
Kidney
Ovary
Testis

Fig. 11 *The adrenal glands release the hormone adrenalin in response to a threatening or stressful situation*

Summary questions

14 Name the hormone released by the adrenal medulla during a threatening situation.

15 Name two divisions of the autonomic nervous system.

16 Using an example, explain what is meant by the fight or flight response.

17 Give two actions of the sympathetic nervous system and two actions of the parasympathetic nervous system.

18 Billy is an A Level psychology student. He has been asked by his teacher to give a short presentation to the other psychology students in his class. Just before his presentation, Billy feels his mouth go dry and he starts to sweat. After the presentation has ended, Billy feels his breathing slow down and he begins to feel thirsty. Use your knowledge of the autonomic nervous system to explain Billy's behaviour before and after the presentation.

slow down and the palms of your hands stop sweating: your parasympathetic nervous system is now acting to restore your bodily functions to their normal state. Even though the threat has gone away, you may still find yourself shaking all over as the hormones in your bloodstream, for example adrenalin, take longer to disperse.

■ The endocrine system

The endocrine system is composed of a number of glands that release hormones directly into the bloodstream. Unlike the fast-acting nervous system, the endocrine system acts more slowly to transport these hormones around the body. One of the major endocrine glands is the pituitary gland, also known as the 'master gland', as it controls the release of hormones from all other endocrine glands in the body. During a threatening or stressful situation, the pituitary gland releases adrenocorticotropic hormone (ACTH) which is the body's major stress hormone. ACTH is then carried around the bloodstream and, in turn, stimulates the adrenal glands, in particular the adrenal medulla, to release adrenalin directly into the bloodstream. In conjunction with the sympathetic nervous system, the adrenalin aids in the fight or flight response by constricting blood vessels in the stomach which inhibits digestion (and gives you that 'sick' feeling) and by increasing the heart rate.

■ Effects of the stress response

Although the fight or flight response is undoubtedly valuable to us in a threatening or stressful situation, prolonged exposure to these stress hormones can be particularly damaging not only physically, but psychologically. Common side-effects include disruption to one's sex life, problems associated with digestion and, in more severe cases, heart disease.

Although our autonomic nervous system is thought to be involuntary, this is not necessarily the case when observing the practices of Zen Buddhists. During meditation, Zen Buddhists are able to control a number of autonomic functions including their heart rate and oxygen consumption. These changes are not due to the decrease in physical activity associated with the meditation because the physical changes exceed that which occurs during sleep or hypnosis. Zen Buddhists are therefore able to control any potential negative effects of stress.

Key points:

- The autonomic nervous system operates involuntarily.
- The sympathetic nervous system prepares the body for fight or flight.
- The parasympathetic nervous system acts to restore the body to its normal state.
- The endocrine system works in conjunction with the sympathetic nervous system by releasing hormones, for example adrenalin, into the bloodstream.

Genotype and phenotype

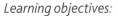

Learning objectives:

- Understand what is meant by the term genotype.
- Understand what is meant by the term phenotype.
- Suggest some examples of disorders that can be used to explain the difference between these two terms.

Key terms

Genotype: the genetic make-up of an individual.

Phenotype: the characteristics shown by an individual that are a result of both genes and the environment.

Heterozygous: the genotype consists of two different genes for example Bb.

Homozygous: the genotype consists of two genes that are the same, for example BB.

AQA Examiner's tip

Make sure you can define and provide examples of both genotype and phenotype.

Summary questions

19 What is meant by the term genotype?

20 What is meant by the term phenotype?

21 Using an example, distinguish between genotype and phenotype.

22 Explain why monozygotic twins, who share exactly the same genotype, may have different phenotypes.

Genotype refers to an individual's genetic make-up, that is the particular set of genes that the individual possesses. **Phenotype** refers to the observable characteristics, or traits, shown by the individual, for example height, weight or eye colour.

The individual's genotype is the major influencing factor in the development of their phenotype, but it is not the only one. Phenotype is affected not only by genes, but also by the environment:

$$\text{Genotype } + \text{ Environment } = \text{ Phenotype}$$

If identical twins, who share the same genotype, were separated at birth and raised in different environments, one twin may show a completely different phenotype from the other twin. For example, if one twin were fed a more nutritious diet, it would be physically much taller and stronger than the other twin.

Psychologists have referred to various disorders to try to explain the difference between genotype and phenotype. An example of such a disorder is phenylketonuria (PKU) which is characterised by a deficiency in the enzyme phenylalanine hydroxylase (PAH). PKU is a recessive genetic disorder which means that each parent must have at least one defective gene for PAH which the child then inherits. It is possible for a parent with a PKU phenotype to have a child without PKU if the other parent has a functional PAH gene. A child who has two parents with PKU will always inherit two defective genes and therefore the disorder.

If undetected and untreated at birth, individuals tend to fail to accomplish important developmental milestones. However, if PKU is diagnosed early, a newborn can develop normally if given a special diet, low in phenylalanine, for the rest of its life.

The distinction between an individual's genotype and phenotype can also arise from studies of hereditary diseases, such as haemophilia. Haemophilia is a recessive, genetic illness that impairs the body's ability to control blood coagulation. The disease is more common in males than in females and is sometimes known as 'the royal disease' as Queen Victoria was a carrier!

In the case of haemophilia, a **heterozygous** individual is a carrier. The individual has a normal phenotype but has a 50:50 risk of passing the gene onto its offspring. A **homozygous** dominant individual has a normal phenotype and has no risk of passing the gene onto its offspring. A homozygous recessive individual has an abnormal phenotype and is guaranteed to pass the gene onto its offspring.

Key points:

- Genotype refers to an individual's genetic make-up.
- Phenotype refers to the characteristics shown by an individual that are determined by genetics and the environment.
- PKU is a genetic disorder which, when treated with a special diet, can mean the individual will develop normally.
- Haemophilia does not always mean the individual will develop the disease, that is they can be a carrier.

Monozygotic and dizygotic twins

Learning objectives:

■ Understand what is meant by monozygotic twins and dizygotic twins.

■ Explain why psychologists are interested in studying twins.

Key terms

Monozygotic: one zygote. These twins are formed when a fertilised egg cell splits into two and forms two separate embryos.

Zygote: a fertilised cell (union of an egg cell and a sperm cell).

Dizygotic: two zygotes. These twins are formed when two separate eggs both become fertilised by different sperm cells.

Fig. 12 *Monozygotic twins Sam and Amanda Merchant from Big Brother 2007*

Monozygotic twins

Monozygotic (or MZ) twins are more commonly known as identical twins.

Monozygotic twins occur when a single egg, which is fertilised to form one **zygote**, divides to form two separate embryos. These two embryos continue to develop into foetuses whilst sharing their mother's womb. If the zygote divides into two embryos at around two days after fertilisation, then the embryos may develop separate placentas and amniotic sacs. Usually, in monozygotic twins, the zygote divides after two days, resulting in a shared placenta but two separate amniotic sacs. Around 1 in 50,000 pregnancies results in conjoined twins – twins who are physically united (joined) in some way. The reason is thought to be due to the zygote dividing too late – around 13 days after fertilisation. Monozygotic twins are genetically identical, that is they share exactly the same DNA. Although they generally look similar, monozygotic twins often become less alike as they grow older due to lifestyle choices, etc.

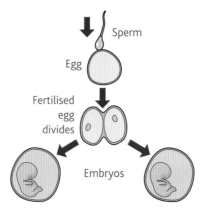

Fig. 13 *Monozygotic twins form when a zygote divides to form two embryos*

Dizygotic twins

Dizygotic (or DZ) twins are more commonly known as non-identical or fraternal twins.

Dizygotic twins occur when two egg cells are fertilised by two different sperm cells. Unlike monozygotic twins, who share the same DNA, dizygotic twins are no more genetically alike than are ordinary siblings (brothers and sisters).

Psychologists are interested in studying monozygotic and dizygotic twins in order to investigate the genetic basis of behaviour. For instance, if one set of monozygotic twins were separated at birth and raised in different environments, what is the likelihood of them both developing a mental disorder such as schizophrenia? If both twins were to develop schizophrenia, should this lead psychologists to conclude that schizophrenia is therefore a genetic disorder?

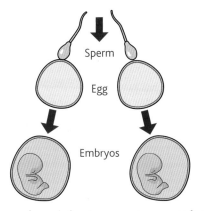

Fig. 14 *Dizygotic twins are formed when two separate eggs are fertilised*

AQA Examiner's tip

An easy way of remembering the difference between MZ and DZ twins is to learn that *mono* means 'one' (one egg) and *di* means 'two' (two eggs).

Key points:

- Monozygotic (MZ) twins are formed when a zygote divides to form two separate embryos.

- Dizygotic (DZ) twins are formed when two eggs are fertilised by two different sperm cells.

- Psychologists are interested in studying twins in order to investigate the genetic basis of behaviour.

💡 Summary questions

23 What are monozygotic twins?

24 How genetically alike are:

 a MZ twins

 b DZ twins?

25 Why are psychologists interested in studying twins?

26 Richard has an identical twin, Samuel. This means they have exactly the same genetic make-up. Like his father, Richard can play tennis to a very high standard whereas Samuel cannot. Use your knowledge of genotype and phenotype to explain why Richard can play tennis but Samuel cannot.

Investigating the genetic basis of behaviour

Learning objectives:

- Explain why psychologists are interested in studying the genetic basis of behaviour.

- Explain what twin, family, adoption studies and selective breeding methods tell us about the genetic basis of behaviour.

Key terms

Concordance: agreement between; the extent to which a pair of twins share similar traits or characteristics.

Meta-analysis: statistical analysis of the results of a number of the same or similar studies.

AQA Examiner's tip

Make sure you can explain the rationale underlying the different methods used to investigate the genetic basis of behaviour.

Link

For more on correlation coefficients, see p101.

The field of behaviour genetics uses both genetics and psychology to study whether behavioural characteristics are inherited. It is evident that physical characteristics, such as our eye colour, or height, are inherited from our parents. What psychologists are interested in is whether characteristics such as intelligence, sexual orientation, addiction, etc. are also inherited.

Twin studies

We know the saying that certain traits 'run in families', for example musical ability. However, the problem in assuming that musical ability must therefore be heritable is that families also share exactly the same environment. We are therefore left unsure as to whether musical ability is a result of inheritance or parental influence. To try to answer this problem, psychologists have looked at twin studies, particularly of monozygotic (identical) twins.

The rationale for using twins to investigate the genetic basis of behaviour is that if one monozygotic twin has a particular characteristic and so does the other twin, then that characteristic may be genetic as they share exactly the same genotype: there should be 100 per cent **concordance** between them. Dizygotic twins, who are no more genetically alike than siblings, should show a much lower concordance rate. If the environment plays a significant role in determining our behaviour, then monozygotic twins, who have been reared apart, should show a low concordance rate for traits such as intelligence.

Intelligence

Wilson (1978, 1983) conducted a longitudinal study and found that by the age of 18 months, monozygotic twins were more similar than dizygotic twins on tests of infant intelligence. The follow-up data over the next 13 years showed that the monozygotic twins were more similar than dizygotic twins in their intellectual performance. Plomin (1990) tried to account for these intellectual differences in dizygotic twins by stating that their different genotypes may in fact have directed them along separate developmental paths which would account for their 'poorer' intellectual performance compared to monozygotic twins who share the same genotype.

Bouchard and McGue (1981) conducted a **meta-analysis** of twin studies and the degree to which IQ scores are inherited with the results shown in Table 4.

Table 4 *Meta-analysis of twin studies and IQ*

Combination of twins	Correlation coefficient for IQ
MZ twins reared together	0.86
MZ twins reared apart	0.72
DZ twins reared together	0.60
Siblings (including DZ twins) reared apart	0.24

Source: Bouchard and McGue (1981)

Sexual orientation

There is some evidence from twin studies to suggest that homosexuality may be genetically determined. Bailey and Pillard (1991), in a study of male twins where at least one of the pair was gay, found that 52 per cent of monozygotic brothers were concordant for homosexuality compared to 22 per cent of dizygotic brothers. Bailey, Dunne and Martin (2000) obtained a sample of 4,901 twins from an Australian twin registry. They found a 30 per cent concordance for homosexuality in MZ twins.

Criticisms of sexual orientation studies, like the ones above, have included the way in which participants were recruited, for example, through gay media, whose target audience is clearly homosexual. This would account for the high response rates to take part in such studies compared to the potential recruitment of homosexuals through more traditional forms of media. Bearman and Bruckner (2002), however, argue against a genetic basis for sexual orientation. They argue that such low concordance rates (as shown in Table 5) do not account for a genetic similarity in homosexual twins. Overall, most researchers suggest that it is unlikely that there is a single 'gay gene'. Instead, our sexual orientation is more likely to be the result of a combination of genetic and cultural factors.

Table 5 *Percentage concordance for homosexuality*

Study	Males	Females
Hershberger (1997)	0%	48%
Bailey *et al.* (2000)	30%	30%
Kirk *et al.* (2000)	30%	50–60%
Bearman *et al.* (2002)	7.7%	5.3%

■ Family studies

As early as 1869, Francis Galton conducted the first empirical research in human behavioural genetics when he published *Hereditary Genius*. His assumption that all natural abilities were inherited was rather overstated, however. By his own admission, Galton had to conclude that any resemblance between family relatives could be a result of both genes and a shared environment.

Addiction

Gianoulakis, Krishnan and Thavundayil (1996) found that sons of alcoholic fathers were more likely to be alcoholics themselves compared to people selected at random. The researchers discovered that when sons of alcoholics drank alcohol, they tended to release more of the neurotransmitter endorphin compared to other people, therefore suggesting a biological predisposition towards alcoholism.

Family size and birth order

There is evidence to suggest that the environment plays a more significant role than genes in determining behaviour. For example, Zajonc and Markus (1975) researched IQ data of 40,000 Dutch males who were born in 1944. They found that IQ is related to birth order and family size. The researchers suggested that this was largely due to the degree of attention given by parents: larger families may mean that each child has a smaller amount of parental attention and perhaps more of a physically deprived environment and hence a lower IQ.

■ Adoption studies

Adoption studies are particularly useful for investigating the genetic basis of behaviour. These studies involve comparing a trait or characteristic between adopted children and their biological or adoptive parents. Adopted children in one family may be compared with biological children in another family, or studying families with both adopted and biological children. If a trait or characteristic has a genetic basis, then the adopted child should show the same trait as its biological parent. However, if a trait or characteristic is environmentally influenced, then the adopted child should show similar characteristics to their adoptive parents.

Age

As children grow older, it is assumed that their cognitive and verbal abilities would develop to become more like their adoptive parents than their biological parents. However, Plomin, Fulker, Corley and DeFries (1997) found that, as adopted children approached the age of 16, they became more similar to their biological parents in cognitive and verbal ability compared to their adoptive parents, therefore suggesting a genetic influence.

Intelligence

In the Minnesota Adoption Study of black children, Scarr and Weinberg (1976) found evidence that intelligence was strongly linked to environmental influence. Black children from low socio-economic backgrounds were adopted into white middle-class families where the adoptive parents had at least one biological child. Scarr and Weinberg initially found that the black children were more intellectually similar to their biological parents (0.43) than to their adoptive parents (0.29) therefore supporting a genetic basis for intelligence. However, Scarr and Weinberg found that inter-racial (black and white) siblings also showed intellectual similarities. As these inter-racial siblings have no genes in common, their similarities in intelligence must be due to the environment and not genetics.

Findings from adoption studies must be viewed with caution, however. Adoptive families are usually smaller, financially richer and may provide a more stimulating environment compared to some biological parents. This would therefore account for an increase in IQ scores.

■ Selective breeding

One method of studying whether a trait or characteristic has a genetic basis is through selective breeding. This method involves artificially selecting male and female animals for a particular trait. These animals are then put together in order to breed and produce offspring. The advantage of this method is that it is a quick way to select for particular traits with the effects of artificial selection being seen within just a few generations of breeding. Plomin (1989) suggests that if selective breeding does not alter the trait or characteristic, then we must assume that the trait or characteristic is entirely dependent on environmental factors.

Selective breeding has been used to demonstrate how a number of behavioural characteristics may have a genetic basis. For example, fruit flies have been bred to be more or less sensitive to light; mice have been bred to be more or less dependent on alcohol; dogs have been bred to be excitable or lethargic; and chickens have been bred to be aggressive and sexually active.

Tryon (1940) conducted an experiment with the aim of investigating whether genetics influenced learning in rats.

He trained a large number of rats to run a complex maze. Those rats that were the quickest through the maze were selected as well as those rats that were the slowest. Tryon then bred the 'bright' (quickest) rats with other 'bright' rats and 'dull' (slowest) rats with other 'dull' rats (the independent variable). He continued this breeding process for a number of generations. The dependant variable was the number of errors made and speed with which the rats learned their way through the maze.

'Maze bright' rats learned to run the maze faster and made fewer errors compared to 'maze dull' rats.

From this we can conclude that learning is a heritable characteristic which can be controlled and manipulated through selective breeding.

These findings seem to suggest that learning has a genetic basis. We must be careful, however, in generalising the findings in this study to explain human behaviour since humans interact very differently within their own environment.

Cooper and Zubeck (1958) conducted a similar study to Tryon but found very different results. They reared 'maze dull' rats in one of two environments:

 an impoverished, or boring environment consisting of a barren wire-meshed cage

 a stimulating environment containing tunnels, ramps, etc.

When the rats reached maturity, the 'maze dull' rats that had been reared in a stimulating environment made the same number of learning errors as the 'maze bright' rats in a stimulating environment. This study therefore shows that the environment is also an important factor in determining behaviour.

Key points:

 There is evidence from twin, family and adoption studies to suggest that certain behaviours, for example intelligence, are genetically determined.

 Research has shown that the environment can play more of a role in determining behaviour than genetics.

 Selective breeding studies have demonstrated how a number of behavioural characteristics, for example aggression, can have a genetic basis.

Fig. 15 *Tryon found that 'maze bright' rats could be selectively bred to make fewer errors through a maze*

Link

For more information on experimental methods, see Chapter 4, Research methods.

AQA Examiner's tip

In your examination answers, consider the issues surrounding the extrapolation of findings from animal research in order to explain human behaviour.

✔ Summary questions

27 What is meant by the terms:
a concordance
b correlation?

28 Explain why MZ twins are useful for investigating the genetic basis of behaviour.

29 Outline one criticism of adoption studies.

30 Explain one limitation of using family studies to investigate the genetic basis of behaviour.

💡 End-of-chapter activity

You could conduct an experiment to investigate gender differences in reaction time. Place a metre ruler against the classroom wall. Ask your partner to hold the ruler against the wall at the zero end of the ruler. You should place your preferred hand level with the 50 cm mark on the ruler but not actually touching the ruler. When your partner suddenly lets go of the ruler, you must catch it with your thumb and index finger. Your score is the number just above your index finger.

In order to carry out this experiment, you should consider the type of experimental design and any extraneous variables that you will need to control. It is always important to consider ethical issues such as gaining consent from your participants before conducting any experiment.

1 (a) What is meant by a defence mechanism? Illustrate your answer with an example.

(2 marks)

(b) Explain two limitations of the psychodynamic approach in psychology. *(4 marks)*

(c) Naveed is 24 years old. He has low self-esteem and feels worthless. As a child, he felt that no matter how hard he tried to please people, no one ever approved of him.

With reference to one assumption of the humanistic approach, explain a possible cause of Naveed's problems. *(4 marks)*

(d) Describe and discuss methodological and/or ethical issues which might arise when investigating cortical specialisation in the brain. *(10 marks)*

AQA specimen question

2 (a) What is meant by the term genotype? Give an example. *(2 marks)*

(b) (i) Explain one methodological strength of the biological approach in psychology. *(2 marks)*

(ii) Explain one methodological limitation of the psychodynamic approach in psychology. *(2 marks)*

(c) Jemima is 15 years old and has always enjoyed going to school. This term, however, her teachers have noticed a change in her behaviour. Jemima has become very withdrawn and displays fear and anxiety every time she has to go to school. When her teachers question why she no longer likes going to school, Jemima says that she was bullied last term.

Referring to features of the behaviourist approach, suggest how Jemima's fear of school developed. *(4 marks)*

(d) Sally and her family are at a theme park. They are waiting in a queue to ride a scary ghost train. Sally starts to feel sick and her hands become hot and sweaty. As Sally moves near to the front of the queue, she feels her heart thumping. After the ride, Sally feels very tired and thirsty.

Describe the role of the autonomic nervous system (ANS) and the adrenal glands in a stressful situation. Use your knowledge of the role of ANS and adrenalin in stressful situations to analyse Sally's response before and after the ride. *(10 marks)*

3 (a) What is meant by the term phenotype? Illustrate your answer with an example. *(2 marks)*

(b) Some psychologists believe that human and non-human behaviour can be explained in terms of evolutionary processes.

(i) What is meant by the term evolution? *(2 marks)*

(ii) Give an example of one behaviour. Suggest how this behaviour can be explained in terms of evolutionary processes. *(2 marks)*

(c) Evaluate the use of post-mortem examinations when used to identify areas of cortical specialisation in the brain. *(4 marks)*

(d) Describe and evaluate the cognitive approach in psychology. Refer to at least one other approach in your answer. *(10 marks)*

4   (a)   Explain one limitation of the humanistic approach in psychology.   *(2 marks)*

       (b)   Psychologists use many methods to identify areas of cortical specialisation in the brain.

            (i)   Explain one methodological problem which might arise when using neurosurgery to identify areas of cortical specialisation in the brain.   *(2 marks)*

            (ii)   Explain one ethical issue that might arise when using PET scans to identify areas of cortical specialisation in the brain.   *(2 marks)*

AQA specimen question

       (c)   (i)   Briefly describe one defence mechanism.   *(2 marks)*

            (ii)   Suggest how the defence mechanism that you have described in (c)(i) might be used to explain a person's behaviour.   *(2 marks)*

       (d)   Describe and evaluate the behaviourist approach in psychology. Refer to at least one other approach in your answer.   *(10 marks)*

Gender development

Introduction

Nearly all parents-to-be must wonder whether they are going to have a boy or a girl. Nowadays, many cannot wait to discover the sex of their child and find out via a scan. They may then decide to decorate the nursery a certain way or to buy particular clothes or toys. More importantly, they can discard half of the names in their 'Name Your Baby' book!

If parents do not know the sex of their child before birth, it is one of the first things they are told when it is born. It is also one of the first things that friends and relatives ask about. Then many go out and buy cards congratulating parents on having a boy or a girl (rather than a baby!). No doubt many of the 'boy cards' will be blue and the 'girl cards' will be pink.

The above examples illustrate that there is a difference between sons and daughters, otherwise why would it matter what parents had? But are there real differences between the sexes? Maccoby and Jacklin (1974) carried out a meta-analysis into differences between the sexes, and concluded that there were only four consistent differences, i.e. in verbal, visual-spatial and mathematical skills, and in aggression. However, other research suggests there are many more differences between the sexes.

If males and females are not the same, then this raises another interesting question for psychologists. Do these differences exist before a child is even born, which is why parents prepare for their sons and daughters differently? Or is it because parents and society decide to treat girls and boys differently that leads them to behave differently?

Evidence suggests that society does accept that some sex differences are natural. For example, we accept that mothers should be allowed to stay at home with a new baby for longer than fathers. Imagine discriminating in the same way between middle-class and working-class parents. We also accept single-sex schools, but would be appalled by separate schools for different ethnic groups. We do not expect to share public toilets with the opposite sex but would be shocked if there was a toilet for over 40s only! We seem to recognise that some differences are essentially created by society and so we should not discriminate because of them. However, we seem to believe that the sexes really are different and may have different needs as a consequence. Or does society over-emphasise these differences and create a distinction that does not really exist?

This is an important question to answer because if we raise our sons and daughters to be different, then in theory we could raise them to be the same. For example, could more women be in higher positions in society, and could men be taught to be as sensitive as women? In short, if females and males could be brought up more similarly, then there would be greater equality of opportunity for both sexes. However, it might be that males and females were never destined to lead the same kinds of lives and we should appreciate and accept this.

Specification	Topic content	Page
Sex and gender: androgyny; sex-role stereotypes; cultural variations in gender-related behaviour; nature and nurture	The difference between sex and gender	44
	The nature–nurture debate in gender development	48
	Explaining gender development	55
Biological explanations: typical and atypical sex chromosome patterns, including Klinefelter's syndrome and Turner's syndrome; influence of androgens (including testosterone) and oestrogens	Biological explanations of gender development	56
Social learning theory: reinforcement; modelling; imitation and identification	Social learning theory	63
Cognitive approach: gender schema theory; Kohlberg's cognitive-developmental theory, including gender identity, gender stability and gender constancy	The cognitive approach	68
Psychodynamic approach: Freud's psychoanalytic theory; Oedipus complex; Electra complex; identification	The psychodynamic approach	74

3 Gender development

The difference between sex and gender

Hint

Draw up a table with the headings 'Sex' and 'Gender'. Identify as many differences between the two concepts as you can. This is useful because the exam paper often asks you to draw a distinction between the terms as well as to describe them separately.

Key term

Androgynous: displaying roughly equal levels of masculine and feminine traits/behaviours.

AQA Examiner's tip

If you are asked to give an example of androgyny then remember to give **both** a masculine and a feminine trait. It does not matter what sex the individual is, but they do need to display both masculine and feminine behaviour. A common mistake is for candidates to say something such as 'A girl who is aggressive'. This may mean the girl is just masculine – it does not tell us in which ways she is feminine. You cannot assume just because she is female that she is feminine. This is the point of distinguishing between sex and gender.

In everyday life, people do not necessarily make a clear distinction between sex and gender. For example, some job application forms may ask for a person's sex, while others may ask for a person's gender, even though they will be requesting the same information. Strictly speaking, if a future employer wants to know whether a person is male or female, then they should be asking for their sex not their gender.

In psychology, it is important to draw a distinction between sex and gender. Although sex and gender are often related, they are not the same thing. Sex refers to whether an individual is female or male, whereas gender refers to whether an individual is masculine, feminine or **androgynous**. Sex relates to the physical differences between men and women or boys and girls, whereas gender relates the differences in their attitudes or behaviours.

We cannot assume that all males 'behave male' and all females 'behave female', and that sex and gender amount to the same thing. It is true that most males behave in more masculine ways and most females behave in more feminine ways and so there is a strong relationship between a certain sex and a certain gender. However, this is not a consistent finding. For example, two men will be the same sex and therefore share similar physical characteristics, such as the same genitals and a similar physique. However, they will not have the same gender if one displays more masculine behaviour and the other displays more feminine behaviour.

There are a significant number of people whose gender is not consistent with their sex. Psychology has to be able to explain these less common patterns of gender development as well as the more typical ones. Indeed, increasingly, members of both sexes are displaying more androgynous behaviour which also does not follow the traditional patterns of female or male behaviour.

Fig. 1 *The media uses the term 'metrosexual' to describe men who display androgynous behaviour. Robbie Williams is sometimes described as a metrosexual because of his masculine and feminine traits*

Androgyny

In psychological terms, androgyny is used to describe a flexible gender role. An androgynous individual displays similar levels of masculine and feminine behaviour. It is not associated with a particular sex – males or females can be androgynous.

Whether a person is androgynous, or just feminine or just masculine, can be assessed by questionnaires or **inventories**. Bem (1974) compiled one of the most well-known inventories for measuring gender.

Key term

Inventory: a list of statements used to test for certain characteristics in people.

Research study: Bem (1974)

Aim: To construct an inventory to measure masculinity, femininity and androgyny.

Method: Fifty male and 50 female judges rated 200 traits for how desirable they were for men and women. Based on judges' ratings, 20 traits were chosen for a masculinity scale and 20 for a femininity scale.

Feminine traits included compassion, sympathy, warmth, shyness and gullibility.

Masculine traits included ambition, athleticism, being analytical, self-sufficiency and aggression.

These traits were then used on the Bem Sex Role Inventory (BSRI) where people had to rate themselves between 1 and 7 on each trait.

Results: When the BSRI was tested on over 1,000 students it showed itself to be valid when checked against the sample's own description of their gender identity.

A smaller sample of students were tested again a month later and got similar scores indicating the inventory was reliable.

Conclusion: Having established the BSRI was reliable and valid, Bem found that some people do score highly on masculine and feminine traits. Men normally scored higher on masculine traits and women on feminine traits. However, many people were more androgynous than at the extremes and these people tend to be psychologically healthier. A small number of people scored low on both sets of traits and were described as 'undifferentiated'.

Evaluation: The problem with inventories or questionnaires is that they rely on people having insight into their personality and behaviour which not all respondents have. Respondents may also lie or exaggerate to give socially desirable answers – particularly in the case of gender which is a sensitive issue for many. However, Bem's inventory was confidential which reduces the likelihood of dishonest responses.

This study also shows that people cannot simply be categorised as either masculine, feminine or androgynous. There are different levels of each behaviour. For example, one person may be very masculine whereas another may be moderately masculine. In addition, it is not easy to measure gender precisely. Gender is more subjective than sex. Whereas an individual's sex can be objectively defined by their genes and physical appearance, their gender may be more open to interpretation.

Gender development

■ Link

Subjective and objective are defined on p2.

■ Sex versus gender

If sex is whether an individual is male or female, then this is decided at conception when a sperm fertilises an egg. A newly formed foetus has the chromosomes that determine whether it will be born a girl or a boy. Whether a baby is actually born with its masculine or feminine traits is much more open to debate.

If sex is genetic, then it follows that an individual's sex is fixed. Genes cannot be changed. So-called 'sex change' operations therefore do not really change a person's sex. However, an individual's sex is partly determined by their anatomy (for example, genitals) and this can be changed in gender re-assignment surgery.

A **transsexual** woman may have a penis surgically constructed and her breasts removed so she appears as a man. She may also be given hormones to stop her menstruating, to deepen her voice and to encourage growth of body and facial hair. Yet, internally, both in terms of genetics and sexual organs, she will always be female. Arguably, this is not a problem as long as she feels 'like a man'. Indeed, this is exactly why she would be undergoing gender re-assignment in the first place. In other words, her sex would be female but her **gender identity** would be masculine. This suggests that gender is fixed like sex, since people who undergo gender re-assignment have not been able to simply adopt the gender role of the sex that they were born. (See Figures 2 and 3.)

There is a debate about whether gender is fixed or not. There is a body of evidence that suggests a person's gender can change.

■ Research study: Imperato-McGinley *et al.* (1979)

Aim: To demonstrate that individuals can change their gender role and identity.

Method: A case study was carried out on 18 males who were part of the same extended family living in rural communities in the Dominican Republic. They had been born with a hormone deficiency which meant their genitals appeared to be female and so they were raised as girls. The evidence suggested they had no problem with adopting a feminine identity and role until puberty. At puberty, the increased production of male hormones caused their testicles to descend and their clitoris-like organs to grow into penises.

Results: Following their biological transformation at puberty, nearly all of the boys easily adapted to their true sex. They adopted masculine identities and began to 'behave like men'.

Conclusion: This shows that sex and gender are distinct concepts. The individual's sex had clearly not changed over time, but their gender had. When investigated they had fully embraced the gender role, showing gender is flexible.

Evaluation: The problem with any case study is that samples are small – in this case, one small community. It might be that other cultures would respond differently to the disorder and we cannot assume that all people would adapt so easily to their new gender role. For example, in the case of this community, roles were seen as God-given and part of one's destiny. In additon, the Dominican Republic was a very patriarchal society so the boys in this study may have been pleased to discover they were actually male.

■ Key terms

Transsexual: a person who desires to be a member of the opposite sex.

Gender identity: an individual's perception of their own masculinity and/or femininity.

Fig. 2 *James Harries was a child TV star when he was a young boy*

Fig. 3 *James was not happy with his sex and as an adult had gender re-assignment surgery and now lives his life as a woman, Lauren*

However, the researchers did not meet the participants until they were adults so had to rely on **retrospective** accounts of their childhoods. Therefore, they could not reliably say that the boys had fully adopted the feminine gender role before puberty.

Key term

Retrospective: from the past.

Further evidence for the flexibility of gender comes from Rekers *et al.* (1974). They described how they used a three-year programme of treatment to extinguish the highly feminine behaviour of an eight-year-old boy and replace it with masculine behaviour. When the boy was assessed at the age of 16 he was described as a normal gender-appropriate adolescent. This had been achieved by reinforcing masculine traits in the boy, again showing that a person's gender can be changed.

To conclude, psychologists are more interested in the concept of gender because it relates to people's perception of themselves and to their behaviour. Essentially, gender is a psychological concept, whereas sex is a biological concept. There is little dispute about the origins of an individual's sex, but what makes a person masculine, feminine or androgynous is much more debatable.

Links

The Imperato-McGinley study shows how a case study can be carried out on a group of people as well as on individuals. See Chapter 4, Research methods, for more information.

The principles of behaviourism were used to treat the boy in this study. See Chapter 1, Key approaches, for more information.

Key points:

- Sex is a biological term referring to whether someone is male or female.
- Gender is a psychological term referring to whether someone is masculine, feminine or androgynous.
- Masculine behaviours are traits associated with being male, and feminine behaviours are traits associated with being female.
- Androgyny is when individuals display high levels of both masculine and feminine behaviours.

Summary questions

1. Give an example of a feminine behaviour.
2. Give an example of a masculine behaviour.
3. Outline what is meant by androgyny.
4. Explain the differences between sex and gender.

Gender development

The nature–nurture debate in gender development

Learning objectives:

- Understand what is meant by nature in relation to gender.

- Understand what is meant by nurture in relation to gender.

- Explain how cultural variations in gender-related behaviour support the nurture argument.

- Describe how sex role stereotyping plays a part in the nurturing of gender roles.

- Consider the evidence for the role of nature in gender development.

Key term

Innate: in-born; present at birth.

Hint

It is easy to confuse the words 'nature' and 'nurture'. Remember that nature refers to something being natural, that is it does not have to be learnt. However, if we nurture something then we help it to grow – it will not 'grow' naturally by itself.

AQA Examiner's tip

Candidates often write about nature and nurture but do not say which is which. If you are describing the debate, make sure that you explicitly show which ideas are associated with nature and which are associated with nurture.

Link

Evolutionary psychology is part of the biological approach. See Chapter 1, Key approaches, for more information.

If a person displays masculine, feminine or androgynous behaviour, then what determines this? The two main arguments are that either gender is **innate** or it has been learnt. These two different perspectives represent a famous debate that occurs throughout psychology: the nature–nurture debate.

The nature argument

The nature side of the debate states that gender is biological. This would explain the strong relationship between a person's sex and their gender. The theory is that because each sex shares the same physiology and anatomy, they have many psychological traits in common too. In the same way that genetics and hormones determine an individual's sex, they also determine whether a person will behave in a more feminine or masculine way. Males are born masculine and females are born feminine. In other words, men and women, and girls and boys, are naturally different.

The physical differences between females and males (for example, in sexual organs) serve an important evolutionary function. They allow males and females to come together and reproduce. The desire to reproduce and pass on genes is one of the basic instincts of any animal including humans. On this basis, masculine and feminine behaviours may also be instinctive. For example, are women more careful and more caring because biologically they are the sex equipped to carry and then care for children? Are men more aggressive and more competitive because biologically they are the sex that has to look after and provide for their partners and children? Indeed, there is some evidence that women seek out such men when 'choosing a mate'. Similarly, men are interested in women who are in a good position to provide them with offspring.

Research study: Buss (1994)

Aim: To investigate the heterosexual mate preferences of men and women.

Method: The survey was carried out in 37 countries across all continents. Respondents were asked to rate the importance of a wide range traits in a potential mate.

Results: Men in all of the countries surveyed rated good looks, youth and chastity higher than women did. Meanwhile, women rated good financial prospects, industriousness and dependability higher than men did.

Conclusion: This supported the evolutionary theory that women and men instinctively seek out different traits in potential mates. For men, good looks and youth are good indicators of a woman's health and fertility, and of her ability to carry and care for a baby. Chastity is also important to men because an unfaithful mate may carry another man's baby: there is no evolutionary benefit in a man securing the survival of someone else's genes. For women, a man who has good financial prospects and is industrious should be able to provide well for them. Dependability is also important as it would suggest a man who will stay around during pregnancy and after the baby is born.

Evaluation: This survey used a questionnaire which means the questions (or traits) were pre-set. This means that respondents were not able to offer other traits that they may have regarded as important besides the ones that Buss had listed. As a Westerner, Buss may not have identified traits that other cultures may seek in a mate making findings unreliable.

Cross-cultural research, such as that of Buss, is useful in the nature–nurture debate. If a behaviour is a product of human nature, then it should occur across the world regardless of experience and upbringing. For example, sleeping is a natural behaviour and is therefore universal. Buss's research indicates that sex-based mate preferences are also **universal** and so must be determined by nature.

There are problems with the nature argument. How does nature explain those cases where a person does not adopt the **gender role** expected of their sex even when there are no genetic abnormalities? In addition, if males and females are naturally different, then how do we explain the finding that both sexes are becoming more similar as gender roles become more androgynous? There is also a body of evidence to show that males and females have different roles in different societies.

Cultural variations in gender-related behaviour

Although Buss (1994) found some universalities in gender-related behaviour, other cross-cultural research has highlighted cultural variations in gender-related behaviour. One of the earliest and most well known pieces of cross-cultural research into gender is detailed below.

Research study: Mead (1935)

Aim: To investigate the similarities and differences across gender roles in different cultures.

Method: Mead carried out a detailed **ethnographic** study by living with various tribes in New Guinea for six months.

Results: In the Arapesh tribe, both sexes were feminine, for example caring, expressive and co-operative. Both parents were said to 'bear a child' which meant the men also took to bed while the baby was born.

In the Mundugamor tribe, both sexes were masculine, for example assertive, arrogant and fierce. Both parents detested childcare so much that sleeping babies were hung out of the way in dark places.

In the Tchambuli tribe, gender roles were reversed compared to **Western society**. Females were very independent and took care of trading. Meanwhile males sat around in groups, gossiping and preening themselves. It was the males who were considered sentimental and not capable of making serious decisions.

> ### Key terms
>
> **Cross-cultural research:** investigations carried out across more than one society.
>
> **Universal:** occurring around the world.
>
> **Gender role:** the behaviours (masculine or feminine) that an individual displays.
>
> **Ethnographic:** the scientific description of specific cultures.
>
> **Western society:** mainly North American, European and Australasian countries.

Gender development

When describing cultural variations, do not just describe the findings from one country but actually compare them to other cultures. It is easy to describe another culture from your own and assume that the difference is obvious. However, you need to be explicit about what westerners think and do and as well as what other cultures think and do.

Fig. 4 *The berdache was neither masculine nor feminine and represented a third gender in Native American tribes*

Conclusion: Gender roles depend on culture. In most societies, women are the carers and the men the breadwinners, but this is not the case all over the world. Mead showed there were 'exceptions to the rule'. Gender-related behaviours are not universal suggesting that they are not determined by nature.

Evaluation: Mead carried out a very detailed observation of the tribes she lived with but in doing so she may have become too involved. For this reason, her findings are sometimes criticised for being too subjective.

There were some problems with Mead's research. She was accused of bias in the way that she interpreted her findings. She apparently exaggerated the similarities between the sexes in the Arapesh and Mundugamor tribes. She also under-stated the fact that males were more aggressive than females in all of the tribes. Even in the Tchambuli tribe, it was the men who did the majority of fighting in times of war. This may support the theory that some gender-specific behaviours are innate.

Although the reliability of Mead's research has been questioned, there are many other cross-cultural studies that show variations in gender-related behaviour, as demonstrated in Table 1.

Studies, such as those listed in Table 1, continue to challenge the idea of natural patterns in male and female behaviours.

To conclude, gender roles do not appear to be common across different societies as we would expect if they were innate. The evidence above strengthens the case for gender being culturally determined and therefore associated with nurture.

Table 1 *Studies challenging Western assumptions of gender*

Researchers	Study	What Western assumption does this challenge?
Best *et al.* (1994)	Observed parent–child interactions in playgrounds across Italy, France and Germany. Found that French and Italian fathers engaged in more play than mothers. However, the opposite was true of German fathers.	That males and females are naturally different in their parenting roles. Women do not necessarily focus mainly on caring.
Pontius (1997)	Investigated Pakistani school children and found no significant difference in spatial skills.	That males have innately superior spatial skills.
Roscoe (1998)	Studied Native American tribes and discovered that berdaches were common-place in these cultures. Berdaches were individuals who combined male and female gender roles and had a unique set of traits (Figure 4). Native Americans therefore acknowledged three genders.	That there are just two genders.
Sugihara and Katsurada (1999)	Used Bem's inventory to measure the traits of Japanese students. They found no significant differences between the sexes. Both males and females scored high on femininity.	That males are born masculine and females are born feminine.

The nurture argument

The nurture side of the nature–nurture debate states that gender is essentially a product of **socialisation**. It is dependent on environmental experiences. Family upbringing and society's expectations would therefore play a key role in a person's gender. This would mean, of course, that most boys learn to behave in masculine ways and most girls learn to behave in feminine ways.

The nurture argument can explain why some people adopt the gender role not expected of their sex. In theory, a feminine boy would have had a set of experiences which have led him to acquire a different gender role from most boys. If gender roles are nurtured, it also explains why an individual's gender may change over time as anything that is learnt can be unlearnt and replaced with a new set of behaviours.

The nurture argument can also explain cultural variations in gender-related behaviour. What distinguishes one culture from another is the fact that they have their own set of beliefs, values and **norms**. There is evidence that people's behaviour is influenced by the standards and expectations of their society. Gender is a behaviour and so is also open to this kind of influence.

💡 Sex-role stereotyping

There is a theory that beliefs, values and norms are transmitted by **agents of socialisation**, such as parents, peers, the education system and the media. These influential groups work collectively to reinforce certain behaviours and discourage others, depending on society's expectations.

In the case of gender, there is often a clear set of expectations of how males should behave which differ from how females should behave. On this basis, the two sexes may be treated differently and this is the root of **sex-role stereotyping**.

Sex-role stereotyping leads to a situation where individuals are expected to behave in ways associated with their sex. Males are expected to be masculine and females are expected to be feminine. As cultures have developed, they have identified what it is to be masculine and what is to be feminine. These ideas come from what males and females typically do. For example, in Western society, females are typically the main carer and are more sensitive, whereas males are typically the main breadwinner and are more competitive.

ℹ️ Sex-role stereotypes are frequently observed in the media's output. Evidence for this comes from content analyses of sources such as children's books (for example, Kortenhaus and Demarest, 1993), teenage magazines (for example, Peirce, 1993), and television advertisements.

Research study: Furnham and Farragher (2000)

Aim: To demonstrate that sex-role stereotypes are used as part of British television advertising.

Method: Samples of TV adverts were taken across the day over one month. Over 200 adverts were analysed according to the sex of the central figure. A male and female researcher coded the adverts for the role and location of the central figure, the type of product being advertised, use of humour and sex of voice-over.

Key terms

Socialisation: a process whereby individuals are taught and encouraged to adopt certain values and roles.

Norms: standard or appropriate ways of behaving.

Agents of socialisation: individuals and groups in society involved in the socialising of others.

Sex-role stereotyping: treating females and males differently according to a set of expectations.

Sex-role stereotypes: culturally determined beliefs about what a particular sex's gender role should be; often an over-generalisation.

Hint

You may find it useful to record these cross-cultural findings on a map of the world. This will help you to identify the countries. Presenting information visually also helps to make it easier to remember.

AQA Examiner's tip

If you get asked for an example of a sex-role stereotype in the exam, or want to describe one, then do give obvious examples. Some candidates seem to worry they are revealing their own prejudices or that they might offend the examiner. It is OK to say things such as 'women are more sensitive' or 'men are more arrogant'. These are well-recognised stereotypes. It does not mean they are necessarily true or that you believe them!

Link

This research study shows an example of how a content analysis is used in investigation. See Chapter 4, Research methods, for more information.

Fig. 5 *Women are more likely to be presented in a domestic role in TV adverts*

Link

A more detailed description of the influence of the media and other agents of socialisation is covered by social learning theory. See Chapter 1, Key approaches for more information.

Findings: Men were most likely to be presented in autonomous roles (for example, as professionals, celebrities) whereas as women were most likely to be presented in familial roles (for example, as mothers, as home-makers). Women were also most likely to be presented in domestic locations, whereas men were most likely to be presented doing leisure activities and to be seen in work settings more. Women were more likely to be used to sell household products and body products, whereas men were more likely to be used to sell motoring products. Male figures were more likely to be presented as humorous. In addition, nearly 70 per cent of voice-overs were male.

Conclusion: These findings represented many stereotypes that society has about females and males. The fact that men are less likely to be presented in a domestic role suggests they are less capable of running a home or bringing up children. Similarly, the fact that so few women are used for voice-overs may imply they lack the status and authority to be able to sell a product.

Evaluation: Findings from content analyses are open to interpretation. Indeed, in the Farragher study, the two coders did not always agree on categories. However, even if the findings are reliable and adverts do use sex-role stereotyping, we cannot assume people are influenced by this. Firstly, viewers will not perceive adverts in the same way as academic researchers. Viewers may extract different meanings from adverts (if any at all!). Secondly, even if viewers are aware of stereotypes, we cannot assume they passively respond to them. They do not necessarily just copy the gender roles they see without questioning them. Having said this, there is a large body of evidence that shows that people do often identify with and imitate what they see in the media.

Sex-role stereotyping can also occur in a more active way through the direct actions of groups, such as parents. This is demonstrated in the study below.

Research study: Fagot (1978)

Aim: To investigate the effect of parental behaviour upon gender role development.

Method: Two researchers observed 24 different families in their homes. Half the families had young sons and half had young daughters. Each set of parents and children were only observed on five separate one-hour periods.

Results: Parents reacted more favourably to their child when he or she was engaged in gender-appropriate behaviour, and reacted negatively to gender-inappropriate behaviour. For example, parents gave girls more negative responses when they engaged in active behaviour.

Conclusion: Parents reinforce certain behaviour through socialisation by sex-role stereotyping their daughters and sons.

Evaluation: Of course, because parents knew they were being observed they may have behaved differently. This means the findings may have not been a valid reflection of what normally happened in the homes. Parents may have stereotyped more (or less) in reality.

Fagot's findings may be out-of-date as today's parents may treat their sons and daughters more equally. Indeed, the nature of sex-role stereotypes means that they can change with time as attitudes change. For example, Furnham and Farragher (2000) compared their analysis of TV adverts with Manstead and McCulloch's (1981) analysis and found there was less evidence of stereotyping 20 years later.

Stereotypes vary across cultures as well as time. Furnham and Farragher (2000) also conducted their research in New Zealand and found that its TV adverts did not necessarily portray the same stereotypes as Britain's.

In contrast, Willams and Best (1982) asked respondents from 27 different countries to categorise a list of traits as masculine and feminine and found there was broad agreement. In other words, sex-role stereotypes seem to be the same around the world. This then begs the question: are our expectations of males and females really to do with our culture? Or do 'stereotypes' really describe real differences between the sexes that are in fact natural?

Gender: nature or nurture?

The basic assumption of the nurture argument is that babies are born without a gender identity. In theory, a baby boy could be raised as a 'girl' and vice versa. Of course, it would be unethical to put this theory to the test experimentally. However, there are real-life cases where children have been raised as the 'opposite sex' which has given psychologists useful insights into the origins of gender.

Research study: Diamond and Sigmundson (1997)

Aim: To investigate the role of biology in the development in gender roles.

Method: The researchers reviewed the case of an eight-month-old baby who accidentally lost his penis during a routine circumcision operation in the 1960s. On the recommendation of a psychologist called Money (who initially followed and reported on this case), the boy's parents decided to reassign his gender. The boy had an operation to construct a vagina and became Brenda. She was socialised as a girl from then onwards.

Results: Initially, Brenda appeared to adapt well to the female role by behaving in a feminine way. Money reported that the gender re-assignment had been a success. However, as she reached puberty she began to lose interest in feminine activities and felt different from other girls, that is she had a masculine gender identity. In her teens, Brenda discovered she had been born male and from then on began to live her life as a man called David Reimer, eventually having a penis reconstructed.

Conclusion: The effects of nature outweighed attempts to nurture this male into the feminine gender role.

Evaluation: This study supports the role of nature in gender development. However, it is based on one case and we cannot be sure that other boys would resist their new gender in the same way. This particular case was compounded by the fact that the boy had an identical twin brother. Without such an obvious male role model in close proximity so much of the time, the gender re-assignment may have worked. In addition, the boy's gender was not re-assigned until he was nearly two and so his masculine gender identity may stem from the fact that he was **not** raised as a girl from birth.

Link

The Fagot study is an example of a how an observation is used in investigation. See Chapter 4, Research methods for more information.

Hint

It is worth trying to remember the dates of studies that investigate sex-role stereotypes. If they are older studies, it is easy to criticise their results as being out-of-date. This is because stereotypes do not stay the same over time.

Gender development

Key term

Interactionist approach: combines two or more perspectives to explain a behaviour or event.

In contrast to the above, Money and Ehrhardt (1972) reported on cases where children were successfully raised as the opposite sex from birth. In one example, a new-born girl had been identified as a boy because her genitals appeared male due to exposure to male hormones in the womb. At the age of three, when the child's true biological sex became apparent, it was decided to continue to raise him as a boy. This was because he already had a firm masculine identity. The 'boy' had surgery to make his genitals look more male and was given hormone treatment during puberty. As an adolescent, he associated with other males and was sexually attracted to females suggesting the role of nurture was more significant in his gender identity.

To conclude, there is evidence to support both the role of nature and nurture in gender development. Many psychologists nowadays adopt an **interactionist approach** to explaining gender, and recognise that gender is a product of both biology and environmental experiences.

Key points:

- If gender is the product of nature, then it is innate and biological.
- If gender is the product of nurture, then it is learnt from the environment.
- Cultural variations in gender-related behaviour suggest that gender roles are dependent on environmental experiences and therefore are a product of nurture and learning.
- Individuals may learn their gender roles as a consequence of sex-role stereotyping.
- Despite strong evidence supporting the role of nurture in gender development, there is also convincing evidence to support the role of nature.

Summary questions

5 Give three terms associated with the concept of nature.

6 Give three terms associated with the concept of nurture.

7 Compare the gender roles of British culture with one other culture.

8 Outline how a young girl may be influenced by sex-role stereotyping.

9 Imagine you have to do a presentation on the nature nurture debate in relation to gender development. Weigh up the evidence that supports both the role of nature and nurture in gender development and come to a conclusion in favour of one of the arguments.

Explaining gender development

Learning objectives:

- Know the key theories for explaining gender development.

- Outline how these theories relate to the nature/nurture debate.

So far, we have established that sex has its origins in biology. Gender, meanwhile, may be rooted in biology (nature) but may instead be a product of socialisation (nurture).

The nature–nurture debate in gender research suggests there are only two explanations of how gender develops. However, this tends to over-simplify this field of study. There are, in fact, a number of theories which have been put forward to explain gender development. Some theories give more support to the nature argument. Others give more support to the nurture argument. The key theories of gender development will be explored further in the rest of this chapter. They are:

- the biological explanations, which emphasise the role of chromosomes and hormones in gender development. These explanations strongly support the role of nature in gender development

- social learning theory, which essentially sees gender roles as being learnt from others. This theory strongly supports the role of nurture in gender development

- the cognitive approach, which focuses more on the mind and how individuals think about their gender. The approach holds that gender identity develops as part of an innate process (nature) but that concepts of gender depend on familial and cultural experiences (nurture)

- the psychodynamic approach, which focuses more on the unconscious elements of gender development. This approach maintains that gender develops instinctively (nature) but that childhood experiences (nurture) moderate this.

Figure 6 illustrates where these different theories stand in the nature–nurture debate.

Fig. 6 *Where theories stand in the nature–nurture debate*

These theories tend to challenge each other since they look at gender from quite different perspectives. However, many researchers would agree that they each have their own strengths and limitations in terms of how well they explain gender development. As suggested earlier, it may be wise to take a more interactionist approach to explaining gender by using elements of all the theories.

Summary questions

10 With which key theory would you associate each of the following terms:

   a learning through imitation

   b unconscious

   c thinking

   d hormones?

11 Outline how each key theory relates to the concepts of nature and nurture.

Key points:

- Biological explanations support the role of nature in gender development, whereas social learning theory supports the role of nurture. Cognitive and psychodynamic explanations consider the role of both nature and nurture.

Biological explanations of gender development

Learning objectives:

- ▨ Describe how biological theories explain gender development.

- ▨ Outline the role of chromosomes and hormones in gender development.

- ▨ Consider the evidence for the biological explanations of gender development.

- ▨ Demonstrate how atypical chromosome patterns support biological explanations of gender development.

- ▨ Explain the limitations of the biological explanations of gender development.

Link

Biological explanations focus on genes and biological structures. For more information on the biological approach, see Chapter 1, Key approaches.

Key terms

Hormones: chemical substances produced by the body that control and regulate the activity of certain cells or organs.

Embryo: an organism in the early stages of development.

Hint

It is easy to confuse the male and female chromosome patterns. It might help if you remember than men wear Y-fronts and it is males that have the Y chromosome!

Biological explanations, perhaps obviously, focus on the biology behind gender. They see sex and gender as being inter-related. In the same way that sex is determined at conception, so is the pattern for gender development.

Why are females and males innately different?

Evolutionary theory offers a biological explanation for the consistent differences between females and males. Human beings have evolved so that males and females possess different chromosomes that trigger the production of different levels of certain **hormones**. Hormonal differences between the sexes lead to differences in behaviour. This allows males and females to perform different roles in reproduction thus ensuring the survival of their genes and, in turn, their species. Women have evolved physiologically, anatomically and psychologically to be the carers of their young. Meanwhile, men have evolved in a similar way to be the main providers for the mother and her young.

The effect of chromosomes

Each cell in the human body contains a total of 46 chromosomes arranged as 23 pairs. Twenty-two of these pairs are matched, and are the same in males and females. However, the 23rd chromosome pair differs between the sexes. Females have two similar chromosomes, known as XX chromosomes. Males have two dissimilar chromosomes, known as XY chromosomes.

An individual's sex is determined by the chromosomal make-up of the sperm that fertilises the egg. If the sperm carries an X chromosome, the **embryo** will be female. If it carries a Y chromosome, the embryo will be male.

In the first weeks after conception, a male and female embryo appear the same. There is no difference in their **gonads**. At six weeks, however, the gonads begin to develop differently. A gene on the Y chromosome is responsible for triggering the events that transform the male embryo's gonads into **testes**. In the absence of this gene, the gonads will automatically develop into **ovaries**.

Once the testes and ovaries develop they begin to release their own sex hormones. Male hormones are known as **androgens**. Female hormones are mainly **oestrogens**.

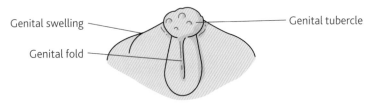

Genital swelling — Genital tubercle

Genital fold

Fig. 7 *Before six weeks, the gonads of a male and female embryo look the same*

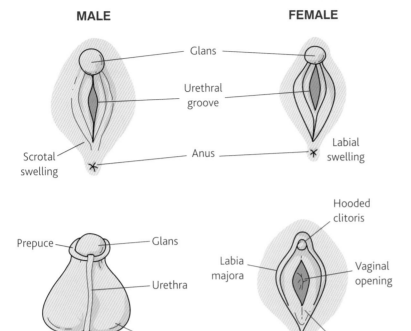

Fig. 8 *At nine weeks, the gonads of male and female foetuses begin to look different*

The psychological effects of hormones

Biological explanations state that sex hormones have an effect on the **pre-natal** development of the brain. Since male and female **foetuses** produce different amounts of certain hormones, this could imply that the male and female brain develop differently. Research does show that there are key structural and functional differences in the brains of males and females. This, in turn, could account for the psychological differences between the sexes (Maccoby and Jacklin, 1974). For example, baby boys show more interest in mechanical objects while baby girls show more interest in faces (Connellan *et al.*, 2000). Since such differences occur in the first few months of life, they are unlikely to be the result of socialisation.

Sex differences in the brain involve the **hypothalamus**. It has two specific regions – labelled the BST and the SDN-POA – which are larger in adult heterosexual males compared to adult heterosexual women. One biological theory is that these differences in brain structure may relate to the differences in female and male sexual behaviour, for example women tend to be more coy whereas men tend to be more promiscuous.

Sex differences have also been found in the structure of the **cerebral hemispheres** of the brain. Biological theorists suggest that this could explain the consistent finding that females develop superior language, emotional and **fine motor skills**, while males develop superior visual–spatial and mathematical skills.

It is also interesting to consider the effects of abnormal hormone production in understanding pre-natal brain development. Females with **adrenogenital syndrome** have normal XX chromosomes but are exposed to excessive androgens in the womb from a malfunctioning of

Gender development

Key terms

Gonads: sex organs.

Testes: the male sex organs (which produce sperm).

Ovaries: the female sex organs (which produce eggs).

Androgens: the group of male sex hormones.

Oestrogens: the group of female sex hormones.

Pre-natal: before birth.

Foetus: a developing embryo (after eight weeks) until birth.

Hypothalamus: a small structure at the base of the brain that regulates many body functions.

Cerebral hemispheres: the two halves of the brain which specialise in different functions, for example the left side for language and the right side for spatial ability.

Fine motor skills: practical skills requiring precise, small movements usually of the hands and fingers, for example using scissors, typing or threading a needle.

Adrenogenital syndrome: a set of symptoms associated with the excessive secretion of adrenal hormones.

Hint

It might help you remember that androgens are the male hormones if you associate them with a boy's name: Andrew. Also, be careful not to confuse androgens (the hormones) with androgyny (the gender).

■ Key terms

Adrenal glands: a group of cells (in the body) that produce and release hormones.

Testosterone: the main male sex hormone.

■ Link

The case of David Reimer shows that gender may be determined long before birth. The fact that he had XY chromosomes that had already affected the development of his brain may explain why he could not successfully adopt a feminine gender. See Research study: Diamond and Sigmundson (1997) on p53 for more information.

their **adrenal glands**. Despite having male-like genitals, these babies are normally identified as females at birth and raised as such. However studies have shown that a significant number of these girls later identify themselves as 'tomboys' (Money and Ehrhardt, 1972). These findings suggest that hormones have a pre-natal effect on the brain which later affects gender-related behaviour.

Of course, sex hormones may not just have an effect on brain organisation in the womb. Hormones are produced throughout an individual's life time and so may continue to affect behaviour. For example, there is evidence that boys experience a surge of **testosterone** around the age of four and that this is responsible for the fact that boys are notably more active and boisterous than girls at this stage of development.

There is a wide body of evidence demonstrating the effect of hormones on gender development.

■ Research study: Van Goozen *et al.* (1995)

Aim: To investigate the effects of sex hormones on adult behaviour.

Method: They used the experimental method to study transsexuals of both sexes who were undergoing hormone treatment, that is were being injected with hormones of the opposite sex. They were given a range of tests to complete before treatment and then three months later.

Results: Male-to-female transsexuals show decreases in aggression and visual–spatial skills but increases in verbal fluency. Female-to-male showed the opposite.

Conclusion: This suggests that sex hormones do affect gender-related behaviours.

Evaluation: This was not a controlled experiment so the changes may have been due to other uncontrolled variables, such as the transsexuals' own expectations.

Slabbekoorn *et al.* (1999) question these findings, and demonstrated that sex hormones do not have consistent effects on gender-related behaviour. Critics also argue that we should be careful about generalising from such an unusual sample. Hormones may not be having the same effect on a typical population of men and women. In addition, there is always a debate about how we reliably measure aggression, verbal fluency and visual–spatial ability.

Other related studies are summarised in Table 2.

Studies, such as the one above, suggest the impact of sex hormones on behaviour. Interestingly, a lot of these sex differences correspond with well recognised gender differences.

Table 2 *Studies showing hormonal effects on behaviour*

Researchers	Study
Hampson and Kimura (1988)	Investigated the fluctuations in oestrogen and **progesterone** that occur during women's menstrual cycles. They found that when these hormone levels were high, women performed better in fine motor tasks and worse in visual–spatial tasks compared to when the levels were low.
Galligani *et al.* (1996)	Investigated the effects of **steroids** which are known to increase levels of testosterone. Using a variety of measures, they found that male athletes who used steriods showed higher levels of aggression than a control group.
Waber (1976)	Investigated the effects of sex hormones in puberty on verbal ability. She found that late maturing boys had better verbal ability than boys who were early developers.

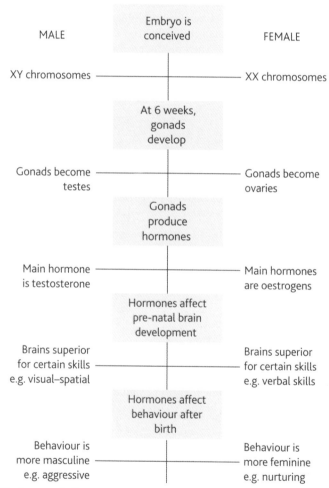

Fig. 9 *The hormonal effects on male and female developmental stages*

Key terms

Progesterone: a female hormone.

Steroids: synthetic, 'man-made' hormones.

Link

Imperato-McGinley *et al.*'s (1979) study of the 'girls' that became boys at puberty also demonstrates what a strong effect hormones can have. These boys would have experienced an increase in testosterone at puberty which could account for the fact that they adopted a masculine role and identity over a feminine one. See p46 for more information.

Link

For more information on genes and the biological approach see Chapter 1, Key approaches.

Atypical chromosome patterns

We have considered a range of evidence suggesting that chromosomes and, in turn, hormones affect gender development. However, it is difficult to establish cause and effect in psychology, and gender is no exception. Can we be sure that it is an individual's XY chromosomes that are largely responsible for his masculinity? Or is it because people know that he is male, that he is socialised to be masculine? Does having an

Key terms

Turner's syndrome: a disorder where a person has the atypical chromosome pattern XO.

Klinefelter's syndrome: a disorder where an individual has the atypical chromosome pattern XXY.

X chromosome rather than a Y chromosome really make an individual much more feminine? Or is it because girls appear different to boys that we expect them to behave differently?

It might be easier to establish the real effects of chromosomes if researchers could manipulate them in some way. What would happen to a person's gender if they had an extra chromosome, or if a chromosome was missing? Fortunately for psychologists, atypical chromosome patterns do occur naturally. Although it can potentially cause difficulties for people born with these disorders, it does offer useful insights into how gender develops.

Two key atypical chromosome patterns are detailed below.

Turner's syndrome

Individuals with **Turner's syndrome** identify themselves as female and have similar interests and behaviours to biologically normal females. This suggests that a feminine gender identity can develop in the absence of ovaries and the oestrogens they produce.

Table 3 *Features of Turner's syndrome*

Atypical chromosome pattern	XO
Frequency	1 in 2,000 births
Sex identity	Female
Physical characteristics	No ovaries, so do not menstruate at puberty and are sterile. Do not develop breasts at puberty. Unusually short stature. Short, webbed neck. Low set ears.
Psychological characteristics	▪ Higher than average verbal ability ▪ Lower than average spatial ability, visual memory and mathematical skills ▪ Difficulties relating to peers

Klinefelter's syndrome

Individuals with **Klinefelter's syndrome** have the XX combination associated with normal females. However, anatomically they are male. This shows the importance of the Y chromosome in triggering the formation of male structures.

In both of the above examples, it is evident that chromosomal abnormalities have an effect on behaviours (via the effect of hormones). More interestingly, the affected behaviours are often related to gender, for example spatial skills, verbal skills, ambition. This demonstrates a strong association between chromosomes, hormones and gender development.

Table 4 *Features of Klinefelter's syndrome*

Atypical chromosome pattern	XXY
Frequency	1 in 500 births
Sex identity	Male
Physical characteristics	Undescended testes and undersized penises. Some breast development at puberty and 'rounding' of body contours. Little body hair. Long limbs. Clumsy.
Psychological characteristics	Lack of interest in sexual activity
	Tend to be passive, shy and lacking in ambition
	Poor language skills and poor reading ability
	Poor judgement and handle stress badly
	Higher than normal level of gender-identity confusion

Analysis and evaluation of biological explanations

Social learning theory would dispute the fact that gender is a product of nature. For example, if men are biologically similar and women are biologically similar, then why do the two sexes not behave in more consistent ways? Social learning theory would argue that men and women display a range of gender-related behaviours depending on their unique learning experiences. This would also explain why different cultures seem to have different gender roles, and why men's and women's typical behaviours have changed over time. For example, biological explanations would suggest that women are destined to stay at home and raise children, whereas nowadays many more women decide not to have children and/or go out to work.

The cognitive approach would argue that the biological explanations are too **reductionist** because they attempt to explain complex behaviours simply in terms of chromosomes and hormones. The cognitive approach would argue that we have to understand the thought processes behind gender development. Although thinking is more abstract and more difficult to study than biological mechanisms, it does not mean it should be avoided. The cognitive approach would also accuse the biological explanations of being too **deterministic**. The cognitive approach would question the idea that we are 'at the mercy' of our biology and would argue that we have some choice in how we think about our gender and how we behave.

The psychodynamic approach would agree that there are innate elements to gender development and that they are related to the sexual differences between males and females. However, it would also emphasise the importance of childhood experiences and familial relationships in gender development. The psychodynamic approach would object to the biological idea that gender develops in isolation from society.

Critics often question the evidence provided by the biological approach. Although not detailed above, a lot of the research on the effects of hormones is demonstrated on animals, which may not be generalisable to human beings. Do animals really have a sense of being masculine and feminine like humans do? Even when humans are studied, they are often unusual cases which may not represent typical gender development. Beyond this, a number of findings have not been replicated. This questions the reliability of an approach which claims to be objective.

AQA **Examiner's tip**

In the exam, you may be asked to describe the effects of an atypical chromosome disorder. It is better to describe the psychological effects as you are studying psychology! In fact, it is good practice to do this, as you may be specifically asked for the effects on behaviour. If this happens, then examples relating to the sex organs or other physical characteristics will not get credit.

Key terms

Reductionism: the belief that complex systems can be explained in terms of their components.

Determinism: the belief that events are controlled by actions that come before them, therefore everything is predictable.

▨ Hint

'Analysis and evaluation of biological explanations' makes reference to approaches that you may not yet have studied. It would be useful to re-read these points once you are familiar with all of the approaches addressed.

AQA Examiner's tip

For a high mark in an essay, it is better to refer to other approaches when criticising a theory. Rather than just listing the limitations of a theory, try to say what other theorists would argue.

▨ It would follow that in cases of atypical gender development there should be evidence of chromosomal or hormonal abnormalities, but this does not always appear to be the case.

▨ As we move through the generations, more individuals from both sexes are identifying themselves as androgynous rather than strictly masculine or feminine. However, these individuals have the same patterns of chromosomes and hormone production as their ancestors. This would indicate that society and culture are having an effect as they do change over time.

Key points:

▨ The biological theories explain gender in terms of innate factors related to the sex of a person.

▨ Males and females have different patterns of sex chromosomes (XY for males and XX for females). Different genes trigger different levels of hormones which affect brain and behaviour. A high level of androgens (including testosterone) makes males more masculine, while a high level of oestrogens makes females more feminine.

▨ Evidence shows that consistent differences between male and female brains may account for gender differences. In addition, hormonal changes (whether manipulated or natural) appear to affect gender-related behaviours.

▨ Turner's syndrome (XO) and Klinefelter's syndrome (XXY) are atypical chromosome patterns. They demonstrate the effects of chromosomes on gender, as individuals with these disorders behave differently from typical males and females.

▨ The biological explanations are accused of being too deterministic, too reductionist, and for ignoring the effects of culture and socialisation.

▨ Summary questions

12 State the male chromosome pattern.

13 Name two atypical chromosome disorders.

14 Outline three features of human development affected by sex hormones.

15 Outline two criticisms of biological explanations of gender development.

16 Describe research that supports biological explanations of gender development.

Social learning theory

Learning objectives:

- Describe how social learning theory explains gender development.

- Know and understand the role of modelling, identification, imitation and reinforcement in gender development.

- Evaluate the evidence for the social learning theory of gender development.

- Explain the limitations of the social learning theory of gender development.

Link

Social learning theory focuses on learning from others. For more information on social learning theory, see Chapter 1, Key approaches.

Key terms

Construct validity: the degree to which a test measures the construct or concept that it is supposed to measure.

Temporal validity: the degree to which findings apply across time.

Link

An independent groups design is one where different participants are allocated to separate conditions. See Chapter 4, Research methods for more information.

Social learning theory (SLT) states that gender is essentially learnt from others. It implies that there are no psychological differences between males and females when they are born. Therefore, gender differences develop because of the way society treats the two sexes.

The differential treatment of children, according to perceived sex, was well demonstrated in the following study.

 **Research study: Smith and Lloyd (1978)**

Aim: To investigate whether mothers acted differently towards a baby depending on the perceived sex of that baby.

Method: An experiment was carried out using 32 mothers who were told the study was investigating play. They were video-taped playing with six-month-old babies. Sex-typed and sex-neutral toys were available for play. Two male and two female babies were presented equally as their own sex and as the opposite sex using stereotyped clothes and names.

Results: Babies perceived to be boys received more encouragement to play actively. Only babies perceived to be girls were offered dolls initially and only babies perceived to be boys were offered hammers initially.

Conclusion: Mothers were involved in the process of differential treatment of boys and girls. It was suggested that boys learn that they should be strong and athletic through sex-typed play. Type of play was not dictated by the child, as boys and girls appeared content to play in masculine and feminine ways depending on what sex they were perceived as being.

Evaluation: There are some problems with this research. To avoid the mothers guessing the aim of the study, an independent groups design was used. Consequently, it may be that the differences in the way mothers played with girls and boys were really down to the individual differences between the participants. Measuring play in terms of the 'first toy offered' and 'length of toy use' lacked **construct validity**. This was a very narrow way of measuring a complex phenomenon. In addition, the study only reflects how mothers behaved at one point in time. The study also lacks **temporal validity** as mothers may not show the same level of stereotyping in today's society.

Of course learning about gender does not just take place through play. Nor does it only involve mothers. Nor does it just happen to children. The argument is that individuals learn about gender-appropriate behaviour throughout their lifetime and from a variety of sources.

- Idle *et al.* (1993) found that fathers reacted more negatively to their sons' feminine toy play than mothers did.

Gender development

It is good practice, but not essential, to cite the names of researchers when describing studies. There are a lot of names to remember in psychology so try to make links between the names and the studies.

For example, for the Idle study you could picture a father lazing in an armchair while his son plays with a car. For the Eccles study, you could picture a teacher giving out Eccles cakes to tidy girls. And for Fagot, you could picture little girls throwing faggots at each other (in a rather masculine way!).

Fig. 10 *Children may learn about gender from something as simple as the toys that we give them to play with*

■ Key terms

Attention: observing someone else carrying out a behaviour.

Retention: storing observed behaviours so that they can be retrieved at a later date.

Model: a person displaying an observable behaviour.

■ Hint

When you have lists to learn, it sometimes helps to use silly sentences to help you to do this. For example, the four conditions to social learning:

Attention

Retention

Reproduction

Motivation

could be remembered by the phrase 'Attractive Rabbits Reproduce Monthly'.

■ Fagot (1985) found that children were more critical of their male peers when they engaged in feminine activities than they were when their female peers engaged in masculine activities.
■ McGhee and Frueh (1980) found that people who view a lot of television have stronger gender stereotypes than people who view little.
■ Eccles (1987) found that teachers tend to praise boys for academic achievement and girls for tidiness and compliance.
■ Pfost and Fiore (1990) found women in traditionally masculine occupations were evaluated more negatively than men in traditionally feminine occupations.

From play activities through to occupations, there are many behaviours which make up an individual's gender. According to SLT, each of these behaviours has to be learnt through the same processes. There are two main processes in learning:

■ acquisition of a behaviour.
■ performing that behaviour.

■ The acquisition of gender roles: modelling and identification

According to SLT, the two conditions to acquiring a behaviour are:

■ **attention**, for example a boy watches his older brother playing football
■ **retention**, for example a girl recalls the things her mother does when preparing a meal.

An individual learns their gender from the people that they come into contact with. Contact may be live (for example, family members, peers) or symbolic (for example, TV celebrities, characters in books). All of these people are potential **models**.

Modelling

When models perform certain activities they are **modelling** behaviour, for example, a mother washing the family's clothes, or a superhero fighting on TV. Modelling behaviours, whether intentionally or unintentionally, gives others the opportunity to learn from them.

However, individuals do not simply copy all of the models they observe. People become **role models** when others identify with them.

Identification

There is evidence that an individual identifies more with same-sex models (Bussey and Bandura, 1984). However, level of **identification** can also be affected by factors such as power, popularity and attractiveness. For example, if a teenage girl desires her pop idol's status, she is likely to attend to that idol's behaviour. In contrast, if a boy does not admire his father then he is not likely to pay much attention to what his father does yet alone retain anything.

The performance of gender roles: imitation and reinforcement

SLT argues that an individual ultimately learns their gender role by acting in ways that they have seen their models acting.

According to SLT, the two conditions to performing a behaviour are:

- (motor) **reproduction**
- **motivation**.

Imitation

Imitation occurs when a behaviour is reproduced. For example, a young girl goes into her older sister's bedroom and attempts to put on make-up just like she has seen her sister do. Or a boy fetches his toy gun and uses it to 'shoot' his neighbour because this is what he saw the 'cop' do to the 'baddie' on his computer game.

We have already established that not all behaviours are imitated. Individuals are more likely to imitate someone they identify with. They also need the **self-efficacy** to imitate that behaviour. Imitation is also motivated by **reinforcement**.

Reinforcement

Reinforcement occurs when a behaviour is strengthened by positive outcomes. For example, a young girl may be motivated to imitate (reproduce) caring behaviour if she sees her mother is happy when looking after a relative's baby, or a young boy may be more likely to imitate competitive behaviour if he sees a man win a prize for 'knocking out' his opponent. But wouldn't a girl also imitate competitive behaviour if it gets her a prize? Not necessarily. She may not identify with the model nor with the prize. Or, because of sex-role stereotyping, she may not believe that she is capable of competitive behaviour. She may also avoid imitating the behaviour if she thinks that she will get punished as a result. For example, her parents may scold her for not being 'lady-like'. This shows that social learning is also affected by what **directly** happens to individuals when they imitate a behaviour.

Gender development

Fig. 11 *An individual could show they are as 'macho' as James Bond by diving from a plane. However, many people would not possess the self-efficacy to imitate this behaviour!*

Key terms

Punishment: a behaviour being followed with negative consequences (reducing the likelihood of that behaviour occurring again).

Internalisation: a process whereby behaviours become an integrated part of an individual's identity.

Social construct: an abstract concept created by society.

Hints

There are four key terms to remember when describing SLT: modelling, identification, imitation, reinforcement.

It sometimes helps to make up bizarre scenarios to help you link words together. For example, you could imagine that a super**model** has been arrested for **imitating** a police officer. She is then put in **identification** parade behind **reinforced** glass!

Remember that the words in a scenario may have a different meaning to the psychological terms and they are just cues to memory.

When an individual imitates a behaviour because they have seen it being rewarded elsewhere, this is known as vicarious reinforcement. However, a person can also be directly reinforced for their behaviour which will also make it more likely to occur again. For example, if a woman is praised by her friends for 'playing hard to get' on a date she may do it each time she has a new boyfriend. Or if a young boy gets adulation from his peers for his sporting ability he may be more likely to keep up his training. Of course, the reverse of reinforcement is **punishment**, and this also has a role in social learning. For example, if a woman is rejected for a promotion time and time again, she may eventually stop applying for higher positions. Or if a boy is ridiculed by his peers for playing with dolls he will be less likely to do it again.

According to SLT, there is a point when certain behaviours do not have to be continually reinforced to be maintained. If a behaviour is well-rehearsed then it becomes **internalised**. Internalised behaviours become an integrated part of a person's personality. In the case of gender, a person's identity will be made up of the behaviours that they have learnt through imitation and reinforcement. Of course, once an individual has a sense of their gender identity, this will dictate what kinds of behaviour they choose to display in the future. Social learning is therefore an on-going and dynamic process.

To conclude, SLT suggests that individuals learn from each other. People both model and imitate at the same time. Through their interactions, people socially construct what it is to be masculine and feminine. Since gender is a **social construct** it can change over time as society changes, and it can vary between societies. SLT can therefore explain changing gender roles, for example why it is acceptable for women to be assertive now when it was not in the past. It can also explain the cultural variations that have been observed in gender-related behaviour.

Analysis and evaluation of social learning theory

- Biological explanations would question whether gender is learnt. They believe that it is largely pre-determined before birth. If gender identity is innate this would explain a number of phenomena which cannot be accounted for by SLT, that is it is not generally possible to raise someone as the opposite sex; when parents try to raise their children in non-stereotyped ways that their sons and daughters still show preferences for gender typical activities; two children of the same sex can be socialised similarly within the same family yet have different gender identities.

- The cognitive approach would argue that gender develops in stages. This goes against SLT as it implies that gender-related behaviour can develop at any point in an individual's life depending on their experiences. However, the cognitive approach has demonstrated that elements of gender are acquired at certain points in a child's lifetime regardless of their upbringing and environment. The cognitive approach also argues that imitation of same-sex role models occurs after gender is acquired. However, SLT sees gender identity as being a consequence rather than the cause of imitation.

- The psychodynamic approach would also argue that gender develops in stages – in fact, in 'one fell swoop'. This goes against SLT's idea that it develops more gradually. The psychodynamic approach would also accuse SLT of focusing too much on behaviour and of ignoring the importance of the unconscious in gender development.

Critics are concerned that most of the evidence for SLT is experimental. For example, in lab-based studies, participants often get the opportunity to imitate a modelled behaviour **immediately** after observing it and often in the **same context**. However, how often does this situation arise in real life?

If gender develops through observation and reinforcement, then how do we explain the significant number of individuals that display 'gender-inappropriate behaviour'? If parents discourage their children from behaving 'like the opposite sex' then where do their models come from? Many groups and communities are intolerant of feminine males and masculine females. However, despite a lack of reinforcement, their behaviours persist. SLT struggles to explain this.

SLT fails to adequately explain where gender stereotypes come from in the first place. Even if it is true that behaviours are reinforced in females and males, why is it these behaviours rather than others? Indeed, the fact that gender stereotypes are so similar across cultures would suggest that gender is less to do with nurture and more to do with nature.

Key points:

- Social learning theory explains gender development in terms of learning experiences.

- Individuals develop gender by identifying with people who model gender behaviour for them. This behaviour is imitated and continues to be displayed if it is reinforced.

- Numerous studies have shown that people of all ages imitate gender-appropriate behaviour. Observations have shown that gender-appropriate behaviour is reinforced by many groups in society, including parents, peers, the media, teachers and work colleagues.

- SLT has difficulty explaining cases where an individual's gender identity is at odds with their environmental experiences. A lot of its evidence may also not reflect real life.

AQA Examiner's tip

There are a lot of key concepts to learn to help you to describe SLT. It is common for candidates to focus so much on describing these concepts that they forget to apply them to the idea of gender development. SLT can be used to explain many behaviours so make sure you are using it to explain gender development (by giving examples) in this part of the exam.

Having read about SLT, you might think that a lot of it is common sense. However, make sure that you use the key concepts to describe SLT rather than using everyday phrases such as 'girls copy their mums', 'we bring up kids differently', 'children get given boy toys or girl toys', etc. You may think that you would never write about a theory like this, but some candidates do!

Summary questions

17 What is meant by the term imitation in SLT?

18 Name three groups that may model gender-appropriate behaviour.

19 Give four ways in which gender-appropriate behaviour may be reinforced.

20 Outline three reasons why some behaviours are more likely to be imitated than others.

21 Two 6 year old classmates – Daisy and Megan – display quite different gender roles. Daisy is very feminine whereas Megan is more of a 'tomboy'. Outine how social learning theory would explain this difference between the girls.

The cognitive approach

Learning objectives:

■ Describe how the cognitive approach explains gender development.

■ Explain how Kohlberg's cognitive-development stages of gender identity, gender stability and gender constancy relate to gender.

■ Describe how gender schema theory explains gender development.

■ Explain the limitations of the cognitive approach to gender development.

Key term

Cognitive development: the idea that the mind develops and changes over time.

Link

For more information on the cognitive approach, see Chapter 1, Key approaches.

The cognitive approach focuses on the thinking behind gender development. It recognises that an individual's gender role is essentially a product of their gender identity. To understand how gender develops, we must understand what is happening in the mind.

There are two key cognitive theories of gender development:

■ Kohlberg's cognitive-developmental theory

■ gender schema theory.

Kohlberg's cognitive-developmental theory

Kohlberg was interested in **cognitive development** generally. He believed that children's minds develop in set stages broadly related to age. He applied this to gender by arguing that a child's understanding of their gender will increase in line with their cognitive abilities. When children are very young, their understanding of the world is basic and so is their understanding of gender. When children are older, their understanding of the world is more sophisticated and so is their understanding of gender.

Kohlberg proposed three stages of gender development as summarised in Table 5.

Table 5 *Kohlberg's gender development stages*

Stage of development	Age of development	Description
Gender identity	2–3 years	Children are able to identify (or label) their own sex. They can also identify others' sex.
Gender stability	3–4 years	Children are able to understand that their own gender is stable; they know that they will stay the same sex forever.
Gender constancy	4–7 years	Children are able to understand that gender is generally constant.

Hint

To help you remember the correct order of the stages you may find it useful to relate them to the word DISC: Gender **D**evelops through **I**dentity, **S**tability and **C**onstancy.

Kohlberg believed that these stages of cognitive development were universal. Wherever children are in the world, they will go through the same stages at about the same age. The difference is that they may learn different things about what it is to be feminine and masculine depending on their culture's norms.

Gender identity

Kohlberg believed that children first begin to think about gender around the age of two. At this stage, they demonstrate **gender identity**. Children are able to say whether they are a 'boy' or a 'girl'. A few months after this, they can also identify other people's sex, for example they may recognise their sister is a 'girl', or their daddy is a 'man'. However, at this stage, gender is just a label and does not mean any more to children than somebody's name. In the same way that children can easily re-name something, they also believe that you can reassign a person's sex. It's not unusual for two- and three-year-olds to think that they could end up as the opposite sex, for example a girl may state that when she grows up she is going to be a daddy. They are also easily fooled by outward appearances. For example, if a three-year-old boy puts on his mum's shoes, he may claim that he is now a girl. Similarly, if his mother gets her hair cut short, he may say that she is now a man. This also shows that three-year-olds are beginning to associate certain characteristics with certain sexes. Boys and girls may also begin to show an interest in playing with their own
sex – but this is only because they share the same label of being a 'boy' or a 'girl', that is they are part of the 'same gang'. The implication is that if we did not have different terms for females and males then young children would perceive themselves as belonging to the same group.

Gender stability

Children move out of the identity stage and into the **gender stability stage** when they understand that their own sex is stable and will not change over time. This happens around about the age of 4. However, children at this stage are still **egocentric** in lots of ways e.g. they cannot picture something from another's point of view. Although they understand their sex will stay the same, they do not have the cognitive ability to understand that this 'rule' must apply to others. Thiey are also still fooled by appearance. So, for example a boy may believe that he has turned into a girl if he puts on a dress. Or children may believe that a female firefighter is really a man. In other words, people's sex is determined by whether or not they behave in a masculine or feminine way.

Gender constancy

When children reach the **gender constancy stage**, then they begin to understand gender as adults do. Around the age of 5, children begin to **de-centre** and appreciate the world from other people's point of view. As this happens, they understand that everybody's sex is constant and not just their own. By now they have also realised that changing their outward appearance does not change how they feel inside and so they have some idea of their own gender being constant. As they reach the end of this stage, they are no longer fooled by others' outward appearance either. This relates to the fact that they demonstrate the cognitive ability to **conserve**. So children at this stage might think that it is unusual that a girl wants to play rugby or that a boy wants to wear pink, but they would not assume that a person has changed their sex because of that. In other words, they understand that sex is consistent across time and across situations. Whether a person is masculine or feminine has no bearing on their sex. This has been related to the fact that children at this stage begin to use genitals as a way of determining sex, and realise that genitals (unlike appearance) are unchangeable. Kohlberg also argued that at the gender constancy stage, children begin to **actively** seek out role models. Children imitate and internalise the behaviours of these role models, to help them develop their sense of gender.

■ **Key terms**

Gender identity stage: when children are able to label themselves and others in terms of their sex (Kohlberg).

Gender stability stage: when children understand their own sex remains stable over time (Kohlberg).

Egocentric: only understanding things through subjective experience; the inability to view the world from another's perspective.

Gender constancy stage: when children understand that each person's sex is consistent across time and across situations.

De-centre: means developing the ability to view the world from another's perspective.

Conserve: to understand that the properties of an object are conserved (stay the same) even if appearance changes.

Examiner's tip

Be careful how you describe the difference between gender stability and gender constancy. Candidates often use a phrase like 'when you understand gender remains the same' for either stage. This is not clear enough. Does it mean remains the same over time (gender stability) or or over situations (gender constancy)? Don't leave phrases open to interpretation.

Fig. 12 *A child in the gender stability of Kohlberg's stages would probably say this character is a girl because he has a dress on*

Research study: Marcus and Overton (1978)

Aim: To show that as children get older they develop gender constancy.

Method: In this experiment, the sample consisted of three year groups from a school: five- to six-year-olds, six- to seven-year-olds and seven- to eight-year-olds. Children were shown a puzzle with a male and female character in it. It was possible to change the hairstyle and the clothes of the characters so they looked like the opposite sex. The same thing was done with a puzzle where photographs of the children's faces were superimposed onto the characters' bodies. The researchers tried out different combinations of the puzzles with the children (for example, the male character with a girl's hairstyle and boy's clothes, etc.). Each time they asked children what sex they thought the character was. When photographs of the actual children were used, then they were asked whether their own sex had changed.

Results: Younger children tended to demonstrate gender constancy for their own sex (for example, when a female child was given a boy's hairstyle she still said she was a girl). However, younger children showed lower levels of gender consistency when the character's appearance changed. Older children showed high levels of gender constancy when both their own and the characters' appearances were changed.

Conclusion: The findings showed that young children, just moving into the gender constancy stage, only saw their own sex as stable under change. However, older children had fully developed gender constancy as they understood sex always stayed the same.

Evaluation: Like many experiments, this one used an artificial task which may have little bearing on real life.

Other findings supporting Kohlberg's cognitive-developmental theory are detailed in Table 6.

Table 6 *Studies supporting Kohlberg's cognitive-developmental theory*

Researchers	Findings
Slaby and Frey (1975)	They observed children watching a split screen with a male model on one side and a female model on the other side who were performing the same activities. Young children spent their time looking at both sides of the screen. However older children (who had high gender constancy) spent longer looking at the model who was the same sex as themselves.
Damon (1977)	He read children a story about a boy who liked to play with dolls, and asked for their opinion on this. Findings showed that young children had no concept of gender appropriate behaviour and thought it was acceptable for a boy to play with dolls. However, older children tended to say it was wrong or unusual because of their more developed idea of gender.
McConaghy (1979)	She showed children pictures of characters with see-through clothes so that children could see the characters' genitals. Younger children, who would not have reached the gender constancy stage, recognised gender by appearance rather than genitals. So a male character (with a penis) was seen as female if he was wearing a see-through dress.
Munroe *et al.* (1984)	They tested children from Kenya, Belize, Samoa and Nepal and found that children in all countries moved through Kohlberg's stages of gender development.

Gender schema theory

Like Kohlberg's theory, gender **schema** theory also emphasises the importance of children **actively seeking** gender-related information. However, this theory disagrees with Kohlberg's in the respect that it believes that children seek out this information long before they have achieved gender constancy.

Gender schema theory suggests that once children have established their gender identity (at around two or three), they search their environment for information which will help them develop their gender schemas. As children build up schemas in their minds, it helps them to interpret and organise what is happening in their world.

The first gender schemas that children form relate to the activities associated with each sex. Children are essentially forming stereotypes and may begin to learn what females and males should and should not be doing. For example, boys should play rough but should not play with dolls. Children also go on to form gender **scripts**, such as making dinner (for females) and doing DIY (for men).

Once children have these gender schemas and scripts, they begin to pay more attention to activities associated with their own sex than the opposite sex. For example, girls become aware that playing with train sets is 'for boys' so they avoid trains and learn little more about them. As a result, gender appropriate behaviour becomes part of children's thinking.

Information which is consistent with children's gender schemas continues to be **assimilated** into their thinking. However, if children encounter behaviours which are inconsistent with their gender schemas, they often fail to **encode** that information. This allows their stereotypes about male and female behaviour to remain intact.

Research study: Martin and Halverson (1983)

Aim: To demonstrate that children do distort inconsistent information to fit their gender schemas.

Method: Using the experimental method, the researchers showed five- and six-year-old children pictures of people carrying out activities. Sometimes these activities were schema-consistent (for example, a girl playing with a doll) and sometimes they were schema-inconsistent (for example, a girl playing with a gun).

Results: Children's recall of the pictures was tested a week later. Findings showed that recall for schema-consistent pictures was generally good. However, when schema-inconsistent pictures were recalled they were often distorted so that the expected sex was remembered as carrying out the activity (for example, children recalled a boy playing with the gun rather than a girl).

Conclusion: Children do use schemas to help them to make sense of their world. They will sometimes use schemas to reorganise information so that it is consistent with their view of gender even if it is not accurate.

Evaluation: As means of control, children's understanding of gender was measured quite precisely. However, this may not be a valid measure of a complex phenomenon.

Key terms

Schema: an internal mental representation of the world which is used to make sense of experiences.

Script: an internal representation of a set of actions that make up a routine.

Assimilation: taking in and making part of.

Encode: to register information for later retrieval.

Gender development

Fig. 13 *The picture on the left would be consistent with most children's gender schemas. However, the picture on the right would be inconsistent with most children's gender schemas*

Around the age of six, children have developed quite a sophisticated set of associations for their own gender e.g. what children of their gender like and do not like, how they talk, etc. Only between the ages of eight and ten do children develop an equally sophisticated view of the opposite gender.

Children's need to understand and then conform to the distinctions between the sexes is well demonstrated in an experiment carried out by Bradbard *et al.* (1986). Four- to nine-year-olds were presented with gender-neutral objects. They were told some were 'boy' objects and others 'girl' objects. Interestingly, children then spent significantly more time playing with the objects they had been told were associated with their sex.

■ Analysis and evaluation of the cognitive approach

■ The cognitive approach suggests that gender develops in age-related stages which would imply that it is related to biological maturation. Although the biological explanations would accept this, they would not agree that children are so active in developing their gender. For biological psychologists, gender is determined by factors outside of the child's control, for example genes, hormones.

■ Social learning theory would argue that children respond to role models in their environment and this leads to gender development. However, the cognitive approach argues that children develop their gender identity almost independently of the environment. Only when their gender is established do they actively seek out role models for themselves. For SLT, there is too much focus on the part that an individual plays in their gender development. There is not enough focus on the social context.

■ The psychodynamic approach would criticise the cognitive approach for focusing too much on the conscious elements of gender development. It would argue for more consideration of the unconscious elements. However, broadly speaking, both approaches agree on the idea that gender develops following set stages. However, according to the psychodynamic approach, gender develops much later than proposed by the cognitive approach.

■ Cognitive theories are often accused of describing but not really explaining gender development. For example, why does gender begin to develop at the age of two and how are schemas actually formed in the first place?

■ Cognitive theories are not very clear on why an individual may adopt a gender identity that leads to gender inappropriate behaviour. Cognitive theories need to offer more adequate explanations of why some children actively seek out role models of the opposite sex.

■ The evidence for cognitive theories has its limitations. Children are often assessed under experimental conditions which may distort reality. Measures of children's cognitive development may not be reliable, as they depend on the way that questions are asked and how answers are interpreted. Gender constancy cannot be objectively measured; it is based on a judgement. There is also the possibility that children do understand the consistency of gender at an earlier age but are **not** able to express this. Differences in gender development may really reflect differences in language development. For example, when a young child suggests a boy has become a 'girl' are they really trying to convey the idea that the boy is behaving in a feminine way but do not have the means to express this?

Key points:

■ The cognitive approach focuses on the thinking behind gender development.

■ Kohlberg's cognitive-development theory suggests children's gender develops through three stages: gender identity (where they can label their own and others' sex); gender stability (where they understand their sex stays the same forever); gender constancy (where they understand that each person's sex is constant regardless of time and situation).

■ Gender schema theory argues that children develop gender as early as two years of age when they begin to categorise and make sense of the world in terms of gender-appropriate behaviour.

■ Cognitive theories tend to describe rather than explain, and critics are concerned that the theories do not pay enough attention to factors that individuals have little control over, for example biology, social context.

Summary questions

22 Outline what is meant by a gender schema.

23 a Identify three features of Kohlberg's gender identity stage of development.

   b Identify three features of Kohlberg's gender stability stage of development.

   c Identify three features of Kohlberg's gender constancy stage of development.

24 Describe the similarities and differences between Kohlberg's cognitive-development theory and gender schema theory.

25 Outline how a child at each stage of Kohlberg's cognitive-development theory would respond to a 'pantomime dame'.

The psychodynamic approach

Learning objectives:

- Describe how the psychodynamic approach explains gender development.

- Outline the role of the Oedipus complex, Electra complex and identification in gender development.

- Consider the evidence for the psychodynamic explanation of gender development.

- Explain the limitations of the psychodynamic approach to gender development.

Key terms

Unconscious forces: drives that motivate behaviour which individuals are not aware of.

Phallic stage: a stage of development where children begin to focus on their own and others' genitals (Freud).

Oedipus complex: an unconscious conflict that occurs in boys when they desire their mother yet fear their father.

Castration anxiety: the fear experienced by boys when they believe they will have their penis removed.

Link

The psychodynamic approach focuses on the unconscious forces which drive changes and development in behaviour. For more information on the psychodynamic approach, see Chapter 1, Key approaches.

The psychodynamic approach emphasises the importance of change and development in behaviours. It believes that this development is mainly driven by **unconscious forces**.

The most famous psychodynamic explanation is Freud's psychoanalytic theory and this can be used to explain gender development.

Freud's psychoanalytic theory

Freud proposed that we move through a number of age-related stages of development encountering different conflicts along the way. These conflicts need to be resolved at each stage to ensure healthy psychological development. Establishing our gender identity is part of this healthy psychological development and this should occur around the age of five.

The first two stages of development are the oral stage (up to one year of age) and the anal stage (from one to three years). At these stages, gender identity is said to be flexible, and there are no clear differences between girls and boys as both sexes focus on seeking pleasure through the mouth and then the anus. Up to the age of three, children have no real sense of being masculine or feminine. However, when they move into the **phallic stage** of development, their understanding of gender begins to change.

The phallic stage lasts from three years of age until five or six years of age. During this period, the child seeks pleasure from playing with his or her own genitals. At the same time, they begin to pay attention to others' genitals and so become aware of the physical differences between females and males. This is the start of children's developing gender identity.

According to Freud, the main force behind a child's gender development is their relationships with their parents. The mother is the first love object for both boys and girls. However, for three-year-old boys this love turns to lust. This gives boys an **Oedipus complex**.

The Oedipus complex

The Oedipus complex describes the conflict that all young boys experience when they develop a passionate desire for their own mother. The conflict arises because boys will want to possess their mother for themselves but they see their father as a rival who stands in their way. As a result, boys become jealous of their fathers.

Boys' feelings go beyond jealousy, and they actually wish their father dead. However, boys also fear their father and as a consequence they develop **castration anxiety**. Castration anxiety occurs because boys are afraid that their father will discover their desire for their mother, and will punish them by removing their most prized possession – their penis. Boys recognise that their father is more powerful than them, partly because their father has a bigger penis. Not only this, but the father is likely to have already reprimanded his son for playing with himself – perhaps even threatening to cut off the boy's penis if he doesn't stop. In addition, boys believe that their mother has already been castrated by their father (as their mother is without a penis) and so the threat appears real. In short, the conflict for boys is between their lust for their mother and their feelings of hostility towards their father.

The Electra complex

Freud was less clear on girls' gender development but his predecessors did propose the **Electra complex** as an alternative to boys' Oedipus complex. When they are in the phallic stage, girls are also said to experience a conflict between a desire for their opposite sex parent and resentment towards their same sex parent. The reason why girls resent their mothers is because girls realise males have penises and they feel cheated because they do not have one. Girls believe that they have been castrated already, and then blame their mother for this.

According to Freud, girls experience **penis envy** where they long for a penis. However, they soon discover they cannot have one and so they substitute their desire for a penis with a desire for a baby. Girls want their fathers to provide this baby (and preferably a male baby) and this is why they lust after their father. However, girls are anxious about their mother finding out about the feelings that they have for their father. While boys fear aggression from their father, girls fear losing their mother's love. This is the conflict that needs to be resolved.

Fig. 14 *When a young boy insists on sleeping between his mummy and daddy in their bed, this may be a sign of the Oedipus complex*

Identification

The way that both girls and boys resolve the conflicts that they have with their respective parents is to **identify** with the same sex parent. By identifying with the same sex parent not only do they develop a **superego** (which allows them to adopt the morals of their parents) but they also adopt their same sex parent's gender identity and role. This may explain why five- and six-year-olds, at the end of the phallic stage, may appear to behave in similar ways to their parents. For example, a boy may begin to follow the same sports as his dad and a girl may help her mother with the household chores.

Freud stated that boys use the **defence mechanism** of repression to push their desires for their mother and their hostility towards their father into the **unconscious**. This reduces the tension between a son and his father, allowing the son to identify with the father. In doing so, boys also reduce the threat of castration.

Key terms

Electra complex: an unconscious conflict that occurs in girls when they desire their father yet worry about losing their mother's love.

Penis envy: a feeling experienced by girls because they are jealous of the fact that men and boys possess a penis when they do not.

Identify: to adopt the attitudes and values of another.

Superego: a part of personality which monitors moral behaviour.

Defence mechanism: a process which protects an individual from unresolved conflicts.

Unconscious: the part of the mind that individuals are not aware of.

Fig. 15 *When a young girl says she is going to marry her daddy when she grows up, this may be sign of the Electra complex*

AQA Examiner's tip

When describing Freud's theory make sure that you use technical terms. Candidates should not use phrases such as 'boys fancy their mums' or 'boys are afraid their dads will chop off their willies' as these are too informal and not appropriate for an A Level examination!

Gender development

Candidates often make the mistake of thinking that Freud only wrote about dual-parent families. Even in Freud's day there were some one-parent families (often because of death or because of fathers who were frequently away from home) so he did comment on this.

Meanwhile, girls also identify with their mother, although Freud argued that their motivation was not as strong therefore they develop a weaker gender identity. By identifying with their mother, girls retain their mother's love. It can also be argued that by internalising the mother's role, the daughter is unconsciously hoping still to attract her father in the same way that her mother does.

Freud was writing at a time when most children lived with both parents but he did theorise about what would happen in the case of families where one parent was absent. He suggested that such children would be unable to experience the Oedipus/Electra complex, and therefore would not be in a position to resolve the conflict necessary to develop a healthy gender identity. For example, he argued that boys without a father would have difficulty developing a masculine identity and would be more likely to become homosexual. Rekers and Moray (1989) offered some support for Freud's ideas. They investigated a sample of boys with gender identity disorders and found that in many cases their fathers were absent from birth or had left home before the age of five. Even where fathers were around, they were often described as psychologically remote.

Freud provided limited evidence to support his theory which is one of the limitations of this explanation of gender development. The theory was mainly based around one case study of a five-year-old boy named Hans.

Research study: Freud (1909)

Aim: To demonstrate the existence of the Oedipus complex.

Method: Hans had developed a phobia of horses. He was the son of Freud's friend. Freud asked the father to write and tell him about his son's development so that he could interpret it in terms of his psychoanalytic theory.

Results: The correspondence showed that Hans was particularly afraid of large white horses with black blinkers and black around the mouth. He was terrified to leave the house and believed that the horses might either bite him or fall down on him.

Conclusion: Freud described Hans's phobia as an outward expression of his unconscious castration anxiety. His fear of horses was really a displaced fear of his father – especially since Hans's father wore dark glasses (like blinkers) and had a beard (like a dark muzzle). According to Freud, Hans's fear was particularly strong because his mother was pregnant. This made Hans very jealous and his fear of horses falling was actually an unconscious desire to see his own father drop down dead.

Evaluation: Critics have questioned the evidence provided by the case study of Hans. It is difficult to generalise from a study of one subject – other boys would not necessarily show the same anxiety as Hans. Freud was also accused of interpreting the case to support his theory. The fact that he never actually met Hans makes the evidence very unreliable. In addition, it later transpired that Hans had witnessed a horrific horse and cart accident just before the onset of his phobia which would offer a much more valid explanation for his fear!

Link

This is an example of a how a case study is used in investigation. See Chapter 4, Research methods for more information.

■ Analysis and evaluation of the psychodynamic approach

■ Biological explanations would support the psychodynamic idea that 'anatomy is destiny' and the idea that gender development is driven by nature. However, biological explanations would question the validity of unconscious forces which cannot be easily tested. They would also not recognise the role of family experiences in the way that the psychodynamic approach does.

■ Social learning theory would agree that parents can have a large influence on the development of gender, but they would disagree that a same-sex parent needs to be present for healthy gender development. SLT would suggest that young children can learn from other same-sex role models besides parents. This would explain why most empirical evidence shows that children from single-parent families do indeed develop normal gender identities (for example, Golombok *et al.*, 1983). Social learning theory would also question whether gender develops at a certain stage in childhood, and instead would argue that gender development depends on environmental experiences rather than maturation.

■ The cognitive-development theory would agree with Freud that gender develops in stages, but would argue that it develops gradually over time rather than in 'one fell swoop'. They would also argue that there is a large body of evidence that children demonstrate some awareness of gender as young as three rather than five or six. The cognitive approach would also emphasise the conscious component of gender and would criticise the psychodynamic approach for focusing too much on the unconscious component.

■ If psychodynamic theory is correct, we would expect sons of strict or harsh fathers to develop stronger masculine gender identities than other boys. However, research evidence suggests it is the sons of more liberal and supportive fathers who have more secure gender identities (for example, Mussen and Rutherford, 1963).

■ Malinowski's (1927) study of the Trobriand Islands suggested that the Oedipus complex was a Western phenomenon rather than a universal one. He found that the boys in these islands still developed a masculine gender despite being disciplined by their mothers' brothers rather than their own fathers.

■ Freud is accused of not giving an adequate account of females' gender development. This is further evidence that the theory is too subjective, arising from his own male perspective rather than a more objective viewpoint. Some critics also disliked the notion of infant sexuality arguing it seemed unlikely that such young children would have the kind of feelings described by Freud. Overall, the psychodynamic approach suffers from the problem that it is unscientific. It is difficult to generalise from, lacks reliable evidence and is not objective enough.

■ Hints

When you have a list of evaluation points to remember, try to summarise them by listing them using short key phrases. For example, the criticisms of the psychodynamic approach could be listed as:

■ unconscious cannot be tested

■ not just parents influence gender

■ children have gender identity before five

■ strict fathers do not have more masculine sons

■ boys disciplined by uncles still develop normally

■ unscientific.

Gender development

Key points:

■ The psychodynamic approach explains gender development as occurring in stages driven by unconscious forces.

■ Boys experience the Oedipus complex where they desire their mother but fear castration by their father as a result.

■ Girls experience the Electra complex where they desire their father but fear losing their mother's love as a result.

■ Both sexes resolve these conflicts by identifying with the same sex parent at the age of about five or six.

■ Freud presented the case of Hans as evidence of the Oedipus complex. Hans's fear of horses represented his fear of his father.

■ Psychodynamic theories are generally unscientific and lack convincing evidence.

 Summary questions

26 Give the stage of Freud's psychoanalytic theory at which children develop their gender identity.

27 Explain what is meant by the term 'identification' in Freud's theory of gender development.

28 Outline the role of the unconscious in Freud's theory of gender development.

29 Describe one similarity and one difference between the Oedipus complex and the Electra complex as described by Freud.

30 Outline three criticisms of Freud's psychoanalytic theory of gender development.

31 A three-year-old girl is playing with her mummy and daddy. She decides that they will act out a story in which she is the princess. Her mummy is a wicked witch who locks the princess in her tower. Her daddy is going to be the knight who arrives, sword in hand, to save her from the wicked witch.

How might Freud's psychoanalytic theory be used explain this scenario?

💡 End-of-chapter activity

You can investigate sex-role stereotyping for yourself by carrying out a content analysis of TV advertisements similar to that of Furnham and Farragher (2000) (see p51). You could aim to see whether females and males are still presented in sex stereotyped ways. You will need to start with a coding system where you identify the different types of role you will be looking for, for example positions of authority, domestic roles. You will also need to clearly operationalise those roles so that you can be objective about what you are looking for. You then need to decide on a sample of advertisements that are going to be a good representation of advertisements in general. For example, you will need to think about the time of day you will watch the adverts and on which channels. If you count the number of times that you observe males and females in different roles then you should be able to present your findings in a table or graph. You may want to make notes on the style and content of the adverts as you go along which would give you some qualitative data to support your quantitative data.

Link

For more on content analysis, see p105.

1 (a) (i) Identify one way in which Klinefelter's syndrome might affect an individual. *(1 mark)*

      (ii) Explain how studying people with atypical sex chromosome patterns can contribute to our understanding of gender. *(4 marks)*

  (b) A number of students have a disagreement about which of the three definitions below is a definition of the term identification.

     (i) A person's desire to be like another person or to be part of a particular social group

     (ii) A procedure whereby a person attaches himself/herself to a model who possesses qualities seen as rewarding

    (iii) The process by which a response is strengthened

     Which of these ((i), (ii) or (iii)) illustrates the term identification? *(1 mark)*

  (c) Madeleine and Naomi were discussing their friend Harry, who is very good at mending cars. Madeleine commented, 'I think boys are naturally good at that sort of thing.'

    State what is meant by nature and nurture in relation to gender. Refer to the example of Harry in your answer. *(4 marks)*

  (d) Describe and evaluate one cognitive explanation of gender development. Refer to one other explanation of gender development in your answer. *(10 marks)*

AQA specimen question

2 (a) Name one sex hormone and give an example of how this hormone might affect a person's behaviour. *(2 marks)*

  (b) Outline two criticisms of the psychoanalytic explanation of gender development. *(4 marks)*

  (c) Victoria is five years old and she is different from other girls of her age. She is smaller in height and has a webbed neck. At school, her teachers have commented that she has good verbal skills but her mathematical skills are poor. Medical tests have revealed that Victoria has a sex chromosome pattern XO.

     (i) Name the atypical sex chromosome syndrome described above. *(1 mark)*

     (ii) Identify how Victoria's sex chromosome pattern differs from that of most girls. *(1 mark)*

    (iii) Explain how studying people like Victoria can contribute to our understanding of gender. *(2 marks)*

  (d) Discuss the social learning theory explanation of gender. Refer to at least one other explanation of gender development in your answer. *(10 marks)*

3   (a)   Outline Freud's explanation of the Oedipus complex.   *(3 marks)*

       (b)   A number of students have a disagreement about which of the three definitions below can be applied to the terms modelling and reinforcement:

- a person's desire to be like another person or to be part of a particular social group
- the process by which a response is strengthened
- a procedure whereby a person observes another person and then attempts to imitate his or her behaviour

           Write down the definition which illustrates each of the following:

           (i)   modelling

           (ii)   reinforcement   *(2 marks)*

       (c)   Describe one study in which the cognitive developmental theory of gender was investigated. Indicate in your answer why the study was conducted, the method used, results obtained and conclusion drawn.   *(5 marks)*

       (d)   Describe and evaluate one biological example of gender development. Refer to one other explanation of gender development in your answer.   *(10 marks)*

                                              AQA, 2006

4   (a)   Below are statements made by three children.

- My name is Michael. I have long, brown hair.
- My name is Valerie. When I grow up, I am going to be a mummy.
- My name is Kate and I am a girl.

           Write down the statement which illustrates the concept of:

           (i)   gender identity

           (ii)   gender stability.   *(2 marks)*

       (b)   Identify one atypical sex chromosome pattern and outline how it might affect an individual.   *(3 marks)*

       (c)   Describe one study in which the development of gender was investigated. Indicate in your answer why the study was conducted, the method used, the results obtained and the conclusion drawn.   *(5 marks)*

       (d)   Describe and evaluate the social learning theory of gender. Refer to one other explanation of gender development in your answer.   *(10 marks)*

                                              AQA, 2005

Research methods

Introduction

Is psychology common sense? If psychology is the study of the human mind and behaviour, then most people could claim that they are psychologists. Many people have their own theories of why an individual thinks or acts in a certain way. These may be theories about their own self, for example 'I can't give up gambling because I have an addictive personality', or theories about others, for example 'He is a jealous person because he is not happy with his own life'. However, in psychology, theories should apply more generally rather than be based on 'one-offs'. But people can come up with this kind of theory. For example, they may have their own explanations of why women are more likely to stay at home than men, or what causes football fans to riot.

Psychology is also about collecting evidence to support theories. So, once again, many people could claim they do this. If a person concludes that women stay at home because of pressure from society, this may have come from talking to friends and family. Or if somebody theorises that football riots are due to poor policing, this could be from personal experience of attending matches. Although this is close to what psychologists do (for example, interviewing people, observing a situation), psychology would claim that data is collected in a more systematic way. This would generally involve being objective rather than relying on personal experience, leading to more reliable findings.

In an attempt to be more systematic, research goes through a number of processes that are detailed further in this chapter.

- In the planning stage, psychologists identify the aim of their research. Before starting their research, they test themselves and their theories by making predictions about the outcome of the study. In doing this, they will identify the key variables under investigation.

- Psychologists also have to make choices about how evidence will be collected. Experiments are often chosen by psychologists because they are highly systematic. However, alternative methods can be reliable too.

- Another important decision is with regard to whom to collect evidence from. Obviously, this will normally be from other human beings. However, psychologists need to decide where people will be drawn from and also how they will be selected. Psychologists are normally keen to select participants fairly. They also want to make sure that the participants can represent the views and actions of other people not being studied.

- When people are under investigation, there are certain guidelines that psychologists will follow. This is generally to ensure that participants are being treated appropriately while being subjected to research.

- Once evidence has been collected, it will need to be analysed and presented in a way that clearly demonstrates findings. If a psychologist is lucky, then the data will support their theory. If not, they may need to rethink their theory!

The point is, whether a theory has been supported or refuted, it has to be done in a way that is **reliable**. This is the goal of psychological research. Understanding how to use research methods in psychological investigations is what allows us to go beyond common sense and produce **valid** findings.

Key terms

Reliability: the consistency of the findings; how much findings can be trusted.

Valid: accurate or true, measures what it claims.

Specification	Topic content	Page
Methods of research		
Qualitative and quantitative research: the distinction between qualitative and quantitative data collection techniques; strengths and limitations of quantitative and qualitative data	Qualitative versus quantitative research	**106**
Formulating research questions; stating aims; formulating hypotheses (null and experimental/alternative/research)	Planning research	**84**
Populations and sampling; sampling techniques, including opportunity, random, stratified and systematic	Sampling	**107**
Experiments: field, laboratory and quasi-experiments; issue of ecological validity	Experimental methods	**87**
Independent and dependent variables; manipulation and control of variables in experiments; extraneous and confounding variables	Planning research Experimental methods	**84** **87**
Experimental designs: repeated or related measures, matched pairs, independent groups and appropriate use of each	Experimental methods	**87**
Controls associated with different designs, including counterbalancing; strengths and limitations of different experimental designs	Experimental methods	**87**
Strengths and limitations of experimental methods	Experimental methods	**87**
Self-report methods: questionnaire construction, including open and closed questions; types of interviews: structured and unstructured	Non-experimental methods Methods of self-report	**94** **95**
Pilot studies and their value	Methods of self-report	**95**
Correlation studies: the difference between an experiment and a correlation study	Correlation studies	**101**
Observational studies: natural and laboratory settings; covert and overt; participant and non-participant observation	Observational studies	**98**
The process of content analysis	Content analyses	**105**
Case studies: the role of case studies in psychology	Case studies	**104**
Strengths and limitations of these methods	(see above)	
Representing data and descriptive statistics		
Appropriate use of the following tabular and graphical displays: bar charts, histograms, graphs, scattergrams and tables	Representing data	**114**
Calculation and use of measures of central tendency (mean, median, mode) and measures of dispersion (range and standard deviation)	Descriptive data	**117**
Correlation as a description of the relationship between two variables; positive, negative and zero correlations	Correlation studies	**101**
Ethics		
An awareness of the code of ethics in psychology as specified by the British Psychological Society	Ethics	**111**
The application of the code of ethics in psychological research	Ethics	**111**

4 Research methods

Planning research

Learning objectives:

- Know how research questions are formulated.
- Know how aims are formulated.
- Know how hypotheses are formulated.
- Distinguish between an independent variable (IV) and a dependent variable (DV).

Key terms

Hypotheses: testable statements making predictions about what will happen in an investigation.

Operationalise: to offer a clear set of criteria to describe how something will be set up or assessed or measured.

Variables: factors that can change (or vary).

Psychologists, like anybody, observe events in their environment and ask why they happen. These may be single events, for example how a particular person developed a phobia of chewing gum. Or they may be events that occur more frequently, for example why people form impressions based on appearance. They may even have theories as to why these things happen. For example, a psychologist may theorise that the person with a phobia had experienced a threatening event while chewing gum. However, psychology is made up of more than theories. Psychologists seek evidence to test and support their theories. This is 'doing research'.

Formulating research questions

Research starts with a research question: something that a psychologist wants to find out. For example:

- How do phobias occur?
- Is it easier to remember sounds or images?
- What makes some people more obedient than others?

If we take the last example, there are a number of possible answers to this question which is why research needs to be carried out. Obedience levels may depend on personality. They may depend on the setting. They may depend on who is giving the orders. It would be difficult to investigate all of these factors at once, so a psychologist would narrow down their field of research in order to come up with an aim.

Formulating aims

An aim is a general statement which describes what a psychologist intends to investigate. Using the previous example, an aim would focus on one factor affecting obedience. For example, the psychologist may decide to focus on personality and more specifically on confidence. The aim of their research would therefore be 'to investigate whether a person's confidence level has an effect on the likelihood of them obeying'. Similarly, a psychologist may aim 'to investigate whether people recall more words depending on whether they are presented acoustically or visually'.

Formulating hypotheses

Having stated an aim, a psychologist then formulates **hypotheses**. The aim is based on a theory, and the theory should allow predictions to be made. For example, the psychologist investigating obedience may predict that people who are more confident are less obedient. This does not constitute a hypothesis yet. A hypothesis also needs to **operationalise** the **variables** that are being tested. In the example, there are two variables being tested: level of confidence and likelihood of obedience. The psychologist may decide to determine level of confidence by using a questionnaire on participants, and to measure likelihood of obedience by observing whether the same participants follow an unreasonable request made by a stranger in uniform.

Now the psychologist can make a very precise prediction, known as a **research hypothesis** (abbreviated to H_1):

> H_1: Participants who score above average on a questionnaire measuring confidence are significantly less likely to follow an unreasonable request made by a stranger in uniform compared to participants who score below average.

The psychologist then tests their hypotheses by collecting data through carrying out an investigation. They then have to make a key research decision. If the results suggest that the prediction was correct, then the research hypothesis is retained. If the results suggest the prediction was wrong, then the research hypothesis is rejected.

As it is possible that a psychologist may have to reject their H_1, they will need to also formulate a **null hypothesis** (abbreviated to H_0) which predicts no difference rather than a difference:

> H_0: There is no significant difference in the number of times participants follow an unreasonable request from a stranger in uniform whether they score above or below average on a questionnaire measuring confidence.

The H_0 is retained if the H_1 is rejected.

The following further illustrates how hypotheses may be formulated:

> H_1: There will be a significant difference in the number of words recalled in two minutes depending on whether those words are read to participants or whether they read the words themselves.

> H_0: There will be no significant difference in the number of words recalled in two minutes whether those words are read to participants or whether they read the words themselves.

As the above examples show, it makes sense to use the word 'significant' when predicting a difference between conditions. For instance, imagine if participants recalled 12 out of 20 words on average when hearing them and 13 out of 20 on average when reading them. There is a difference between 12 and 13 but it is not significant. Because it is not significant, a researcher would not conclude that one way of presenting words is better than the others in terms of recall.

All of the hypotheses so far have predicted differences (for example, between likelihood of obedience, recall of words). However, it is also possible for a hypothesis to predict a **correlation**. For example:

> H_1: There is a significant correlation between participants' scores on a self-esteem test and the number of friends they have.

In this case, the null hypothesis would be:

> H_0: There is no significant correlation between participants' scores on a self-esteem test and the number of friends they have.

The hypothesis predicting no correlation or no difference is always known as the null hypothesis. However, the hypothesis predicting a difference is not always known as a research hypothesis.

If the H_1 is formulated specifically for an experiment it can be known as an **experimental hypothesis**. Experimental hypotheses only predict differences as correlations cannot be tested experimentally.

Key terms

Research hypothesis: a hypothesis that predicts a difference in the measured variable (change in DV due to the IV, see next heading) or correlation between variables.

Null hypothesis: a hypothesis that predicts no difference in a variable or no correlation between variables.

Correlation: a relationship between two variables.

Experimental hypothesis: a hypothesis used only in experiments which predicts a difference and has an IV and DV.

Hint

When writing a hypothesis, make sure both conditions (of the IV) are stated (not just one).

AQA Examiner's tip

You may remember H_0 is the abbreviation for a null hypothesis as it predicts nothing (zero) will change or no relationship.

It is good practice to use the word 'significant' when writing a hypothesis. However, you can only ever be sure that a difference is significant by carrying out a statistical test on data. This is something you will have to be able to do in A2 Psychology but do not have to concern yourself with at AS.

Research methods

Key terms

Alternative hypothesis: a hypothesis which predicts a difference or correlation following a null hypothesis which predicts no difference/correlation.

Independent variable: something manipulated or set up in an experiment.

Dependent variable: something that is measured after the independent variable may have had an effect on it.

AQA Examiner's tip

Candidates are often able to identify the variables (the things that will change in an experiment) but sometimes get the IV and DV muddled. Does the IV you have identified affect the DV you have identified? Does the change in the DV depend on the action of the IV?

affects IV depends on DV

Fig. 1 *How the IV and DV are related in an experiment*

Summary questions

1. Give the alternative to retaining a hypothesis.

2. Outline one difference between a research question and an aim.

3. Identify three types of H_1.

4. Describe the difference between IV and DV.

5. Imagine you have been asked to investigate what makes a good leader?

   a Outline a possible aim.

   b State an appropriate research and null hypothesis.

   c Suggest how the IV and DV might be operationalised.

Although less common, a psychologist may predict no difference before carrying out their research. For example:

H_0: There is no significant difference in the ability of men and women to solve anagrams under timed conditions.

In this case, the second hypothesis is known as the **alternative hypothesis** (abbreviated to H_A):

H_A: There is a significant difference between the ability of men and women to solve anagrams under timed conditions.

Independent variables and dependent variables

As stated, experimental hypotheses always predict a difference. This is because in experiments a variable is manipulated to test whether it causes a change (or difference) in another variable. This is the variable that is measured. The manipulated variable is the **independent variable** (IV) and the measured variable is the **dependent variable** (DV). The DV gets its name because, if the experimenter's prediction is right, this variable depends on the activity of the IV. In other words, the IV has an effect on the DV. This is why only experiments can reliably establish cause and effect.

Table 1 *The independent variables and dependent variables in the hypotheses stated above*

Independent variable	Dependent variable
Whether participants have an above or below average score for confidence levels	Whether participants follow an unreasonable request from a uniformed stranger or not
Whether words are read to participants or they read them themselves	Number of words recalled in two minutes
Whether participants are male or female	Number of anagrams correctly solved under timed conditions

The hypothesis predicting a correlation is not included in Table 01 because it does not predict a difference and therefore does not contain an IV and DV. It is simply predicting a relationship between two variables but is not stating which variable affects which.

Key points:

- Research questions arise from observations and psychologists use research to try to answer them.

- Research starts with an aim which is a broad statement about what is being investigated.

- Research uses a H_1 (research/experimental/alternative hypothesis) which predicts a difference or correlation and will be retained if evidence supports it. If H_1 is rejected then the H_0 (null hypothesis) is retained instead as this predicts no difference or no correlation.

- Experimental hypotheses contain an independent variable which will be manipulated by the experimenter. The independent variable is predicted to have an effect on a dependent variable which will be measured by the experimenter.

Experimental methods

Learning objectives:

- Understand what is meant by the experimental method.

- Distinguish between extraneous and confounding variables in experiments.

- Explain how variables can be controlled.

- Know about the different types of experiments.

- Know about the different types of experimental designs.

- Understand the strengths and limitations of different experimental designs.

- Understand the strengths and limitations of using the experimental method.

AQA Examiner's tip

It is worth considering the issues in this section on experimental methods (including the use of the IV and DV) in the context of the social, cognitive and individual differences topics at AS. This is because the exam paper PSYB2 will always include a question on experimentation in relation to these topics.

Key terms

Experiment: a process of manipulating an IV and measuring a DV, while all other variables are controlled.

Confounding variable: a variable besides the IV which may have affected the DV.

Extraneous variable: a variable besides the IV which could affect the DV.

Experimental methods offer one of the most common ways of collecting evidence in psychology.

Experimental methods do not all apply one particular method of data collection; there are several types. Experimenters may use observation or more direct questioning. With **experiments**, it is the **process** which is important, and not how the data is collected. What all experimental methods have in common is the fact that an independent variable (IV) is manipulated to cause a change in a dependent variable (DV). The DV is then measured.

Generally, in experiments, the ideal is to control all relevant variables whilst changing only the IV. Every attempt is made to even out **confounding variables** (for example, balancing out the number of men and women in each condition), and to eliminate any **extraneous variables** which may affect the results (for example, noise, poor eyesight of participant). The reason for this is that if all other variables are controlled, only the IV can be responsible for changes in the DV. Therefore, the experiment is the only method which can reliably state that one thing (the IV) has caused another thing to change (the DV).

The reasoning here is not restricted to experimentation but is used as common-sense thinking in many everyday situations. Imagine a person who can hear a humming sound which seems to be coming from a piece of electrical equipment in their room. Most sensible people would not turn off every piece of electrical equipment to get rid of the noise. We would expect them to turn off one piece of equipment at a time while keeping everything else switched on until the source of the humming was found. This is the logic of doing experiments. Switching off one piece of equipment and turning it back on again is like manipulating the IV. Listening to see whether the humming stops or not is like measuring the DV. Keeping everything else switched on is like controlling all other variables.

Controlling variables

As stated above, experimenters need to control unwanted variables which may affect the DV, otherwise this questions the reliability of research. These unwanted variables are called extraneous variables. Imagine a psychologist who wants to compare girls' and boys' performance in a maths test. They might want to control variables that could affect their performance besides their sex, such as their intelligence levels, how much revision they do, and where the test takes place. These are all examples of extraneous variables.

If certain variables are not controlled (for example, who their maths teacher is) or cannot be controlled (for example, some of the boys feel sick on the day), they may later affect the outcome of a piece of research. When variables have had an impact on findings, then these are described as confounding variables. Confounding variables make results less reliable.

So the effects of extraneous variables should be eliminated to stop them from becoming confounding variables. However, this is not always

Key terms

Standardisation: the process of keeping variables the same.

Counterbalancing: the process of ensuring variables occur in all possible combinations an equal number of times.

Randomisation: the process of deciding the order or use of variables by chance.

Order effect: where behaviour is affected because participants take part in two or more conditions in a particular order.

Practice effect: where participants' performance improves across conditions through familiarity with a task or environment.

Fatigue effect: where participants' performance worsens across conditions because of tiredness/ boredom.

Demand characteristics: features or cues in an experiment which help participants work out what is expected of them (the aim of the experiment). Helpful participants may respond according to what they think is being investigated.

Hint

It is common to confuse extraneous and confounding variables as they are both variables that could operate on the DV besides the IV. Remember the **extraneous** variable is an **extra** or additional variable that gets in the way **before** the experiment but is then controlled. A con**found**ing variable is one that the researcher **found** out affected the findings **after** the experiment.

AQA Examiner's tip

When candidates are asked a question about controlling variables, they tend to think there are numerous ways of doing this. If you remember there are only three main ways – standardisation, counterbalancing or randomisation – then you can at least use one of these ideas to start your answer.

possible, in which case, it is common to attempt to minimise their effects.

There are three ways of controlling extraneous variables:

- **standardisation**
- **counterbalancing**
- **randomisation**.

Standardisation

Standardisation means making things the same (or standard) across conditions. An experimenter may standardise factors such as participants, the environment, tasks, measures and instructions. Imagine an experiment comparing recall of images and words. If participants were given different instructions for recalling the images rather than the words, then this may affect their performance rather than the nature of the material.

Counterbalancing

Counterbalancing is often used in repeated measures designs, that is where the same participants are used in all conditions. In such experiments, there is a danger that **order effects** may affect results. Order effects include the **practice effect**, the **fatigue effect** and recognising **demand characteristics**.

Imagine an experiment comparing 20 participants' recall in familiar and then unfamiliar settings. If the same participants are used in both conditions, they may do better in the second condition than expected because they are getting used to the task (practice effect). They may do worse, not because of the change in setting, but because they are getting tired (fatigue effect). Since they are taking part in both conditions and can see what has changed, they may deduce the aim of the experiment (recognising demand characteristics). When this happens, participants often behave in the way they think is expected of them (for example, recall fewer words), although sometimes participants will go out of their way (if they can) to behave not as expected. Either way, the experimenter does not get a true measure of behaviour.

Counterbalancing simply means that the order in which conditions are encountered is balanced out across all participants. This means that every possible combination of order of conditions occurs the same number of times. For example, with two conditions (for example, A and B), 50 per cent of participants would do condition A and then condition B and 50 per cent would do B then A. This does not get rid of the problem of order effects but it does stop the same condition being affected every time. In the above example, assume that participants' performance does partly improve with practice in the second condition. If counterbalancing is used, then this confounding variable would be shared across both conditions. Ten participants' recall would be tested in a familiar setting first and then an unfamiliar setting. For the other 10, conditions would be reversed. This means both settings are affected by practice rather than it consistently benefiting one.

Randomisation

Imagine a psychologist wants to test whether where a word is in a list has an effect on its chance of being recalled. They predict that the first and last three in a list of 12 will be better recalled than the middle six. However, they want to make sure that the first three and last three are not recalled more because they are easier words to remember – as this would be an extraneous variable. It therefore makes sense to control this variable by changing where each word occurs in the list. Rather than try to work out all the possible combinations of word order, the psychologist would be likely to randomise the order of the words. This would mean that each word would have an equal chance of appearing at any position in the list. Probability would suggest that each word would occupy most places in the list over a number of trials.

Randomisation basically means controlling variables by use of chance. If researchers use chance to control variables, this means they cannot be accused of biasing the investigation.

Randomisation can also be used to decide the order of conditions as an alternative to counterbalancing. Researchers may also use randomisation to allocate participants to conditions.

Types of experiment

There are three different types of experiment:

- **laboratory experiment**
- **field experiment**
- **quasi-experiment**.

As they are all experiments, they all involve the use of an IV and DV. However, they differ in the level of control they have over variables.

Laboratory experiment

A laboratory experiment is one that is carried out under controlled conditions. Many memory and perception experiments are carried out under controlled conditions because psychologists are keen to control situational variables which may affect attention and thinking, such as noise, heat and lighting. These factors can be kept constant under laboratory conditions.

A laboratory experiment also allows **random allocation** of participants to conditions where appropriate. This makes it a true experiment as the psychologist cannot influence who participates in which condition. In this sense, findings cannot be accused of bias.

Behaviourists also favour laboratory experiments. Controlled conditions allow behaviourists to manipulate one stimulus to elicit a response, while keeping all other stimuli the same (for example, the number of people in the environment, other reinforcers in the environment).

Since a laboratory setting makes it easy to control most extraneous variables, it has the advantage that it is easier to reliably establish cause and effect. In other words, if an experimenter observes a change in the DV it is highly likely to be due to the IV (the only variable that should have changed). However, the limitation is that a controlled environment gives an artificial setting. This means that behaviour that occurs in the laboratory may not necessarily happen in real life. For example, a person may show high levels of obedience under controlled conditions but these would not be replicated in everyday life. This means that the findings from laboratory experiments tend to lack **ecological validity**.

Field experiment

An obvious alternative to conducting an experiment in the laboratory is to conduct it 'in the field'. A field experiment is one carried out in the

Research methods

AQA Examiner's tip

Candidates often mistakenly assume that demand characteristics occur in participants rather than in the actual experiment. Participants' behaviour may change because of demand characteristics, but they do not refer to the actual change in behaviour.

Link

For more on behaviourists, see Chapter 1, Key approaches.

AQA Examiner's tip

Lack of ecological validity is one of the most commonly quoted criticisms in an exam, but is not always creditworthy. Remember it only applies when a situation/environment is artificial and subsequently affects behaviour. For example, a field experiment would not lack ecological validity as the environment is natural. Laboratory experiments carried out on animals would not lack ecological validity. Animals are not as aware of their environment as humans, so do not change their behaviour because they 'know' they are in a lab!

natural environment of those being investigated – perhaps a school, a factory, or a street. The IV is still manipulated by the experimenter.

A number of obedience experiments have been carried out in natural environments. As in the earlier example, research assistants dressed in uniforms have approached people in shopping centres to see if they will follow requests, say, to pick up litter or give money to strangers. This gives findings more ecological validity as the people are in real-life settings and are more likely to behave as they normally would do.

Field experiments also have the advantage of having some control over extraneous variables. In the above example, the psychologist could keep the person in the uniform the same and could ensure participants are asked to do the same task in the same way. However, the psychologist will not have control over environmental factors (for example, how many people are around at the time) and this makes it more difficult to reliably establish cause and effect compared to a laboratory experiment.

Quasi-experiment

A quasi-experiment may take place in a laboratory or in the field. Like other experiments, they have an IV but in this type of experiment the experimenter does not directly manipulate the IV.

Some IVs are not open to manipulation as some conditions are pre-decided by fixed characteristics. For example, if a psychologist was comparing men and women's driving skills, she could not randomly allocate participants to be male or female! The IV is naturally occurring.

The IV may be naturally occurring in the sense that it is reliant on the forces of nature. For example, imagine a psychologist who wanted to compare the reactions of people suffering from brontophobia (fear of storms) during stormy and calm weather. They could not manipulate the IV (the weather) so would have to wait for it to occur naturally.

Sometimes conditions are set up, but not by the psychologist. This would also give a quasi-experiment. For example, a school may be testing a new regime with a new year group and comparing it with the old regime used on other year groups. A psychologist may visit the school to study this but they would not be directly in control of the IV.

Some psychologists prefer quasi-experiments for ethical reasons as participants are not being manipulated as much as in laboratory or field experiments.

■ Experimental designs

Any experiment will have at least two conditions – often an **experimental condition** and a **control condition**. The experimental condition describes the condition where a variable is actually being tested whereas the control condition is where nothing is manipulated and all things are kept the same as normal. For example, a psychologist may want to investigate how cues affect people's recall of a list of items. The experimental condition would test recall with cues and compare this with recall in the control condition where no cues would be used.

Having established conditions, the next decision an experimenter needs to make is how they are going to organise participants across conditions. In other words, they have to choose an **experimental design**.

■ Key terms

Experimental condition: the condition where a variable is actually tested.

Control condition: the condition that acts as a comparison; where nothing changes.

Experimental design: the way participants are used in conditions within an experiment.

There are three types of experimental design:

- **repeated (or related) measures design**
- **independent groups design**
- **matched pairs design.**

Repeated (related) measures design

In a repeated measures design, the same participants are used in each condition, for example participants' recall is tested with cues and then without cues.

Strengths

The strengths of this design are that:

- any differences between conditions are likely to be due to changes in the IV and are not due to **participant variables**
- fewer participants need to be recruited as they are used twice (or more).

Limitations

The limitations of this design are:

- order effects (for example, practice effect, fatigue effect, recognising demand characteristics) as participants take part in all conditions.

However, order effects can be reduced (but not eliminated) by counterbalancing or randomising the order of conditions.

Independent groups design

In an independent groups design, different participants are used in each condition. This would normally be decided by random allocation, for example participants are allocated to the cues or no-cues conditions based on the toss of a coin. In other words, there is no attempt to match participants across conditions.

Strengths

The strengths of this design are that:

- there are no order effects as participants only take part in one condition so cannot get better through practice, or under-perform from fatigue, or change their behaviour due to demand characteristics
- it allows task variables to be controlled, for example participants can be given the same word list in each condition so that this does not become a confounding variable.

Limitation

The limitation of this design is that:

- any differences between conditions could be due to the individual differences of participants, for example one condition could do better on recall not because of cues but because of the motivation of its participants.

However, the larger a **sample** is, the lower the probability of a significant difference in the characteristics of participants. For example, what is the chance that 50 participants randomly allocated to one condition would be that different from the 50 participants allocated to the other condition?

Key terms

Repeated (related) measures design: an experimental design where the same participants are used in all conditions.

Independent groups design: an experimental design where different participants are randomly allocated to different conditions.

Matched pairs design: an experimental design where different participants are used in each condition, but where they are matched in terms of key characteristics.

Participant variables: the differences between the characteristics of participants.

Sample: the group of people who are selected (from a population) to take part in an investigation.

Research methods

Matched pairs design

In a matched pairs design there are different participants in different conditions but they are related in the sense they are matched up on important psychological characteristics. These characteristics will depend on the nature of the study, but typical ones are gender, age, intelligence and personality. In short, for every participant in one condition, they have a partner they have been matched with in the second condition (hence matched pairs). For example different participants are used for the cues and no-cues conditions, but they are matched for intelligence.

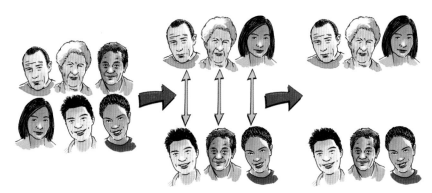

Fig. 2 *Paired for similar psychological characteristics*

Link

Construct validity is explained in Chapter 3, p63.

AQA Examiner's tip

Sometimes you are asked to **discuss** the strength or limitation of a method, like an experiment. This means you need to describe the strength/limitation first but then evaluate by considering a relative limitation/strength. For example a strength of an experiment is its high level of control which allows researchers to establish cause and effect **but** the control may distort reality leading to low ecological validity.

Strengths

The strengths of this design are that:

▓ there are no order effects as participants only take part in one condition

▓ individual differences between conditions are reduced as participants have been matched up.

Limitations

The limitations of this design are that:

▓ it is time consuming and expensive to match participants (especially when random allocation to conditions tends to give a balance of participants between conditions anyway).

▓ Evaluating the use of experimental methods

There are a number of strengths and limitations to using the experimental method (as opposed to non-experimental methods) in psychology.

Table 2 *Strengths and limitations of using the experimental method*

Strengths	Limitations
Experiments offer a **high level of control** over extraneous variables, especially laboratory experiments where the environment is also controlled. Control over variables makes it easier to **reliably establish cause and effect**, that is to be surer the IV is affecting the DV.	Many experiments are laboratory based, meaning the environment is artificial. Findings therefore **lack ecological validity**. (However, this problem is solved by field experiments which take place in natural environments.)
If cause and effect is established, it is possible to predict and control behaviour. This is the goal of scientific research making experiments **highly scientific**.	Since experiments are highly controlled, they measure variables in very precise ways. However, this gives results that **lack construct validity** as variables are often assessed more narrowly than they would be in real life.
Experiments are also **objective** because they are not easily influenced by the experimenter once they are set up. This means results are not open to bias.	Participants are often aware they are taking part in experiments. They may then respond to the **demand characteristics** of the experiment by behaving differently from normal. Demand characteristics tend to be a problem with experiments because they are so 'set-up' that the aim of the research often becomes obvious.

Key points:

- The experimental method involves manipulating an IV to measure a change in the DV when all other variables are controlled.

- Extraneous variables are other variables (besides the IV) that could affect the DV if not controlled. Uncontrolled variables that could have affected the DV during an experiment are known as confounding variables.

- Unwanted variables can be controlled through standardisation, counterbalancing or randomisation.

- There are three types of experiments: laboratory, field and quasi-experiments.

- There are three types of experimental designs: repeated measures, independent groups and matched pairs designs.

- Repeated measures designs have the problem of order effects when the independent groups and matched pairs do not. Independent groups designs have the problem of participant variables which is reduced in matched pairs designs and eliminated by repeated measures designs. Matched pairs designs are more time-consuming than the other two.

- The main strength of the experimental method is its ability to reliably establish cause and effect though high levels of control. However, controlling situations and other variables may distort reality and can result in a lack of ecological validity in the case of laboratory experiments.

Summary questions

6 'It is possible to control a confounding variable.' True or false?

7 Explain why it would be necessary to use a quasi-experiment to compare the personalities of people with and without phobias.

8 Outline the similarities and differences between a laboratory experiment and a field experiment.

9 Describe how a researcher would use counter balancing in an experiment with 3 conditions and 24 participants.

10 Imagine you are asked to design an experiment to investigate whether sleep deprivation affects performance in an examination.

   a Outline three controls that you would use in this experiment.

   b Discuss the relative strengths and weaknesses of different types of experimental designs for this investigation.

Research methods

Non-experimental methods

As mentioned previously, experimental methods allow researchers to reliably establish cause and effect because they are highly controlled. However, do experiments involve **too much** control? Some researchers believe that controlling variables distorts reality because in real life many variables operate together to affect human thought and behaviour. They would say that isolating some variables and manipulating others is too artificial. Therefore, they prefer to use more valid methods of investigation that reflect real life more accurately. These other methods are sometimes known as non-experimental methods.

Non-experimental methods may also be used because they are seen as more ethical. They do not necessarily manipulate and change participants' behaviour in the same way that experiments can do.

Sometimes experiments are not an option and non-experimental methods have to be used anyway. There are some situations that cannot be set up experimentally and can only be studied as they occur. For example, a child cannot be made to be autistic so that the effects of the disorder can be studied. This can only happen naturally.

Non-experimental methods are essentially methods that do not involve the direct manipulation of a situation or behaviour. Instead, they investigate phenomena as they occur.

There are a number of methods that can be categorised as non-experimental methods:

■ self-report methods, where participants report on their own thoughts or behaviour using specific methods such as questionnaires and interviews

■ observational studies, where participants' behaviour is recorded through watching

■ correlation studies, where two naturally occurring variables are measured to establish if there is a relationship between them or not

■ case studies, where one person, group or organisation is studied in detail

■ content analyses, where secondary material is analysed in order to given insight into human thought or behaviour.

Key points:

■ Variables are not directly manipulated in non-experimental methods. Instead, they investigate phenomena as they occur.

■ Non-experimental methods may be used to increase validity and to avoid ethical problems associated with manipulating behaviour. They are also used when experiments are not practically possible.

■ The main non-experimental methods are self-report methods, observational studies, correlation studies, case studies and content analyses.

Summary questions

11 State why non-experimental methods might be seen as more ethical than experimental methods.

12 Outline two differences between experimental methods and non-experimental methods.

13 Briefly explain why each of the following is classed as a non-experimental method:

a self-report method

b observational study

c correlation study

d case studies

e content analysis.

Methods of self-report

- Understand what self-report methods have in common.

- Know how questionnaires are used in research.

- Explain the difference between structured and unstructured interviews.

- Explain the difference between open and closed questions.

- Understand the role of pilot studies.

- Explain the strengths and limitations of using self report methods.

Key terms

Questionnaire: a list of pre-set questions often presented in written form.

Structured interview: participants are directly questioned using pre-set questions.

Unstructured interview: participants are directly questioned based on the answers they give.

Respondent: a person who answers a questionnaire.

Generalise: the extent to which findings are applicable to a wider population.

Response bias: where respondents represent certain types of people but not others.

AQA Examiner's tip

Candidates often assume questionnaires are posted out and evaluate them on this basis. This is fine, but you should make it clear to the examiner that this is what you are assuming.

Methods of self-report quite simply require participants to report on themselves. This is done by getting them to answer questions.

There are three key methods which allow psychologists to ask questions:

- **questionnaires**
- **structured interviews**
- **unstructured interviews**.

Questionnaires

Questionnaires are made up of a list of pre-determined questions to which participants respond. Questions may focus on:

- opinions, for example 'Do you think first impressions are important?'
- past experiences, for example 'Have you ever voted for something you did not really believe in?'
- certain scenarios, for example 'How would you respond if a teacher told you stand out in the cold?'

Questionnaires can be administered in a number of different ways. For example:

- face-to-face in a private or public place
- *en masse* to a group in a particular setting
- through the post
- via the internet
- over the telephone.

Evaluation of questionnaires

- Large numbers of questionnaires can be administered at once making them more cost-efficient and less time-consuming than interviews. It is also easier to reach a wide range of people if methods such as postal or internet surveys are used. However, if questionnaires are sent out, this relies on **respondents** returning them. Response rates tend to be low making it difficult to **generalise**. In addition, researchers often get a **response bias** with questionnaires. Only certain people return questionnaires (for example, people with 'time on their hands') or they may only returned by people who are motivated to comment on a subject. Either way, this gives an unrepresentative sample.

- Questionnaires are often completed privately and can easily be made anonymous. This should mean more honest (or valid) responses are given. However, it may lead to less honest responses because there are no researchers monitoring answers.

- Another problem is that respondents may misunderstand or misinterpret questions without a researcher present. This, again, could lead to invalid responses.

Interviews

Interviews involve the researcher directly asking participants questions and recording their responses. This is often done on a one-to-one basis.

Key terms

Interviewer: the person asking the questions.

Interviewee: the person answering the questions.

Hint

Structured interviews get their name from the fact that they have a structure, that is the questions (and possibly answers) are in place already. Unstructured interviews have no real structure or plan.

AQA Examiner's tip

It is very common to be asked to distinguish between structured and unstructured interviews in the exam. This is often worth 3 marks. To gain all 3 marks, you will need to say something about structured interviews, then something about unstructured interviews and then finally draw a difference between them (that you have not already stated).

AQA Examiner's tip

Candidates often make the mistake of thinking structured interviews always used closed questions and unstructured always use open questions. Although most unstructured interviews use open questions, many structured interviews do too.

Structured interviews

Structured interviews use pre-determined questions. The **interviewer** has already decided what they are going to ask about.

Unstructured interviews

Unstructured interviews may start with some common questions, but generally the interviewer just has a topic that they want to cover. The interviews are basically like conversations, with a broad framework to guide discussion. They tend to be directed by the participant rather than the researcher. The questions are determined by the answers that the **interviewee** gives.

Comparing structured and unstructured interviews

- Structured interviews have set questions which make it easier to compare interviewees' answers. This makes it easier to identify patterns and trends in responses.
- However, because unstructured interviews do not have pre-set questions, the interviewer can follow new lines of enquiry. Interviewees may introduce relevant ideas that the researcher would not have thought to ask about in the original design.
- Unstructured interviews allow interviewees to go into more depth, giving more valid results. It is certainly likely to give researchers a clearer idea of their participants' view of the world. Critics of the structured interview argue that this is preferable to the researcher imposing their view of the world on participants through their questioning. However, if the researcher is in control of the questioning, it does mean they are more likely to access the information they want rather than irrelevant or useless information.

Open versus closed questions

Self-report methods clearly rely on questioning. Questions can be open or closed.

Closed questions are questions where participants are offered a fixed set of responses to choose from. Common ways of closing questions are:

- yes/no responses
- rating scales, for example:

    Agree 1 2 3 4 5 Disagree

- multiple choice, for example:

    Very often [ ]   Often [ ]   Rarely [ ]

Open questions do not restrict responses. Participants are free to answer a question how they wish, for example 'What were the effects of introducing uniform into your school?', 'How do you feel when you encounter spiders?'

Open questions are clearly better for exploring answers in more depth which may help researchers get closer to the truth. They may also allow researchers to discover new lines of enquiry.

However, closed questions make it easier to compare answers, and to identify patterns and trends. They will also help researchers stay focused on the aims of the investigation.

▮ Pilot studies

Researchers may want to test their questions to make sure they are valid measures of the concept under investigation, for example do a set of questions really measure masculinity? Or will a particular question allow participants to demonstrate their prejudices? It may simply be a case of making sure questions are understood or that all options are covered by a closed question.

When a researcher trials their questions this is known as a **pilot study**. It generally involves a smaller sample of people and sometimes just a sample of questions.

Pilot studies are not just used for self-report methods. Psychologists can practise any part of any method, for example a procedure in an experiment, a coding system for an observation, a measure in a correlation. The general purpose of a pilot study is to identify any factors that might negatively affect the outcome of a study. This saves the researcher from wasting time and money on a piece of research that could be unreliable.

▮ Key terms

Pilot study: a small scale, trial study.

Socially desirable responses: responses which are not necessarily true but are given because the respondent wants to 'look good' in front of others.

▮ Evaluating the use of self-report methods

Table 3 *Evaluation of self-report methods*

Strengths	Limitations
Unlike observations, it is possible to **access people's thoughts and feelings** through asking questions.	Methods of questioning need participants to possess a number of qualities to be reliable. They can be ineffective if participants are dishonest, inarticulate, lack confidence, lack insight or have a poor memory.
Questions allow researchers to **find out what people would do in certain situations without having to set them up.** (However, what participants say they would do in a given situation may be different from what they actually would do.)	It is possible that participants' **responses are influenced by researchers** when using interviews or questionnaires. For example, in face-to-face interviews participants may feel pressured to give **socially desirable responses**, or where questions and possible answers are pre-set this may lead participants to give certain responses.

Research methods

Key points:

- Methods of self-report require participants to answer questions.

- Questionnaires use pre-set questions which are normally written down and answered privately.

- Structured interviews also use pre-set questions, whereas unstructured interviews base questions on interviewees' answers.

- Open questions allow participants to answer questions freely whereas closed questions offer fixed responses.

- Pilot studies are practice studies which allow researchers to trial questions and other procedures.

- The main strength of self-report methods is they give access to thoughts and feelings, but this relies on participants being able or prepared to express them.

■ Summary questions

14 What do self-report methods have in common?

15 Outline two limitations of open questions.

16 Outline two limitations of closed questions.

17 Describe three differences between structured and unstructured interviews.

18 Discuss different ways of administering questionnaires to assess people's attitudes towards sex.

Observational studies

Learning objectives:

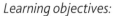

- Understand what observational studies have in common.
- Distinguish between a laboratory and a natural observation.
- Distinguish between a covert and overt observation.
- Distinguish between a participant and non-participant observation.
- Explain the strengths and limitations of using observational methods.

Key terms

Covert: undercover; people are not aware of being watched.

Overt: open; people are aware of being watched.

Participant observation: when the researcher observes people whilst joining in their activities/situation.

Naturalistic observation: an observation taking place in a natural environment as opposed to a laboratory.

Observational studies simply involve watching and recording people's behaviour. This may be done in a number of ways, including:

- using a scoring system, for example rating a teacher's level of discipline
- using a check list of criteria, for example checking how many certain behaviours an autistic child displays
- keeping a tally, for example counting the number of times a doll is picked up by a girl or a boy
- making notes
- video recording.

When a psychologist decides to use an observation, there are a number of decisions that they have to make about how they will carry out their observation:

- Should it be in a laboratory or a natural setting?
- Should it be **covert** or **overt**?
- Should it be participant or non-participant?

For example, a psychologist may decide to carry out a covert, **participant observation** in a natural setting.

Laboratory versus natural observations

Observations can take place in one of two main settings: a laboratory or a natural setting.

Observations that take place in a laboratory would basically be laboratory experiments. In other words, it is an observation in a controlled environment. For example, observing whether people perform better in a task in the presence or absence of an audience that has been brought into the laboratory.

Observations that take place in a natural setting are sometimes called **naturalistic observations**. They involve observing people in their natural environment. This means the behaviour observed is relatively unconstrained and people have a choice in how they behave, for example, observing boys' and girls' toy choice in a nursery setting.

- Doing an observation in a laboratory offers a high level of control which means it is easier to reliably establish cause and effect. However, the artificial environment means that findings lack ecological validity.
- Doing an observation in a natural environment offers a high level of ecological validity. People are being observed going about their usual behaviour in a situation which is not set up. This means any findings should be generalisable to real life. However, observing without intervention means there are many uncontrolled variables making it difficult to draw any conclusions about causation. For example, imagine a researcher who observes a class of disobedient children. She may be able to see that they are not following rules but may not be able to be definite as to why.

▨ Covert versus overt observations

Observations can either be conducted covertly or overtly.

Covert observations describe observations where the psychologist observes an individual, group or situation without people being aware of this. For example, a psychologist may pretend to be part of a group without revealing their true identity or aim, for example going undercover to become a member of a gang of hooligans to study conformity. Alternatively, a psychologist may observe from a hidden viewpoint, for example watching how parents play differently with boys and girls from behind a two-way mirror.

Overt observations describe observations where the psychologist is open about their observation. In other words, they make their presence obvious and people know that their behaviour is being recorded. For example, participants taking part in an experiment often know they are being observed.

- ▨ Doing a covert observation means participants do not know they are being watched. This means they should behave as they normally would do, giving valid results. However, there are **ethical concerns** surrounding this type of observation. Is it right to watch someone without their consent, particularly just for the purpose of psychological research?

- ▨ Doing an overt observation is more ethically sound as people are now aware they are being observed but may withdraw themselves as a consequence. However, the most obvious limitation is **observer effect**: where people behave differently because they are being observed, giving unreliable results.

▨ Participant versus non-participant observations

Participant observations are observations where the psychologist joins in with the group or situation they are observing while also recording data. For example, a psychologist may volunteer to help a team of carers to see how they support children with autism.

Non-participant observations are observations where the psychologist is not directly involved in what is being observed and records behaviour 'from a distance'. For example, sitting in the corner of a bar to observe whether men and women use different body language when interacting with one another.

- ▨ Doing a participant observation allows the researcher to experience a situation as the participants do. This gives the researcher a greater insight into the lives of the people being studied, increasing the validity of findings. However, the researcher may become too involved in what they are investigating and lose their ability to be objective. There is also the practical problem of recording data while taking part in the study – which is even more difficult if it is also covert!

- ▨ Doing a non-participant observation allows the researcher to remain objective as they are not directly involved. However, they may not have a true understanding of behaviour if they are too removed from the situation.

Fig. 3 *Covert observations are undercover as participants do not know they are being observed*

▨ Hint

It is easy to muddle covert and overt observations. Remember **covert** observations are under**cover**. Meanwhile **overt** observations are **open**.

▨ Key terms

Ethical concerns: concerns about how participants are treated in a study in terms of their health and well-being.

Observer effect: where participants do not behave normally/naturally because they are aware of being observed.

AQA Examiner's tip

If asked to give a strength of an observation, candidates often suggest it is ecologically valid. This is true of many observations as they tend to take place in a natural environment. However, some observations take place in laboratories which lack ecological validity. You can use ecological validity as a strength, but make sure it applies in a question or at least qualify it for the examiner.

Evaluating the use of observational studies

Table 4 *Evaluating the use of observational studies*

Strengths	Limitations
Findings from observations are more reliable as the **researchers can see for themselves how participants behave** rather than relying on self-reports.	It is difficult to make judgements about **thoughts and feelings** when using this method as these features **are not clearly observable.**
Most observations take place in a natural setting so have **high ecological validity**. People are even more likely to behave normally if it is a covert observation too.	**Observer bias** can be a problem as the researcher may only perceive things from a certain perspective. (However, using more than one observer increases **inter-rater reliability**.)
	If participants are aware they are being observed then they may act differently giving invalid results: this is known as the **observer effect**.

Key points:

- Observational methods simply involve watching and recording behaviour.
- Laboratory observations are carried out in controlled environments whereas natural observations are carried out in the field.
- Covert observations are undercover whereas overt observations are open and participants know they are being observed.
- Participant observations involve the observer becoming involved in the group or situation they are observing, whereas in non-participant observations the observer just stands back and watches.
- The main strength of observations is that researchers can observe behaviour first-hand rather than having to trust self-reports. However, there are potentially problems with observer bias and the observer effect.

Summary questions

19 State why a natural observation has high ecological validity.

20 Outline the difference between observer bias and observer effect.

21 Outline one solution for:
   a observer bias
   b observer effect.

22 Compare the use of participant and non-participant observations.

23 Compare the use of observational studies and self-report methods for investigating people's tendency towards aggression.

Correlation studies

Learning objectives:

- Understand what is meant by a correlation study.

- Explain the difference between a positive, negative and zero correlation.

- Explain the strengths and weaknesses of using a correlation study.

Key terms

Correlation analysis: the analysis of data to test for a relationship between two variables.

Quantitative data: data in numerical form.

Scattergram: a graph for representing correlations.

Correlation co-efficient: a number measuring the strength and direction of a correlation.

Correlation studies, like experiments, describe a **process** rather than an actual method. Correlation studies use methods such as self-report or observations to collect data, but it is how data is analysed which is important.

Correlation analyses look for a relationship between two variables. For example:

- A psychologist investigates whether there is a relationship between how often ethnic minority groups are shown on television and the level of racism within a society. They measure one variable by counting how often individuals from ethnic minority groups appear on television in one day across three channels. The other variable is measured using an interview to assess participants' racist attitudes.

- A psychologist investigates whether there is a relationship between levels of cortisol (a hormone) and how anxious people are. They measure one variable by calculating the percentage of cortisol in a blood sample. The other variable is measured using a questionnaire assessing anxiety levels.

- A psychologist investigates whether there is a relationship between the length of time spent rehearsing material and people's ability to recall it. They measure one variable by controlling and timing how long a participant rehearses for. The other variable is measured by counting the number of items recalled in a set time.

Correlational analyses can only be done on **quantitative data** as it is essentially a statistical process. In the above examples, it is clear to see that most of the variables would be quantitative, e.g. percentage of cortisol, amount of time spent rehearsing. Racist attitudes and anxiety levels would also have to be scored. For instance, the psychologist could not simply decide that a participant was 'very anxious' or 'moderately anxious' but would have to decide on some kind of rating scale, for example 10 = very anxious, 1 = not anxious.

The reason that correlation studies rely on quantitative data is because they actually measure the strength and direction of the relationship between two variables. They do more than simply state if two variables are related.

This relationship can be shown graphically using a **scattergram**. It can also be measured by a **correlation co-efficient**, which is always between +1 and −1. Correlations can be broadly categorised into positive, negative and zero correlations.

Positive correlation

If two variables show a positive correlation, it means as one variable increases then so does the other variable. Similarly, as one variable decreases then so does the other. For example, if anxiety levels increased in relation to cortisol levels increasing, then this would give a positive correlation. This also means that when cortisol levels are low then levels of anxiety are low.

A perfect positive correlation has a co-efficient of +1. This occurs when two variables increase (and decrease) in exact relation to one another.

r = 0.8

Fig. 4 *This scattergram shows a strong positive correlation with a co-efficient of +0.8*

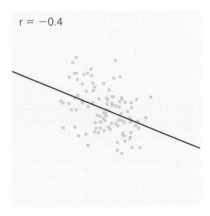

r = −0.4

Fig. 5 *This scattergram shows a moderate negative correlation with a co-efficient of −0.4*

▨ **Hint**

It is easy to confuse positive and negative correlations. Think of variables having a 'positive relationship' in a positive correlation. They travel everywhere together; if one goes up so does the other. If one goes down, so does the other. Meanwhile variables in a 'negative relationship' want to go in the opposite direction from each other!

▨ Negative correlation

Despite its name, a negative correlation still shows an actual relationship between two variables. In this instance, it means as one variable increases then the other variable decreases, and vice versa. For example, if levels of racism were higher in societies where fewer individuals from ethnic minority groups were shown on television but lower in societies where more individuals were shown, then this would give a negative correlation.

A perfect negative correlation has a co-efficient of −1. This occurs when one variable increases at exactly the same rate as the other decreases.

▨ Zero correlation

If there is no clear relationship between two variables then it is described as no correlation. For example, if some people recalled lots of items after rehearsing for a long time yet others did not and if others recalled little after rehearsing for a long time, then this would suggest there is no correlation between rehearsal time and recall.

A zero correlation has a co-efficient of 0. This occurs if there is absolutely no indication of a pattern between variables.

▨ Evaluating the use of correlation studies

Correlation studies are often mistaken for experiments because they both employ strict measures and statistical analysis. However, correlation studies have a key limitation compared to experiments; they cannot reliably establish cause and effect.

Unlike an experiment, a correlation study does not have an IV and DV. It simply measures the relationship between existing variables and nothing is set up. However, this does demonstrate the advantage of correlation studies: they do allow researchers to statistically analyse situations that could not be manipulated experimentally for ethical or practical reasons. For example, it would be wrong to inject a person with cortisol to see if it made them anxious but both variables can be measured after the event. Or it would not really be possible for a researcher to set up 'societies' to investigate whether presenting individuals from ethnic minorities on television has an effect on the audience's attitudes towards race.

It is because correlation studies take place after the event that it is difficult to reliably state that one thing causes another thing to happen. To establish cause and effect, the researcher needs to be there at the beginning and monitoring any changes as they go along – as in an experiment.

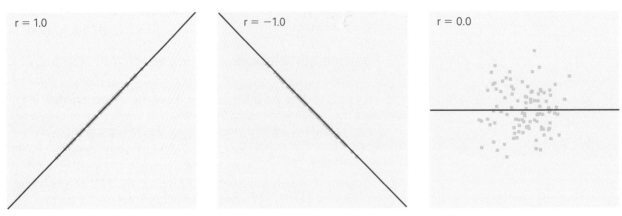

r = 1.0   r = −1.0   r = 0.0

Fig. 6 *Scattergrams showing (a) a perfect positive correlation, (b) a perfect negative correlation, (c) a zero correlation*

Table 5 *Evaluation of correlation studies*

Strengths	Limitations
Correlations can establish the strength and direction of the **relationship** between variables.	Correlations **cannot reliably establish cause and effect**.
They allow researchers to **statistically analyse naturally occurring phenomenon** which could not be set up ethically or practically.	Variables have to be quantified which means the measures may **lack construct validity**, for example can anxiety simply be scored?

If a correlation shows a relationship between two variables, then one probably is affecting the other. However, it is not necessarily clear which. For example, if there is a positive correlation between cortisol levels and anxiety levels, are high levels of cortisol the cause of anxiety or an effect of it? Although it is possible to show an individual has high levels of both, it is not possible to say which occurred first. For example, imagine there is a negative correlation between the number of individuals from ethnic minority groups on television and levels of racism. Does seeing these individuals make people less racist, or is it because people are less racist that television producers decide they can show more individuals from ethnic backgrounds?

With correlation studies, the lack of control over other variables also causes problems. It could be that other factors account for the relationship between two variables, that is they are both being affected by a third, unaccounted for variable. For example, if there was a positive relationship between rehearsal and recall, both could be high or low depending on an individual's motivation. Meanwhile, government policy may be influencing levels of racism and incidence of individuals from ethnic minorities on television so that the variables are not really directly related.

Sometimes variables are not really related at all – they appear to be, but it is just a coincidence. For example, if we used a scattergram to plot the number of mobile phones stolen and the number of sexually-transmitted infections diagnosed over the last 10 years, it would show a positive correlation. It does not mean they are necessarily connected in any way!

Link

Correlation studies predict a relationship between variables rather than a difference since they have no IV and DV. See 'Planning research' p86.

 Examiner's tip

Candidates often confuse experiments and correlations. Remember, if variables are measured on two scales it will be a correlation. If one of the variables describes two distinct conditions (for example, Condition A and B), then it is an experiment (as it is looking for a difference, for example between A and B, not just a relationship).

Research methods

Key points:

- A correlation study measures the relationship between two variables.

- A positive correlation means two variables change in the same direction, a negative correlation means they change in opposite directions and a zero correlation means they show no pattern of relationship.

- Correlations do not allow researchers to establish cause and effect. However, they do allow them to statistically analyse naturally occurring events that could not be set up experimentally.

Summary questions

24 Give the direction of a correlation where one variable increases as the other decreases.

25 Describe the strength and direction of a correlation with a co-efficient of +0.3.

26 'Tall people make better leaders than short people.'
  a Explain why this hypothesis could not be tested using a correlation study.
  b Outline how the theory could be tested using a correlation study.

27 Outline the differences between a correlation study and an experiment.

28 A common finding is the positive correlation between the number of life changes a person experiences (in a time period) and their levels of stress. Outline the different ways in which this relationship can be explained.

Case studies

Learning objectives:

■ Understand what is meant by a case study.

■ Explain the strengths and limitations of using case studies.

Key terms

Case study: an in-depth investigation of one person or group or organisation.

Subject: an out-dated term for participant which is still sometimes used for case studies since the individuals under investigation are quite passive in the research rather than actively volunteering to take part.

Link

■ Diamond *et al.*'s case study of David Reimer shows how studying atypical behaviour can be useful. It showed that normally gender is not socialised. See Chapter 3, Gender development, p53.

Summary questions

29 Give two reasons why it is difficult to generalise from a case study.

30 State three ways in which data can be collected for a case study.

31 Discuss the strengths and weaknesses of the case study method using the Diamond and Sigmundson (1997) case study (see p53) as an illustration.

Case studies have two main features:

■ They focus on a sample of either one individual, group or organisation.

■ They study that sample in-depth.

Case studies often use unstructured interviews, observations and past records (for example, medical histories, school files, diaries) to carry out an in-depth analysis of the **subject**. Since samples are small, it should be possible to find the time to do this.

Case studies are often used to investigate atypical behaviour or unusual situations. Studying what happens when 'things go wrong' can give insight into normal patterns of behaviour. This includes investigations into the effect of brain damage on memory, the development of autism in children and the rise of the Nazi party. Each of these cases focuses on a rare event. This explains why samples tend to be small, as they do not affect many individuals or organisations. However, when they do happen, they may show psychologists how they can help a child with autism or how they can stop something like the Holocaust happening again.

Case studies do not always have to focus on unusual subjects. Sometimes they are used just because a psychologist wants to have more insight into a particular individual.

Evaluating the use of case studies

Table 6 *Evaluation of case studies*

Strengths	Limitations
Case studies offer high levels of **validity** as they go into depth and give insight.	Since case studies are based on small samples, it is **difficult to generalise**.
They allow researchers to study **events that they could not practically or ethically manipulate.**	The researcher can become too involved in case studies and **lose their objectivity**. They may misinterpret or influence outcomes.
Case studies are efficient as **it only takes one case study to disprove a theory**.	Since case studies are often 'picked up' after the event (for example, after someone has suffered brain damage), **it can be difficult to establish cause and effect**.

Key points:

■ Case studies are in-depth investigations of one person or group of people.

■ Case studies are detailed enough to give valid findings but it is difficult to generalise from them.

Content analyses

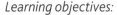

Research methods

Learning objectives:

- Understand what is meant by a content analysis.
- Distinguish between a quantitative and a qualitative content analysis.
- Explain the strengths and weaknesses of using content analyses.

Key terms

Content analysis: the process of interpreting secondary material as a means to understanding people.

Coding: operationalising variables for analysis.

Qualitative: descriptive (data).

Content analyses are different from other research methods in the sense that they are processes where people are studied indirectly rather than directly. This is done by investigating materials that people produce rather than investigating the actual people themselves. For example, the processes may involve:

- exploring media output to investigate gender stereotypes
- scrutinising teenage magazines to investigate peer pressure
- examining graffiti in public toilets to investigate gender differences in behaviour.

Content analysis can be quantitative which means data collected is numerical. This may involve simply **counting** the occurrence of a particular feature, or **coding** material in some way, for example:

- keeping a tally of the **number** of black characters that appear in a selection of children's books
- calculating the **percentage** of male and female voice-overs used in TV adverts
- **rating** an autistic child's drawing for its aggressive content.

Content analysis can be **qualitative** which means data collected is more descriptive, for example:

- deconstructing the themes within a newspaper
- uncovering the thinking behind a woman's letter to her husband
- identifying the unconscious thoughts in an agoraphobic's diary.

Evaluating the use of content analyses

Table 7 *Evaluation of content analyses*

Strengths	Limitations
Content analyses allow researchers to **study people they would have no or little access to**. They also have **few ethical issues** as there is no or little direct contact with 'participants'.	Since researchers have no direct contact with people, it **easier to misinterpret their thoughts and behaviour** without being able to see or speak to them. **Qualitative content analyses** are particularly open to interpretation because they are **mainly based on opinion**. (This is why it is useful to have a number of researchers carrying out an analysis, so they can seek agreement.) **Quantitative content analyses** are more objective because coding systems are used. However, these may **lack construct validity**.

Key points:

- A content analysis involves interpreting secondary material.
- Quantitative content analyses produce numerical data whereas qualitative content analyses produce descriptive data.
- Content analyses allow researchers to study people they cannot access, but because of this, findings are more open to interpretation.

Summary questions

32 Give three examples of types of people who could be studied through content analysis to get around problems of access.

33 Outline how gender stereotyping in films could be investigated using both quantitative and qualitative content analyses.

34 Describe the similarities and differences between quantitative and qualitative content analyses.

35 Outline five categories you might code and score if you were carrying out a content analysis of computer games to assess them for their level of violence.

Qualitative versus quantitative research

Research methods

Learning objectives:

- Distinguish between qualitative and quantitative research.

- Know what methods are used in qualitative research.

- Know what methods are used in quantitative research.

- Understand the relative strengths of qualitative and quantitative research.

Hint

It might help to remember that **quant**itative data refers to **quant**ities, amounts or numbers. **Quali**tative data has more '**quali**ty' because it is more detailed/ descriptive.

Content analyses show how research can be both qualitative and quantitative. In other words, it is a method that can produce descriptive (qualitative) data and numerical (quantitative) data.

Other methods can also produce both types of data, whereas some methods tend to produce one type of data more than another. This is summarised in Table 8.

Quantitative data has the advantage in that it can be easily summarised into graphs or statistics, so that researchers can identify patterns and trends, for example is there an increase or decrease in levels of obedience? Quantitative data can also be more objective as scoring systems are not open to interpretation, for example the number of anagrams a participant gets right in an experiment cannot be disputed.

Qualitative data is generally seen to have more construct validity. This is because describing behaviour (rather than scoring it) is what happens in real life, for example describing how bad an individual's phobia is. Qualitative data is also richer and more detailed, and therefore gives more depth and insight into a subject.

Table 8 *Data produced by different methods*

Method	Type of data produced
Experiment	Experiments use mainly quantitative data because the DV has to be measured to establish cause and effect. To measure a DV, the researcher often needs to quantify it, for example number of words recalled.
Self-report	If closed questions are used this can produce quantitative data, for example the percentage of respondents that said yes. Open questions tend to produce qualitative data because responses tend to be individualised and in detail.
Observation	If structured observations are carried out (for example, using coding systems or checklists) then quantitative data can be produced. When researchers simply describe what they see, this produces more qualitative data.
Correlation	The method has to produce quantitative data so that a correlational analysis can be performed. Correlational analysis is a statistical process so can only be applied to scores.
Case study	Case studies generally produce qualitative data since they are in-depth and detailed investigations.

Summary questions

36 Name a method that produces both qualitative and quantitative data.

37 Outline the disadvantages of using qualitative data.

38 Outline the disadvantages of using quantitative data.

Key points:

- Qualitative research produces descriptive data whereas quantitative research produces numerical data.

- Self-report methods, observations, case studies and content analyses can be used as part of qualitative research.

- Experiments, correlations, self-report methods, observations and content analyses can be used as part of quantitative research.

- Qualitative research provides rich, valid data whereas quantitative research provides objective data that is easier to analyse.

Sampling

Learning objectives:

- Understand the difference between a population and a sample.
- Distinguish between random sampling, systematic sampling, stratified sampling and opportunity sampling.
- Explain the relative strengths and weaknesses of different sampling methods.

Key terms

Target population: the wider group of people that research findings should apply to.

Biased sample: a sample that is not representative of the target population.

AQA Examiner's tip

When asked to define a representative sample, candidates sometimes respond by stating that it is a sample which is representative. This is known as a tautological answer because it just uses the same terms to define the concept. It will not earn you any marks. You need to think of another term for sample (for example, a selection of the population) and another term for representative (for example, cross-section).

Psychologists do not only have to choose a research method for collecting data. They also need to decide who they are going to collect data from.

Population

Before deciding who to collect data from, psychologists need to identify who they are **generally** interested in investigating. In other words, who they want to be able to generalise their findings to. This is known as the population or, more precisely, the **target population**.

In many investigations, the target population is the human population because psychologists want to comment on people generally, for example what is the capacity of human memory? Or why do people in every society feel a pressure to conform? However, in other investigations, the target population may be more specific. For example, a psychologist who is interested in the gender development of girls could have a target population of females under the age of 16. Similarly, a psychologist interested in effects of amnesia on memory could have a target population of people who have suffered brain damage.

Sampling

Unless a target population is very small, it is impossible for a psychologist to study everybody they want to apply their findings to. Imagine the practicalities of investigating the whole of the human population! Even when the target population is small (for example, boys raised as girls), not everyone in that population will necessarily be identifiable or accessible. For these reasons, it is often enough for a psychologist to investigate a sample of a population. Indeed, the participants in an investigation are often called the sample.

Since psychologists can rarely study the whole of the population, the ideal is to obtain a sample of people that are representative of a population. If a sample is representative it reduces the need to investigate everybody because all necessary views or behaviours will be represented by that group. So if 50 per cent of a representative sample agree that 'first impressions count', then the assumption is that 50 per cent of the population would say the same.

However, sometimes samples may not represent the population that well. For example, imagine a psychologist wants to investigate the intellectual abilities of children with autism. If she took a sample of 10 children who were all male she would not be representing all children. Although it is more unusual for girls to be diagnosed with autism, they still need to be represented in the sample – especially since sex is another factor that may influence intellectual ability. If a sample is not representative and there are more of certain types of people than others then it can be described as a **biased sample**.

In theory, it would seem that a larger sample is a more representative sample. Logically speaking, the more of a population that is included in a sample then the more like the population the sample is! However, this is not always true. For example, if a psychologist was studying obedience in the human population, it would be better to have 30 participants from a range of different cultural backgrounds rather than 100 participants from the same cultural background. The point is that the size of the sample is not as important as the composition of the sample.

The composition (or make up) of the sample partly depends on the technique used to choose the participants from the target population. First a **sampling frame** is chosen. Then, there are a number of sampling techniques that can be used to select from the sampling frame. These are listed below.

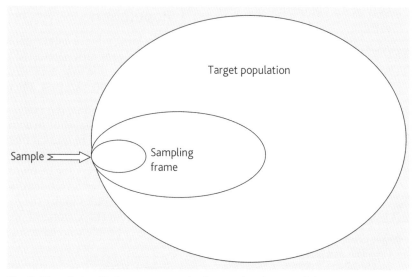

Fig. 7 *The relationship between a sample, the sampling frame and the target population*

Random sampling

A random sample is made up of participants chosen mathematically, using chance. Every person in the sampling frame has an equal chance of being selected for the sample. This is equivalent to choosing 'names out of a hat' although a computer is more likely to make the choice nowadays!

Strengths

- It avoids bias as the researcher has no control over who is selected.
- The law of probability says that the researcher will normally get a representative sample. For example, what is the chance of drawing 20 females from a population which is 50 per cent male and 50 per cent female?

Limitations

- There is a chance, although unlikely, of a 'freak' sample which would not be representative.
- Compared to other methods, it is time-consuming because all potential participants have to be identified in the first place before the 'draw' can be made.

Systematic sampling

A systematic sample is also made up of participants chosen mathematically. This is done by taking every nth person in the sampling frame for the sample. For example, imagine a researcher had a sampling frame of 100 people from which she wanted to select 20 participants. Using systematic sampling, they would list the participants (say alphabetically) and then select every fifth one to obtain her 20

Key term

Sampling frame: a section of the target population from which the sample is literally drawn.

AQA Examiner's tip

Candidates often make the mistake of thinking that random sampling is 'grabbing' anyone 'at random'. If a researcher is just using anyone who is available, then this is actually opportunity sampling. Random sampling is actually a very sophisticated sampling technique.

Fig. 8 *A random sample is equivalent to 'pulling names out of hat'; everyone has an equal chance of being selected*

participants. This is very similar to random sampling but, theoretically, is not random. This is because each person in the sampling frame **does not** have the same chance of being selected. This is because once the researcher has decided she is going to take, say, every third person, then the people who are first and second on the list, then fourth and fifth, and so on – in theory – do not have chance of being selected!

Strengths

▥ It avoids bias as, once the researcher has decided what number they are going to use for selection, they have no control over who is selected.

▥ The law of probability says that the researcher will normally get a representative sample. For example, what is the chance that every fifth person is a male if the list of people is 50 per cent male and 50 per cent female?

Limitations

▥ There is chance, although unlikely, of a 'freak' sample which would not be representative.

▥ It is not as objective as random sampling, because the researcher may decide on how people are listed before selection and on what number to use for the 'system'.

Stratified sampling

A stratified sample is made up of participants who have been selected **after** the sampling frame has been stratified or layered. This basically means that the sampling frame is divided into groups that the researcher wants to make sure are represented in the final sample. A certain number of participants are selected from these groups (normally randomly) so that they are proportionately represented in the sample.

For example, imagine that a psychologist investigating conformity decides that sex and sociability are important factors in his study. He then decides that he wants them to be represented proportionately in his sample:

i   He divides his sampling frame into males and females.

ii He then subdivides these groups into out-going and shy people.

iii In his sampling frame of 100 people, he has 50 males and 50 females.

iv Of the 50 males, 40 are classed as out-going and 10 are classed as shy.

v   Of the 50 females, 30 are classed as out-going and 20 are classed as shy.

vi The psychologist decides to select a sample of 10 participants, so to achieve the right proportions of people he selects:

   4 from the out-going males

   1 from the shy males

   3 from the out-going females

   2 from the shy females.

vii This gives him the same percentages of people, by sex and sociability, as found in the sampling frame.

Strengths

▥ It avoids the problem of 'freak' samples, more or less guaranteeing a representative sample by making sure all key characteristics are present.

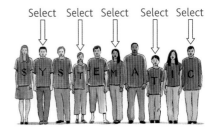

Fig. 9 *A systematic sample involves selecting every nth participant from the sampling frame*

▥ Hint

Systematic and stratified sampling are often confused, but if you think about it logically their names tell you how they work. Systematic sampling selects people using a system, that is select every nth person. Stratified sampling stratifies (layers) the sampling frame.

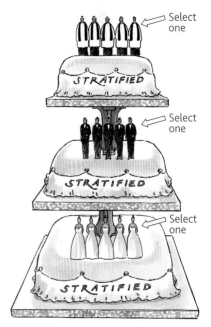

Fig. 10 *A stratified sample involves stratifying the sampling frame into key groups of people and then selecting from each of these*

It is relatively objective because once the sampling frame is stratified, it is normally left to chance who is selected from each strata.

Limitations

It is more time-consuming than other techniques because all potential participants need to be assessed and categorised before a sample can even be drawn.

The researcher may not identify all the key characteristics for stratification meaning the sample is still not representative.

Opportunity sampling

An opportunity sample is made up of participants who have been chosen because they are convenient. This means they might have been selected because they have actively volunteered, because they are in the locality, or because they are known to the researcher. In short, the researcher uses anybody they have the opportunity to use.

Strength

It is less time-consuming than other techniques because time is not spent planning and using sophisticated systems for selection.

Weaknesses

It is quite likely that the sample will be biased because only certain types of people will volunteer to be chosen. For example, only certain people may volunteer for psychological research (e.g. be confident). Similarly, if people come from the same locality they may be similar in terms of their characteristics (e.g. all university students), or if they are acquaintances of the researcher they may share similar characteristics to them (e.g. be middle class).

The researcher may show bias when selecting the participants, whether intentional or not. For example, they may choose people that they know are going to behave in a way that they have predicted.

Once in a lifetime opportunity to take part in my psychology experiment!

Fig. 11 *An opportunity sample involves selecting anyone who is readily available*

Summary questions

39 'A target population and a sample can be made up of the same people.' True or False?

40 Explain what is meant by a representative sample.

41 Explain why larger samples are not always more representative than smaller samples.

42 Look at the following sampling techniques: random, systematic, stratified, opportunity.

   a State which sampling technique is most likely to give a representative sample and explain why.

   b State which sampling technique is least likely to give a representative sample and explain why.

Key points:

- A population describes the entire group of people that research findings should be generalised to. Meanwhile, a sample is a group drawn from the population that a researcher actually studies and generalises from.

- Random sampling is when every person in the sampling frame has an equal chance of being selected. Systematic sampling is when every nth person is selected from the sampling frame. Stratified sampling is when the sampling frame is stratified into different sub-groups and then people are selected from each sub-group in proportion to their occurrence in the population. Opportunity sampling is when people are selected on the basis of convenience.

- Random, systematic and stratified sampling tend to give representative samples, although the first two techniques can occasionally result in 'freak' samples. Opportunity sampling tends not to produce very representative samples but is much less time-consuming than the other methods.

Research methods

Ethics

Learning objectives:

- Understand what is meant by ethical research.

- Describe the main ethical guidelines when carrying out psychological research.

- Understand how unethical research can be justified.

Hint

The website for the BPS (http://www.bps.org.uk) should be checked for the most up to date 'Ethical principles for conducting Research within Human Participants' available in the 'Code of Conduct and Ethical Guidelines' section of the website.

Key terms

Ethical: appropriate; morally correct.

Confidential: anonymous; private.

Consent: agreement.

Informed consent: consent based on awareness of the aims of an investigation.

Deception: misleading of participants through lies or withholding information.

AQA Examiner's tip

If an exam question asks you to identify an ethical problem with a study then start your answer by actually identifying the problem by using the appropriate term, for example consent, confidentiality, etc. You then earn further marks by actually applying it to the study in question.

It is not enough to simply select participants for a study. Psychologists are obliged to consider the psychological well-being, health, values and dignity of their participants. Bearing in mind that the goal of most psychological research is to support the welfare of human beings, it would be wrong to mistreat specific individuals in the process. If psychologists do not deal with their participants appropriately, their research is described as unethical. This may lead to psychologists being stopped from practising psychology.

Researchers should seek to make their investigations as **ethical** as possible. To help them do this, various organisations produce codes of ethics. In the UK, most psychologists will follow the Code of Conduct and Ethical Guidelines produced by the British Psychological Society (BPS). The guidelines fall under a number of headings, as summarised below.

Respect

Psychologists should value the dignity and worth of all individuals. This includes the following guidelines:

- Researchers should avoid unfair or prejudiced practices.
- Data collected on a participant should be kept **confidential** so that others cannot identify it as theirs (for example, names should not be used).
- If confidentiality cannot be ensured (for example, if a participant discloses something illegal, if there is a threat to someone's safety), then participants must be warned of this in advance of an investigation.
- Audio, video and photographic recordings should only be made with **consent**.
- Participants should give **informed consent**.
- Participants under the age of 16 should give their own consent where possible but consent of parents or other guardians (for example, teachers) should be sought as well.
- Adults with impairments should give their own consent to participate in research where possible but the researcher should also consult with a person who is well-placed to appreciate the participant's reaction (for example, a family member, an independent adviser).
- Detained persons (for example, in prison) must have the freedom to give their own consent.
- Researchers should not pressurise people to consent to an investigation nor use payment to encourage them to agree to do something they would not normally choose to do without payment.
- It is possible to carry out an investigation without consent in situations where people would expect to be observed by strangers (for example, in a night club). However, researchers need to be wary about observing people who, even while in a public area, may believe they are unobserved (for example, in a public toilet).
- Psychologists should avoid **deception**. Participants should not generally be misled about the nature of an investigation. However, the BPS does recognise that in some circumstances research may not be valid if participants know that they are being studied or know why they are being studied. Therefore researchers should ensure participants are informed as early as possible that they are being studied or why they are really being studied.

Key terms

Right to withdraw: ability to not continue with an investigation.

Protection of participants: avoiding causing participants unnecessary harm.

Debrief: to inform participants of the aim of research after the event.

AQA Examiner's tip

It is very difficult for you to judge whether a researcher is working within their competencies, so avoid raising this issue in an examination. Focus on more obvious issues – such as when consent is not sought or confidentiality not ensured.

Participants have the **right to withdraw** from the research at any time during the investigation, for whatever reason.

Competence

Psychologists should work within the limits of their knowledge, skill, training, education and experience.

Responsibility

Researchers have the responsibility of the **protection of participants**, that is protecting them from physical and mental harm, misuse and abuse during an investigation. More specifically:

- The risk of harm should be no greater than in everyday life.
- If a researcher is not sure whether a risk (for example, deception, distress) is justifiable or not, it is recommended that they consult with individuals that are similar to the participants (that is, socially and culturally) and ask them about how they would feel if they were a participant in the planned investigation.
- Wherever possible, the right to withdraw should be made clear to participants at the start of the research.
- This right to withdraw applies even where participants have been paid to take part.
- In the case of children, if they appear to be avoiding a situation it should be taken as their need to withdraw.
- Researchers should deal with any negative affects of an investigation at the end of the research, and should be available to help deal with any longer term consequences.
- During an investigation, a researcher may find evidence of psychological or physical problems which a participant is unaware of. In such a case, the researcher has a responsibility to inform the participant if they believe that by not doing so the participant's future well-being may be at risk. In these cases, the researcher can offer advice or, if not qualified, should recommend an appropriate professional.

Participants should be **debriefed** following their participation in a piece of research. This would also normally apply when they have taken part in an investigation they have not been aware of. More specifically:

- Researchers should make sure participants have fully understood the (true) nature of an investigation.
- Even if a participant has completed the investigation, they have the right to withdraw their own data or have it destroyed – this may be particularly important for participants who realise they have been deceived once debriefed.
- Researchers should ask the participants about their experience of the research in order to check for any negative effects or misunderstandings that may not have been expected.
- Researchers may have to use counselling as part of their briefing to ensure that participants leave in a healthy state of mind (especially if they have been deceived) or that they at least leave in the same state as which they entered.

Debriefing a participant does not necessarily excuse an unethical piece of research.

Some psychologists choose to use **non-human animals** as part of their research and there are a number of ethical guidelines with this field of study.

▮ Researchers should choose a species which is scientifically suitable for an area of study and which will suffer the least from investigation. Researchers should also use the smallest number of animals possible.

▮ As much as possible, researchers should avoid procedures which cause pain, suffering, distress or lasting harm. Where such procedures are used, they need to be fully justified and require a Project Licence.

▮ Where animals are kept in captivity for research purposes, researchers should make sure they are well housed and cared for. Normal feeding and breeding habits should be not be disrupted.

▮ Researchers are encouraged to investigate free-living animals as much as possible, rather than studying them in controlled conditions. When this happens, researchers should try to interfere with the natural habitat as little as possible.

▮ Integrity

Psychologists should value honesty, accuracy, clarity and fairness in their interactions with participants and the public.

🔢 Unethical research

Despite the ethical guidelines, research that breaches ethical guidelines may still be carried out. For example, deception is relatively common in conformity experiments where psychologists want to test genuine behaviour, or in memory experiments where they want to use surprise recall tests. In turn, this may cause distress, discomfort or embarrassment for the participant.

Unethical research may be carried out if the psychologist can show that the means justify the ends. For example, if a group of participants are deceived in an experiment investigating prejudice this may be justified if it shows us the cause of prejudice. Why? Because the findings may show us how to reduce prejudice which would benefit wider society. In other words, a large number of people at the expense of a small minority. This may become even less of a problem if the participants are treated ethically after the event. For example, if they are counselled, ensured privacy, and given the right to withdraw data if they wish.

Key points:

▪ Ethical research is research that protects the welfare of participants.

▪ The main ethical guidelines covering psychological research are: consent, deception, debriefing, withdrawal from an investigation, confidentiality, protection of participants and working with animals.

▪ Unethical research can be justified if the costs are outweighed by the benefits of the findings.

Research methods

▮ Key term

Non-human animals: any animal species excluding human beings.

▮ Hints

When you have a list of terms to learn (such as those in the code of ethics), it sometimes helps to associate them with a more familiar list. One way of doing this is to associate terms with a route you know well. For example:

▮ You pass the churchyard; there is **conf**etti on the ground – **conf**identiality.

▮ You pass the prison; prison houses the **cons** – **cons**ent.

▮ You pass your friend who lives at number 10; 10 = **dec** – **dec**eption.

▮ You pass the bank; you **withdraw** some money from the cashpoint – **withdraw**al from investigation.

▮ You pass the fizzy drink factory; it makes **pop** – **p**rotection **o**f **p**articipants.

▮ You pass the hairdresser's; her shop is called **Debra's** – **debr**iefing.

▮ You pass the vet's; the vet treats **animals** – working with **animals**.

AQA Examiner's tip

Sometimes in the exam you get a parted question where they first ask you to identify an ethical problem in part (i) and then ask you for a solution to the problem in part (ii). Make sure you answer part (i) with an issue you know how to deal with in (ii).

💡 Summary questions

43 Give two examples of people who may not be able to give their own consent in psychological research.

44 Explain how psychologists may sometimes justify deceiving their participants.

45 Describe how ethical guidelines help to promote the welfare of human participants.

Representing data

Learning objectives:

- Know how graphs are used to represent data.

- Understand the differences between bar graphs, line graphs, histograms and scattergrams.

Key terms

Transcript: word-for-word written account.

Graph: pictorial representation of data.

Raw scores: the original scores collected for individual participants.

Discrete data: data in categories.

Continuous data: numerical data from a scale where, in theory, there are no intervals between scores.

Link

For an example of a summary table see summary question 52 at the end of the section on Descriptive data, p121.

AQA Examiner's tip

Sometimes you have to interpret a graph in the exam. Remember you are looking to describe general patterns (for example, increases, common responses, etc.) rather than quoting specific details from the graph (for example, how many participants got each score).

When research is qualitative, data is sometimes presented in its original format (for example, a **transcript** of an interview) or is summarised (for example, a synopsis of what happened during an observation).

Quantitative data is easier to summarise as there are various tools for doing this. **Graphs** offer one way of summarising or representing data. Data can also be represented in a summary table. A summary table is different from a table of **raw scores** because it presents descriptive data (for example, averages) rather than individual scores. This is normally enough to see the pattern of results.

Bar graphs

Bar graphs are used to represent data which is divided into categories. This is sometimes known as **discrete data**. Examples of discrete data include:

- answering yes or no to a question
- deciding whether a child's play is competitive, co-operative or independent
- identifying a participant as extroverted or introverted.

On a bar graph:

- each bar represents a different category. These are listed along the horizontal (x) axis.
- the frequency each category is chosen or occurs is measured up the vertical (y) axis, and is shown by the height of the bar.
- bars should be drawn separately to indicate that each category is separate and discrete.
- even if a category is not chosen or observed, it should be still represented on a bar graph to show readers that its frequency is zero.

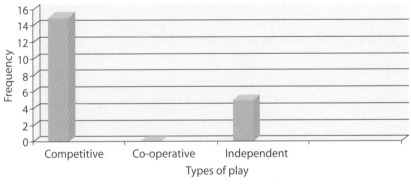

Fig. 12 *A bar graph to show the frequency of different types of play observed in three-year-old boys*

Line graphs

Line graphs are used to represent data which is in numerical form. This is sometimes is known as **continuous data**. Examples of continuous data include:

- respondents rating on a scale of 1 to 6 how much they agree with a statement
- the number of words recalled in a memory experiment
- the age of person.

On a line graph:

- The scale of measurement (for example, rating, number of words, time) would be placed along the horizontal (x) axis.
- The frequency of each score is measured up the vertical (y) axis, and is represented by a point on the graph.
- When all points are plotted a line is drawn between each of them. This shows data is continuous.

Since data is continuous, a line graph can be used to make estimations about the frequency of scores between those represented on the graph. For example using the line graph in Figure 13, it would be possible to estimate the obedience score of a child between the ages plotted.

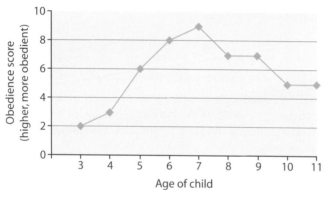

Fig. 13 *A line graph to show the obedience level of children at different ages*

■ Histograms

Histograms are an alternative to line graphs as they also represent continuous data. Bars represent each score rather than a point. Bars are drawn touching to show that data is continuous.

Histograms are useful when there is a large range of data. Rather than representing every score on a scale on the graph, they can be grouped and represented by one bar. Each group of scores is known as a class interval, and this gives the width of the bar. As a general 'rule-of-thumb' a histogram should have six to eight bars.

For example, imagine a piece of research that produced the data shown in Table 9.

Research methods

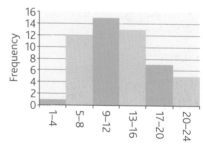

Fig. 14 *A histogram to show the frequency of scores in a word recall test (using the data in Table 9)*

Table 9 *Number of words recalled and their frequency*

Number of words recalled	1	2	3	4	5	6	7	8	9	10	11	12	13	14	15	16	17	18	19	20	21	22	23	24
Frequency	0	1	0	0	2	3	3	4	3	4	4	4	3	5	3	2	3	2	0	2	1	2	1	1

It would not be that useful to represent the data on a line graph as none of the scores are achieved that frequently. In other words, the line graph would show a relatively flat line.

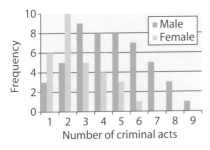

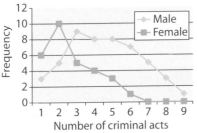

Fig. 15 *Data represented in two ways: a compound histogram and a line graph*

■ **Research methods**

■ Key term

Compound histogram: a histogram representing two or more sets of data.

■ Link

Scattergrams are used for correlational analyses. See Correlation studies on p101.

■ Hint

When interpreting a scattergram **never** state that it shows that one variable is affecting another. Remember, scattergrams only show relationships not causation.

AQA Examiner's tip

You may be asked to sketch a graph in the exam. Remember a sketch does not have to be neat but it does need to be relatively accurate as there will be marks available for it 'looking right'. Do not forget to label the graph and to give it a title as this is what normally gets you the most credit. The data you have to use to construct a graph is normally given in a table, so adapt its labels and titles to fit your graph.

However, if the scores were grouped in class intervals of four (that is, 1–4, 5–8, 9–12) then the data could be represented using a histogram. This would show a clearer pattern of recall (see Figure 14).

Line graphs do have their advantages over histograms (see Figure 15):

■ As mentioned earlier, the line can be used to make estimations.

■ It is easier to visually represent and compare two or more sets of data on a line graph (using two or more lines) whereas **compound histograms** are generally more difficult to read.

■ Scattergrams

As demonstrated earlier, scattergrams are used to represent relationships between variables. This is different from the other graphs which are used to display differences.

Both variables need to be measured using a numerical scale. One variable is represented on the x-axis and the other on the y-axis. It does not matter which way around this is done as data is being analysed for a relationship not for cause and effect.

Key points:

■ Graphs are used to represent quantitative data pictorially.

■ Bar graphs are used to show differences in discrete data. Line graphs and histograms can both be used to show differences in continuous data. Scattergrams are used to show relationships between two sets of continuous data.

💡 Summary questions

46 Name the type of graph used to represent a correlation.

47 State the class interval a researcher should use on a histogram to represent scores ranging from 40 to 51.

48 Briefly explain why bars are drawn touching on a histogram but not on a bar graph.

49 Sketch a line graph to represent the data in Table 10.

Table 10 *The number of feared objects reported by a sample of agoraphobics*

Number of feared objects	1	2	3	4	5	6	7	8	9	10
Frequency	0	2	4	6	6	4	3	2	0	1

50 a Look at Figure 12. Give the number of times three-year-old boys were observed playing independently.

b Look at Figure 13. Estimate the obedience level of a child of four years and six months.

c Look at Figure 14. Identify the most common range of scores in the memory experiment.

d Look at Figure 15. Describe the pattern of results.

Descriptive data

Learning objectives:

- Understand what is meant by a measure of central tendency.

- Distinguish between the mode, median and mean when measuring central tendency.

- Understand what is meant by a measure of dispersion.

- Distinguish between the range and standard deviation as a measure of dispersion.

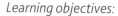

Key term

Measure of central tendency: a measure of average.

Descriptive data is quantitative data that has been analysed to show patterns. This therefore includes data presented in graphs.

Quantitative data can also be presented in a table. It is conventional to present a table that summarises data rather than one that contains all of the raw scores. Generally speaking, people do not want to see evidence of all of a psychologist's research. They want to see the main trends.

For example, imagine an investigation where two groups of participants' recall scores are compared. One group is tested in the same situation that they learnt information and the other is tested in a different situation. People do not necessarily want to know how each individual participant has done. They are more interested in which group did better **on average**. This is where **measures of central tendency** are useful.

Measures of central tendency

Measures of central tendency describe a data set by identifying one score that represents the general trend of that data. This score will tend to be somewhere 'central' to other scores. In other words, a measure of central tendency identifies a typical or average score.

Look at the following data set which shows the number of baskets scored by participants in a basketball game when in front of a crowd:

4   5   1   4   3   11   27   0   1   4   4   3   2   1   3   8

This data set, like most others, can be summarised using one of three measures of central tendency. They are:

- the mode
- the median
- the mean.

The mode

The mode simply identifies the most common score in a data set. Using the above data set this would be 4, as it occurs the most times (four times).

The median

The median is calculated in two stages.

1 All scores need to be ordered numerically (either ascending or descending). Using the example data set, this would give:

0   1   1   1   2   3   3   3   4   4   4   4   5   8   11   27

2 The median is then identified by locating the middle score in the data set. If there is an odd number of scores it is literally the score in the middle. If there is an even number of scores (as in the above data set) then it is the number that would occur between the two scores in the middle. This can be worked out by adding the two middle numbers together and dividing by two. In the example data set, the middle number would be 3.5 (3 + 4 ÷ 2):

0   1   1   1   2   3   3   3   [3.5]   4   4   4   4   5   8   11   27

The mean

The mean is sometimes known as the arithmetic average because it calculates the measure of central tendency by:

1 adding together all of the scores in a data set

2 then dividing that sum by the total number of scores in the data set.

Using the example data set, the first stage would give the sum of 81:

$$(0 + 1 + 1 + 1 + 2 + 3 + 3 + 3 + 4 + 4 + 4 + 4 + 5 + 8 + 11 + 27)$$

Then the second stage involves dividing 81 by 16 (the total number of scores). The mean $(\bar{X}) = 81 \div 16 = 5.1$ (to 1 decimal place).

It is interesting to note that with the example data set, different measures of central tendency give different results. Although the mode (4 baskets) and median (3.5 baskets) are similar in this case, the mean is noticeably higher at 5.1 baskets. This is because the mean takes into account every score and, here, is skewed by a particularly high score (27). Meanwhile, the mode is unaffected by any outliers because it is only interested in the most common score (not unusual ones). The median is also unaffected because it is only interested in what occurs in the middle of a data set and not at the extremes.

Comparing the measures of central tendency

The fact that the mean uses all of the scores in a set has strengths and weaknesses. Some researchers argue that even extreme scores should be accounted for by a measure of central tendency because they play an equally important part in 'telling the story' about data. On this basis, the mean is better than the other two measures because it misses nothing out and gives a more valid measure. However, other researchers argue that extreme scores make measures unreliable as they misrepresent the true tendency of a data set by skewing it so it is too high or too low. In the above example, the mean makes it look as though participants are relatively good at scoring baskets in front of a crowd. However, in fact, the mean is inflated by one particularly high-scoring participant.

Some researchers also dislike the mean because the average is often a decimal score, which they say is meaningless. For example, how can someone score 5.1 baskets? Meanwhile the median is normally one of the scores in the data set and the mode is always one of the scores in the data set.

The main problem with the mode is that it relies on there being a score which occurs more than others. However, sometimes each score in a data set occurs only once so there is no mode as such. Alternatively, there may be two or more scores that occur equally frequently which gives a number of averages. Sometimes these can be at either end of a range of data so do not really help in measuring the central tendency!

💡 Measures of dispersion

Whatever measure of central tendency is chosen, it only really tells a person what is happening on average. Take the example of the mean of 5.1 baskets from above. If someone did not have access to the rest of the data set, then what would this average tell them? Does it mean that most participants score around about 5 baskets, or does it mean that there is a wide spread of scores that tend towards 5 in the middle?

If people are interested in how spread out a set of scores are, then they can take a **measure of dispersion**.

■ Hint

Remember:

■ The **mode** takes the **most** common score.

■ The **median** takes the **mid** score.

■ The **mean** is nasty – because you have to do some maths to calculate it!

AQA Examiner's tip

You may be asked to calculate a measure of central tendency in the exam so be prepared for this. However, you are more likely to be asked to justify why a certain measure should or should not be used, so make sure you know the strengths and limitations of using each one.

■ Key term

Measure of dispersion: a measure of how spread out data is.

Table 11 *Scores for two classes for a psychology test*

Class	Set of scores	Median
A	43% 48% 50% 50% 51% 52% 55% 55% 56% 57% 60%	52%
B	25% 30% 32% 39% 45% 50% 58% 59% 65% 72% 80% 82%	54%

The importance of measuring dispersion is illustrated above. Imagine, the results in Table 11 are the test results of two psychology classes.

Using the median as a measure of central tendency, it is possible to say that the two classes have done equally well in the test as there is no marked difference between the two medians.

However, although on average the groups' performances are similar, the spread of their scores is quite different. Class A have very similar scores to the average showing their scores are not that spread out. Class B have very different scores from each other and the average, showing their scores are more spread out.

It is not easy to use the spread of scores to say which class is better. They are just different. The point is that it is not really fair to compare them as one class appears to have a group of students of very similar ability whereas the other group has a wider range of abilities.

This shows why researchers often take a measure of dispersion (as well as an average) when analysing data. They want to assess whether it is reasonable to compare two groups.

The range

The **range** offers one measure of dispersion and is normally used in conjunction with the median. While the median analyses what is happening in the middle of a data set, the range analyses what is happening at either end!

The range measures the spread of data by simply identifying the highest score then subtracting the lowest score and adding 1 (to count back in the lowest score). So, using the data set of the two psychology classes:

▥ Class A would have a range of 18 (60 − 43 + 1)
▥ Class B would have a range of 58 (82 − 25 + 1).

The fact that Class B has a much higher range than Class A tells us that their scores are more dispersed.

Of course, where a repeated measures design is used, a researcher may expect the range of scores to be very similar across conditions as the same participants are being used. Take the example of the participants taking shots at a basket in front of a crowd. The range of their scores is 28. The researcher would expect a similar range of scores without a crowd observing. Even if everyone did better without a crowd, the participant who scored zero would still probably score low and the participants who scored 27 would still probably score high.

The standard deviation

The range offers quite a basic measure of dispersion because it does not take into account what is happening between the highest and lowest score.

The **standard deviation (s.d.)** is a more sophisticated measure of dispersion because it uses all scores in a data set to calculate the spread of scores. This is why it is often used in conjunction with the mean which

AQA Examiner's tip

You may be asked to compare two averages in the exam. Remember, you are looking for a notable difference between them to retain a research hypothesis. If the difference is small, you should consider retaining the null hypothesis.

▥ Key terms

Range: a measure of dispersion that finds the difference between the highest and lowest score in a data set.

Standard deviation (s.d.): a measure of dispersion that calculates how much each score (in a data set) deviates from the mean.

AQA Examiner's tip

You will not have to actually calculate a standard deviation in the exam. However, you do need to understand how it is calculated and what it shows.

$$\sigma = \sqrt{\frac{\Sigma\,(X - \overline{X})^2}{n - 1}}$$

σ = standard deviation

X = score $\overline{X}$ = mean

Σ = sum of   n = number of scores

Fig. 16 *The formula for calculating the standard deviation*

also uses all scores. Indeed, the s.d. uses the mean in its calculation. It essentially uses a formula to calculate how much each score deviates from the mean (or standard) on average. When scores deviate a lot from the mean (are very spread out) it gives a high s.d. When scores do not deviate that much from the mean it gives a low s.d.

The formula for calculating the s.d. is given in Figure 16.

The data in Figure 17 uses the mean and standard deviation to compare the personal space (closest physical distance people are comfortable being to another person) of a group of male and female participants.

The findings in Figure 17 show that males, on average, require significantly more personal space (a distance of 34.5 cm) than females (who require an average distance of 29.2 cm).

Males	Personal space (cm)	Deviation from mean $(x-\overline{X})$	$(x-\overline{X})^2$
1	30	−4.5	20.25
2	31	−3.5	12.25
3	33	−1.5	2.25
4	28	−6.5	42.25
5	25	−9.5	90.25
6	36	1.5	2.25
7	42	7.5	56.25
8	50	15.5	240.25
9	37	2.5	6.25
10	33	−1.5	2.25
	$\overline{X} = 34.5$		$\Sigma\,(x-\overline{X})^2 = 474.50$

$$\sigma = \sqrt{\frac{474.5}{(10\text{-}1)}} = \frac{52.722222}{9} = 7.26$$

Females	Personal space (cm)	Deviation from mean $(x-\overline{X})$	$(x-\overline{X})^2$
	27	−2.2	4.84
	26	−3.2	10.24
	30	0.8	0.64
	30	0.8	0.64
	26	−3.2	10.24
	27	−2.2	4.84
	33	3.8	14.44
	35	5.8	33.64
	28	−1.2	1.44
	30	0.8	0.64
	$\overline{X} = 29.2$		$\Sigma\,(x-\overline{X})^2 = 81.6$

$$\sigma = \sqrt{\frac{81.6}{(10\text{-}1)}} = \frac{9.06666}{9} = 3.01$$

Fig. 17 *Working for determining s.d.*

However, the standard deviations show that the scores for males are more dispersed than females as the s.d. for males (7.26) is more than double the females (3.01). In other words, females are more consistent in how much personal space they need. However, closer analysis of the male scores shows that Participant 8 requires a large amount of personal space. This would skew the mean for males and account for their high standard deviation.

The general point is that the standard deviation gives useful information that takes us beyond the mean. For example, a mean may not even change between two conditions but the standard deviation might. This could indicate that the IV has affected individuals differently to give a greater variation of scores rather than affecting the average score.

Key points:

■ A measure of central tendency describes the trend of data by calculating a typical or average value for a data set.

■ The mode does this by identifying the most common score. The median finds the middle score. The mean calculates the arithmetic average by adding together all scores and dividing by the total number of scores.

■ A measure of dispersion describes the spread of a set of scores (around the average).

■ A range does this by working out the difference between the highest and lowest score. The standard deviation basically calculates the average by which each score deviates from the mean.

 Summary questions

51 Look at the following data set:

5 15 3 10 5 2 11 12 8 6

  a Calculate its mode.

  b Calculate its median.

  c Calculate its mean.

52 Look at Table 12. Explain what the table shows about cues and recall.

Table 12 *The means and standard deviations of participants recalling words in the presence and absence of cues*

	Cues present	Cues absent
Mean number of words recalled	17.3	10.2
Standard deviation	4.5	2.0

53 Outline one similarity and one difference between the range and the standard deviation.

54 Discuss the relative strengths and weaknesses of different measures of central tendency.

End-of-chapter activity

Choose a topic from the AS topics you have studied. Think of a research question you would like to answer within this topic area. This will give you the aim of your research.

From this plan an investigation to test your hypothesis (which should arise from your aim).

You will then need to make decisions about how to operationalise your variables and control other variables. Decide what method to use to collect your data, as well as the experimental design (if appropriate). You then need to choose an appropriate sampling technique and plan how your are actually going to execute your research. Remember to consider ethical issues as part of your planning.

When you have carried out your research, present your investigation in the form of a report as detailed below.

1 Under the heading 'Introduction', outline the theory and research that has been carried out in your topic area; state your aim; state your research and null hypothesis.
2 Under the heading 'Method', describe all the design decisions you made (that is, about method, operationalising variables, controlling variables, experimental design, ethical considerations, sample, materials used) and justify these choices; outline the procedure, that is how your investigation was actually carried out.
3 Under the heading 'Results', present your data in a summary form, for example graphs and/or table of descriptive statistics; comment on your findings including whether you should retain or reject your research hypothesis.
4 Under the heading 'Discussion', try to explain your findings; consider the reliability of your findings by discussing the limitations of the methods/controls/designs/samples/procedures that you used.

AQA Examination-style questions

1 A psychologist wanted to investigate whether mood had an effect on the recall of information. She expected that participants who rated themselves as 'happy' would recall more words from a list than participants who rated themselves as 'unhappy'.

Fifty people, selected by opportunity sampling, were asked to complete a mood state questionnaire. From these 50 people, the psychologist selected 10 participants who had rated themselves as 'happy' and 10 participants who had rated themselves as 'unhappy'.

The 20 participants were required to learn a list of words such as 'pencil', 'door', 'necklace' and 'thermometer'. The mean number of words recalled by both groups is given in Table 1 below.

Table 1 The mean number of words recalled by participants rating themselves as 'happy' and participants rating themselves as 'unhappy'

	Participants who rated themselves as 'happy'	Participants who rated themselves as 'unhappy'
Mean number of words recalled	15.3	7.4

(a) What do the mean scores indicate about the recall of words by these two groups of participants? Justify your answer. *(2 marks)*

   (i) The mean is a measure of central tendency. Name two other measures of central tendency. *(2 marks)*

   (ii) Name one measure that the psychologist could use to find out about the spread of scores in each group. *(1 mark)*

(b) (i) Identify the type of experimental design used in this study. *(1 mark)*

   (ii) Explain one disadvantage of the experimental design that you have identified in your answer to (b)(i). *(2 marks)*

(c) (i) Outline what is meant by the term extraneous variable. *(2 marks)*

   (ii) Explain why the psychologist used the same word list with both groups of participants. *(2 marks)*

(d) The psychologist used opportunity sampling, rather than random sampling, to select the original 50 people for this study.

   (i) Outline what is meant by random sampling. *(2 marks)*

   (ii) Explain why random sampling might be a better technique to use than opportunity sampling. *(2 marks)*

(e) The questionnaire used to measure mood state contained both closed and open questions.

   (i) Write one closed question that might be used to obtain information about a person's mood state. *(1 mark)*

   (ii) Write one open question that might be used to obtain information about a person's mood state. *(1 mark)*

   (iii) Outline one disadvantage of using questionnaires in psychological research. *(2 marks)*

AQA, 2006

2 A psychologist wanted to investigate differences between the language development of five-year-old girls and boys.

Ten girls and 10 boys were selected from a local primary school.

To assess each child's language development, the psychologist administered a test. A high score on the test indicated good language development and a low score indicated poor language development. The results are given in Table 2 below.

Table 2 The scores, means and standard deviations for girls and boys on a test of language development

Participant	Girls' scores	Boys' scores
	46	52
	58	32
	90	51
	41	86
	52	42
	73	62
	81	47
	79	65
	47	70
	82	48
Mean	64.9	55.5
Standard deviation	18.0	15.5

(a) In your answer book, sketch a bar chart of the mean scores presented in Table 2. Provide a suitable title and correctly label your bar chart. *(3 marks)*

(b) What do the mean scores indicate about language development in these girls and boys? Justify your answer. *(2 marks)*

(c) (i) Outline what is meant by the term standard deviation. *(2 marks)*

(i) What do the standard deviations indicate about the language development of these girls and boys? Justify your answer. *(2 marks)*

(d) Before the investigation, the psychologist conducted a pilot study. State what is meant by a pilot study. *(1 mark)*

(e) The psychologist used a random sampling technique to select the children for this study. State one advantage and one disadvantage of random sampling. *(2 marks)*

(f) Outline and explain one ethical issue that should have been considered when this study was being conducted. *(4 marks)*

(g) The psychologist decided to conduct an unstructured interview with one child who achieved a high score on the language test. State one strength and one limitation of an unstructured interview. *(2 marks)*

(h) Following the investigation, the psychologist conducted a non-participant observation at the primary school. Outline what is meant by non-participant observation. *(2 marks)*

AQA, 2006

3 A psychologist wanted to investigate the relationship between pet ownership and stress. It was predicted that the more pets a person owned the less stress a person would report.

To assess each participant's level of stress, the psychologist administered a questionnaire. The maximum possible score on the stress questionnaire was 70. A high score on the questionnaire indicated a high level of stress, and a low score a low level of stress. The results obtained are given in Table 3 below.

Table 3 The number of pets owned and stress score for each participant

Participant	Number of pets owned	Stress scores
1	0	59
2	1	51
3	2	45
4	3	31
5	4	40
6	5	38
7	6	28
8	7	27
9	8	21
10	9	12
11	10	11

(a) (i) Sketch a scattergram of the data presented in Table 3. Provide a suitable title and correctly label your scattergram. *(3 marks)*

 (ii) Identify the type of correlation shown in your scattergram and state what it shows about the relationship between pet ownership and stress. *(2 marks)*

(b) State one strength and one limitation of the correlation method. *(2 marks)*

(c) The psychologist obtained the participants for this study through opportunity sampling. State one strength and one limitation of using opportunity sampling. *(2 marks)*

(d) The questionnaire used to measure stress contained both open and closed questions.

 (i) Write one closed question that might be used to obtain information about how stressed a person feels. *(1 mark)*

 (ii) Write one open question that might be used to obtain information about how stressed a person feels. *(1 mark)*

 (iii) Write one open question that might be used to obtain information about how stressed a person feels. *(1 mark)*

(e) The psychologist decided to conduct a case study by observing and interviewing one of the participants who reported a very high level of stress.

 (i) State one advantage of observational studies. *(1 mark)*

 (ii) Distinguish between a structured and an unstructured interview. *(3 marks)*

 (iii) Briefly discuss one limitation of the case study method. *(3 marks)*

AQA, 2006

Social psychology

Introduction

Social psychology is about people's social behaviour. It concerns itself with those aspects of human behaviour which involve other people. It is based on the fact that we are social animals, that we constantly interact with others and our behaviour is influenced by their presence.

Social psychology is based on scientific enquiry. Its aims are to understand, explain and predict behaviour using empirical methods.

It is concerned primarily with human behaviour. Not all 'behaviour' can be objectively observed. Social psychology also concerns itself with internal processes, for example thoughts and feelings.

Social psychology is concerned with how behaviour is influenced by 'others'. This can be as a result of their actual presence. Examples of this will be seen in the chapter on social influence. Nevertheless, even when we are not in the presence of others we use knowledge of social behaviour to make sense of our social world. Examples of this will be seen in the chapter on social cognition. A brief overview of these chapters should make this clearer.

Obedience to authority is one type of social influence. Here a person acts in response to a direct order. However many forms of social influence are indirect and unintentional. In conformity we see how beliefs, attitudes and behaviour can be influenced by being a member of a group and the topic of social facilitation examines the physical presence of others on behaviour. Although social influence brings benefits to society it can also create problems, for example in obedience to a destructive authority. By studying the processes of social influence, psychologists can understand the principles underlying their solutions such as in defiance of authority.

Social cognition uses concepts from cognitive psychology to explain how cognition influences our social behaviour and our understanding of the social world. In a way social cognition is a sub-area of cognitive psychology combining themes from cognitive psychology with the study of people in social settings. The cognitive concept of a 'schema' is used to explain impression formation and stereotyping which underlies prejudice. Other related cognitive themes are 'limited capacity processing' and 'categorisation'. Cognitive factors are also evident in attitudes and attribution biases.

Social psychology is a relatively young branch of psychology. In 1897, Triplett carried out what is usually considered the first experimental study in social psychology but it was not until the mid-1920s that social psychology began to take a firm hold in psychology. A watershed event was the publication of Allport's book *Social Psychology*, which argued that social psychology would only flourish if it became an experimental science. This was in tune with Watson's (1913) behaviourist principles for psychology as whole. The rise of Nazism and the Holocaust had a further impact on the interest in social psychology. Adorno's work on the authoritarian personality (1950) and Milgram's work on obedience to authority (1963) are just a few examples of significant research carried out in an attempt to understand some of the fundamental questions about human behaviour.

Specification	Topic content	Page
Social facilitation, dominant responses, causes of arousal: evaluation, apprehension and distraction Effects of arousal on task performance	Social facilitation	128
Types of conformity, including internalisation and compliance	Conformity	132
Explanations for conformity, including informational social influence and normative social influence	Conformity	132
Factors affecting conformity, including those investigated by Asch	Conformity	132
Explanations of obedience	Obedience and defiance of authority	138
Situational factors: conditions affecting obedience to authority as investigated by Milgram	Obedience and defiance of authority	138
Dispositional explanation: the authoritarian personality	Obedience and defiance of authority	138
Explanations of defiance of authority	Obedience and defiance of authority	138
Ethical and methodological issues in studying social influence	Ethical and methodological issues in studying social influence	143
Factors affecting impression formation, including social schemas, primacy and recency effects, central traits and stereotyping	Impression formation	148
Concept of attribution: dispositional and situational attributions; attributional biases, including the fundamental attribution error, the actor-observer effect and the self-serving bias	Attribution	154
The structure and function of attitudes: cognitive affective and behavioural components; adaptive, knowledge and ego-expressive functions	Attitudes	159
Explanations of prejudice, including competition for resources, social identity theory and the authoritarian personality	Prejudice	163

Social psychology

5 Social influence

Social facilitation

Social psychology

Learning objectives:

- Understand what is meant by social facilitation.
- Describe the effects of arousal on task performance.
- Describe and evaluate theories of social facilitation.

Hint

Facilitation means to make things easier. This is measured by how long it takes to do a task or the number of errors made.

Key terms

Co-action: when people work alongside each other on the same task.

Social facilitation: the tendency for people to perform better on tasks in the presence of others than when alone.

Audience effect: impact on the individual task performance of the presence of an audience.

Social inhibition: the tendency for people to perform less well in the presence of others than when alone.

Dominant response: the response which is most likely to be given in a situation, that is most usual, appropriate or best practised. It takes priority over all other possible responses.

What is meant by social facilitation?

Students revising for exams often have a preference for how to revise. Some revise better on their own whereas others believe they revise more efficiently if others are present, for example in a classroom or library. Is performance affected by whether one does a task alone or in the presence of others? The first known psychologist to investigate this question was Norman Triplett (1898). He observed that cyclists rode faster when racing together than when alone. Triplett thought that perhaps it was the competitive element between people that improved performance. To test this hypothesis he recorded the time it took children to turn a fishing reel 150 times. Sometimes they were alone in a room but at other times two children worked at the same time in the same room each with their own reel. He found that many children worked faster in **co-action**.

Numerous similar experiments on humans and animals have showed improved performance as a result of others' presence. Allport (1920) found that college students completed more multiplication problems in co-action than when alone. Ants digging in groups have been found to dig more than three times as much sand per ant than when alone (Chen, 1937). Allport (1920) referred to this effect as **social facilitation**. However he was not convinced that competition was necessarily involved. In one experiment he asked participants not to compete with one another in tasks such as crossing out the vowels in a page of writing. Social facilitation still occurred (Allport, 1924). Of course the problem here is that even if people are instructed not to compete they may still do so. Dashiell (1930) found that just the presence of an audience (**audience effect**) could result in social facilitation.

Some research produced the opposite effect: impaired performance. This is referred to as **social inhibition**. In the 1960s, Zajonc provided a theory which attempted to explain these contradictory findings.

Arousal theory of social facilitation

People are relatively unpredictable so their presence instinctively causes a person to be in a state of alertness or arousal. This 'preparedness' is a clear advantage to the species and leads to a readiness to respond with the most adaptive response. According to Zajonc, arousal acts as a drive that brings out the **dominant response**. In an easy or well practised task, dominant responses tend to be correct so social facilitation occurs, but in a task which is difficult or not well learned the dominant responses tend to be incorrect so social inhibition occurs.

This theory explains the contradictory findings mentioned earlier. For example, on a multiplication problem, there is only one correct answer but many incorrect ones. For someone who finds such a task easy, arousal is low; in everyday terms the task is 'boring'. The presence of others increases arousal and brings out the dominant response; the correct answer. However, for a person who struggles with the task then the presence of others still increases arousal and brings out the dominant response: an incorrect answer.

Research study: Michaels et al. (1982)

Aim: To investigate the presence of an audience on the performance of average and below average pool players.

Method: Pool players were observed from a distance in a college student union and classified as either average or below average. Researchers recorded the number of successful shots (the operational definition of performance) by six identified as average and six identifed as below average. At this stage the players did not know that they were being observed. Four researchers then walked up to the tables of the players so that it was obvious that they were observing their game.

Results: The players identified as average in ability increased their shot accuracy by 9 per cent whereas those who were below average showed a decrease of 11 per cent in shot accuracy when watched.

Conclusion: The presence of an audience results in social facilitation when the task is well known but social inhibition when the task is more difficult.

Evaluation: By focusing on behaviour in its natural setting, the experimenter increases the ecological validity of the findings. Furthermore because the participants were unaware of their participation in a study they were less likely to react to demand characteristics. But this lack of awareness raises ethical concerns such as the invasion of privacy and lack of informed consent.

Similar findings were observed in research on animals. Zajonc (1969) put cockroaches into a runway. They had to run down a straight corridor into a darkened goal box to escape a bright light. Sometimes they ran in pairs (co-action) and other times on their own. They reached the goal box more quickly when in pairs. If the task was made more difficult by putting a right angle turn in order to reach the goal box, the cockroaches were faster when running on their own. The experiment was also conducted with cockroaches running on their own but with an audience of cockroaches placed alongside the runways. Again the presence of other cockroaches resulted in social facilitation in the easy task when the dominant response (running down the straight runway was correct) and impaired performance in the difficult task because the dominant response was incorrect.

Evaluation of arousal theory

▦ The theory does not explain why a person who is very competent at a task can still perform poorly in front of an audience. This is better explained by the **Yerkes-Dodson law.** According to this law, such a person may benefit from an audience to raise the arousal level but only up to the optimum level. Too much arousal impairs performance.

▦ The theory does not acknowledge cognitive processes as important, for example what the presence of others might mean to the person doing the task. Certainly results from animal studies suggest that these are not necessary. Nevertheless some believe that the thought of competition in the case of co-action and the thought of being judged in the case of audiences are important factors in social facilitation.

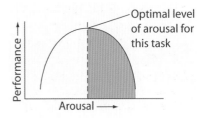

Fig. 1 *Graph showing inverted-U relationship between arousal and performance*

Evaluation apprehension theory

Cottrell (1968) argued that it is not the presence of others that causes arousal but the apprehension (anxiety) of being evaluated by others. Increased arousal in the presence of others is not an innate response but a learned one; people associate the presence of others with evaluations of their performance on a task. Thus the mere presence of others is not enough to raise arousal and the dominant responses which follow.

Research study: Henchy and Glass (1968)

Aim: To investigate whether concern about being evaluated is necessary to produce dominant responses.

Method: Participants' performance on tasks, for example typing, was assessed in one of four conditions:

1 alone – this was the control condition
2 in the presence of two 'experts'
3 in the presence of two non-experts
4 alone but filmed for later evaluation by experts.

Results: Facilitation of dominant (well-learned responses) only occurred in conditions 2 and 4. Moreover in conditions 1 and 3 performance was similar.

Conclusion: Some concern about evaluation is necessary to produce dominant responses. The results supported Cottrell's theory.

Evaluation: This experiment raises ethical issues. In order to test apprehension, participants were subjected to stress. The strength of this experiment is the use of four groups; one control and three experimental groups. These were all needed to separate the effect of the presence of others from evaluation apprehension.

Evaluation of evaluation apprehension theory

- There is further support for this theory from studies in which the audience is blindfolded. As the theory would predict, there is no social facilitation on well-learned tasks.
- The theory does not explain social facilitation in animals that presumably do not experience evaluation apprehension.
- Evaluation apprehension may be one cause of arousal in the presence of others, but may not be the only factor.

Distraction-conflict theory

Baron (1986) suggests that the presence of others is distracting because attention is divided between the task and the audience or co-actors (response conflict). Two distinct effects occur:

- Distraction leads to a negative effect on task performance regardless of whether it is simple or complex because one is less able to concentrate on the task.
- The conflict increases arousal making a dominant response more likely.

Together these processes impair the performance of complex tasks (distraction plus dominant response which is incorrect) but improve performance on simple tasks (correct dominant response outweighing the negative effect of distraction).

Research study: Sanders *et al.* (1978)

Aim: To investigate whether distraction would result in social facilitation on a simple task and social inhibition on a complex task.

Method: Participants were given a simple and complex digit-copying task. This was done alone or in co-action with the co-actor performing the same task (distracting) or different task (not distracting). The researchers believed that someone doing the same task would be a relevant source of social comparison and therefore distracting.

Results: Participants in the distraction condition made more mistakes on the complex task but copied more digits correctly on the simple task than in the other two co-action conditions. The dependent variable was measured by the number of mistakes made.

Conclusion: The results supported the distraction-conflict theory. Performance on simple tasks was facilitated by distracting others, but inhibited by distracting others on more complex tasks.

Evaluation: There is degree of subjectivity in deciding what is 'distracting' and in distinguishing between a 'simple' and 'complex' task. Nevertheless the study is highly controlled experiment involving six conditions.

Evaluation of distraction-conflict theory

- This theory can be applied to any distracting stimulus. Experiments show that any form of distraction, for example noise, movement, not only social presence, can cause social facilitation/inhibition.

- The theory can explain results from studies on social facilitation in animals. It is possible that cockroaches and other animals do become distracted.

Key points:

- People tend to perform better on easy or well-learned tasks in the presence of others than on their own.

- People tend to perform worse on difficult or poorly learned tasks in the presence of others than on their own.

- There are several theories for this effect: arousal theory, evaluation apprehension theory and distraction-conflict theory.

- According to arousal theory, the mere presence of others leads to the production of dominant responses and social facilitation/inhibition.

- Evaluation apprehension theory stresses that the presence of others causes evaluation anxiety.

- Distraction-conflict theory suggests that the presence of others is distracting.

AQA Examiner's tip

In a question on distraction-conflict theory, it is crucial to refer to the 'conflict' aspect. Notice that arousal features in all theories and it can get quite confusing. Learn the distinctive elements of each.

Link

It is important to operationalise the dependent variable (DV) to make sure that it is precisely defined and clear how it can be measured. In this study, the operational definition of the DV (social facilitation or inhibition) was the number of mistakes made. See Chapter 4, Research methods.

Summary questions

1 What is meant by social facilitation?

2 Give an example of a dominant response.

3 According to arousal theory, why does performance of a simple task in the presence of others result in social facilitation?

4 Studies of social facilitation in animals can be explained by some theories but not by others. Identify one theory that can explain the effect and one that cannot. Explain your answer.

Social psychology

Conformity

Learning objectives:

- Understand what is meant by the term 'conformity'.

- Describe research carried out into conformity.

- Know and understand the factors that affect conformity.

- Know and understand why people conform.

Key terms

Conformity: a form of social influence where group pressure, real or imagined, results in a change in behaviour.

Group: two or more people who share a common goal.

Membership group: a group to which we belong; a group we are in.

Reference group: a group that is psychologically significant (important) for our behaviour and attitudes.

Autokinetic effect: visual illusion in which a pinpoint of light shining in complete darkness appears to move about.

AQA Examiner's tip

When asked what is meant by the term 'conformity', do not use the term or similar in your answer, for example, 'conforming to others in a group'. You are simply saying the same thing in different words and not explaining what it means.

What is meant by conformity?

Conformity is a word commonly used when people try to explain why a person is doing what everyone else is doing. For psychologists the term has a very precise meaning and includes the following features:

- **Change in behaviour** A person at a social gathering may find himself in total disagreement with the rest of the group on a sensitive issue, for example capital punishment. It is not uncommon for the person to conform; to behave as if in agreement.

- **A group** Any **group** important to the individual in some way at a given time can cause the change in behaviour. This may be a **membership group**, one we belong to, or a **reference group**. This is a group we do not belong to but consists of people we like or admire, for example British youths adopting aspects of American gang culture such as music, dress, jewellery and language (famously parodied by the fictional television personality Ali G).

- **Pressure** This can be imagined or real. Imagined pressure is not expressed by the group and might just be in the mind of the person who experiences it. A typical example is being asked to sponsor someone for charity. Usually there is no direct pressure to sponsor the person; one can refuse. But on seeing the list of sponsors, people often do conform and add their name to the list. Pressure can of course be much more direct or real. For example, picket lines are often used during strikes to ensure workers conform to the strike.

Fig. 2 *Tied down by convention*

Research into conformity

Research study: Sherif (1935)

Aim: To investigate whether people would be influenced by others in a situation where the answer is not clear.

Method: The design used was repeated measures. Participants, tested individually, were shown a point of light in a totally darkened room. The light was not moving. Each participant was asked to estimate how far and in which direction the light moved. In a darkened room a stationary spot of light does appear to move. This is known as the **autokinetic effect**. Participants were tested

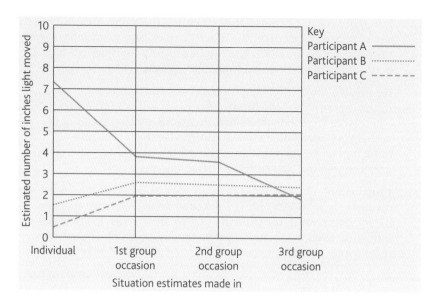

a large number of times (that is, trials) and gave different but consistent answers; some said the light did not move very far, others said that it moved by several inches. In the second part of the experiment, participants were put into small groups of about three people. Each was asked to describe the movement of light in the presence of others. This procedure was repeated over several trials.

Results: Over a number of trials, the participants answers converged and they gave very similar estimates.

Conclusion: In an ambiguous situation, participants are influenced by the judgement of others.

Evaluation: Sherif did not ask participants to arrive at a group estimate. This is a good illustration of conformity due to imagined pressure. However there are several criticisms. The main criticism is that it is not unusual for people to be influenced by the judgement of others when they are uncertain about their own judgement. There was good reason for the uncertainty: participants were in a darkened room, there was nothing against which to judge the movement of light, the light was in fact stationary. Sherif's experiment therefore does not reveal anything surprising about human behaviour. It was this problem which prompted another psychologist, Asch, to conduct an experiment involving a definite right answer. Would people conform to the judgements of others when they were actually wrong?

Link

The design here was repeated measures. Estimates of the distance the light moved when participants were alone were compared with their estimates when they were in a group. See Chapter 4, Research methods, for more about experimental designs.

Social psychology

Research study: Asch (1951)

Aim: To investigate whether people would conform to the judgements of others in situations where such judgements were clearly wrong.

Method: Male students were asked to take part in a study of visual discrimination. They were tested in groups of seven to nine. In each group there was only one genuine or 'naïve' particpant. All the other participants were in fact stooges. The participants were seated in a semi-circle and their task was to decide which one of three comparison lines was the same length as a standard line (see Figure 4). They had to give their judgement aloud in the order in which they were seated with the naïve participant answering second to

Hint

The reason why one third of the trials were 'neutral' (that is, the stooges gave the right answer) was so that the participant did not become suspicious and work out what was really going on (demand characteristics of the experiment).

Link

Asch needed to establish the percentage error when participants did the visual discrimination task on their own. Otherwise he could not establish if any difference in the percentage error when participants did the task in groups was likely to be due to the manipulation of the independent variable. See Chapter 4, Research methods, for more information on demand characteristics, control conditions and independent variables.

AQA Examiner's tip

When asked to describe a study, include the aim of the study, the method, the results and the conclusion. However, when referring to a study in a discussion, this level of detail is not needed, only an outline of the study and its relevance to the discussion.

Hint

In conformity, an individual is influenced by a group. The group is sometimes referred to as 'the majority' and conformity as 'majority influence'. Sometimes a small group can be influenced by one which is larger.

AQA Examiner's tip

In answering a discussion question, there is a strong tendency to be negative about research. A balanced discussion needs to present positive as well as negative points.

last. There were 18 trials. On six 'neutral' trials, the stooges all gave the correct answer but on the other 12 trials they unanimously gave the same wrong answer. There was a control condition in which 37 participants made their judgements in private.

Results: In the control condition, 0.7 per cent errors were made. In the experimental condition, 37 per cent errors were made. There were large individual differences. About 25 per cent of the participants made no mistakes. Twenty-eight per cent gave eight or more (out of 12) incorrect answers and the remaining participants gave between one and seven incorrect answers.

Conclusion: The task was obviously easy as the error rate in the control condition was only 0.7 per cent. Asch concluded that the 37 per cent error in the experimental condition was due to social influence. Even in situations where the judgements of others appear to be wrong, conformity occurs.

Asch's findings have been referred to as 'the surprise of Solomon Asch' (Hewstone *et al.*, 1996). Asch's participants, unlike Sherif's, were in a situation where the information from others in the group was clearly wrong. The results go against common sense predictions. They reveal the powerful influence of an **incorrect** majority on the judgements of an individual. Asch reports that more than one-third of the time, his 'intelligent and well-meaning college students were then willing to call white black' by going along with the group.

Why did people conform in Asch's experiment?

After the experiment Asch asked his (naïve) participants how they felt in the group. All said that they felt uncomfortable and doubtful about their own judgements, even lonely. When asked why they had conformed, they reported the following:

- Their perception must have been inaccurate and the majority's accurate. Perhaps they were suffering from eye strain or sitting in a bad position.
- Not to stand out and look inferior or stupid.
- Not to be an outcast.
- To convey a good impression of themselves.
- Not to spoil the experiment or upset the experimenter.

Fig. 4 *The naïve participant was placed second to last*

Such responses led Asch to believe that a major factor in conformity was to avoid conflict and social disapproval. Asch (1956) investigated these fears of social disapproval directly by doing a further experiment. The procedure of the experiment was similar to his original one with the difference that one stooge gave incorrect answers in the presence of 16 naïve participants. Asch found that the naïve participants acted in disbelief and laughed and ridiculed the stooge. Even the experimenter found it difficult to control his laughter. It does therefore seem that the participants were justified in fearing conflict and social disapproval.

Evaluation of Asch's work

The findings of Asch's work have implications for many aspects of group behaviour such as decision-making and social interaction. His experiment can be seen as an example of the rigorous standards required in psychological research: participants were studied under highly controlled conditions, Asch was able to carry out statistical analyses on the data collected and his study has been replicated and similar results produced (Neto, 1995).

There are however a number of criticisms both of Asch's research and interpretations of his findings. His research has been criticised for its lack of validity and there are concerns over ethical issues. Asch's experiment is almost always described as a study of conformity yet almost two-thirds of the judgements made by participants were in fact correct. Conformity is presented as a negative characteristic but does have beneficial effects. It is important for social stability; group norms provide a standard and expectations of behaviour ensuring a structure and order for social groups.

Variations to Asch's experiment

Asch conducted several variations to his original research to investigate factors that affect conformity.

- **Size of the majority** Asch (1951) ran groups in which the size of the majority was changed from one to 16. One person (stooge) had no real effect on conformity. Two stooges in the majority produced 13 per cent errors. Three stooges produced 33 per cent errors. The addition of further stooges did not lead to further increases in conformity.

- **Unanimity** Asch wondered if the unanimity of the group made the naïve participant feel isolated, increasing the tendency to conform. Asch broke unanimity and gave the participant a 'supporter', that is a stooge who answered before the participant and who gave a different answer to that of the group. The results showed that a break in unanimity, even when the answer was wrong, reduced conformity to around 5.5 per cent. Allen and Levine (1971) arranged for the 'supporter' to appear as if they had extremely poor vision. Even in such situations conformity was reduced though not quite as much as when the 'supporter' appears convincing.

- **Task difficulty** The more difficult the task, the greater the conformity. Linked to this is belief in one's competence. Research has found that those who perceive themselves as competent in a task conform less than others. Perrin and Spencer (1981) replicated Asch's experiment using British students who were studying engineering, maths and chemistry (they wanted to avoid students who might have been familiar with Asch's experiment). These students remained independent, reporting correct answers even though they faced a unanimous majority. In several hundred trials only one error was made. One possible explanation is that these students considered themselves to be competent. Engineering students in particular need to be precise when using lines.

Links

- Further evaluative points are dealt with under 'Ethical and methodological issues in studying social influence' on p143–6. These two general issues apply to much of the research in social influence.

- Norms are explained on p136.

Hint

Help yourself to remember information by making it relevant. Asch's research on the size of the majority suggests that if you want to influence someone you only need two supporters.

Link

One other interpretation of the results of this study is that it was conducted in the 1980s and that there was a change in the value placed on conformity. See p143.

AQA Examiner's tip

- Be economical with your learning! You can use the Perrin and Spencer study to illustrate more than one point: task difficulty and historical climate.

- In questions asking what factors tend to increase or decrease conformity, make sure that this is clearly stated in the answer, for example if a task is difficult, conformity is likely to increase. There is a tendency to simply identify the factor, for example task difficulty.

Hint

It is important to use the correct terminology. However, do not confuse anonymity with unanimity. Anonymity means that you cannot be identified. Unanimity means that all are in agreement/one mind (from *unus* meaning 'one' and *animus* meaning 'mind').

Social psychology

Key terms

Normative social influence: an explanation of conformity which is a result of people's need to be seen as part of the group and not going against the norms of the group. The individual wants to be liked and respected by the group.

Informational social influence: an explanation of conformity which is a result of people's need to be right. The individual turns to others in situations of uncertainty and conforms because others are thought to have more knowledge.

Compliance: a type of conformity: conforming to the majority but not really agreeing with them; public agreement but private disagreement.

Hints

- Normative influence contains the word 'norm'. The reason for conformity is to fit in with the norms – what is acceptable to that group.

- Informational influence contains the word 'information'. Because when we are unsure we look for information from others.

- **Self-esteem** Asch (1956) suggested that people with low self-esteem (few positive feelings about themselves) conform more than people with high self-esteem. This is possibly linked to a strong need for social approval.

- **Anonymity** When the incorrect majority called out their judgements but the single naïve participant wrote his down privately, conformity dropped to just over 12 per cent. This suggests that we are still influenced by others even when asked for our private views. An example of this is voting behaviour. Even though we can vote in private, our views may still be influenced by the media and our friends before reaching a decision. Campaigners are aware of this, which is why they use facts selectively to influence people's vote.

Why do people conform?

Asch's research has revealed two main explanations for conformity: **normative social influence** and **informational social influence**. (Deutsch and Gerard, 1955).

Normative social influence

Normative social influence occurs when people conform because of the very powerful need for social approval and acceptance; to be liked and respected by others in the group and to avoid rejection. The group is seen as powerful and important to the individual. Normative social influence results in public agreement but is not likely to change private opinion. Normative social influence was probably the main reason for conformity in Asch's experiment. After the experiment participants said that they wanted to please the experimenter, did not want to be different, look stupid and stand out. They were responding to group norms. This type of conformity is known as **compliance.** Because the conformity is only superficial, the change in opinion or behaviour lasts only as long as the group pressure itself.

Informational social influence

People conform because they believe that the group knows better; that the group has more knowledge, expertise or evidence. People are motivated by the need to be right; to feel confident that what they perceive, feel and believe is right. Informational social influence comes into play when people are uncertain and was probably partially responsible for the effect Sherif (1936) found in his autokinetic studies. It was an ambiguous situation, the effect was an illusion and participants were uncertain. Informational social influence tends to result in private agreement with the group as well as public agreement with the group. This type of conformity is known as internalisation; incorporating or taking in others' attitudes, values or beliefs; agreeing with the group privately as well as publicly. Because the new norms are internalised, this type of conformity persists even when group pressure is removed.

A two-part study by Baron based in more realistic settings than Sherif's and Asch's demonstrates both informational and normative social influence (Baron, Vandello and Brunsman, 1996).

Research study: Baron, Vandello and Brunsman (1996)

Aim: To investigate if conformity would increase when being right is important.

Method: The participants were students from Iowa University. There were two stooges and one naïve participant in each group.

Particpants were shown a slide of a stimulus person (suspect) followed by a slide of a four person line-up. The task was to identify the 'suspect' in the line-up. One group of participants was told that their results were very important (of scientific value) and another group was told that their results were not particularly important (just a pilot study). This was an independent groups design and the independent variable was whether or not the results were believed to be of importance.

The task was made difficult by giving all participants one second only in which to view the line-up and then identify the suspect. This was done in a group situation with the two stooges giving the wrong answer.

In a follow-up study with different participants, the task was exactly the same but this time the task was made easy by giving all participants five seconds to view the line-up and then identify the suspect.

Results: In the first part of the study, where the task was difficult, the error rate was 51 per cent for those who believed that the task was important and 35 per cent for those who believed it was unimportant.

In the follow-up, where the task was easy, the error rate was only 16 per cent when the task was believed to be important and 33 per cent (similar to Asch's findings) when it was believed to be unimportant.

Conclusion: When we are unsure what is correct (difficult task) and being right matters, we look to others for guidance. Thus the first part of the study demonstrates informational influence.

When the task is easy but accuracy is not important, it is better to be wrong than risk social disapproval. The follow-up demonstrates normative social influence.

Evaluation: One obvious ethical issue raised by this study is deception. Furthermore the participants were all students so it is not possible to generalise to a non-student population from such a biased sample. However all variables were carefully operationalised; conformity was measured by percentage error and task difficulty was operationalised by the number of seconds of viewing time.

Key points:

- Conformity involves a change in behaviour due to group pressure.

- Sherif investigated whether people are influenced by others in a task where the answer is not clear. Asch's study looked at conformity in a situation where the answer was obvious.

- Asch carried out variations to his basic study. He investigated factors that may affect levels of conformity such as group size and unanimity.

- Deutsch and Gerard have identified two main reasons for conformity: informational social influence and normative social influence.

- Two types of conformity are internalisation and compliance. Compliance can be linked to normative social influence and internalisation can be linked to informational social influence.

Social psychology

Summary questions

5 Identify a key feature of conformity.

6 In Sherif's study, how did the participants' group estimates differ from their individual estimates?

7 Identify two factors that can affect the level of conformity.

8 Outline one reason for conformity in Asch's experiment. Explain your answer.

9 What is the difference between 'compliance' and 'internalisation'?

10 Ed is a member of a team of six experts who are judging an art exhibition. He favours a landscape painting for first prize but the others all favour an abstract painting. Using your knowledge of psychology, explain why he might conform.

Obedience and defiance of authority

Learning objectives:

- Know and understand how situational factors affect obedience to authority.

- Explain why people obey.

- Explain why people defy authority.

Key term

Obedience to authority: a type of social influence where someone acts in response to a direct order from authority.

Fig. 5 *Milgram's electric shock generator*

Social psychology

138

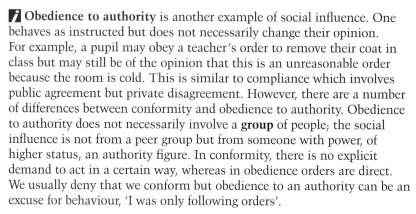

Obedience to authority is another example of social influence. One behaves as instructed but does not necessarily change their opinion. For example, a pupil may obey a teacher's order to remove their coat in class but may still be of the opinion that this is an unreasonable order because the room is cold. This is similar to compliance which involves public agreement but private disagreement. However, there are a number of differences between conformity and obedience to authority. Obedience to authority does not necessarily involve a **group** of people; the social influence is not from a peer group but from someone with power, of higher status, an authority figure. In conformity, there is no explicit demand to act in a certain way, whereas in obedience orders are direct. We usually deny that we conform but obedience to an authority can be an excuse for behaviour, 'I was only following orders'.

Obedience to an authority figure is generally desirable. As in conformity, this form of social influence helps society run smoothly. However, there are also many cases of obedience to an unjust authority figure, the outcome of which may be disastrous, for example the Holocaust and the killings of innocent women and children under military orders in My Lai, Vietnam. It was the events during the Second World War in Nazi Germany which prompted Milgram's famous but controversial experiments into obedience to authority. Adolph Eichmann, a Nazi war criminal, had recently been sentenced to death for his part in the Holocaust. His defence was that he was simply 'obeying orders'. Certainly he and others on trial did not appear to be 'evil' men. Eichmann was described as dull, ordinary, sane and normal in personal relationships. It was this 'banality of evil' which intrigued Milgram. Is obedience to a destructive authority something we are all capable of?

Research study: Milgram (1963)

Aim: To investigate how far people would be prepared to go in obeying an authority figure.

Method: Forty men aged 20 to 50, from a range of occupations, volunteered to take part in a study on learning and memory. The study took place at Yale University. On arriving at the psychology department, the participant was greeted by the experimenter who was always dressed in a grey lab coat. The participant was paid and then introduced to another 'participant' who was really a stooge. They were told that the experiment was concerned with the effects of punishment on learning and that they would draw lots to decide who would be the teacher and who would be the learner. In fact the draw was fixed and the participant was always the teacher.

The participant watched as the learner was strapped into a chair, attached to electrodes linked to a shock generator and given a mild sample shock. The learner complained of a slight heart condition but was assured that although the shocks may be painful they would not be harmful.

The teacher was then taken to another room and seated in front of a shock generator. The shocks ranged from 15 volts to 450 volts in 15-volt intervals. There were verbal descriptors beneath some of the shocks such as 255 'intense shock' and 375 'danger: severe shock'. The job of the teacher was to test the learner on word pairs and every time a mistake was made to deliver a shock beginning at 15 volts and moving one level higher as necessary. The teacher was given a sample 45-volt shock before the study started.

The learner did not really receive any shocks but just acted as if he did. At 315 volts the teacher let out a violent scream and at 330 volts there was complete silence. If the teacher hestiated in giving a shock, the experimenter had a list of verbal prods which could be used such as 'the experiment requires that you continue'.

Results: Before the study, Milgram asked staff, psychiatrists and students to predict how many of the participants would continue to the final 450 volts. The prediction was that most particiants would refuse after 150 volts and less than one percent would go up to 450 volts. The results were that all participants went as far as 300 volts and 65 per cent continued to the end.

Conclusion: Ordinary people are capable of following orders even if these could result in killing another person.

Evaluation: This study is well known for the ethical issues it raises: deception, protection of participants and the right to withdraw. These as well as several methodological concerns are discussed in detail under 'Ethical and methodological issues'.

💡 Situational factors affecting obedience to authority

In order to find out why obedience levels were so high, Milgram conducted several variations to the basic experiment:

- **Location** Many participants reported that they continued to deliver shocks because the research was carried out at a prestigious university. Milgram moved the experiment to a run-down inner-city office building. Obedience dropped to 47.5 per cent. This suggests that location played some part in levels of obedience but was not a crucial factor.
- **Proximity of the victim (learner)** The learner was in the same room as the teacher at a distance of one and a half feet. The obedience rate dropped to 40 per cent. When the teacher was required to force the learner's hand down onto the shock plate, the obedience rate dropped to 30 per cent. The more direct the person's experience with the victim the less they obey. However, although there is a drop in obedience, it is still high considering the amount of information available to the participant.
- **Proximity of the authority figure** The experimenter left the room and instructions were given by telephone. Obedience dropped to 20.5 per cent. In some cases the participant either pretended to give a shock or gave a lower one.
- **Social support** The participant was a member of a team of three 'teachers'. The other two teachers were in fact stooges. The real participant delivered the shocks and the other two teachers read out the list of word-pairs and informed the participant if the answer was correct. At 150 volts one of the stooge teachers refused to continue and at 210 volts the other stooge teacher also refused. Obedience dropped to 10 per cent.

Link

Predictions that few people would go to the final level demonstrate the fundamental attribution error; over-estimating the role of personal characteristics and under-estimating the role of situational factors. See p154.

Hint

This study can be quite confusing. The real participant is the teacher and the stooge is always the learner. Sometimes these terms are used interchangeably depending on the context.

Proximity means closeness. In the above context; how close the victim is to the participant or teacher.

Social psychology

■ **A peer administers the shock** The participant was paired with a stooge teacher who delivered the shock. The participant had to read the word pairs and informed the stooge teacher whether or not to administer a shock. Obedience rose to 92.5 per cent.

■ Why do people obey?

Personal responsibility

Milgram suggested that when we are obeying the wishes of authority, we feel less responsible for our own actions. We are in the **agentic state**; acting as 'agents' of the authority figure. Obedience levels therefore are high. This effect is clear in Milgram's studies. When the participant asked the experimenter who would take responsibility for any harm done to the learner, he was reassured that the responsibility was the experimenter's. In such instances, the participant would usually continue to deliver shocks. When the participant had peer support and the peer administered the shock, obedience was very high. The participant felt even less responsible. When the experimenter left the room, the participant felt more responsible for his actions. It was harder to act against conscience so obedience levels dropped. The participant was now in the **autonomous state**. The agentic state can be seen in everyday situations, for example when people claim that they are not responsible for their actions; that they are merely 'following orders'.

Perception of a legitimate authority and legitimate orders

🛈 Milgram maintained that for a group to function effectively, individuals must defer to those of higher status in the group hierarchy. From an early age we are socialised to recognise the authority of people like our parents and teachers. These people are seen as legitimate or justified authorities and we accept that they have the right to tell us what to do. The experimenter at a prestigious university was accepted as legitimate. His impersonal prods and grey laboratory coat were additional reminders of his position and authority. Bickman (1974) also demonstrated the power of a uniform. When an experimenter was dressed in the uniform of a guard and told passers-by to pick up paper bags or give a coin to a motorist wanting to park, there was 80 per cent obedience compared with 40 per cent when the experimenter was not in uniform. However, the orders given by the authority figure must also be seen as justified. In Milgram's experiment the order to continue to shock the learner was accepted as justified as it was given by an experimenter in the pursuit of scientific knowledge. When Milgram ran his study away from Yale University, obedience rates were lower.

Social norms

By responding to the advertisement, agreeing to the study and accepting payment at the start, the participant had agreed to a social contract. This implied contract was to continue until completion and is a very strong social norm. This was made more difficult by the gradual increase in shock level; once started, when does one stop? Moreover the participant was well aware of his social role, that of a participant, and the experimenter's, as the person in charge. Disobedience would mean breaking the social norm of being polite to the authority figure and effectively accusing him of being immoral. According to Milgram, social norms and roles produce obedience not just in his experiment but obedience in general.

■ Key terms

Agentic state: lacking a sense of personal responsibility and feeling under the control of an authority figure.

Autonomous state: taking control of one's own behaviour; feeling responsible for and aware of the consequences of the behaviour.

Dispositional explanations of obedience to authority

The above factors focus on situational factors in obedience to authority. Milgram did not think that an 'obedient personality character' exists. Anyone can carry out orders if they feel that the authority is legitimate. However Adorno published a book in 1950 which aimed to explain the psychological basis of prejudice. This book also provided some insight into a possible dispositional explanation of obedience to authority.

Questionnaires were devised to measure prejudice and other characteristics of an individual. The findings from these questionnaires supported the idea of an authoritarian personality. Such a person is characterised by:

- hostility to people perceived to be of lower status
- respect for people perceived to be of higher status
- a preoccupation with power
- blind respect for authority.

The authoritarian personality is believed to result from harsh parenting, including punishment for disobedience. In Milgram's experiment, those who gave the highest shock level did tend to have stronger authoritarian characters and were more likely to blame the learner rather than themselves for the obedience. Crutchfield (1955) published the findings of a study into conformity which also lend support to the authoritarian personality explanation. His participants were military and business people who were on an assessment course but became unknowing participants in his research. He tested personality factors as well as conformity. One finding was that conformers tend to have authoritarian views and are generally submissive. As obedience to authority involves compliance to social roles, this explains the link between personality, conformity and obedience. Privately the participant may disagree with the order to deliver a shock but publicly, in the role of the willing and submissive participant, he does as he is told.

Explanations of defiance of authority

During the Second World War in the French village of Le Chambon, Jews destined for deportation to Germany were being sheltered by villagers who quite openly defied orders to co-operate with the new regime. These villagers remained defiant throughout the war. Such stories of defiance to authority are less common than those of obedience but, like empirical studies, are of interest because they contain some clues into why this happens.

Research study: Gamson et al. (1982)

Aim: To investigate whether groups of people would defy an unjust authority.

Method: A fictitious human relations company, supposedly collecting information on community standards, asked groups of participants to discuss the case of a petrol station manager. The groups were told that the manager had recently been sacked by the oil company who employed him because he was living with a woman to whom he was not married. Consequently he was suing the company. The participants were told that the discussion would be video-taped. During the discussion, the coordinator came in, switched off the camera and ordered some of the group members to argue as if offended by the manager's moral behaviour. The camera was then switched on again. This was repeated several times for more group

AQA Examiner's tip

- There is often a temptation to describe the Milgram study in almost any question on obedience. Read the question carefully. A question on 'why do people obey' does not require a description of the study. You can, of course, refer to aspects of the study to illustrate a point, for example the grey lab coat.

- If asked to describe a study of obedience to authority, you may prefer not to select Milgram as it is detailed. Bickman's study and Hofling's described later on in the chapter are both acceptable. Zimbardo's study is not a study of obedience to authority.

Hint

A dispositional explanation is just another way of saying a personality explanation. In other words, are there any aspects of your personality which make you more likely to obey?

Link

Although this type of personality is generally considered as one of the explanations of prejudice, some the features of this personality are considered a predisposing factor in obedience to authority. See also 'Authoritarian personality' under 'Prejudice' in Chapter 6, p165.

Social psychology

■ Hint

Defiance of authority is quite simply rebellion. Other terms you may come across are resistance and disobedience.

AQA Examiner's tip

■ Remember that Milgram identified several factors which reduce obedience to authority such as when the authority seems less than legitimate, or the victim is in close proximity, etc. These too can be discussed if asked for explanations of defiance of authority.

■ If asked to describe a study of defiance to authority, you can use Milgram's variation 'social support'.

💡 Summary questions

11 Identify one difference between conformity and obedience to authority.

12 Outline the role of the teacher in Milgram's experiment.

13 Which of Milgram's variations produced the highest level of obedience? Explain why the obedience levels were so high.

14 Distinguish between a situational and dispositional explanation of obedience to authority. Give an example of each.

15 A group of protesters is fixing a banner to the top of a tall crane. A plain-clothes policeman on the ground uses a loudhailer to order them to stop and come down but the protestors refuse. Use your knowledge of psychology to explain why the protestors defy the order.

members. The individuals were also asked to sign an agreement so that the discussion could be used as evidence in a court case.

Results: In 16 of 33 groups everyone rebelled. In nine groups the majority rebelled and in the remaining eight groups a minority rebelled.

Conclusion: Support can help people defy authority.

Evaluation: By studying the effects of increasingly unreasonable orders in an everyday setting, the study avoids the criticism that results cannot be generalised to real situations (though of course one may not be able to generalise to situations quite different to this setting). The major problem is the ethical issues related to this study. Many participants reported high levels of stress and anxiety. As a result, the researchers had to stop after 33 groups had discussed the case though they had planned to run 80 discussion groups.

■ **Social support** In both the key study and Le Chambon, people supported one another, were able to share information and received social support. Milgram also found that when two stooge teachers resisted authority, the participant was more likely to disobey than when facing the authority figure alone.

■ **Role models** When ordered by police to give a list of sheltered Jews, the local pastor modelled defiance by openly refusing. Milgram's stooge teachers acted as models of defiance when they refused to continue with the study. Modelling occurred in Gamson's study. Within each group, it just needed one person to rebel and the rest gradually followed.

■ **Personal experience including education** The villagers' ancestors had themselves been persecuted and church leaders preached resistance to destructive obedience. One of Milgram's participants had experienced a concentration camp and refused to obey after 210 volts because she felt responsible for own behaviour. In Gamson's study, a participant explained his disobedience because of knowledge of Milgram's work.

■ **Questioning motives** In the Gamson study, people began to question the motives of the people in authority. By contrast, Milgram's study was accepted as being of scientific value from the start.

■ **Loss of freedom** In Gamson's study participants felt manipulated and controlled. According to Brehm, we believe that we have freedom of choice and if this is threatened, we disobey to restore our sense of freedom.

Key points:

■ Milgram claimed that we all have the potential to obey destructive orders.

■ Obedience is affected by the proximity and legitimacy of the authority figure, the proximity of the victim and the social support available.

■ There are several explanations for obedience to authority: whether or not the person feels responsible for the consequences of obeying an order, the perceived legitimacy of the authority figure and order, the role of social norms and personality.

■ Obedience can be resisted. This is more likely to occur if people have social support, exposure to disobedient models, knowledge and/or experience of the effects of obedience and question the motive of the authority figure.

Ethical and methodological issues in studying social influence

Learning objectives:

- Evaluate the methodological and ethical issues in studying social influence.

- Understand why ethical and methodological issues are interdependent.

Link

Key features of the experiment are the manipulation and control of variables, preferably in laboratory conditions. See Chapter 4, Research methods, for more information.

Key terms

External validity: whether the findings of a study can be generalised to situations and people other than those in the study, for example other populations, locations, times.

Ecological validity: a specific type of external validity referring to generalisations beyond the immediate setting to the real world.

Internal validity: whether observed effects (measures of dependant variables) are due to the manipulation of the IV.

Individualistic culture: where people prioritise standing out as an individual over fitting in as a group member, for example UK, USA.

Collectivist culture: where people prioritise group loyalty, belonging and fitting into a group over standing out as an individual, for example India, Brazil.

The study of social influence uses the scientific method to investigate how individuals are influenced by the actual or imagined presence of others. Experimentation is the preferred method as this is the best way to study cause and effect. Experiments, however, raise important ethical and methodological issues.

Methodological issues

Methodological issues involve **external validity**, **ecological validity** and **internal validity**.

External validity

Asch's participants were his students, all American males. Findings from such a biased and unrepresentative sample cannot be generalised to other populations. Conformity has been found to be higher in non-student populations and some research findings have suggested that females conform more than males. This, however, is not a consistent finding and can generally be explained by the type of conformity task used (Sistrunk and McDavid, 1971).

Would similar findings be obtained in other cultures and historical periods? These are important questions when considering the validity of the original findings. North America is an example of an **individualistic culture**. In Asch type replications, the percentage of errors made is lower in the studies done in individualistic cultures than in studies done in **collectivist cultures** (Smith and Harris Bond, 1993).

The lowest rate of conformity, 14 per cent, was found with Belgian students (Doms, 1983) and the highest, 58 per cent, with Indian teachers in Fiji (Chandra, 1973).

Asch's studies were carried out during the Cold War. This period in America was characterised by witch hunts for anyone who behaved in an anti-American way. It was sensible to conform; any deviance from expected behaviour and values could result in accusations of Communism. In 1974, Larsen replicated Asch's experiment with American students and did find lower rates of conformity.

Milgram's research was also criticised for its unrepresentative sample and questionable cross-cultural replicability. Participants were a cross-section of men aged 20 to 50 from New Haven, a small though typical American town. Unlike Asch, he later tested women and found similar levels of obedience. Studies in different countries have produced various rates of obedience, but comparisons are difficult to make because methodological procedures differed, for example a study in Holland (Meeus and Raaijmakers, 1986) showed 92 per cent obedience but electric shocks were not used. Instead the participant, conducting a job interview, had to harass and criticise their interviewee.

Ecological validity

Asch's use of line judging and Sherif's illusion are trivial and artificial tasks which bear little if any relevance to everyday life. However, Asch

Link

Demand characteristics are explained in Chapter 4, Research methods, p88.

Hint

■ It may help to remember what ecological validity means if you consider that ecology is the study of things in the natural environment.

■ The more control there is in an experiment, the less its ecological validity.

■ Participants adjust their behaviour to what they think are the 'demands' of the study (demand characteristics).

AQA   Examiner's tip

It is useful to get into the habit of making a list of evaluative points for each 'major' study covered.

Link

There are number of ethical principles relevant to social influence: use of deception, respect for privacy, informed consent, debriefing and protection from harm. There can be a trade-off between these and validity. See Chapter 4, Research methods, for more information.

deliberately chose an unambiguous task because he wanted to measure pure conformity. Critics have argued that Milgram's experiment does not reflect real life; participants carried out a task they were unlikely to come across in real life. Any obedience might simply have been due to demand characteristics. However Bickman's field study of obedience produced similar findings on obedience to Milgram in a more realistic setting. A 'real life' study on obedience to authority also produced high levels of obedience (Hofling, 1966). An unknown doctor telephoned nurses working in several American hospitals and ordered them to give a patient 20 mg of a drug. The maximum dose of 10 mg was clearly labelled on the bottle. 21 of the 22 nurses began to prepare the drug (actually a harmless tablet). Milgram believed that the psychological processes in obedience are essentially the same irrespective of whether the setting is artificial as in the laboratory or naturally occurring.

Internal validity

Critics claim that in a number of experiments participants were displaying demand characteristics. Some of Asch's participants did say that they gave the wrong answer and conformed because they did not want to spoil the experiment or upset the experimenter. In Sherif's study where the task is ambiguous, participants may appear to be conforming but are in fact responding to demand characteristics (others' behaviour). It has been argued that Milgram's participants were not convinced by the experimental set-up and merely obeyed because of demand characteristics. This is unlikely; all participants were given a sample shock and suffered from varying degrees of stress. Bickman's and Hofling's participants were not even aware that an experiment was taking place.

■ Ethical issues

As researchers, psychologists studying social influence confront important ethical issues:

■ How will the participant be used in the research and can this be justified, for example can deception be justified?

■ Is the research important and of value, outweighing any harm done? It is difficult to assess the importance of research; often such judgements are made on the basis of the findings.

To guide researchers, national societies have established a set of ethical principles. In the UK, the British Psychological Society (BPS) has developed a code of ethics based on these principles. These relate to what is acceptable in pursuit of scientific goals.

Use of deception

The principle states that (assuming the research is of importance) intentional deception of the participants over the general nature of the investigation should be avoided wherever possible. Asch and Milgram deceived their participants about the purpose of the study and the role of other participants. Sherif and Gamson also deceived their participants about the purpose of the study. However, without deception the aim of these studies could not be achieved and internal validity would have been compromised. Some psychologists have suggested role playing or simulations to avoid deception, but the potential costs of these approaches need to be weighed up against the potential benefits of experiments using deception. According to Hogg and Vaughan (2005), some deception is 'essential to preserve the scientific rigour of much experimental social psychology'.

Respect for privacy

It is sometimes difficult to decide whether the research topic justifies invasion of privacy. Hofling's and Bickman's participants did not know that they were part of a study. However both internal and ecological validity were strengthened.

Informed consent

Unless participants know the aim and procedure and are fully informed about the study including the right to withdraw, they cannot give informed consent. The deception in the above studies ruled out informed consent and Milgram's participants did not exercise their right to withdraw. On the contrary they were ordered to continue giving shocks. A way round the problem of informed consent is to obtain **presumptive consent**. Milgram did obtain this form of consent from his students and psychiatrists.

Debriefing

Debriefing allows the researcher to obtain informed consent retrospectively and put right any deception that took place. The deception and aims are explained and participants also have the right to withdraw their results. It is as if the participant never took part in the study in the first place. Milgram fully debriefed his participants. But it is questionable if debriefing puts right the deception and the guilt of knowing one was prepared to give electric shocks strong enough to kill a person. In Hofling's study, participants had to live with the realisation that they were prepared to break hospital rules and perhaps harm a patient.

Protection from harm

Participants should be fully debriefed so that they feel no worse about themselves after the study than they did before. Any possible harm should be no greater than in normal life.

Asch's participants suffered from stress. This was confirmed by physiological measures of arousal (Bogdonoff *et al.*, 1961). However, we frequently find ourselves in disagreement with others so any discomfort was nothing out of the ordinary. Milgram's participants suffered from stress; one even suffered from convulsions. However, all were debriefed; 84 per cent said that they were glad to have taken part and none suffered long-term emotional disturbances. Ethical objections were not raised when Milgram sought presumptive consent and no one, including Milgram himself, expected such 'shocking' results. Perhaps the study would not have attracted so much criticism had the results been different.

Is the research important and of value?

Sherif's and Asch's studies have shown that people will conform to implicit group pressure. Findings from studies on obedience to authority go against commonsense predictions, highlighting the power of authority figures and the capacity for ordinary people to carry out terrible deeds. Of course, not everyone accepts the findings as relevant to real-life phenomena and some argue that an obedience explanation for events such as the Holocaust can in itself constitute an ethical issue, misused as an alibi to those guilty of crimes against humanity (Mandel, 1998).

Key term

Presumptive consent: obtaining the views of other people about the acceptability of experimental procedures. If others feel that they are acceptable, then we can presume that the actual participants would have also consented.

Social psychology

AQA Examiner's tip

Do not forget in discussing ethical issues to present both sides of the argument, for example Milgram did deceive his participants but one could argue that he had no choice. Use terms such as 'however', 'but' and 'although' to flip from one side of the argument to the other.

Key points:

- Methodological issues include external, ecological and internal validity.

- The external validity of much research is low, but there is some evidence of high ecological and internal validity.

- There are a number of ethical issues raised by research into social influence: use of deception, respect for privacy, informed consent, debriefing and protection from harm.

- These issues have to be weighed up against a more fundamental issue; the value and importance of the work.

Summary questions

16 Identify two methodological issues in research into social influence.

17 Outline two ethical issues raised by one study into social influence.

18 Explain why it could be argued that Hofling's study is high in ecological and internal validity.

19 Briefly discuss the justification for deception in any one example of research into social influence.

End-of-chapter activity

You can investigate conformity yourself using the method similar to that devised by Asch (1951). Asch asked his participants to judge which one of three comparison lines was the same length as a standard line. Some participants carried out this task individually and other participants carried out this task in groups consisting of about six stooges, all of whom gave the same wrong answer on two-thirds of the trials. Asch compared the number of errors of judgement in each condition to find out if the 'naïve' participant was influenced by the views of other group members. You should not use real stooges in your practical but instead you could create a sheet of made-up responses to a similar task. In order to carry out your experiment you will need to think about which experimental design to use, the controls you will need to put in place and how to adapt it so as not to involve a live group. You should also consider issues around consent, deception, briefing and debriefing.

1   (a)   (i)   Identify two factors that psychologists have suggested result in obedience.   *(2 marks)*

           (ii)   Identify one different factor which usually results in defiance of authority.   *(1 mark)*

     (b)   In the context of social facilitation, explain the relationship between performance and dominant response.   *(3 marks)*

     (c)   Identify one factor which, according to Asch, might influence whether or not a person conforms with a group norm. Explain why this factor tends to increase or decrease conformity.   *(4 marks)*

     (d)   Describe and discuss ethical and methodological issues that have arisen in empirical studies of obedience.   *(10 marks)*

2   (a)   In a study of conformity participants were asked to estimate the number of sweets in a jar. Half of the sample wrote the estimate on a clean sheet of paper. The other half filled in sheets of paper on which six fictitious estimates ranging from 231 to 267 sweets had already been placed. The participant had to fill in the last blank space.

           (i)   Explain how the researcher would use the results from the two groups to investigate whether or not conformity had taken place.   *(4 marks)*

           (ii)   Explain why a study carried out as described above may be said to lack ecological validity.   *(2 marks)*

     (b)   Evaluation apprehension is one factor that can affect the performance of a soloist. Using an example, explain what is meant by evaluation apprehension.   *(4 marks)*

     (c)   Describe and discuss at least two factors that, according to Milgram, influence the likelihood of a person obeying an order.   *(10 marks)*

Impression formation

Learning objectives:

- Understand the psychological importance of impression formation.

- Know and understand factors that affect impression formation.

- Know and understand the psychological explanations for these factors.

- Describe and evaluate research that has been carried out into impression formation.

Key terms

Impression formation: the process by which a general impression of another person is made. Such impressions are based on limited information and are used to produce expectations about the individual.

Social schema: a schema is an organised set of ideas about something. It is a hypothetical and mental representation. A social schema is a schema about people and social events.

We live in a social world and spend time in other people's company, whether it is the family, friends or simply daily encounters. Just as we try to make sense of our physical world, we also try to make sense of our social world. This is not based on passive observations. We actively use the information available to us to try to understand and draw conclusions about others' behaviour. The process by which we develop ideas about what people are like is called **impression formation**. This is important to us. Impressions affect how we feel about others, how we might act towards them and how we think they might act towards us. This gives some feeling of control over what is going on in our social world, making it more predictable and safe.

Impression formation is particularly important when meeting someone for the first time. We make judgements based on what is available to the senses, such as how the person looks (for example, expression, facial features). Other senses are also important; we may attend to how the person 'sounds', for example softly spoken, or smells, for example body odour. These various bits and pieces of information are quickly integrated into a general impression such as whether or not they are trustworthy. We receive an enormous amount of information yet such judgements have to be quick in order to predict their behaviour and know how to respond. How are we able to arrive at such quick judgements?

🔐 Factors affecting impression formation

A very important factor in the general impression of another person is a **social schema**.

Social schemas

Whenever we first meet a person, we compare the incoming information we receive with our memories of previous experiences with similar people. Such memory structures or representations are known as social schemas. Certain cues activate a schema. The schema then fills in the missing details. For example, if you meet someone who is dressed 'loudly', you might use the extrovert schema and infer that they are also impulsive and sociable.

Fig. 1 *First impressions*

Schemas simplify the social world because they:

- help interpret the flow of information reaching the senses
- process and organise large amounts of information swiftly and economically
- help with the retrieval of information; schema consistent information is better remembered than schema inconsistent information
- quickly enable the individual to know what to expect in social situations and guide behaviour.

There are many types of social schema; all influence the encoding of new information, memory of old information and inferences about missing information. Fiske and Taylor (1991) have identified a number of social schemas:

- **Person schemas** These contain knowledge about specific individuals, for example the prime minister or a best friend. These are likely to include stereotypes, such as politicians are liars. Such a schema may alert one not to trust a politician.
- **Role schemas** These are knowledge structures about role occupants, for example doctors are allowed to ask personal questions as long as they relate to health. These too are likely to contain stereotypes, for example doctors are caring. Such schemas lead to expectations from people in these roles.
- **Event schemas** These are sometimes referred to as 'scripts' and contain knowledge of the sequence of events in social situations, for example a script for going to a rock concert may contain facts such as buying a ticket beforehand, turning up early to get a good place at the front, singing, clapping, dancing when appropriate. Such knowledge guides behaviour and makes it easier to cope.
- **Self schema** This contains self-concepts stored in memory, for example I am intelligent, politically aware. Such a schema might enable a person to decide whether to stand as a candidate for local government.

Research confirms that schemas help us to process information. If participants are explicitly told to remember as much information as they can about a person, they actually remember less than if they are simply told to form an impression (Hamilton, 1979).

Social schemas operate on 'top-down' or concept-driven processing. This means that we rely on prior knowledge rather than seek information directly from the immediate context. Without schemas we would be overwhelmed by the information that inundates us. However, such 'cognitive economy' leads to problems.

- Schemas are an over-simplified representation of reality.
- Crucial information may be overlooked.
- Information consistent with a schema is stored but inconsistent information is forgotten.
- Schemas go beyond the information given and 'fill in the gaps' leading to incorrect judgements of and facts about people and situations, for example after reading a story about a character going to a restaurant, participants recalled statements about a character paying for a meal though this was never mentioned (Bower, Black and Turner, 1979).

Hint

An inference is like a guess. It is based on the information you receive. In other words, you are guessing that if someone is loudly dressed (information received) then they are also impulsive, sociable, etc.

Link

Note the information-processing approach to social cognition: encoding, storage and retrieval of information. See Chapter 1, Key approaches.

Hint

Consider the following question. When teaching a pupil for the first time, does the teacher form an impression based on facts; how they are actually working, behaving, etc. (information from the immediate context) or use prior knowledge, for example stereotypes, what their brother was like, where they live and their parents' profession?

Social psychology

■ Links

Gregory's theory of visual perception is a top-down theory stating that our perceptions of the world are hypotheses based on previously stored information. In eyewitness reliability, Bartlett refers to active constructive memory and one theory of face recognition, holistic theory, also takes a top-down approach.

A prejudice is a biased attitude, often based on stereotypes. Such an attitude can lead to prejudiced behaviour (discrimination). See 'Prejudice', p163.

AQA **Examiner's tip**

Prepare for a question on 'Describe a study investigating social schemas'. Take either the Bower *et al.* (1979) study or the Hamilton (1979) reference and organise that information under: aim, method, results and conclusion. You will need to work out the aim and conclusion.

■ Key terms

Stereotype: a widely shared and simplified belief that all members of a particular group share certain important characteristics, for example that Germans are hard-working.

Central trait: a personal trait or characteristic that strongly influences a perceiver's overall impression of someone possessing that trait.

■ Hint

A trait is an adjective describing any lasting personal characteristic that a person might have, for example, a trait of impulsiveness. This might be used to explain consistencies in behaviour, such as careless spending. It can also be used to describe any inherited characteristic such as eye colour.

Stereotyping

Impressions of people are also strongly influenced by **stereotypes**. In a way, these are schemas about groups of people but are more culturally determined than either person or role schemas. Whereas person schemas contain information about the individual characteristics of a person, stereotypes ignore individual characteristics and a person is assumed to possess traits which are typical of a certain social category. Furthermore stereotypes are often negative.

Typical stereotypes include gender, race, age, occupation and physical appearance. We cannot take every person we come across and study them in detail as an individual, so we categorise people into groups. These snap judgements also guide our behaviour, for example a taxi driver on a Friday night in town if given a choice is more likely to pick up a middle-aged couple than a couple of youths.

We have expectations as to which characteristics are consistent with a stereotype. Haire and Grune (1950) found that people given information consistent with the stereotype of a 'working man' had no problem putting all the information together to compose a paragraph about him. However there was one piece of information that they found difficult to include; the fact that he was 'intelligent'. Either they ignored the information altogether or distorted it, for example promoting the man from a worker to a supervisor.

Central traits

According to Asch (1946), certain traits are more important in forming impressions of people than are other traits. These traits tend to be evaluative rather then descriptive. For example, it is of more use to know that the person who is about to move into the house next door is a 'warm' person than that they are 'tall'. Such traits are known as **central traits**.

Traits that have an insignificant influence on final impressions are known as peripheral traits.

Research study: Asch (1946)

Aim: To investigate whether certain traits are influential in shaping a general impression of people.

Method: The design was an independent groups design. There were four groups of participants.

Group A was given a list of adjectives decribing a fictitious person: intelligent, skilful, industrious, warm, determined, practical, cautious. Group B had the same list only the word 'warm' was replaced by the word 'cold'. For groups C and D the word 'warm' was replaced by either the word 'polite' or 'blunt'.

Participants in all the groups were given a list of traits such as generous, reliable, serious, wise and happy. They had to indicate which of these would also apply to the 'person'.

Results: Participants given the traits 'warm' and 'cold' made extreme judgements, for example 91 per cent in group A judged the person to be also generous compared with 8 per cent in group B. No differences were found between groups C 56 per cent and D 58 per cent.

Conclusion: 'Warm' and 'cold' are central traits which influence general impressions of people. Traits such as 'polite' and 'blunt' are peripheral and do not have this effect.

Evaluation: This study lacks ecological validity. There is limited information about the person and normally we respond to a 'real' person in an everyday situation. Even if one needs to form an impression of someone from a written source, for example an application form, this contains more than just a list of traits.

Research carried out in more naturalistic settings support those of Asch. In a study by Kelley (1950), students were informed that they were going to be taught by a guest lecturer whom they did not know. The students were all given a biographical sketch of the lecturer before class, including that either he was 'warm' or 'cold'. The students who had been told that he was warm before meeting him rated him more favourably after class and also took more part in class discussion than those who were told that he was 'cold'. This study was more realistic and allowed the students to interact. Even so, this study also deals with impression formation over a short period of time. There is no relationship with the person and no further contact takes place.

Primacy and recency effects

Our first impressions of others are influential simply because they are the first. This tendency is known as the **primacy effect**. This relates back to the earlier point about 'cognitive economy'. A schema is quickly constructed about a person and this affects information attended to; people pay less attention to subsequent contradictory information. Information which does not fit the schema tends to be ignored; this is preferable to changing a schema. For example, a person at an interview starts confidently, giving long answers, smiling and making eye contact. The impression made is that of a suitable candidate for the job. As the interview progresses, the interviewee begins to look tense, looks down at the floor and answers are shorter. It is much easier to discount this later information on the grounds that the person must now be tired than to change the schema already formed. Negative first impressions in particular are difficult to change. This is because we are biased towards negativity; we pay more importance to it because it signifies potential danger. Its detection has survival value for the individual and the species.

> **Key term**
>
> **Primacy effect:** information we are provided with first about a person has the most influence on the impression that is formed of the person. First impressions tend to be long lasting.

Research study: Asch (1946)

Aim: To investigate whether the order in which information about a person was presented influenced the judgements others made of the person.

Method: Two groups of participants were presented with lists of six adjectives describing another person. The independent variable was manipulated by changing the word order in the two conditions.

Group A were presented with the list of positive adjectives first: intelligent, industrious, impulsive, critical, stubborn, envious.

Group B were presented with the same list, but the adjectives were in reverse order with the negative ones first, that is envious, stubborn, etc.

All participants were then asked to rate the person on a series of personality measures such as how honest, sociable and happy they thought the person was. The dependent variable – the judgement made of the person – was measured by the number of positive ratings on the personality measures.

Link

The independent variable is the variable that is directly manipulated by the researcher (word order) in order to see if it causes a change in the dependent variable – in this experiment the number of positive ratings. See Chapter 4, Research methods.

Link

The primacy and recency effects in relation to the multi-store model of memory are discussed in Chapter 7, Remembering and forgetting.

Key term

Recency effect: information we are provided with later about a person has the most influence on the impression that is formed of the person.

AQA Examiner's tip

- If asked how the primacy or recency effect might influence the perception of a person, do not discuss these in terms of memory. You will not gain any credit.

- Prepare for a question on how you might investigate the primacy effect in person perception. Design your own experiment, collect and analyse the results.

Results: Group A gave more positive ratings than group B.

Conclusion: The order of presentation influences judgements. Information presented first had more effect than later information.

Evaluation: The study was well controlled but the criticism levelled at this study is the same as that made of the earlier Asch study. Participants did not meet a real person but just read a description. People may behave differently in a real face-to-face situation. In fact in recent versions of this study, participants have complained that they do not have enough information on which to base a judgement.

A study which provided participants with more detailed information about a fictitious character, a young student by the name of Jim, also produced similar findings (Luchins, 1957). He presented students with two paragraphs about Jim. One made Jim sound like an extrovert and the other like an introvert. The two paragraphs could be combined to produce a short story about Jim. Some of the participants read the paragraph which presented Jim as an extrovert first and the others read the introvert paragraph first. There were also two control groups. They read one paragraph only; either the introvert or the extrovert description. These two groups could correctly recognise Jim as either an extrovert or introvert. Findings for the two experimental groups showed that findings for the first part of the description had more influence on the impression formed. Seventy-eight per cent of the participants who read the extrovert paragraph first judged Jim as friendly, whereas only 18 per cent who read the introvert description first judged him as friendly.

One could argue that this study was more ecologically valid. Jim was described in some detail and presented as a real character. However, he was still fictional and they did not actually meet him.

A **recency effect** occurs when later information has more of an impact than earlier information. Luchins found some evidence for the recency effect. If he left a time delay of 15 minutes between the two paragraphs then a recency effect was more likely. Other studies have found that if participants were first warned against jumping to conclusions when making their judgements, a recency effect was also possible (Hendrick and Constanini,1970). A primacy effect can also be reduced if people are warned about the biasing effect of first impressions and the need to attend to all the available information. However, primacy effects are more common with the clear implication that first impressions count.

Research study: Jones et al. (1968)

Aim: To investigate whether the recency effect would occur in a situation involving a person attempting to solve a series of problems.

Method: Participants watched a male student attempting to solve 30 difficult multiple-choice questions. Group 1 saw the student being successful near the beginning of the test and group 2 saw the student being successful towards the end of the test. The study was controlled so that in each condition the student solved exactly 15 out of 30 problems correctly. After the test, participants were asked to assess the student's general ability. It was predicted that participants in group 2 would consider the student more able because he got better as the test progressed whereas group 1would attribute the success simply to beginner's luck.

Results: Although it was arranged that the student solved the same number of problems correctly in each condition, he was judged more capable if the successes came mostly at the beginning of the series rather than towards the end. Moreover, when asked to judge how many problems the student got right, participants who saw the successes clustered at the beginning estimated an average of 21 whereas those who saw the successes towards the end estimated an average of 13.

Conclusion: The participants' impressions of the student's performance were influenced by how they started off rather than how they finished. The results therfore supported the primacy effect.

Evaluation: This study, unlike the Asch and Luchins studies, involves a real person rather than hypothetical people. However, to some extent it is still an artificial situation; there is no relationship with the 'student' and no further contact takes place.

Key points:

- Impression formation is a very rapid process and is based on limited information.
- There are several factors which affect impression formation: social schemas, stereotyping, central traits, primacy and recency effects.
- Social schemas determine how information is encoded and help to process new information quickly.
- Social schemas produce biases in our processing, for example stereotyping and the primacy effect.

AQA Examiner's tip

You may feel overwhelmed by the numerous studies in this section but do not worry about remembering the names of all of the researchers. It is quite acceptable when referring to evidence to state, 'A study investigating ... found ...' or 'A study was carried out ...'.

Social psychology

Summary questions

1 Give two reasons why impression formation is important in social situations.

2 Explain what is meant by a 'schema'.

3 Explain why people rely on schemas when forming impressions of others.

4 Suggest two reasons why the primacy effect occurs.

5 Evaluate any one study investigating impression formation. Include at least one strength of the study and one shortcoming.

6 Amy is going for a job interview. What advice might you give her to maximise her chances of getting the job? Refer to your knowledge of psychological studies of impression formation.

Attribution

Learning objectives:

- Understand what psychologists mean by 'attribution'.

- Understand the distinction between dispositional and situational attributions.

- Know and understand the most common attribution biases.

- Explain why attributions may be biased.

Key terms

Attribution: the process of giving a cause to our own behaviour and that of others.

Dispositional attribution: explaining a person's behaviour in terms of their personality (disposition); also known as an internal attribution – the cause is inside the person.

Situational attribution: explaining a person's behaviour in terms of the environment (situation); also known as an external attribution – the cause is outside the person.

Hint

Free will versus determinism: the parallel with external and internal attributions is that we are not seen to be responsible for behaviours that are not freely chosen (external attributions) but may be seen as responsible where dispositional attributions are made.

People constantly consider possible reasons as to why something has happened. If an accident occurs, for example a train crashes, people want to know why. This is important, because knowing a cause not only explains the past but allows a person to predict and control the future. Explaining why things happen in our social world is equally important (Heider, 1958). In particular, people want to find causes (**attributions**) for events that directly concern them, for example a failed job application. Was this due to the fact that the selection was a 'fix' or some incompetence demonstrated by the applicant? When we are not sure what has caused a behaviour (in this example, failure to get the job), we search for causes that seem appropriate. Being able to explain our social world; **why** we or others behaved as we did, is another example of the need to understand and control our social world.

Dispositional and situational attributions

Fritz Heider (1958) believed that people are intuitive or naïve psychologists. By this he means that people use rational, scientific-like, cause-effect analyses to understand their world. Because people believe that their own behaviour is not random but motivated (caused), they tend to look for reasons for other people's behaviour too in order to understand their motives. There are two types of attribution:

- **dispositional attributions**, also known as internal attributions. Here the cause of behaviour is based on a person's stable characteristics such as attitudes, personality or abilities

- **situational attributions**, also known as external attributions. These assign the cause of behaviour to the situation such as stimuli in the environment. For example, if a shopper in a supermarket runs into you with their trolley, you will either attribute the cause to their disposition, that they are careless (in that case you might well be annoyed!), or to the environment, that it is very busy and they were pushed.

In making a dispositional attribution you are in fact claiming that a person was responsible for the action. However, in making a situational attribution you are saying that the person is not responsible but that the situation was the cause of the behaviour.

Making the correct attribution is important. The type of attribution made has consequences for how responsible a person is seen to be for their actions. If someone makes a dispositional attribution for the cause of an accident, such as a car crash, they are in fact blaming someone.

Attribution biases

Our attempts to make an accurate and logical attribution are not always successful. Sometimes the attribution process is biased. In this section we are going to consider the most common biases: the fundamental attribution error, the actor–observer effect and the self-serving bias.

The fundamental attribution error

People tend to be biased in preferring dispositional to situational attributions even in the face of evidence to the contrary. We prefer to look for a 'stable' reason for behaviour and for explanations that are best able to predict and control the environment. People's dispositions or personalities, unlike situations, do not change so we are better able to predict behaviour. Furthermore we are 'cognitive misers'; it is much simpler to focus on an individual's behaviour and look for explanations relating to their personality rather than think of the numerous situational reasons. For example, we are more likely to think that a friend did not acknowledge our birthday because they are forgetful. Thinking about all the possible situational reasons, e.g. that they had no money for a card, or were pre-occupied with other events, is too complex. An observer rarely has such information about another person's circumstances. Over-emphasising internal dispositional causes is known as the **fundamental attribution error**.

Research study: Jones and Harris (1967)

Aim: To investigate whether participants took account of situational factors when judging the attitude of a writer toward Fidel Castro.

Method: Students read speeches about Fidel Castro (communist leader of Cuba at the time). The speeches were written by other students. The speeches were either pro-Castro or anti-Castro. The participants were informed either that the writer had freely chosen to write the speech or had been instructed to write the speech. The independent variable therefore was whether or not the writer had supposedly freely chosen to write the speech. The speech writer's attitude towards Castro was measured using an attitude scale.

Results: Where the writer had a choice, participants reasoned that those who had written a pro-Castro speech were in favour of Castro and that those who had written an anti-Castro speech were against Castro – an internal, dispositional attribution. However a dispositional attribution was also made when participants knew that the writer had been instructed to write the speech.

Conclusion: People prefer dispositional explanations even when there is clear evidence for a situational attribution to be made.

Evaluation: The use of speeches in assessing someone's attitude towards a person or issue is arguably a method high in mundane realism. In other words, it appears real (mundane) rather than artificial to participants. In everyday situations we often make judgements about people's attitudes to sensitive issues by what they write and say (though usually this is done through choice).

Key term

Fundamental attribution error: a bias in attributing another's behaviour to internal/dispositional causes rather than to situational causes.

Link

Milgram's study of obedience to authority, p138. Predictions before the study were that very few people would administer the final shock because such unprincipled personalities were rare. What people ignored in their predictions was the power of social situations.

Social psychology

The fundamental attribution error can be observed in everyday situations. For example, there is a tendency to attribute road accidents to the driver rather than the vehicle or road conditions, and failing standards in schools to teachers rather than class size, lack of support from parents and government, etc. However, if people focus on the situation to find out about people's behaviour, then a situational attribution is more likely to be made.

There are cultural and developmental variations. Young children in western cultures explain actions in concrete, situational terms and only

Social psychology

■ Link

In studying social influence (see p143), we saw that cultural norms can affect the levels of conformity. Individualistic cultures (North America) focus on the individual as distinct. In collectivist cultures (China), people see themselves as part of a social group so the context in which behaviour (conformity/attributions) occurs is relevant.

■ Key term

The actor–observer effect: the tendency to attribute our own behaviours externally and others' behaviours internally.

AQA   Examiner's tip

Use abbreviations to save time in the exam. Only write the full version once and then the abbreviation in brackets, for example fundamental attribution error (FAE).

■ Hint

To help you remember this bias, consider a well-known illustration of this phenomenon. In the quarter final of Euro 2004 against Portugal, David Beckham missed the first penalty. Most people made a dispositional attribution; a lack of competence. However, Beckham made a situational attribution; the pitch was uneven and the ground gave way.

make dispositional attributions later on in childhood. Furthermore the process may not be universal. Morris and Peng (1994) asked American and Chinese students at American universities to read summaries of two murders. One murderer was a Chinese student who had failed to get a top academic job. The other was a white American postman who had shot his boss. The students were asked to indicate on rating scales likely reasons for the murderers' behaviours, for example the economic recession and mental illness. Results showed that Americans rated dispositional attributions (mental illness) as more important than situational (economic recession). The reverse was found for the Chinese students. These results were irrespective of whether or not the murderer was made out to be Chinese or American.

The actor–observer effect

People are more likely to attribute internal causes to other people's behaviour than they are to their own behaviour. This is known as the **actor–observer effect.** This is so called because you are an 'actor' when you try to explain the causes of your own behaviour but an 'observer' when you try to explain other people's behaviour.

Why does this occur? One reason is that we have more information about ourselves than we have of others. We observe ourselves in many situations so we know, for example, what makes us angry but we don't know that about others. So if a motorist cuts us up, we may well think 'What an aggressive driver!' and make a dispositional attribution. On the other hand, a person is more likely to explain their own excessively fast driving as being late for work; a situational attribution. Another reason why the actor–observer effect occurs is 'perceptual'. When observing others they become 'figures' or 'objects' against a background. Because they stand out, we focus on their personality to explain their behaviour. However, we cannot observe ourselves. What stands out instead is the situation which assumes the role of 'figure' against the background of the self.

■ Research study: Storms (1973)

Aim: To investigate whether:

■ participants' attributions of their own behaviour would differ from the attibutions of others

■ participants' attributions of their own behaviour would differ when taking an observer's view of themselves from when taking an actor's view of themselves.

Method: Participants were videotaped in conversation. After the conversation and before watching the video they were asked why they had said certain things during the conversation and why they thought others with whom they were having the conversation had said certain things. They then watched the videotape and saw themselves in conversation with the others. The questions were repeated.

Results: When taking the actor's view of themselves (before watching themselves on video), participants attributed their own remarks to the situation, for example 'I was responding to what the other person said'. They attributed what others had said to internal, dispositional causes, for example 'He was showing off'. When taking an observer's view of themselves (after watching themselves on the video), there were more dispositional attributions of their own behaviour, for example 'I was trying to act friendly' than when taking the actor's view of themselves.

Conclusion: When people explain their own behaviour, situational causes are emphasised and when explaining other peoples' behaviour, dispositional causes are emphasised. However when observing their own behaviour, people make more dispositional attributions.

Evaluation: This is an ingenious if somewhat complicated study. It was highly controlled. Participants were able to compare their own behaviour from an actor's point of view with the same behaviour from an observer's point of view. However Storm's findings have not always been replicated.

■ Hint

Imagine that you have just failed your driving test. A typical 'actor' explanation might be that the examiner was unfair. Now look at your reflection in the mirror and think of the test. You should find it easier to make dispositional attributions: I'm just not ready yet. This is similar to participants' attributions of their own behaviour from an observer's view of themselves in Storm's experiment.

Other factors have been found to reverse the actor–observer effect, such as positive behaviours (being helpful). This brings us to the next bias: the self-serving bias.

The self-serving bias

People sometimes make exceptions to the actor–observer rule. For example, if a person passes their driving test then they are much more likely to attribute this to their ability, I am a competent driver, than to the situation, the examiner was lenient. However, one may still attribute someone else's success to good fortune.

Self-serving biases protect a person's self-esteem, making them feel better about themselves. Another reason for the bias is that generally people want to succeed so, if successful, claim responsibility for that success.

■ Key term

Self-serving bias: a tendency to attribute one's successes to positive internal attributions and failures to external, situational attributions.

■ Research study: Johnson et al. (1964)

Aim: To investigate whether teachers would make internal attributions for their students' successes and external attributions for their failings.

Method: The 'teachers' were students who were asked to teach maths to two secondary school pupils. After the teaching sessions, each teacher was told that one pupil had performed well and the other had performed poorly. Giving the same information to each teacher was an important variable to control throughout the study. The teachers were then asked to continue teaching each pupil. Following this the teachers were told that:

■ the pupil who had initially done well continued to make progress
■ the pupil who had initially not done well had either improved or continued to do poorly.

The teachers were then asked to explain the performance of their pupils.

Results: Dispositional attributions were given for improved performance, for example the teacher's knowledge of maths or their teaching ability. For pupils who continued to do poorly, the teachers made external attributions, for example lack of effort or the pupil's lack of ability.

Conclusion: The results support the self-serving bias. The teachers explained the results of their pupils' performance in a way which was most favourable to themselves.

Evaluation: The sample of participants was biased. The 'teachers' were all students and thus it is not known if such findings generalise to other teachers and other people. Some research using experienced rather than student teachers failed to produce consistent findings. This study does however have relevance to real-life settings.

Social psychology

Hint

Attribution theory has resulted in a number of practical applications. Learning to make more appropriate attributions and take control can help overcome problems such as depression and addiction.

AQA Examiner's tip

If asked to describe a study in which attribution bias was investigated, make sure you follow the instructions to refer to the aim, method, results and conclusion. This applies to all questions on 'Describe a study'.

There are some exceptions to the self-serving bias:

- When there is public praise for a person's success such as for a heroic deed, people are more likely to be modest and give external attributions. However one could argue that such behaviour in itself is self-serving (Schlenker *et al.*, 1990).
- If a person knows that their future performance will be critically examined then the self-serving bias is reduce (Miller and Schlenker, 1985).
- Depressed people show a reversed bias (Abramson *et al.*, 1978).
- Women are more likely to show a reverse bias than men (Davison and Neale, 1994).

Key points:

- People have a need to find causes for theirs and others' behaviour; attribution of cause.
- There are two types of attribution; dispositional and situational.
- People prefer to make dispositional attributions of others' behaviour as these are more stable and better able to predict behaviour.
- Attempts at attributions are subject to several biases. These are the fundamental attribution error, the actor–observer effect and the self-serving bias.

Summary questions

7 Give one reason why people feel the need to make attributions.

8 What is a 'dispositional attribution'?

9 List the main types of attribution bias.

10 Explain the fundamental attribution error.

11 The manager of a football team attributes the team's successes to his own skill and its failures to the players' lack of effort. Explain why the manager's behaviour is an example of the self-serving bias.

Attitudes

Learning objectives:

- Understand what psychologists mean by attitudes.

- Know and understand the components of attitudes.

- Know and understand the main functions of attitudes.

Key term

Attitude: a learned like or dislike of someone or something that influences our behaviour towards that thing or person.

Hint

Psychologists refer to an 'attitude object' as you always have an attitude to something. However, do not take it literally in such a narrow sense. It can mean people, situations, ideas or events, as well as objects.

The word **attitude** is part of our everyday language. People often discuss their likes and dislikes of objects, of other people, situations, ideas and events and how these may lead to certain behaviours. Disagreements with others over attitudes make us aware of how powerful they are.

We are not born with attitudes; these develop from our experiences and the information we receive. A person may have an unfavourable attitude towards dogs because a dog once attacked them. Someone's attitude towards smoking may be modelled on the attitudes of their parents.

Attitudes are hypothetical constructs that cannot be directly observed but are important in the study of social psychology. The aim of scientific psychology is to explain and predict human behaviour. Because attitudes influence behaviour, they can serve as predictors of behaviour. Therefore changing attitudes is seen as a meaningful starting point for modifying behaviour, for example carefully planned adverts are aimed at potential buyers to convince them of the merits of actually buying the new product. However, as we shall see, attitudes do not necessarily predict behaviour.

So far we have mentioned two inter-related components of attitudes: evaluation of the object, person, situation, idea or event and the behavioural component. Some psychologists argue that there is a third component to an attitude. This three-component model of attitudes (Rosenberg and Hovland, 1960) details the structure of attitudes. The three components are known as the cognitive component, the affective component and the behavioural component.

The structure of attitudes

The cognitive component

This is the belief component. It includes facts: what the person knows, believes or perceives about the attitude object. Of course, this knowledge may be incomplete or inaccurate, but the key point is that it is non-evaluative, for example I believe that the Labour government is interfering.

To convert a belief into an attitude, a value ingredient is added. Values refer to an individual's understanding of what is desirable, good, etc. To continue with the above example, I value freedom so I find interference by the government offensive (not good).

The affective component

This is the emotional component: how the person evaluates or feels about the attitude object, for example likes or dislikes, good or bad. Following on from the above belief, I do not like this Labour government.

The behavioural component

This is sometimes referred to as the conative component and is about how we intend to behave towards the attitude object, for example I will not vote Labour.

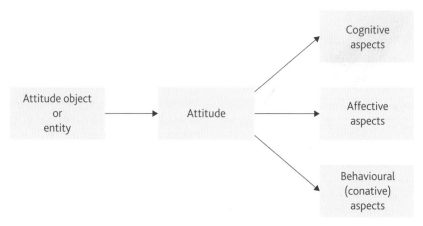

Fig. 2 *The three-component model showing the attitude object and the three components of an attitude (after Eagly and Chakain, 1993)*

Link

Social learning theory and cognitive psychology also consider the important role of mediating variables between stimuli and responses. These topics are revisited at A2.

AQA **Examiner's tip**

Prepare your own example of the three-component model based on thought, feeling and intended action to use in the exam, for example attitude object – cricket: I believe that there is little action in cricket, I dislike cricket and I never watch it on TV.

The three-component model sees an attitude as a mediating variable between observable stimuli (attitude object) and responses (how you might behave towards it). Attitudes influence behaviour; they both guide and bias it. This S-R framework illustrates the influence of behaviourism on social psychology in the 1960s.

Evaluation of the structural approach

The structural approach (the three-component model) provides an understanding of the link between attitudes, beliefs, values, intentions and behaviour. This is represented in Figure 3.

A major problem with this model is that it assumes that the components are highly correlated. In a famous study dating back to the 1930s, a sociologist, Richard LaPierre, escorted a Chinese couple on a three-month trip across the USA. They stopped at 251 hotels, restaurants and similar establishments and were refused service only once even though at that time people in the States were generally hostile towards the Chinese people. After the trip he wrote to all of the establishments and asked if they would be willing to accept members of the Chinese race as guests. Of those who replied (about half), 92 per cent said that they would not accept Chinese customers. This study is often quoted to show that attitudes do not predict behaviour. However, people answering the questionnaire were not necessarily those who had served the couple. They may have responded differently to the questionnaire had they been told that the couple were educated and well dressed. Nevertheless this study is often used to show that factors other than attitudes and intentions determine behaviour. Habits, social norms and group pressure also exert powerful influences. So despite knowledge of beliefs, values, attitudes and intentions, people do not always do as they say they will.

A further problem with the structural approach is that it does not tell us why people hold attitudes; what functions they serve for the individual.

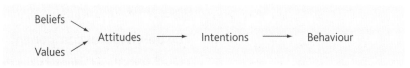

Fig. 3 *Structural analysis of attitudes showing the link between beliefs, values, intentions and behaviour*

The function of attitudes

A number of theorists (for example Katz, 1960) have identified the function of attitudes. In this section we shall consider three such functions.

Adaptive function

This is sometimes known as a utilitarian (practical) function. The attitude expresses our desire to obtain rewards or to avoid punishment, for example if someone wants a promotion at work, they may grovel to the boss by expressing admiration for the company's management policies. Similarity often breeds liking so it may be functional to adopt similar attitudes to those of someone you may want to impress or make friends with. Such attitudes may be publicly expressed but not necessarily believed.

Knowledge function

These are attitudes that bring order and structure to all the information we must deal with in our daily lives. Essentially they are schemas that simplify information processing. They allow us to predict what might happen and give a sense of control. A positive attitude to studying for exams tells you what to expect in this situation: that you should pass. Like other schemas such attitudes often oversimplify reality.

Ego-expressive function

This is also known as the self-expressive function. We are social animals who need to communicate with others and want people to know our opinions and values. For example, a person may want to communicate to others their positive attitude towards private education. This is because of deeply held values about freedom of choice in education. This also helps identify with individuals and groups who share such an attitude. The ego-expressive function also confirms our own sense of identity; we need to hear our attitudes for ourselves. This becomes particularly important in adolescence when the search for identity is a key challenge. Because ego-expressive attitudes derive from a person's underlying values, they do not change easily.

There are of course cultural differences in attitudes which reflect underlying values. These differences also have implications for attitude change.

Links

Notice the link here to normative social influence on p136. People sometimes conform to others because they want to be accepted by the group. Hence certain attitudes may have to be publicly expressed but not necessarily believed.

In impression formation (see p148), we considered the importance of schemata in making sense of our social world. We are basically 'cognitive misers' looking for short cuts and attitudes provide a quick schematic way of interpreting information.

AQA Examiner's tip

Students often confuse the three components of attitudes with the three functions of attitudes. Make sure that you distinguish between these.

Research study: Han and Shavitt (1993)

Aim: To investigate whether participants in different cultures had preferences for different attitudes.

Method: This was a cross-cultural study. Using content analysis, a range of American and Korean commercial advertisements were analysed and shown to Korean and American participants. Korea is a collectivist culture valuing group harmony and collective achievement. America is an individualistic culture valuing personal choice and achievement. The American slogans stressed individualism, for example 'the art of being unique' whereas the Korean slogans stressed group harmony, for example 'sharing is beautiful'. The researchers analysed participants' responses to the advertisements.

Social psychology

Link

A detailed analysis had to be made of the advertisement in order to be able to categorise them as ones stressing individual values or ones stressing harmonious relationships. See Chapter 4, Research methods, for more about content analysis.

Results: The American participants preferred the adveriisements that stressed individual values whereas the Korean participants preferred the slogans that stressed harmonious relationships.

Conclusion: The research showed that there are cultural differences in attitudes. These differences have also been found in a study of political advertisements (Tak *et al.*, 1997).

Evaluation: The advantage of this study is that it takes the research beyond the confines of a laboratory and gives rich insight into how different cultural values can affect attitudes. However, content analysis is prone to subjectivity; it can be difficult to interpret the content of the advertisement.

Understanding the function of an attitude is helpful in knowing how easily it can be changed and how consistent it might be with other attitudes. However the division into separate functions is over-simplistic. Shavitt (1989) recognised that an attitude can serve a number of functions for an individual at the same time, for example a positive attitude to conservation can serve an adaptive function (approved by significant others), as an expression of values (save the planet) and can guide and structure information processing (not buying certain products). Different people might hold the same attitude for different reasons.

Key points:

- The structural approach to attitudes identifies three components: cognitive, affective and behavioural.
- Attitudes do not necessarily correspond to behaviour.
- Attitudes may serve any of three functions: adaptive, knowledge and ego-expressive.
- Knowledge of the function of attitudes has implications for understanding attitude change and the stability of attitudes.

 Summary questions

12 Identify the three components of attitudes.

13 What was the main finding in LaPierre's study?

14 In your own words, explain what is meant by the adaptive function of attitudes.

15 Explain why an attitude serving an adaptive function may lack stability.

16 Explain why an attitude serving an ego-expressive function may be difficult to change.

Prejudice

Social psychology

Learning objectives:

- Understand what psychologists mean by prejudice.

- Understand how competition for resources may lead to prejudice.

- Describe 'social identity theory'.

- Know and understand the 'social identity theory' explanation of prejudice.

- Know and understand the authoritarian personality explanation of prejudice.

Key terms

Prejudice: an unfavourable attitude towards a social group and its members.

Realistic conflict theory: a theory that conflict stems from direct competition between social groups over scarce resources.

Hint

Do not confuse prejudice with discrimination. Prejudice is an attitude whereas discrimination is the behaviour associated with a particular prejudice, for example someone who is prejudiced against people who go to Oxbridge may show discrimination by avoiding a person who goes to one of those universities.

What is prejudice?

Prejudice is a term which has rather negative connotations and is normally taken to mean a hostile attitude towards a person or group, for example older people or a racial group. However, prejudice can also be positive. An obvious example is patriotism. It involves pre-judging an individual or a group and always includes an evaluation (the affective component of an attitude). Although prejudice can be both positive and negative, it is negative prejudice which concerns psychologists.

Prejudice is founded upon and maintained by stereotypes. Thus someone may be prejudiced against all the pupils from a particular school because they believe all of them to be snobbish. Thus prejudices are in fact cognitive schemas which serve to simplify our social world. In keeping with all schemas, they are resistant to change when faced with information which goes against the belief.

There are many explanations for the causes of prejudice and these have tended to concentrate on the more extreme types such as prejudice resulting in violence. At the start of the 20th century, prejudice was very much seen as an instinctive reaction to certain categories of people in much the same way as animals react to the unfamiliar and unusual. This view is no longer popular although it is accepted that there may be an innate component to prejudice. Similarly psychologists have sought explanations in terms of 'nurture'; that prejudices are learned. There is some indirect evidence for this view, for example Barrett and Short (1992) found that young English children aged 5–10 years had clear preferences for different European groups (for example, the French were liked most, but Germans were liked least) even though they had little factual knowledge about these groups. However this nature–nurture approach somewhat simplifies a complex psychological phenomenon. More recent explanations focus on social psychological theories and personality theories.

Explanations of prejudice

Competition for resources

According to Sherif, prejudice in society is caused by competition between different social groups. This can include competition over jobs, money, territory and status. This explanation is also known as **realistic conflict theory**.

Sherif claimed that competition will always give rise to prejudice and conducted a field study to investigate this.

Research study: Sherif et al. (1961)

Aim: To investigate whether intergroup conflict arises where groups compete over scarce resources.

Method: This was a field experiment. Twenty-two 11-year-old, well-adjusted, middle-class boys were selected to go on a summer

Link

The experiment was carried out in a natural setting – a summer camp. However there was still a degree of control, for example allocation of boys into groups. See Chapter 4, Research methods, for more about field experiments.

camp at Robber's Cave State Park in America. The boys were divided into two groups that split up friendships; the Eagles and the Rattlers. This was done by random allocation in order to control for participant variables. For the first week the groups did not know of the other's existence. Time was spent in separate activites which encouraged group cohesion and identity. In the second week of the experiment the researchers set up a series of competitions between the groups and offered prizes for all members of the winning team.

Results: Strong 'in-group' and 'out-group' feelings developed, leading to stereotypes, hos-tility and fights.

Conclusion: Conflict can arise from competition over scarce resources (only one team received the prizes).

Evaluation: The study, of course, raises serious ethical issues; the researchers deliberately created hostility and conflict. Later the researchers did set up tasks for the boys to work co-operatively to solve a common problem. This reduced the hostility. Attempts at replication among scout groups in England have not shown the same dramatic effects (Tyerman and Spencer, 1983) so this raises questions about the extent to which findings can be generalised. Field experiments in general do not afford the same degree of control as laboratory experiments but nevertheless this study has been hailed as 'the most successful field experiment ever conducted on intergroup conflict' (Brown, 1986).

Evaluation of realistic conflict theory

Although the study demonstrates conflict arising from competition, it does not tell us about the mechanism by which conflict then turns into prejudice. One possible explanation is that conflict leads to blame being projected onto scapegoats (the out-group), hostility and prejudice.

This theory can explain changes in prejudice over time and contexts. Brewer and Campbell (1976) conducted a survey of 30 tribal groups in Africa and found that there was greater negativity towards tribal out-groups that lived close by. These were likely competitors for scarce resources such as land and water.

Research suggests that prejudice against immigrants is highly related to whether or not they are seen as a threat to economic well-being, but this does not account for prejudice against groups not associated with competition for resources, for example New Age travellers.

Realistic conflict theory involves two variables: group membership and competition between groups. There does appear to be some evidence that competition is not necessary and that people favour their group just for being categorised as a member of that group. This brings us to the next theory of prejudice.

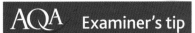 Examiner's tip

Prepare for a question on theories of prejudice. Produce a table. For each theory, identify the key features, the strengths, the weaknesses and one study.

Key term

Social identity theory: social groups to which we belong can have significant impacts on our self-esteem. Identifying with groups and making positive evaluative in-group comparisons enhances one's self-esteem.

Social identity theory

Sherif had shown conflict to be a sufficient cause for hostility. However it is not a necessary cause because hostility can occur in the absence of conflict. **Social identity theory** based on a cognitive approach explains prejudice as a result of the way we process information. Tajfel (1982) proposed a three-component model:

- People categorise themselves and others into groups. Categorisation simplifies interpersonal perception.
- People identify with groups that they perceive themselves to belong to (in-group).

People make comparisons between in-groups and groups they do not belong to (out-groups) in order to boost their self-esteem. This is done by over-estimating the good qualities of the in-group and putting other groups down. Because part of normal psychological functioning is to feel good about ourselves in this sense, the theory is also motivational. People are motivated to see their group as better in order to promote their self-esteem.

In a series of experiments, Tajfel *et al.* (1971) found that simply knowing of another group's existence, **minimal groups**, is enough to produce in-group favouritism and out-group bias. Schoolboys aged 14 to 15 were randomly divided into two groups and told to give coins to members of their own group and members of the other group. They were given choices, for example they could either give 20 coins to a member of their own group and 15 coins to one in the out-group (difference of five) or 15 to one of their own group and eight to one of the out-group (difference of seven). The second alternative was preferred even though it meant that their own group got fewer coins. This study shows that emphasising the distinction between groups enables one's group to come out on top and that mere categorisation is enough to activate prejudice. In this study, the children did not even know who was in their group and who was in the out-group. All they knew was which group they belonged to. The drive towards a satisfying social identity is seen to be at the root of prejudice. This study has been accused of artificiality and may only reflect the norms of competitive societies (see Wetherall, 1982).

Evaluation of social identity theory

The theory may be culturally specific. In a study in New Zealand, Wetherell (1982) found that eight-year-old children of Polynesian origin were much more generous towards the out-group than were children of European origin. This may be a result of the cultural norms of more co-operative societies. This theory also presents prejudice as natural; that we are naturally driven to boost our self-esteem. It thus could easily be misrepresented as a justification of prejudice. However there is much empirical support for the theory both from minimal group experiments and real world inter-group relationships.

■ Authoritarian personality

This theory sees prejudice as 'an expression of deep-lying trends in personality' caused by excessively harsh parenting (Adorno, 1950). Working from a Freudian perspective, he proposed that the child's natural aggression as a result of strict discipline was displaced onto weaker targets. At the same time, the prejudiced person would be over-respectful towards authority figures as these symbolised the parents. Along with these characteristics, a number of other components develop which collectively make up the **authoritarian personality.** To measure these characteristics, a questionnaire known as the F-scale was developed (F stands for fascism). This has widely been used as a research tool.

Evaluation of authoritarian personality

Some studies have found support for the F-scale and the relationship between authoritarianism and prejudice, for example against AIDS sufferers and the homeless.

However the F-scale has been criticised. One reason is that the scores could be explained by the level of education rather than personality. Research has found that the authoritarian personality is more likely to exist amongst the

■ Key terms

Minimal group: people are classified into groups but have little if any interaction with other members of their group. Nevertheless group members still identify with their group and show in-group favouritism and out-group prejudice.

Authoritarian personality: a person who holds rigid beliefs, is submissive to authority and hostile towards out-groups.

■ Hint

Do not confuse social identity theory with realistic conflict theory. It may help to bear in mind that this theory concerns social competition whereas realistic competition is when groups compete over real resources and there is interdependence between groups.

Social psychology

Links

■ The authoritarian personality is also discussed under 'Obedience to authority' (p138) as a dispositional explanation of obedience.

■ The method used to measure the authoritarian personality (Authoritarianism or F-scale) was a questionnaire. Questionnaire construction and the strengths and weaknesses of questionnaires apply here. See Chapter 4, Research methods.

AQA Examiner's tip

In an extended question on explanations of prejudice, actually name the theories. You will be credited for this and it will help you focus. Do make sure you can evaluate these. If asked for evidence, you must include it otherwise you will automatically lose marks.

less well educated. Another is response bias. Respondents were asked whether they agreed with items on the scale and agreement implied an authoritarian personality, for example obedience and respect for authority are the most important virtues that children should learn. Some people do not like to disagree so a high score could simply be a measure of acquiescence (how much someone agrees) rather than authoritarianism.

The theory ignores cultural factors. Pettigrew (1958) illustrated this point in his study of prejudice in South Africa. White South Africans showed high levels of anti-black prejudice but not authoritarianism. This suggests that a better explanation is the current norms rather than personality dysfunction. Harsh parenting cannot explain sudden and dramatic changes in prejudiced attitudes. Furthermore it is unlikely that a whole social group would suffer from a personality disorder.

Key points:

■ Prejudice is an attitude. It predisposes an individual to act in an unfavourable way towards others.

■ There are several explanations of prejudice. One is where two or more groups are in competition for resources (realistic conflict theory).

■ Social identity theory states that social categorisation results in prejudice because people make evaluative comparisons between their in-group and out-groups.

■ Authoritarian personality explains prejudice as a consequence of a harsh style of child-rearing.

✓ Summary questions

17 Give one reason why prejudice is resistant to change.

18 Explain the difference between prejudice and discrimination.

19 Identify a strength and a weakness of realistic conflict theory.

20 Explain why social identity theory is both a cognitive and a motivational theory.

21 Explain two flaws with the authoritarian personality explanation of prejudice.

💡 End-of-chapter activity

Investigate the primacy effect yourself using the method similar to that devised by Asch (1946). Asch asked participants to make a judgement about a fictitious person using a rating scale. The scale included a series of personality measures such as how sociable and how honest they considered the person. Participants were first presented with a list of six adjectives describing the person, for example industrious, stubborn. Half of the participants were presented with a list where the positive adjectives were at the beginning of the list followed by the more negative adjectives. The other half were presented with the same list of words in the reverse order. Asch was able to compare the ratings of the person by the two groups to see if they had been influenced by the order of words.

In order to carry out this experiment, you need to think about which experimental design to choose, the controls needed, up-to-date adjectives and how you are going to construct your rating scale. Consider also issues around consent and debriefing.

1   (a)   Identify two components of an attitude.   *(2 marks)*

    (b)   Using an example outline what social psychologists mean by a dispositional attribution.   *(2 marks)*

    (c)   Anna goes for a job interview. Explain how both

        (i) the primacy effect, and

      (ii) stereotyping

           might influence how the interviewers perceive Anna.   *(6 marks)*

    (d)   Discuss two explanations of prejudice. Refer to evidence in your answer.   *(10 marks)*

2   (a)   Refer to any one experiment which investigated the primacy or recency effect in impression formation.

        (i) Identify one experiment that investigated the primary recency effect in impression formation.   *(1 mark)*

      (ii) Explain whether the study was a field or laboratory experiment.   *(2 marks)*

     (iii) Explain one methodological strength of the study.   *(3 marks)*

    (b)   Attitudes serve several functions. Name and explain which function each of the following attributes serves:

        (i) 'Everyone in my office is football mad so I go to some games with them.'

      (ii) 'I'm a vegetarian and proud of it. Eating meat is wrong.'   *(4 marks)*

    (c)   Describe and discuss two types of attribution bias. Refer to empirical evidence in your answer.   *(10 marks)*

Cognitive psychology

Introduction

Hint

For AQA specification B, only 'Perceptual processes' and 'Remembering and forgetting' are required for AS Level.

Fig. 1 *A basic information flow model based on a computer analogy*

Key terms

Monocular depth cue: information from one eye that gives an indication of distance and depth.

Binocular depth cue: information from two eyes that gives an indication of distance and depth.

Constancy: the tendency of visual perception to remain the same in spite of differences in observation conditions, for example whether an object is far away or close by it is perceived as the same size.

Cognitive psychology is the study of processes that go on in the brain, including thinking, language, problem-solving, decision-making, perception, attention, memory and forgetting. Although cognitive processes are often studied separately, they are interdependent. For example, in order to come to a decision, we have to think about a problem and this uses other cognitive processes such as memory and attention.

Cognitive processes are unobservable and so psychologists have proposed models of how they think they operate. An early influence on cognitive psychology was the analogy of a computer. Computers operate via a sequence of stages through which information flows and is processed (Figure 1).

Psychologists have used this flow chart to model the processes that go on in the brain. The multi-store model of memory proposed by Atkinson and Shiffrin in 1968 modelled memory as a sequence of stages based on the computer analogy. One of the problems with sequential stage models is that they rely on stimulation of the sensory system from the environment. The brain is a much more sophisticated system than a computer and a stage model based on a computer analogy is over-simplified. This is because incoming stimuli from the environment may be affected by processes in the brain such as motivation, emotion and expectation. For example, read the following weather forecast:

'Today there will be sunshine and …'

There is no stimulus in the final word and yet you probably automatically added 'showers'. This is because your brain automatically fills in what it expects in a particular context.

'Perceptual processes' refers to the way stimuli entering our sensory system are perceived. The brain analyses the raw input (sensations) and helps us to make sense of the world. Sensation is the information received, and perception is how that information is interpreted in the brain. The information received by our senses is often confusing and disorganised. In order to perceive depth and interact with the environment appropriately, our brain uses a number of cues, including **monocular** and **binocular depth cues**. Additionally, the information received by the visual system is in a variety of strange shapes and sizes. The brain makes use of a number of **constancies** in order to interpret the world in a stable way.

The topic 'Remembering and forgetting' is extremely relevant to our everyday lives. Think about what you have done today, from getting out of bed to where you are and what you are doing now. In every task you performed, memory has played a crucial role. Memory is not just where we store facts, but where we actively work on information held – even making plans for the future.

Specification	Topic content	Page
Models of memory including the distinguishing features/components of each of the following: the multi-store model (Atkinson and Shiffrin), working memory model, levels of processing	Models of memory	170
Types of long-term memory: episodic; semantic; procedural Autobiographical memory	Types of long-term memory	179
Explanations of forgetting, including decay, interference, retrieval failure (absence of context and cues), displacement, lack of consolidation and motivated forgetting, including repression	Explanations of forgetting	182
Perceptual set and the effects of motivation, expectation, emotion and culture on perception	Perceptual set	206
Perceptual organisation: the Gestalt principles	Perceptual organisation: the Gestalt principles	191
Gibson's and Gregory's theories of visual perception	Theories of perception	201
Depth cues, monocular and binocular. Types of perceptual constancy, including size constancy and shape constancy	Depth cues in perception	194
Distortion illusions, including the Muller-Lyer illusion and the Ponzo illusion	Perceptual set	206
	Theories of perception	201
	Visual illusions	198
Ambiguous figures, including the Necker cube and Rubin's vase	Theories of perception	201
	Visual illusions	198
What distortion illusions and ambiguous figures tell us about perception	Visual illusions	198

Cognitive psychology

Models of memory

Learning objectives:

▪ Understand the main features, including the strengths and limitations, of:

▪ The multi-store model of memory.

▪ The levels of processing theory.

▪ The working memory model.

Key terms

Modality: refers to the sense, for example sight, touch, smell.

Rehearsed: repeated, and this is a key control process which acts as a buffer between SR and LTM, and also enables information to be transferred to LTM.

💡 The multi-store model of memory

Atkinson and Shiffrin (1968) proposed a multi-store model of memory which had two distinct stores: a short-term store and a long-term store. In addition to these two stores, this model proposed that stimuli from the environment are held for a very brief time (less than one second) in a sensory register.

Main features

Sensory register

The sensory register is **modality**-specific, which means information is held in the same sense that it is registered – a taste is held as a taste, a visual image is held as an icon (picture). The capacity of this sensory register is quite large, but its very brief duration (approximately half a second) means information is lost before there is time to measure its full capacity. The processing in sensory memory is largely unconscious and therefore has to be deduced from experiments. A series of experiments by Sperling in 1960 have indicated that sensory register holds at least nine items, but only for a brief period of time.

Short-term memory

From sensory register information can be lost, or is passed onto short-term memory (STM). In 1956 Miller published a famous paper called 'The Magical Number Seven' in which he presented research evidence to show the limit of short-term memory to be between five and nine items, or an average of seven items. The capacity of short-term memory can be extended through 'chunking'. This is where items are 'chunked' into meaningful wholes, for example B,B,C,C,4,I,T,V,A,A, R,A,C becomes BBC, C4, ITV, AA, RAC. If information in short-term memory is **rehearsed**, it can be retained in short-term storage and then can be transferred to long-term memory for potentially indefinite storage.

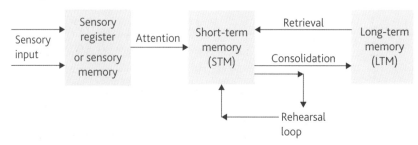

Fig. 1 *The multi-store model of memory (Atkinson and Shiffrin, 1968)*

Long-term memory

Long-term memory (LTM) refers to anything that we can remember for a period of time lasting from minutes up to a life-time. Our long-term memory has a huge capacity and seems to be able to store memories in a number of forms. The code is largely abstract/semantic, and there is evidence that information is stored in an organised and meaningful way.

Evaluation of multi-store model

Research evidence

▨ The duration of STM was investigated by Peterson and Peterson (1959) who gave participants trigrams (for example, MXT) which they had to recall after varying amounts of time from 0–18 seconds. Only 10 per cent of the trigrams were recalled after 18 seconds and it was therefore deduced that the duration of STM is approximately 18 seconds. The duration can be extended by rehearsal and, according to the model, it is as a result of rehearsal that information is transferred to LTM. As information in LTM can potentially be stored indefinitely, then Peterson and Peterson's findings on the limited duration of STM when rehearsal is prevented can be used as evidence for the **functional separation** of STM and LTM.

▨ Research study: Baddeley (1966)

Aim: To investigate coding in short-term memory (STM) and long-term memory (LTM).

Method: An independent groups design experiment was carried out which had three conditions:

▨ learn a list of acoustically similar words (for example, rain, pain, train)

▨ learn a list of semantically similar words (for example, quick, fast, swift)

▨ learn a list of unrelated words (control condition).

Participants were then asked to recall the words (dependent variable) either immediately (STM) or after 20 minutes (LTM).

Results: When participants recalled immediately, they made most mistakes with the acoustically similar words, whereas after 20 minutes it was the semantically similar words that resulted in more errors.

Conclusion: This was interpreted as showing that an acoustic code was used in STM which made it difficult to remember the similar sounding words immediately. In LTM participants had difficulty with words of the same meaning which suggests in LTM information is stored semantically.

Evaluation: Although findings from this experiment were interpreted as indicating an acoustic code in STM, more recent findings have suggested other codes (for example, visual) can also be used in STM. In addition, this was a highly controlled laboratory situation and any findings may not apply to real life situations. In real life, we rarely have to learn lists of words in such a fashion and therefore the study lacks ecological validity.

Link

See the study by Bower *et al.* (1969) on p179 for evidence of organisation in LTM.

Key term

Functional separation: the two stores are used for different tasks (or functions) – STM for rehearsal, LTM for storage.

AQA Examiner's tip

▨ You should know the properties associated with each store and some of the evidence on which they are based.

▨ In addition to being specifically asked about properties, this information is useful as evidence for the functional separation of the two types of memory stores (STM and LTM).

Link

For more information on independent groups design, number of conditions, control condition, dependent variable and ecological validity, see Chapter 4, Research methods.

Cognitive psychology

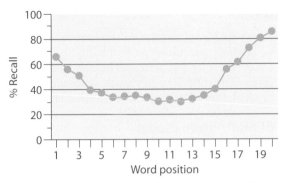

Fig. 2 *Graph to show the serial position effect (the percentage recall of each word according to its position on the list) on a free-recall memory experiment*

Link

The primacy and recency effects are also discussed in Chapter 6, Social cognition (pp151–153), in relation to impression formation.

Key terms

Displaced: pushed out of STM due to its limited capacity of only five to nine items – this is explained in the section on forgetting.

Consolidated: the time that it takes for information that has left STM to be reprocessed for storage in LTM, during this process information can be lost – this is explained in the section on 'forgetting'.

Anterograde: a type of memory failure for information after an event (for example, surgery).

There is experimental evidence for the functional separation of STM and LTM from a study carried out by Murdock (1962). In this study, lists of words that varied in length from 10 to 40 words were presented at intervals of 2 seconds for each word. When participants were asked to recall them in any order, the results showed that more words were recalled from the beginning and the end of the list, irrespective of the length of the list. When plotted on a graph this shows a serial position curve, sometimes referred to as the primacy/recency effect:

– primacy effect: the better recall of words at the beginning of a list (these have been rehearsed and transferred to LTM)

– recency effect: the better recall of the last few words at the end of the list (still in STM).

The words in the middle of the list have been **displaced** from STM but not yet **consolidated** into LTM. The primacy and recency effects are considered to be strong evidence for the existence of two separate memory stores.

Clinical studies of amnesiacs show that it is possible for STM or LTM to be damaged independently, for example a patient known as HM underwent surgery in 1953 in an attempt to stop his seizures. As a result of the surgery, HM was left with **anterograde** amnesia. He had some memory from before the surgery but very limited memory of events occurring after surgery. His STM was normal but he was unable to learn new material (impaired LTM), again suggesting these two stores function separately.

Further clinical evidence comes from individuals who suffer from Korsakov syndrome (usually caused by alcohol poisoning). Patients with this syndrome forget all new material within seconds of receiving it, although their LTM is generally intact. They seem to have a specific difficulty in transferring information from STM to LTM.

Further evaluative comments

The multi-store model of memory proposed that rehearsal was the key for transferring information from STM to LTM. Although rehearsal may be important in some cases, for example memorising a telephone number, in everyday life we very rarely rehearse information and yet we seem to be able to store lots of things. We may, for example, remember a part of a psychology lesson because it was funny or we found something really interesting. This can be better explained by Craik and Lockhart's levels of processing theory (below).

The multi-store model of memory has been criticised for being over-simplified with its view of STM and LTM structures operating in a single, uniform fashion. We now know that this is not the case. The working memory model proposed by Baddeley and Hitch (1974) is a more active model of human processing where STM is more than one unitary store but comprises a number of different stores.

▥ Case studies of patients with brain damage suggest that the multi-store model is over-simplified. For example, a patient known as KF suffered brain damage following a motorcycle accident, and underwent brain surgery. Some years later he was found to have normal LTM storage but an STM capacity of only two items. If STM was necessary for the transfer of information to LTM, then KF's LTM should also have been affected.

▥ Many of the studies supporting the multi-store model of memory use laboratory experiments, and can therefore be criticised in terms of ecological validity and demand characteristics. Findings from such experiments may tell us very little about how memory works in real life.

▥ The levels of processing theory of memory

Main features

The multi-store model of memory was largely concerned with the structural components of memory (that is, the distinction between STM and LTM), whereas Craik and Lockhart (1972) proposed that **process** rather than **structure** was important and that words can be processed at a number of different levels:

▥ shallow/structural level – a visual level, for example physical properties of the stimulus

▥ intermediate/phonetic level – an auditory level, for example the sound of the stimulus

▥ deep/semantic level – the meaning of the stimulus and connections to other stimuli.

Craik and Lockhart argued that it is what is done with the material during rehearsal which determines whether material is remembered, not simply the repetition of the words. They proposed that any stimulus can be processed in a number of stages which move from low levels of analysis (for example, analysis of shape/structure) to higher levels that may involve meaning or connections to other items in memory. It is the higher levels of processing that give more durable memories, rehearsal just prolongs the memory trace without on its own leading to a permanent memory. For example, if you see the word BOOK, you may focus on the individual letters, or on the sound of the word, or on its meaning – the latter being a deeper level of processing.

A major experimental technique used to study levels of processing is when different tasks are performed on a list of words. One or more of the tasks requires the processing of meaning, for example 'Think of an adjective to go with the word BOOK.' In order to think of a word to describe BOOK, you would first need to process what a book is, and this would entail making connections with material already stored in LTM. Other tasks might only require shallow processing, for example 'Is the word in capital letters?' You would be able to answer this very quickly without the need to process the meaning of the word 'book'.

Craik and Lockhart (1972) argued that it is preferable for participants not to know beforehand that there will be a recognition (or recall) test (incidental learning) because then they will be less tempted to perform additional analyses upon the words. Such an incidental learning experiment was carried out by Craik and Tulving in 1975 to support the levels of processing theory.

▥ Link

For information on ecological validity and demand characteristics, see Chapter 4, Research methods.

Cognitive psychology

Craik and Lockhart also suggested that Atkinson and Shiffrin's model of memory gave a simplified view of rehearsal. They argued that, when material is encoded, there are two types of rehearsal that can take place and it is the **kind** of rehearsal that is important for long-term retention. They distinguish between two types of rehearsal:

▌ maintenance rehearsal – simple rote repetition, repeating the words as they have been presented

💡 elaborative rehearsal – analysing the meaning of the rehearsed material, perhaps linking it with stored knowledge in LTM.

The crucial theoretical assumption made by Craik and Lockhart is that the depth of processing determines the persistence of a memory trace in long-term store, and elaborative rehearsal will entail deeper processing and thus a more durable memory.

Evaluation of levels of processing theory

Research evidence

> ### ▌ Research study: Craik and Tulving (1975)
>
> **Aim:** To investigate depth of processing by giving participants a number of tasks requiring different levels of processing and measuring recognition.
>
> **Method:** This was a repeated measures design experiment with three conditions. Participants were given a list of 60 words, one at a time and were required to process each word at one of three levels (the independent variable).
>
> ▌ At a deep level they might be asked a question, such as 'Does this word fit into the sentence …?'
>
> ▌ At an intermediate level, they might be asked, 'Does this word rhyme with …?'
>
> ▌ At a shallow level, they might be asked, 'Is this word in capital letters?'
>
> Following the task, participants were (unexpectedly) given a list of 180 words, which contained the original 60 words processed and 120 'filler' words, and were asked to identify the ones they recognised from the original 60 (the dependent variable).
>
> **Results:** Significantly more words were recognised if they had been processed at a deep level (approximately 65 per cent) than either phonetic (37 per cent) or shallow (17 per cent) levels.
>
> **Conclusion:** As deeper processing resulted in better recognition, then the level at which material is processed must be related to memory.
>
> **Evaluation:** This study relies on incidental learning (the participants did not know they would be asked to recall the words), rather than intentional learning, which has the advantage of being more true to real life. This means participants are unlikely to engage in extra processing which could invalidate the results. However, there is a necessary level of deception required in such a design which raises ethical issues.

▌ Hint

With respect to Craik and Lockhart's theory, the terms 'level' and 'depth' are used interchangeably.

▌ Link

For more information on repeated measures design, independent/dependent variables, demand characteristics and the meaning of confound, see Chapter 4, Research methods.

Cognitive psychology

Further evaluative comments

- Craik and Lockhart argued that perception, attention and memory are interdependent because memory traces are formed as a result of perceptual and attentional processes. They focused attention on these processes and by doing so they have made a major contribution to our understanding of memory.

- The theory is open to **empirical** testing and generally the results of studies have supported predictions (for example, Craik and Tulving, 1975). Furthermore, these studies have generally involved incidental learning rather than intentional learning, which is more ecologically valid.

- A problem for the theory is the difficulty in determining what level of processing actually occurs in any particular case. There is no adequate measure of processing depth. Depth is usually defined as 'the number of words remembered' and the 'number of words remembered' is taken as a measure of depth. This is circular because what is being defined forms part of the definition!

- More recently, Craik (2002) has acknowledged that the original levels of processing theory was over-simplified and has accepted a number of research findings. For example, he accepts the findings of the transfer-appropriate processing theory (Morris *et al.*, 1977). Morris found recall depends on the relevance of the processing to the memory test, and that semantic processing is not always superior to phonetic processing.

The working memory model

Main features

The multi-store model of memory proposed a single (unitary) and passive short-term store, whereas the working memory model emphasises the active nature of a short-term store which has more than one component. The term 'working memory' refers to a system for the short-term maintenance and manipulation of information. Baddeley and Hitch (1974) proposed a model which consisted of three components allowing for temporary storage of verbal and visuo-spatial material. The component that stores verbal material was originally called the articulatory loop, but is now known as the phonological loop (Baddeley and Logie, 1992). The phonological loop is concerned with auditory and speech-based information. The component that allows storage of visuo-spatial material is called the **visuo-spatial scratchpad** (sometimes called sketchpad). Overseeing the co-ordination of these stores is an attentional control system known as the **central executive**.

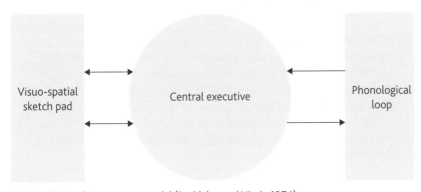

Fig. 3 *The working memory model (Baddeley and Hitch, 1974)*

Key terms

Empirical: in this sense, scientific studies can be carried out, for example experiments.

Visuo-spatial scratchpad: allows the temporary storage and manipulation of visual and spatial information. It is limited in capacity, typically holds about three to four items, and is known as the 'inner eye'.

Central executive: a limited capacity attentional system that has a controlling force over the sub-systems (phonological loop and visuo-spatial scratchpad).

Cognitive psychology

The central executive

The central executive is required to perform a number of tasks, including:

■ focus and switch attention

■ co-ordinate the sub-systems – phonological loop and visuo-spatial scratchpad

■ connect working memory with long-term memory.

It is named the 'central executive' because it allocates attention to inputs and directs the operation of the other components – not unlike a business executive. It is a flexible system that can process information in any sensory modality in a variety of different ways. It can also store information for brief periods of time.

The visuo-spatial scratchpad

The visuo-spatial scratchpad can be divided into two components:

■ a visual component – deals with objects and features such as shape and colour

■ a spatial component – deals with locations and movements in space. The spatial component is involved in, for example, planning your way through a shopping centre.

The phonological loop

The phonological loop has two components:

■ a phonological store, which holds auditory memory traces for a few seconds before they fade

■ an articulatory rehearsal process, which is essentially sub-vocal speech, and has a limited capacity of about three to four items.

Auditory verbal information enters automatically into the phonological store. Visually presented language (for example, text that we read) can be transformed into phonological code by (silent) articulation and placed in the phonological store. The phonological store can be regarded as an 'inner ear' because it remembers vocal sounds in their temporal order. The articulatory process can be regarded as an 'inner voice' as it repeats the words in order to prevent them from fading away after about 2 seconds.

There has been a lot of research carried out into the phonological loop and evidence for this component comes from at least three areas:

■ **Similarity of sound** Studies have demonstrated that similar sounding letters, V P B G, are recalled less well than dissimilar letters, X A Y W. Similarity of sound in words also has a detrimental effect on recall, although similarity of meaning in words is unimportant. This suggests that the code is phonological.

■ **Word-length effect** Research findings suggest lists of short words are remembered better than longer words. Short words can be (silently) articulated faster than longer words and therefore more of them can be articulated in the time (approximately 2 seconds) before the trace decays.

■ **The effect of articulatory suppression** If participants in a study are asked to say something aloud at the same time as they are rehearsing material in a phonological loop, then memory for the rehearsed material is impaired.

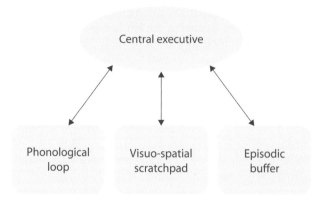

Fig. 4 *The working memory model with episodic buffer*

The episodic buffer

The three-component model of working memory has recently been revised and a fourth component, the **episodic buffer** has been added (Baddeley, 2000). It was considered necessary to add this fourth component because a number of problems were beginning to emerge with the original model:

▧ The three-component model had difficulty explaining the interaction between the working memory and long-term memory.

▧ On the original working memory model, there was no mechanism for allowing the sub-systems to interact.

Evaluation of the working memory model

Research evidence

▧ Evidence for a general attentional processor like the central executive, in addition to the sub-components of the model, is provided by dual-task experiments:

– Performing two tasks at the same time (concurrent). If the two tasks are using the same sub-system, performance is poorer when performed at the same time than when performed separately. If the two tasks require separate sub-systems (for example, visuo-spatial scratchpad and phonological loop), then they are usually performed equally as well together as separately.

– Articulatory suppression – this is saying something aloud (for example, repeating a word) which makes use of the articulatory loop thereby making it difficult to perform a simultaneous task using the same sub-system due to its limited capacity.

▧ There is an increasing amount of evidence to support the relationship between the phonological loop and the acquisition of language (Baddeley *et al.*, 1998). In a clinical study of a patient with a phonological loop deficit, but normal verbal long-term memory, Baddeley found a failure to acquire the vocabulary of a new language. In addition, the phonological loop is proving to be a good predictor of the ability of children to learn a second language.

▧ Key findings from studies identifying the brain regions associated with the use of the phonological loop have provided evidence for the functional separation of phonological store and articulatory processes. **Functional imaging** studies have identified the phonological store within **Wernicke's area** and the articulatory rehearsal process located within **Broca's area**. Such imaging studies have also produced clear

Key terms

Episodic buffer: a limited capacity store that binds together information from a number of fields – verbal, visual, spatial and chronological information. It can use access to the different sub-systems, and from conscious awareness.

Functional imaging: when a scan of the brain is carried out whilst tasks are being performed.

Wernicke's area: a region in the temporal region of the brain (usually left hemisphere) that is important to language.

Broca's area: a region in the frontal lobe (usually left hemisphere) that is important to speech production.

Link

For more about the brain see Chapter 1, Key approaches, p24.

Cognitive psychology

evidence that verbal and spatial working memories are separate. Verbal memories appear to be located in the left hemisphere (side) of the brain whereas spatial memory is located in the right hemisphere of the brain.

Link

To understand what a repeated measures design experiment is, refer to Chapter 4, Research methods.

Research study: Hunt (1980)

Aim: To investigate evidence for a limited capacity central executive.

Method: This was a repeated measures design experiment. Participants performed a psychomotor task – gliding a lever between two posts with only the use of thumb and index finger – and at the same time completed an intelligence test consisting of spatial patterns.

Results: As the problems became more difficult on the intelligence test, performance on the psychomotor task deteriorated.

Conclusion: Hunt interpreted the deterioration in performance as evidence that both tasks were making use of the same central processor (rather than sub-components) and both were competing for the same limited capacity available.

Evaluation: The experiment requires participants to perform two concurrent tasks that are most unlikely to take place togther in the real world and therefore it can be said to lack ecological validity. Furthermore, it is inferred that the two tasks are using the one central component, but could it be the visuo-spatial scratchpad that is in use?

Summary questions

1. On the multi-store model of memory, what is the duration of (a) sensory register, (b) short-term memory?

2. Describe a study that provides evidence for the duration of short-term memory.

3. Outline one limitation of the multi-store model of memory.

4. Identify the key component of the working memory model and explain the function of this component.

5. Qasim failed his recent maths module even though he tried to learn the formulae by repeating them over and over again. He did not understand the concepts and could not apply them in the exam. In geography he gained a grade A, and he understood the geographical concepts well because he had investigated them on a geography field trip.

   How might the levels of processing theory explain Qasim's failure at maths and success at geography?

Further evaluative comments

- The concept of the central executive has remained vague, even though this is the most important component of the working memory model. For example, the central executive is considered to have a limited capacity (Hunt, 1980), but there is no evidence provided as to what this capacity is.
- Much of the evidence provided for the working memory model is derived from laboratory studies with a high level of experimental control. This artificial environment may give us a detailed insight into theoretical models but may not generalise to complex real-life situations.
- This contemporary model of memory is still being researched and modified, and has provided valuable insight into the complexity of short-term memory processes.

Key points:

- The multi-store model of memory consists of a sensory register, a short-term memory (STM) and a long-term memory (LTM).
- Each component of the multi-store model has different properties, that is differences in code, capacity, duration.
- According to the multi-store model, the key process for transferring information from STM to LTM is rehearsal.
- The levels of processing theory emphasises that depth of processing is the key to long-term retention.
- The working memory model is a model of short-term memory only.
- The working memory model has a central executive and a number of sub-systems, including the visuo-spatial scratchpad and phonological loop; more recently the episodic buffer has been added.

Types of long-term memory

- Know and understand the main components of long-term memory.

- Evaluate the evidence for the separate components of long-term memory.

Key terms

Procedural memory: the skills and habits that people possess, for example how to swim, ride a bike, play the piano.

Semantic memory: our general knowledge about the world and all the facts we know. There is no specific link of time and place of learning the information.

Episodic memory: memories of specific episodes in a person's life. It includes all the personal and autobiographical information of a life and is affected by time, context, organisation and place of occurrence.

The long-term memory holds all the facts you have learned, the skills you have practised and your personal memories. It can store vast amounts of information and there seems to be no finite capacity. People can learn new facts and skills throughout their lives. A distinction has been made between different types of long-term stores: **procedural memory**, **semantic memory** and **episodic memory**:

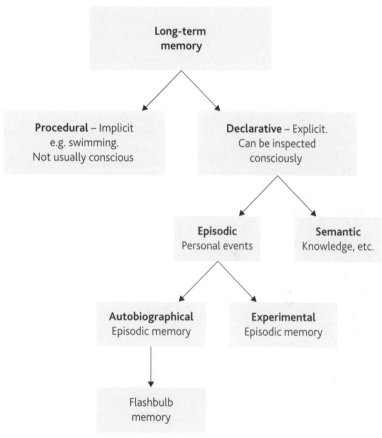

Fig. 5 *The main components of long-term memory*

Procedural memory

When we perform tasks such as swimming we do not call on conscious memory to enable us to do so, we can carry out this task unconsciously. In contrast, both semantic and episodic memories (known as 'declarative' memories) require the **conscious** recall of facts and events.

Semantic memory

To know that the capital of France is Paris, you do not need to know when and where you first learnt this fact. This differs from episodic memory which is closely tied to time and place. Information in semantic memory is thought to be hierarchically organised (Bower *et al.*, 1969). Here information is systematically linked to related information.

Research study: Bower *et al.* (1969)

Aim: To investigate semantic categorisation in long-term memory.

Method: Two groups of participants (independent design) were presented with the same words to learn but the words were presented differently. They were given four trials of 28 words (112 words in total) either hierarchically organised on the page (for example, musical instrument, string, parcel, paper, photocopier …), or randomly on the page. They were then asked to free recall as many words as possible (dependent variable).

Results: The 'organised condition' had significantly higher recall (mean of 73 words) than the 'random condition' (mean of 21 words).

Conclusion: As recall is facilitated by organisation, long-term memory storage is probably semantically organised.

Evaluation: When participants carry out memory experiments, an assumption is made about how the material is encoded. In the Bower study, it is assumed participants make semantic associations between the words in the organised condition, but not in the random condition. In fact this might not be the case. Even in a controlled experimental setting, it is difficult to know precisely what processing is taking place. In addition, such controlled laboratory experiments may tell us little about how memory works in the real world.

Link

For more information on independent design and dependent variable, see Chapter 4, Research methods.

Episodic memory

An example of a question that would require episodic memory is: 'What did you have for breakfast this morning?'

Cohen (1993) argued for a distinction between two types of episodic memory:

- **autobiographical episodic memory** – memory for specific life events that have personal meaning, for example where you went on holiday last year
- **experimental episodic memory**, for example learning lists of words which are already stored in semantic memory but are now tied to the specific episode of processing the list of words for an experiment.

A **flashbulb memory** is a detailed and vivid memory of an event that is stored after one occasion and lasts a lifetime. Such events are often life-changing autobiographical events such as births, deaths, or may be associated with important historical events such as 9/11. There is usually emotional arousal (fear, excitement) when the memory is first encoded and this emotional content makes the memory particularly vivid.

Research study: Conway *et al.* (1994)

Aim: To investigate a flashbulb memory for the memorable event of Margaret Thatcher's resignation.

Method: An opportunity sample of 923 participants were interviewed soon after Mrs Thatcher resigned as leader of the Conservative party, and just over one-third of them were interviewed again 11 months later. Details of the memory of the resignation were assessed for vividness and accuracy.

Results: Eighty-six per cent of the participants had an accurate memory of the event, which could be considered a flashbulb memory.

Conclusion: A flashbulb memory was formed from the distinctive event.

Evaluation: This was a longitudinal study and nearly two-thirds of the original sample were lost. This makes the remaining sample likely to be biased and the results may lack generalisability.

Evidence for separate components of long-term memory

Case studies of brain-damaged patients

■ HM was 27 years old and suffered from severe epilepsy when surgeons decided to carry out a drastic operation and remove most of his **hippocampus**. His memory was affected dramatically – he recalled most events from before the operation but could not store new memories; both episodic and semantic memories were affected. Although he could not remember what he had eaten for breakfast, he could acquire new procedural memories, for example he learned to play tennis. The part of his brain concerned with procedural memories (the **cerebellum**) was not affected by the operation.

■ Clive Wearing was a famous musician who suffered a rare brain infection in 1985 that left him with only a 'moment to moment' memory. However, some of the procedural memories that he had previously stored, such as playing the piano, were still available to him. If you asked him if he could play the piano (declarative knowledge) he would answer 'no', but he could in fact play (procedural memory).

Interactive nature of long-term memory stores

Although the memory systems are considered largely independent, many everyday tasks require an interaction of the stores. For example, if you were going into an examination you would probably draw on your previous experience of procedures to follow, for example where to sit. During the examination you would also be drawing on semantic knowledge and maybe episodic memories of previous examinations.

Key points:

■ Long-term memory holds a vast amount of information for an indefinite period.

■ A distinction has been made between three types of long-term stores: procedural, semantic; episodic.

■ Evidence for the separate components of long-term memory comes from clinical studies.

Links

■ For more information on opportunity sample and longitudinal study, see Chapter 4, Research methods.

■ For more information on case studies, see Chapter 4, Research methods.

■ For more information on structures such as the cerebellum, see Chapter 2, Biopsychology.

Key terms

Hippocampus: part of the limbic system, which is deep inside the brain.

Cerebellum: situated at the back of the brain behind the brain stem and stores the skills we have learnt.

Summary questions

6 Distinguish between procedural and semantic memory. Use an example to illustrate each type of store.

7 Outline what is meant by 'flashbulb memory'. Use an example to illustrate your answer.

8 Explain how one case study of a brain-damaged patient offers support for the distinction between different types of long-term store.

Explanations of forgetting

Learning objectives:

- Know and understand the explanations of forgetting in short-term memory and long-term memory.

- Understand the strengths and limitations of the explanations of forgetting.

Key terms

Trace: the change in neural tissue (in the brain) as a result of a stimulus.

Cue: anything that acts as an aid to retrieval from memory.

Engram: a permanent change in neural tissue (in the brain) that represents what has been learned.

Hint

Some researchers argue, however, that trace decay is a theory of both short-term and long-term forgetting.

Links

- For more information on repeated measures design experiment and ecological validity, see Chapter 4, Research methods.

- For more information on interference as a theory of forgetting, see the Keppel and Underwood (1962) study later in this chapter, p184.

Psychologists have proposed a number of theories for why we forget things. Some of these theories are concerned with problems when storing memories which lead to the memories not being available (for example, the memory **trace** has decayed). Other theories are to do with problems accessing memories that have been stored but for some reason are now not accessible to us (for example, because we have not got the appropriate **cue**). When we think about forgetting we usually mean from LTM, but information might be lost before it even gets there.

Trace decay

Information that enters STM leaves a trace in the brain due to the excitation of nerve cells. This neural activity gradually dies away unless the material is rehearsed. Hebb (1949) argued that whilst learning is taking place, the **engram** which will eventually be formed is very delicate and liable to disruption because it is an active trace. With learning, it grows stronger until a permanent engram is formed (the structural trace).

Some researchers argue that if knowledge and skills (in LTM) are not used and practised, then the engram will decay. According to Hebb (1949), trace decay can only apply to STM, as he believes when we rehearse material the corresponding neural activity causes a structural change in the brain (and therefore it is no longer a trace). Solso (1995) also concluded that there is no evidence that the major cause of forgetting from LTM is neurological decay.

Research study: Waugh and Norman (1965)

Aim: To investigate STM using a serial probe technique and support trace decay as a theory of forgetting.

Method: A repeated measures design experiment was conducted where participants were presented with lists of 16 digits at a rate of one to four per second. The last digit, known as the probe, occurred once before in the list and the task was to recall the digit which had followed it. It was predicted that participants would recall the digit more accurately if they were presented rapidly (four per second), as there would be less time for the trace to decay, than if they were presented more slowly (one digit per second).

Results: There was no relationship between speed of presentation and recall, which suggested trace decay was not a major source of forgetting on this task.

Conclusion: Waugh and Norman concluded that forgetting is probably better explained by interference rather than decay.

Evaluation: Waugh and Norman set out to support trace decay theory but their prediction was not supported. Keppel and Underwood (1962) also supported interference over trace decay theory. Note that both studies lack ecological validity as the tasks set were artificial and therefore may not be relevant to everyday life.

Evaluation of trace decay

▨ It is difficult to test trace decay theory because if participants are tested after different time periods they could be rehearsing and thus strengthening the trace; but if rehearsal is prevented (say with a **distractor task**), forgetting could be due to interference from the task rather than decay of the memory trace.

▨ Trace decay theory has difficulty dealing with situations where items which cannot be remembered at one time can be remembered at a future time, even though no additional presentations have been made. If the trace has decayed it should **never** be available.

▨ The experiment by Peterson and Peterson (1959) is used as evidence for the role of decay in STM, as their findings show that after 18 seconds the trace has almost completely decayed when rehearsal is prevented.

▨ Waugh and Norman, who set out to support trace decay, concluded that interference is the most likely cause of forgetting in STM.

▨ Displacement theory

Displacement theory explains forgetting from short-term memory in terms of the limited capacity of this store. It suggests that there are a limited number of 'slots' for information in short-term memory (approximately seven as found by Miller, 1956) and when the system is 'full' the oldest material is 'pushed out' or displaced by incoming information.

The study by Waugh and Norman (1965), using their serial probe task, offers support for the displacement theory of forgetting. They found that if the probe was one of the digits at the beginning of the list, recall was small because later digits would have displaced earlier ones. However, if the probe was presented towards the end of the list, recall was high, since the last digits would still be available in short-term memory. The poorer recall of items in the middle of the serial position curve could also be attributed to displacement.

Evaluation of displacement theory

Displacement theory seems to give an adequate account of forgetting from STM when applied to the multi-store model of memory. Empirical evidence, such as the Murdock primacy/recency experimental findings, offers support for the displacement theory. However, more recent models of memory, such as the working memory model, have indicated that STM is much more complex than the unitary, limited capacity short-term store first proposed by Atkinson and Shiffrin's multi-store model of memory.

▨ Interference theory

Interference theory is concerned with what occurs before, during and after learning. At the beginning of the storage process, interference can prevent new information from passing from STM to LTM. In LTM, as the store of information grows, there will be increasing interference between competing memories.

There are two types of interference:

▨ proactive interference, where earlier learning interferes with what you are trying to learn at present. For example, you have learnt Spanish and are now having difficulty learning French

▨ Links

▨ See study by Tulving (1968) under the retrieval failure theory of forgetting later in this chapter (p185).

▨ Peterson and Peterson's study was outlined under the STM component of the multi-store model of memory on p171.

▨ Key term

Distractor task: any task that interferes with rehearsal in short-term memory, for example counting backwards in threes from 300.

▮ Hint

Displacement is only concerned with forgetting from STM.

▨ Links

▨ Miller (1956) was discussed with respect to the capacity of STM under the multi-store model of memory on p170.

▨ Waugh and Norman (1965) is the research study in trace decay theory of forgetting on p182.

▨ The serial position curve is discussed in the evaluation of the multi-store model of memory on p172.

retroactive interference, where more recent learning interferes with the recall of earlier material. For example, you know your present mobile phone number but cannot now remember your previous one.

Research study: Keppel and Underwood (1962)

Aim: To investigate the effects of proactive interference on recall from memory.

Method: In a repeated measures design experiment, participants were given a series of trials where they had to learn trigrams (for example, TXK) and then count backwards for 3, 9 or 18 seconds (the independent variable). The order of testing was balanced to control for order effects. The dependent variable was the recall of the trigram.

Results: On the first trial, performance was almost 100 per cent even though some participants had only 3 seconds interval whilst others had 18 seconds. On the second and third trials, performance falls steadily as the interval increases. If decay is the sole explanation for forgetting, performance should fall as the interval increases on the first trial as well as subsequent trials.

Conclusion: The inferior performance on later trials was due to interference; the first trigram learned is remembered perfectly as there is no preceding item to interfere. This type of interference is proactive because earlier learning of trigrams interferes with later learning.

Evaluation: This study has low ecological validity as this situation would not arise in real life.

Link

For more information on independent variable and dependent variable, see Chapter 4, Research methods.

With respect to **retroactive** interference, McGeogh (1942) found the greater the similarity between the two lists, the greater the interference, and this was called 'response competition'. Other researchers have suggested retroactive interference is a type of 'unlearning' of the first list.

Evaluation of interference theory

The strongest support for interference theory comes from laboratory studies such as the Keppel and Underwood study. However, such laboratory studies tend to use nonsense syllables as the stimulus material. When meaningful material is used, interference is more difficult to demonstrate (Solso, 1995). Interference theory suffers as a general theory of forgetting because the situations it best deals with are rarely encountered in everyday life. We do not often have to learn similar verbal responses to the same stimuli in a short period of time. In the laboratory, for example learning takes place in a very limited amount of time and this makes it much more likely that interference will occur (Baddeley, 1990). Such studies, therefore, lack ecological validity. Solso (1995) has pointed out that studies of interference have largely involved episodic memory and although this demonstrates that episodic memory may be subject to interference, semantic memory is likely to be more resistant.

Lack of consolidation

Time-dependent changes occur in the nervous system as a result of learning. In order for information in STM to become an LTM, it must go through a process known as **consolidation**. During consolidation, STM is repeatedly activated. If something interrupts the process, say a bang to the head, then STM cannot be consolidated and memories cannot be 'stored' for long-term access.

Research study: Yarnell and Lynch (1970)

Aim: To investigate memory loss due to concussion.

Method: A field study was carried out with American footballers who were concussed for a brief period of time during a game. They were approached immediately they regained consciousness and asked for details of the events that occurred in the game just prior to the injury. They were asked again 20 minutes later.

Results: Accurate information was given when the footballers were questioned immediately after they regained consciousness, but the same information was not available 20 minutes later.

Conclusion: The consolidation process had been disrupted and therefore the information about the game was not available in long-term store.

Evaluation: As this was a field study it was high in ecological validity but there were problems of control. For example, is it certain they had been concussed? If so, for how long? There are also ethical implications when questioning patients recovering from (even brief) concussion.

Evaluation of lack of consolidation

▥ Patients who have been concussed often suffer retrograde amnesia, which is loss of memory for events prior to the concussion. This may be because the consolidation process has been interrupted.

▥ Electro-convulsive therapy (ECT) causes memory loss for events just before the therapy is given. Evidence suggests that after a one-hour delay between learning and ECT, perfect retention occurs. This suggests that the essential consolidation period required, to ensure information reaches long-term store, is up to one hour. There is evidence from both animals and humans to support the theory that a consolidation process is necessary to prevent memory disruption and loss.

💡 Retrieval failure theory

According to retrieval failure theory, memories cannot be recalled because the correct retrieval cues are not being used. The role of retrieval cues is demonstrated by the 'tip-of-the-tongue' phenomenon, in which we know that we know something but cannot retrieve it from LTM at that particular moment.

An everyday example of retrieval failure might be where you go upstairs to get a pen but once there cannot remember what you went upstairs for. As soon as you go back down to the place you first thought about the pen, you are likely to remember. This is because you now have the **environmental cues** to aid memory.

Tulving (1972) investigated retrieval failure in LTM. He gave participants a list of words and then asked them to write down as many as they could

▮ Key terms

Consolidation: where time is needed for learning to become firmly recorded.

Environmental cue: something in the surroundings that helps you to remember.

▮ Link

For more information on what a field study is, see Chapter 4, Research methods.

Cognitive psychology

remember in any order. Later participants were asked to recall them a second and then a third time. Tulving found that not all of the same words were recalled across the three occasions, and one word was recalled on the third occasion that had not been recalled on the earlier trials. These findings cannot be explained by trace decay because if the trace had decayed it would never be available, but retrieval failure theory would argue that different retrieval cues were used on the three occasions, which resulted in the difference in recall.

Tulving (1974) used the term 'cue-dependent forgetting' to explain that if the same cues are not present at recall as during the original learning, then recall is poor. There are two types of cue-dependent forgetting:

- **context-dependent forgetting**, which occurs if the relevant environmental variables that were present when learning took place are missing at recall; these variables act as external cues
- **state-dependent forgetting**, which occurs in the absence of relevant psychological or physiological variables that were present during learning; these variables act as internal cues. A study by Bower (1981) showed that when the mood (internal cue) of participants at learning and recall was matched (for example, happy at learning and happy at recall) recall was superior to a mismatch of mood at learning and recall.

Research study: Godden and Baddeley (1975)

Aim: To see if cues from the environment affect recall.

Method: A field experiment was carried out with deep-sea divers who learned lists of words either on land or underwater (independent variable). Recall of words (dependent variable) was then tested in the same or a different context.

Results: Those who learned and recalled in different contexts (for example, learned on land and recalled under water, or vice versa) showed more than a 30 per cent deficit compared to those who learned and recalled in the same context.

Conclusion: Environmental context affects memory, and superior recall occurs when environmental conditions at learning and recall match.

Evaluation: Although this was a field experiment which means it is more ecologically valid than controlled laboratory studies, the extreme conditions do not really reflect memory in everyday conditions.

Link

For more information on field experiment, independent variable and dependent variable, see Chapter 4, Research methods.

Evaluation of retrieval failure theory

Retrieval failure theory is able to explain findings that cannot be explained by trace decay theory (Tulving, 1972) and there is a lot of empirical evidence to support cue-dependent forgetting. However, some of this evidence has been criticised. The Bower (1981) study manipulating the mood of participants under hypnosis has never been replicated. This study also suffers from dubious ethics. In addition, studies have often been carried out under extreme conditions (for example, deep-sea divers) or where the states are very different (for example, manipulation of extreme moods via hypnosis), whereas in real life we rarely have to recall things under such extreme conditions. These studies can be said, therefore, to lack ecological validity, and in less dramatic changes in environment only slight differences in recall are produced (Baddeley, 1995).

Motivated forgetting theory

Perhaps forgetting has nothing to do with interference from other items, or failure to consolidate material, but in fact we are **motivated** to forget. According to Freud (1901), some experiences are so painful that if they were allowed to enter consciousness they would produce overwhelming anxiety. Instead, these experiences are **repressed** and stored in the unconscious, thereby becoming inaccessible. Even when a person seems to be trying hard to recall a particular event, they may stop or change the subject when they come near to recalling the original, painful memory.

In motivated forgetting, the original experience has been stored but it has now become inaccessible. Retrieval is not available through conscious efforts to try to remember – in fact the more we try to remember something, the more it is likely to be repressed. The material has been repressed usually because it is upsetting or potentially harmful and can cause anxiety. Access to repressed memories can occur through the use of Freudian techniques, such as free association (a psychoanalytic technique where the patient is encouraged to verbalise all their thoughts to an analyst, no matter how trivial or bizarre they may seem), or sometimes repressed events break though in the form of dreams or parapraxes (slips of the tongue). What is repressed varies from individual to individual but when the event is recalled it is accompanied with an unpleasant emotional reaction (for example, fear, guilt). The memory is retrieved only when the emotional tension associated with it is released (known as catharsis) and this usually occurs during therapy.

Key term

Repressed: pushed below conscious awareness.

Research study: Glucksberg and Lloyd (1967)

Aim: To investigate motivated forgetting.

Method: In a repeated design experiment participants were required to learn a paired-associate list of words (A–B). They were then asked to read a second list of words some of which were related to the B words on the paired-associate list. The related words on the second list were accompanied by an unexpected and unavoidable electric shock. Participants were then asked to recall the original A–B list of paired associate words (dependent variable).

Results: The B words that were related to the second list of words learnt (and which were acompanied by the electric shock) were forgotten significantly more often than the control words.

Conclusion: This supports the motivated theory of forgetting as the words accompanied with an electric shock would have unpleasant associations and would have been repressed.

Evaluation: There are ethical implications around the issues of deception and use of electric shocks in this study. This is also a fairly contrived study as motivated forgetting is usually concerned with personal and emotional events.

Link

For more information on repeated design experiment and dependent variable, see Chapter 4, Research methods.

Evaluation of motivated forgetting theory

In order to investigate motivated forgetting in the laboratory, participants would need to experience something traumatic, and this is unethical. Where mildly upsetting experiences have been

Cognitive psychology

investigated in the laboratory (for example, Glucksberg and Lloyd) evidence has been found for the repression hypothesis.

Support for motivated forgetting is also evident in tests of emotional inhibition. For example, Levinger and Clark (1961) found participants were particularly poor at remembering associations to emotional words (for example, anger).

However, more recent studies have found that it may not be repression but **arousal** that influences the recall of emotionally charged words. Although findings from studies on immediate recall support poorer recall for emotional words, when participants are tested after a delay of seven days or more, the opposite results are found, that is the emotional-arousing words are better recalled (Parkin *et al.*, 1982). This cannot be explained by repressive forgetting but can be explained by the arousal hypothesis. This hypothesis proposes that high arousal inhibits immediate recall but leads to better recall in the longer term (Bradley and Baddeley, 1990).

Table 1 *A summary of the theories of forgetting in short-term and long-term memory*

Short-term memory	Short-term memory and long-term memory	Long-term memory
Decay	Interference	Interference
Displacement	Decay	Lack of consolidation
		Retrieval failure
		Motivated forgetting

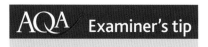

Examiner's tip

Questions can be asked about any named theory of forgetting so you must learn all the theories.

Key points:

Trace decay explains forgetting as the fading of a neurological trace which is formed when a stimulus is encoded.

Displacement is based on the limited capacity of STM because when the seven 'slots' are full, new information pushes out the oldest information in short-term store.

Retrieval failure is concerned with cues, both internal (for example, mood) and external (for example, environment), which aid retrieval of memories. However, the research into retrieval failure has often involved extreme conditions and therefore has lacked ecological validity.

There are two type of interference: retroactive and proactive. Support for interference theory of forgetting comes largely from laboratory studies and these may not be relevant to forgetting in real life.

Lack of consolidation as a theory of forgetting refers to the necessary period of time required so that memories can be 'embedded' in long-term store, and if disruption occurs during the consolidation period then memories of events just prior to the incident are lost.

Motivated forgetting refers to Freud's theory of repression, which is when anxiety-provoking material is pushed into the unconscious and becomes inaccessible.

Cognitive psychology

Summary questions

9 With respect to trace decay theory of forgetting, what is a 'trace'?

10 Outline what is meant by 'displacement' with respect to forgetting.

11 Explain how the Waugh and Norman study: (a) does not support trace decay theory; (b) does support displacement theory of forgetting.

12 Outline one weakness of the retrieval failure theory of forgetting.

13 Use an example to distinguish between retroactive and proactive interference.

14 Outline what is meant by 'consolidation' with respect to memory and forgetting.

15 What is the main problem when trying to study motivated forgetting in the laboratory?

16 Lucy always revised in her bedroom, lounging on her bed with the TV on. When she tested herself at home she remembered all the key facts. In the examination room, Lucy failed to recall a lot of the previously learned facts, but when she returned to her bedroom she remembered all the key facts again.

Outline one theory of forgetting that might account for Lucy's experience. Describe a strategy Lucy could use to ensure this forgetting does not occur in the future.

 End-of-chapter activity

Design an experiment to test the levels of processing theory, based on the study by Craik and Tulving (1975). You will need to make a number of design and implementation decisions, for example whether to use a repeated measures design (as Craik and Tulving did), and you will need to operationalise your variables, that is decide how you will measure recall (the dependent variable) and what the conditions will be (the independent variable). You will also need to think carefully about how you can control potentially confounding variables, and about ethical issues.

Use 20 small cards and on one side write a word for participants to process. Each word should be similar in length and complexity and be a common noun, for example HOUSE. On the back of half of the cards write a deep processing/semantic question, for example 'Does this word fit into the sentence THE DOG RAN OFF WITH THE …?'; and on the other half a shallow processing/structural question, for example 'Is this word in capital letters?' Following presentation of each card (separately at 5-second intervals), participants should recall as many of the words as possible in 2 minutes.

 Link

For more information on design of experiments and ethical issues, see Chapter 4, Research methods.

1 (a) Outline what is meant by context as an aid to retrieving information from memory. Illustrate your answer with an example. *(3 marks)*

(b) The following examples illustrate the three different explanations of forgetting. In each case, write whether the example illustrates displacement, interference or a lack of consolidation.

(i) Alison drove a left-hand drive car all the time she was in Spain. Because the car was left-hand drive, the passenger and driver positions were the opposite to those in her British car. When she came home, she kept going to open the passenger's door instead of the driver's door.

(ii) Ewan listed the ten things that he wanted me to buy him but, by the time he had finished speaking, I had forgotten the first three or four.

(iii) When Olwen recovered consciousness after her operation, she had forgotten all about the magazine article she had read just before the operation. *(3 marks)*

(c) Outline what is meant by the following:

(i) episodic memory *(2 marks)*
(ii) procedural memory? *(2 marks)*

(d) Describe and evaluate the multi-store model of memory. *(10 marks)*

AQA, 2006

2 (a) Outline what is meant by displacement and state why it does not explain forgetting from long-term memory. *(3 marks)*

(b) In a study investigating levels of processing, participants are shown a series of words including SOAK, peach and LATER. After they are shown each word, they are asked one of three questions.

Identify the level of processing that would be triggered by the question:

(i) Does it rhyme with joke?
(ii) Can you eat it?
(iii) Is it in capital letters? *(3 marks)*

(c) Identify four features of the working memory model. *(4 marks)*

(d) Andrea has been studying for examinations in Italian and Spanish, She spent hours revising Italian vocabulary in her bedroom some weeks ago. Unfortunately she cannot remember it very well in the examination and she sometimes writes Spanish words by mistake.

Describe and evaluate two likely explanations for Andrea's forgetting. *(10 marks)*

AQA, 2006

Perceptual organisation: the Gestalt principles

Learning objectives:

Learning objectives:

- Understand the main principles of the Gestalt School.

- Know and understand the Gestalt laws of perceptual organisation.

- Evaluate the usefulness of the Gestalt principles in aiding our understanding of visual perception.

Links

- Monocular depth cue, binocular depth cue and constancy are explained on pp194–197.

- Rubin's vase is discussed further in 'Ambiguous figures', p199.

Key terms

Gestalt: a German word with no exact English translation but is generally used to mean 'unified whole'.

Perceptual organisation: how we structure the information from a stimulus, this occurs at an unconscious level.

Pragnanz: a German word which means that we attempt to perceive a coherent structure.

Sensation is the information that is received by our sense organs from the environment, and perception is how that information is interpreted. The main senses through which we receive information are visual, olfactory (smell), touch, taste and auditory (hearing). This chapter will focus largely on the perception and interpretation of visual sensory information. The information that is received by our senses is often confusing and disorganised, for example the sense receptors in the retina of the eye detect a two-dimensional, flat image, but the interpretation by the brain is of a three-dimensional object. In order to perceive this depth and interact with the environment appropriately, our brain makes use of a number of cues, including monocular and binocular depth cues. Additionally, the information received by the visual system is in a variety of unrealistic colours and forms (that is, strange shapes and sizes). The brain makes use of a number of constancies in order to interpret the world in a stable way.

Our brain and visual system takes the fragmentary information received by the sense organs and forms an organised perception. The **Gestalt** psychologists have offered useful information about how this perceptual organisation occurs.

A group of German psychologists studied **perceptual organisation** and in the 1930s developed the Gestalt school in the USA. They believed that rather than studying the basic sensory experiences, psychologists should study the whole figure ('the Gestalt'). They also believed that people are born with certain tendencies, such as the tendency to organise visual material in predictable ways, and that these can be described.

The basic principle for Gestalt psychologists was the law of **Pragnanz**. This law explains psychological organisation as always extracting the simplest and most stable shape to be perceived in an object. This can be illustrated in examples of 'figure-ground'. When you look at dual-image figures you see one image and the other becomes the background. In the Rubin's vase picture (see Figure 18 on p199), if you 'see' the vase this becomes the object and the faces become the background. Similarly, when the faces are perceived the vase becomes the background.

A main assumption of the Gestaltists is that 'the whole is more than the sum of its parts'. Max Wertheimer (1880–1943), a Gestalt psychologist, compiled a list of Gestalt laws of perceptual organisation which are used to demonstrate the perception of groups (the whole) rather than individual elements (the parts).

Cognitive psychology

Table 1 *The main Gestalt principles*

Law	Explanation	Diagram
Proximity	This principle states that things that are close together are usually seen as belonging together.	**Fig. 1** *In this figure we tend to see four sets of two, rather than a set of eight*
Similarity	The principle of similarity states that we tend to group together things that have similar characteristics.	**Fig. 2** *In this figure we tend to group together the black dots and white dots*
Closure	There is a tendency to close simple figures by filling in the missing information to make a whole figure.	**Fig. 3** *In this figure we tend to close up the boxes*
Good continuation	This principle states that we have a preference for continuous figures.	**Fig. 4** *In this figure we tend to see two continuous wavy lines, rather than lines that break in the middle*

Gestalt laws of organisation

■ **Research study: Navon (1977)**

Aim: To investigate whether the whole is perceived before the parts making up that whole, thus supporting the Gestalt position that 'the whole is more than the sum of its parts'.

Method: In a controlled experiment participants were presented with a number of figures and had to identify either the single large letter or the smaller letters making up the large letters. The small letters were sometimes the same and sometimes conflicting with the large letter. The independent variable was whether the small letters were the same or conflicted with the large letter. The dependent variable was the time taken to identify the small letters and the large letters.

Results: There was no difference in the time taken to identify the large letter, whether it was made up of the same or different letters. However, the time taken to identify the small letters was much greater when the small letters and large letters were different, than when the small letters and large letters were the same.

Conclusion: The identity of the large letter (the whole) was available before information about the parts (small letters) and therefore the results support the Gestalt position.

Evaluation: This is a rather contrived task that has been set up to suit a laboratory situation and does not necessarily reflect how perception works in the real world. Rarely in real life do we have to identify such letters and therefore the experiment, although well controlled, lacks ecological validity.

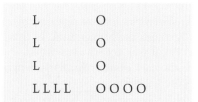

Fig. 5 *Example from Navon's study*

Evaluation of the principles of the Gestalt school

One important contribution made by the Gestalt school is that we have a set of basic laws that explain how we make sense of sensory input. First we perceive a form or figure distinct from the background, then this 'form' is further influenced by our need to organise sensory inputs into meaningful 'wholes'. These Gestalt laws are still valid and can be applied to our understanding of modern developments, including modern media devices such as television and computers.

However, there have been criticisms of the Gestalt school. The laws have been **described** but not **explained**. For example, Gestalt psychologists have never explained the processes that are involved when we 'close' an incomplete figure. A further criticism is that the Gestalt laws can describe organisation of **two-dimensional** objects but have proved inadequate when applied to **three-dimensional** objects, which, of course, is what we are constantly exposed to in real life.

Key points:

- A key assumption of the Gestalt approach to perceptual organisation is that 'the whole is more than the sum of its parts'.

- There are a number of Gestalt laws of organisation which explain how we perceive sensory inputs, these include proximity, similarity, closure and good continuation.

- There is empirical evidence to support the Gestalt principle that the whole is perceived before the parts, such as the study by Navon (1977).

- Although the Gestalt principles are still relevant today, more recent models of perceptual organisation can better explain three-dimensional perception, etc.

Link

For more information on controlled experiment, independent and dependant variables, see Chapter 4, Research methods.

Summary questions

1 What is the law of Pragnanz?

2 Name two Gestalt laws of organisation and give an example of each.

3 Outline one strength and one weakness of the Gestalt principles of perception.

4 Usman was studying psychology and was doing a practical in class. He was given a series of paired figures, like the example below, and was asked first to identify the small letters that made up each large letter, and then to identify the large letter.

It took Usman significantly longer to identify the conflicting small letter (v) than the matching small letter (x) although the identification of the large letter was equally fast for both stimuli. What explanation would Gestalt psychologists give for Usman's results?

Depth cues in perception

Learning objectives:

- Know and understand the main depth cues that allow us to perceive distance.

- Explain how monocular depth cues differ from binocular depth cues.

- Know and understand the main visual constancies that allow us to perceive visual objects accurately.

Key terms

Depth perception: viewing the world in three dimensions.

Depth cue: a clue or signal that gives information about the three-dimensional nature of an object.

Motion parallax: the visual cues picked up by a moving observer.

Depth perception allows us to perceive distance – the distance of objects from us in the environment and from each other. We can determine the relative distance of objects by making use of two kinds of cues: binocular ('two-eye') and monocular ('one-eye'). When something is far away from us, we rely on monocular cues and for closer objects we use both monocular and binocular cues. We live in a world of three dimensions but our retinas are essentially two-dimensional. It is depth perception which enables us to perceive the world in three dimensions.

Figure 6 shows the different types of **depth cue** available to each separate eye (monocular) and both eyes together (binocular).

Monocular depth cues

Monocular depth cues allow a person to judge depth and distance with just one eye.

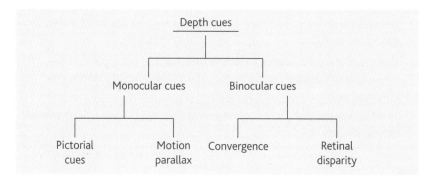

Fig. 6 *Depth cues*

Motion parallax

One monocular cue is **motion parallax**. This involves movement and is therefore experienced in the natural environment (or in a motion picture). When we are moving, say on a train, close objects seem to pass by quickly and distant objects seem to pass by slowly. The visual system uses this information to calculate how far away an object is, as the faster an object passes by the closer it must be to us.

Pictorial cues

The other type of monocular cues can be represented in, say, a drawing; indeed artists use these visual cues to make two-dimensional paintings appear realistic. The main pictorial depth cues are listed in Table 2.

Binocular depth cues

Binocular depth cues occur because the visual fields of both eyes overlap. Only animals that have eyes on the front of their head (for example, primates) can make use of binocular cues; other animals (for example, fish) are restricted to monocular cues. There are only two binocular cues: convergence and retinal disparity.

Table 2 *The main pictorial depth cues*

Monocular pictorial cue	Explanation	Diagram
Linear perspective	Lines that are parallel (for example, railway tracks, roads) look like they come to a point (converge) in the distance. The further the lines are from us, the more they appear to converge.	Fig. 7
Interposition	Objects that are nearer block objects that are further away. If the image of one object blocks the image of another, the first object is seen as closer to us.	Fig. 8
Height in the plane	Objects that are further away appear higher in the visual field.	Fig. 9
Relative size	When an object moves further away from the eye, the image gets smaller. Objects with smaller images are seen as more distant. This cue is only useful if we know the approximate actual size of the object.	Fig. 10
Shadow	A cast shadow is projected onto another surface by an object. This gives the appearance of a solid (three-dimensional) object; when a cast shadow is present but not attached to an object it gives a cue to distance.	Fig. 11
Texture gradient	A coarser texture looks closer, and a finer texture looks more distant. This is particularly useful for perceiving the distance of objects resting on the ground, for example grass, sand.	Fig. 12

Convergence

When you are looking at an object in the distance, the two eyes are parallel, but as the object gets closer the eyes turn towards each other, or converge. As the eyes turn inwards, the external eye muscles stretch and pull, sending impulses to the brain to give you this depth cue. The stretching of the eye muscle is not usually consciously registered but if you hold a pen at arm's length and watch the pen as you bring it forward to touch your nose, you probably will feel the stretch of the eye muscles. Convergence is most important for perceiving the distance of objects in close range. When the eyes converge on a nearby object, the angle between them is greater than when they converge

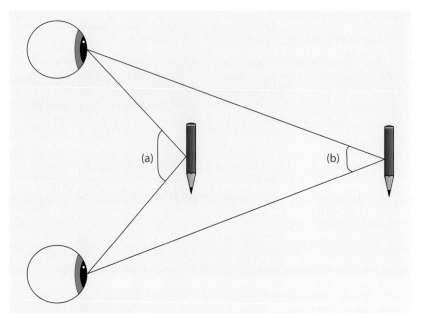

Fig. 13 *Convergence: angle (a) is larger than angle (b), and therefore pen (a) is perceived as closer to the person*

on a distant object. The brain uses this information to determine the distance of the object. In this way how close the pen is to your nose can be assessed.

Retinal disparity

Our two eyes are approximately 6 cm apart and because of this separation, there is a disparity (difference) between the image that falls on each **retina** at the back of the eye. Furthermore, the closer the object is, the greater the disparity of an image is on the retinas. The amount of disparity produced by the image of an object on the two retinas provides an important clue about its distance from us. To demonstrate this retinal disparity, close one eye and line your finger up with the corner of the room. Now close that eye and open the other eye – the finger appears to move!

Visual constancies

Perceptual constancies involve seeing visual objects accurately, regardless of their distance away from us, or other factors that distort the retinal image. For example, when we approach an object we do not perceive it as getting larger in size or different in shape. The image on the retina becomes larger but we adjust this change in size relative to the decrease in distance. When we observe an object, the light falling on the retina is known as the 'retinal image'. Light rays enter through the lens in the front of the eye and are focused on a particular area of the retina at the back of the eye. The intriguing question is 'how does the brain interpret the light image on the retina to arrive at an accurate perception?' This usually accurate perception is partly due to visual constancy.

Size constancy

If you move closer to an object, then the size of the image the object forms on your retina will get larger, but in human vision the perceived size of the object remains constant. To illustrate this, hold both hands in front of you, your left hand at arm's length and your right hand about half way to your face. Both hands are perceived as the same size, but the retinal image of the right hand will be much larger.

How is it that we perceive the hand as being the same size in spite of these differences in the retinal image? One explanation for this (that is, for size constancy) is that the brain receives information both about the size of the retinal image and distance of the object. The visual system seems to automatically make allowances for distance. Taking account of both size and distance in the visual system the brain would conclude that the hands are the same size.

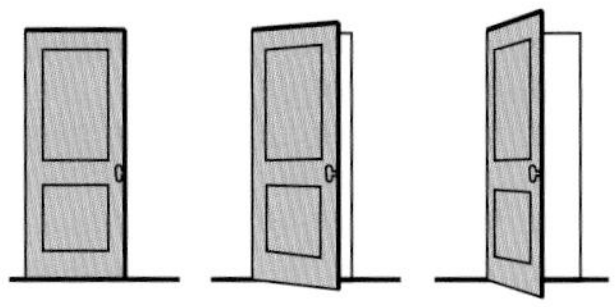

Fig. 14 *Shape constancy; the three doors are perceived as 'normal' shaped*

Shape constancy

Two quite different viewpoints of the same object do not stop us from recognising it. In real life, our viewpoint of objects changes all the time and yet we do not experience differences in the perceived shape of these objects – if we did, it would be very difficult to negotiate our way around! The pattern of lines which form the image on the retina is different for the three viewpoints of the doors in Figure 14, but the object is recognised as one and the same. A door is 'seen' as a rectangular shape even when open and the retinal image is of a trapezium.

Form constancy

The constant perception of an object's size and shape as we move around our environment is known as **form constancy**. This has been explained by Helmholtz (1910) as **unconscious inference**. We are aware of the size and shape of a familiar object, and therefore if the image on our retinas is large the object is perceived as being close, and if the retinal image is small it must be far away.

Key points:

■ There are two kinds of depth cues available to aid perception – monocular and binocular.

■ Monocular depth cues include motion parallax, which is important for perception of movement, and pictorial depth cues, which are applied to static images.

■ The two binocular depth cues are convergence and retinal disparity.

■ Visual constancies, such as size and shape, allow us to perceive objects accurately.

Key term

Unconscious inference: involves a mental judgement (of which we are unaware) based on the limited information we have available.

Summary questions

5 Identify three pictorial depth cues.

6 Use an example to explain one of the depth cues identified in the previous question.

7 Identify one binocular depth cue and explain how this can help us to perceive distance.

8 Identify one example of a perceptual constancy, and explain how this constancy can aid visual perception.

Cognitive psychology

Visual illusions

Learning objectives:

- Describe the Ponzo and Muller-Lyer illusions.

- Evaluate explanations for visual illusion.

- Describe the Necker Cube and Rubin's Vase ambiguous figures.

- Explain what visual illusions and ambiguous figures tell us about perception.

Fig. 15 *An example of the Ponzo illusion*

Key terms

Ponzo illusion: where two equal horizontal lines are perceived as unequal due to the linear perspective from the converging lines.

Linear perspective: a monocular depth cue.

Carpentered environment: one in which buildings are built from long straight pieces of material with right angle joints.

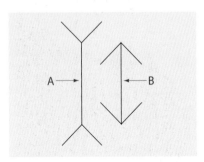

Fig. 16 *The Muller-Lyer illusion*

Normally the visual system receives accurate information about the size and distance of objects, usually by the use of distance cues. Psychologists have been particularly interested in instances when the visual system makes errors, as sometimes it does when conflicting information is received.

💡 Distortion illusions

The Ponzo illusion

In the **Ponzo illusion** the top horizontal line looks longer than the line below it despite the fact that they are the same size and therefore must have the same retinal image. One explanation for perceiving the top line as longer is that this illusion contains false depth cues (**linear perspective**) which trigger the size constancy mechanism inappropriately. In the case of the Ponzo illusion, the converging lines are the false depth cues which 'trick' the brain into assuming the top line is further away than the bottom line. An object that is further away produces a smaller retinal image, but this retinal image is of two lines of the same size. The size constancy mechanism, therefore, expands the perceived size of the top line. In most cases automatic triggering of the size constancy mechanism by a simple depth cue would result in an accurate perception. It is when perception goes wrong that psychologists have been given an insight into how the automatic scaling mechanism might operate.

The Muller-Lyer illusion

The Muller-Lyer illusion requires the observer to look at two lines and decide which is longer. The lines are actually of equal length, but the line with the outgoing fins is perceived as longer. Segall *et al.* (1963) presented the Muller-Lyer illusion to participants from western and non-western cultures and found that people from **carpentered** (western) cultures were more susceptible to this illusion. They concluded that the Muller-Lyer illusion is a result of our experience with angles found at the intersection of walls with ceilings and floors. This type of building is experienced in a western culture but not in a non-western culture.

Evaluation of the Muller-Lyer illusion

There are a number of criticisms with the explanations presented for the Muller-Lyer illusion:

- On the Segall *et al.* study, as the materials were drawings on paper, the differences found between cultures could simply be differences in experiences of interpreting two-dimensional drawings.

- Some critics of the 'carpentered world' hypothesis for the Muller-Lyer illusion point to the fact that children (who have limited visual experience) tend to be more susceptible to the illusion than adults, when in fact you would expect the opposite to be the case if the illusion was simply due to our exposure to a western, angular environment.

The moon illusion

Illusions are rare in the natural world but one illusion that does occur is the moon (and sun) illusion. This is where the moon appears larger when low down on the horizon than when high in the sky. The size of the retinal image does not change. One explanation for why it appears to be much larger when the moon is close to the horizon is again due to constancy scaling. When the moon is high in the sky, there is no depth or distance information available and so you see the moon at its retinal image size. However, when the moon is low down, near the horizon, depth cues operate. The horizon is as far away as it is possible to see, so constancy scaling automatically increases the size. If the moon (whose retinal image remains the same) appears to be further away when it is closer to the horizon, then we conclude it must be larger.

▨ Ambiguous figures

Ambiguous figures give two hypotheses to choose from because the data from the stimulus are insufficient to enable us to make an unambiguous interpretation of what our senses tell us.

The Necker cube

With the **Necker cube**, the same input results in different perceptions of the cube, which appears to have two orientations, and we tend to 'flip' between them. The cube appears to spontaneously reverse if we look at it for about 30 seconds.

Rubin's vase

Rubin's vase is another example of an ambiguous figure; we can perceive either two faces or a vase. Both hypotheses are correct, so your perceptual system cannot reject either.

Old/young woman

A famous ambiguous figure is the old/young woman. Again our perceptual system can form two hypotheses – a picture of a young woman or an old woman, but you do not see them simultaneously. Once you perceive both figures, you can fluctuate back and forth between the two. The origin of this figure is unclear, but this early example is from a German postcard of 1888. E.G. Boring adapted this figure in 1930 and it has now become widely known.

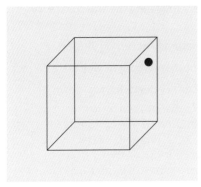

Fig. 17 *The Necker cube ambiguous figure: stare at the dot*

Fig. 18 *Rubin's vase. Did you see the vase or the face profiles first?*

AQA **Examiner's tip**

Both the Ponzo illusion and the Muller-Lyer illusion or the preceding page are named on the specification and therefore could be named in a question.

■ **Links**

- ■ See Gregory's theory of perception (p203) for further discussion of the Muller-Lyer illusion.
- ■ This is an example of the Gestalt psychologist's 'law of Pragnanz' – see p191.

■ **Key term**

Necker cube: a line drawing of a transparent cube that appears to reverse when viewed.

AQA **Examiner's tip**

Both the Necker cube and Rubin's vase are named on the specification and therefore could be named in a question.

Fig. 19 *The original ambiguous figure of the old/young woman. Can you see them both?*

Cognitive psychology

What do visual illusions and ambiguous figures tell us about perception?

Ambiguous figures

▨ Visual perception is an active process whereby the brain is actively trying to extract meaning from the retinal image. This offers support for the top-down explanation for perception as proposed by Gregory (1972).

▨ Research carried out on an adapted version of the old/young woman (Figure 19) offers support for Gregory's theory of hypothesis testing. When participants are first shown a picture of a young woman followed by the ambiguous figure, they are significantly more likely to report seeing the young woman; similarly if shown a picture of an old woman prior to the ambiguous figure they are significantly more likely to report seeing an old woman. Such studies clearly show that our perceptual hypotheses can be affected by what we expect to see – thus supporting both the concept of 'perceptual set', and also Gregory's theory of perceptual hypothesis testing.

Visual illusions

▨ Visual illusions have given psychologists an insight into the automatic scaling mechanisms (for example, size constancy) that are applied in visual perception. The depth cues from the converging lines in the Ponzo illusion (Figure 15), and the arrows in the Muller-Lyer illusion (Figure 16), cause constancy scaling to occur. This results in an error in perception. By making careful adjustments to these depth cues, psychologists have been able to research visual perception in carefully controlled environments and find out more about perceptual processing.

▨ A criticism of the research into visual illusions is that they are often on two-dimensional drawings in laboratory situations where there are limited environmental cues. This means the studies lack ecological validity. In the real world there are a multitude of cues from the environment and perception is usually accurate. We normally have little trouble estimating the size and distance of objects and do not, for example, see people in the distance and think they are miniature humans!

Key points:

▪ Distortion illusions (for example, the Ponzo illusion) are generally explained by depth cues inappropriately triggering the size constancy mechanism.

▪ The moon illusion is an example of a naturally occurring illusion.

▪ Ambiguous figures give rise to two hypotheses, both of which are correct.

▪ Visual illusions and ambiguous figures are evidence for top-down processing.

Links

▪ For more about Gregory, see Theories of perception on p203.

▪ For more information about perceptual set, see p206.

Summary questions

9 Name two distortion illusions.

10 Give a brief explanation for one of the illusions you have identified above.

11 Give two examples of ambiguous figures.

12 Briefly discuss what visual illusions and/or ambiguous figures tell us about perception.

Cognitive psychology

Theories of perception

Learning objectives:

■ Describe the main components of Gibson's theory of visual perception.

■ Understand the strengths and limitations of a bottom-up approach to perception.

■ Describe the main components of Gregory's theory of visual perception.

■ Understand the strengths and limitations of a top-down approach to perception.

Hint

There are a number of different terms given to Gibson's theory of perception, including: direct, bottom-up, data-driven.

Key terms

Texture gradient: a gradual change in the microstructure of a surface.

Bottom-up processing: perception is determined by information coming from the 'raw' stimulus.

Optic array: the complex pattern of light which reaches the perceiver's eye from the environment.

In order to receive information from the environment, we are equipped with sense organs, for example eyes, ears and nose. Each sense organ is part of a system which receives sensory inputs and transmits sensory information to the brain. Psychologists attempt to explain how physical energy received by sense organs forms the basis of perceptual experience. Some psychologists argue that perceptual processes are **direct** and that there is enough information in the stimulus to enable an accurate perception to be gained from the stimulus alone. Others argue that perceptual processes are not direct, but depend on the perceiver's expectations and previous knowledge, as well as the information available in the stimulus itself.

Gibson's theory of visual perception

Gibson (1966) proposed that sensory information from the retina is enough to explain how we perceive objects and events. Gibson's theory is known as a **direct theory** of perception because it emphasises the importance of information direct from the environment which is available for analysis by the receptor cells in the retina of the eye. He proposed that **texture gradients** on the ground are linked to similar gradients found on the retina in the eye. These complementary gradients allow humans to have depth perception. This approach to perception is known as data-driven or **bottom-up processing**, because it starts with sensory input from the object to the retina and works upwards to higher levels of perceptual analysis in the brain.

There are three important components of Gibson's theory:

■ optic flow patterns

■ the role of invariants in perception

■ affordances.

Optic flow patterns

In a natural environment the light source (for example, window or lamp) gives off millions of rays of light in many different directions. Some of these rays come directly from the object to the eye, but some rays may be deflected (for example, from the wall, to the object and then to the eye). Rays also come from the surface on which the object stands. Gibson proposed that the light present as we move our head and eyes over the surroundings (the **optic array**) gives us a lot of helpful sensory data direct from the environment.

Changes in the flow of the optic array contain important information about what type of movement is taking place. For example:

■ Any flow in the optic array means that the perceiver is moving. If there is no flow the perceiver is static.

■ The flow of the optic array will be coming from or moving towards a particular point. The centre of that movement indicates the direction in which the perceiver is moving. If a flow seems to be coming from a particular point, this means the perceiver is moving towards that point; but if the flow seems to be moving towards that point, then the perceiver is moving away.

Aim: To investigate the importance of optic flow in the perception of movement.

Method: A specially prepared 'swaying' room was set up on which the floor moved, and the texture flow could be manipulated (independent variable) under experimental conditions. Adults and children were placed in the room and assessed to see if they could remain upright (dependent variable).

Results: Adults were able to make unconscious mental adjustments so that they could remain upright. Children tended to fall over.

Conclusion: The adult brain can monitor changes in the optic flow and send appropriate signals to the muscles.

Evaluation: It is very difficult to set up an experiment to measure optic flow and this was quite an ingenious idea. However, it is rare to encounter 'swaying', particularly of a room, in real life and therefore the experiment is artificial. In addition, although unconscious mental adjustments were inferred from this experiment, it tells us nothing about how these adjustments are made by the brain.

Link

For more information on independent and dependent variables, see Chapter 4 Research methods.

Key terms

Invariant: the flow of texture always occurs in the same way.

Ecological relevance: findings can be applied to real life

The role of invariants in perception

When we move our head and eyes, or walk around our environment, things move in and out of our viewing fields. Textures expand as you approach an object and contract as you move away. This flow of texture is **invariant** and provides important, direct information about the environment, acting as a cue to distance and depth. For an example of a texture gradient see Figure 12, p195.

Affordances

According to Gibson, the meaning of an object (what it is and what it can be used for) can be directly perceived. Affordances can tell us the properties of an object (for example, whether it is edible or whether we can sit on it) directly from the pattern of stimulation arising from it.

Evaluation of Gibson's direct approach to perception

Gibson's theory has stimulated some interesting empirical research which has **ecological relevance**:

- The analysis of optic flow has provided some understanding of how skilled long-jumpers control their approaches to the take-off position.

- The concept of invariants has proved useful in research into the perception of ageing faces. How is it that we can identify faces we have not seen for 20 years or more? Changes in the shape of the skull are partially responsible for changes in our faces with age. When we apply a mathematical invariant to these changes then we can explain what happens to the face and why we continue to recognise the person.

- Gibson's theory helped to advance the study of perception because the emphasis shifted from laboratory-created situations to real environmental tests.

Cognitive psychology

However, there are some criticisms of Gibson's theory:

▨ Invariants (which are of central importance to direct perception theories) are extremely difficult to detect and extract, and have, therefore, proved difficult to incorporate into a model of vision simulation.

▨ Another important feature of Gibson's direct theory of perception is his idea of 'affordances', but this concept can be misleading. If an object (say, a berry) has an eating affordance and we eat it and become ill, would we eat a similar berry in the future? It would still have the same optic array and thus give off the same affordance. However, it is likely that stored knowledge does play a part in the meaning objects have for us and we would probably avoid eating a poisonous berry next time!

▨ Generally our visual perception is fast and accurate and this provides evidence for Gibson's theory of direct perception. However, his theory cannot explain why perceptions are sometimes inaccurate, such as on visual illusions. For example, there is a tendency for people to overestimate vertical lines relative to horizontal ones (see Figure 20).

Fig. 20 *In this figure, does one line appear longer?*

▨ Gregory's theory of visual perception

Gregory (1972) proposes that perception is an active and constructive process. He believes that the bottom-up sensory information from the retina is not sufficient on its own to explain perception of objects and that stored knowledge about objects is both useful and necessary. This is known as **top-down processing** because expectations stored in the brain (for example, about what objects look like) work downwards to influence the way we interpret the incoming sensory information.

Evidence for top-down processing

One kind of evidence for top-down processing is our ability to make sense of ambiguous information (i.e. information that can be interpreted in more than one way). If an identical input on the retina can be perceived in two ways then the interpretation must depend on prior expectations of what is likely to occur in that context. Read the sentences below. How is the 'S' perceived?

> The Cat 5at on the Mat
>
> Eat 5 fruit and vegetables a day

The dual interpretation of the ambiguous letter/number demonstrates the relevance of perceptual set to Gregory's top-down approach to perception. Perceptual set is outlined in the next section of this chapter.

Perceptions as hypotheses

Gregory has proposed that perceiving is an activity resembling hypothesis formation and testing. He says that signals received by the sensory receptors trigger neural events, and appropriate knowledge which is stored in the brain interacts with these inputs from the stimulus so that we can make sense of the world. Gregory has presented evidence to support this theory:

▨ We perceive objects accurately even when we have only partial sensory information. For example, we might only see a long narrow rectangle if the door is ajar, but we respond to the object as a door.

▨ **Key term**

Top-down processing: the process by which perception relies on information already stored in memory.

▨ **Hint**

There are a number of different terms given to Gregory's theory of perception, including constructivist, top-down, hypothesis-testing.

Cognitive psychology

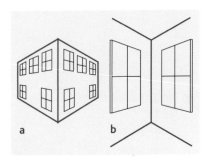

Fig. 21 *Gregory's misapplied size constancy explanation for the Muller-Lyer illusion*

a   b

Sometimes a single physical pattern can produce two perceptions. The Necker cube (see Figure 17) is a good example of this – when you stare at the dot on the cube the orientation can suddenly change or 'flip'. Gregory's theory would explain the perception of an ambiguous figure as the brain actively attempting to make sense of the stimulus.

Applying Gregory's hypothesis theory to the Muller-Lyer illusion

The Muller-Lyer illusion (see Figure 16) is where a line with outgoing fins appears longer than a line with ingoing fins. Gregory attempts to explain why this illusion occurs. He says that the fins provide cues to depth and the outgoing fins suggest the inside corner of a room, ('a' in Figure 21). Look at the ceiling of the room you are in and note how the corner resembles the outgoing fins. The ingoing fins appear to resemble the corner of a building, ('b' in Figure 21). In the real world these inward and outward facing corners are cues to distance. According to Gregory's misapplied size constancy theory, because the outgoing fins are giving off depth cues suggesting this line is further away, but the retinal image is that the two lines are equal in length, the one further away must be longer and is therefore scaled up. Size constancy allows us to perceive things as the same size despite changes in distance, which is usually helpful, but occasionally can be 'misapplied'.

Evaluation of Gregory's top-down approach to perception

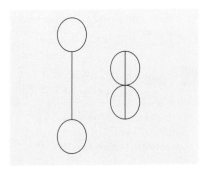

Fig. 22 *Muller-Lyer with the depth cues removed*

- One of the problems with the misapplied size constancy theory that Gregory uses to explain the Muller-Lyer illusion is that when the depth cues (the fins) are removed the illusion still exists. In Figure 22, circles replace the fins and therefore there are no depth cues, but we still perceive one line as longer. This suggests that the misapplied size constancy theory may have been misapplied, and the illusion may simply occur due to the overall longer length of the line with the outgoing fins.

- One of Gregory's main ideas is that perception makes use of hypothesis testing – but what type of hypothesis testing is this? In science when we test a hypothesis we may have to change it on the basis of our findings. However, this does not always seem to occur with Gregory's hypothesis testing. Illusions continue to persist even when we have knowledge of them, surely the hypothesis should have been modified? In the Muller-Lyer illusion we can take a ruler and measure the two lines and confirm that they are actually the same length, but in future exposures to this illusion we would still make an error. There seems to be a lack of relationship between learning and perception, and this is difficult to explain, as the knowledge we have learnt should modify our hypotheses.

- The top-down approach with its emphasis on the role of knowledge in perception makes it difficult to explain infant perception, as the newborn visual experience is very limited.

- A further problem for the top-down approach to perception is that if we have to construct our own world based on past experience, why are perceptions so similar, even across cultures?

- Although the top-down approach can explain some visual illusions and account for when perception goes wrong, much of the research has been carried out in the laboratory situation and a major criticism is that constructivists have underestimated the richness of the sensory information available to perceivers in the real world. Most of the time, perception is accurate, and in the natural surroundings there is a wealth of information available to the perceiver, not just from the image in isolation but also from the other objects, movement etc. in the visual field. This accurate perception can be better explained by Gibson's theory.

Which theory is correct?

Both Gibson and Gregory offer explanations for perceptual processes but there are some major differences between the two accounts. Table 3 gives some of the distinguishing features of each theory and how they can be compared.

Neither Gibson nor Gregory can explain all perception all of the time. Under ideal viewing conditions where stimulus information is clear, Gibson's direct theory can explain perception. However, when stimulus information is limited and viewing conditions not ideal, Gregory's theory, that we construct and test hypotheses, may be more likely. It is probable that top-down and bottom-up processes interact with each other to produce the best interpretation of the stimulus presented.

Table 3 *Comparison of theories of perception*

Gibson's theory	Gregory's theory
Direct, bottom-up	Indirect, top-down
Difficulty in explaining visual illusions	Can explain visual illusions
Can explain accurate perception in good viewing conditions	Difficulty in explaining largely accurate nature of perception
Research largely conducted in natural environment	Research usually laboratory-based

Key points:

- Gibson has a theory of perception which states that information from the stimulus and the environment is sufficient to explain perception. Gibson's theory is concerned with bottom-up processing.

- Gregory has a theory of perception which states that information from the stimulus and environment is not sufficient to explain perception, and memory and experience is also required. Gregory's theory is concerned with top-down processing.

- It is likely that visual perception is a combination of both top-down and bottom-up processing, depending on a number of factors such as viewing conditions.

Summary questions

13 Name three important features of Gibson's theory of perception.

14 Why is Gibson's theory known as a direct theory of perception?

15 Explain why Gibson's theory is considered ecologically valid.

16 Why is Gregory's theory known as a top-down theory of perception?

17 Gregory states that the Muller-Lyer illusion is a question of misapplied size constancy. Explain what he means by this.

Cognitive psychology

Perceptual set

Learning objectives:

- Understand what is meant by perceptual set.

- Describe some of the factors that affect how we perceive stimuli.

- Evaluate how researchers have investigated these factors.

Key term

Perceptual set: a readiness to perceive particular aspects of a stimulus.

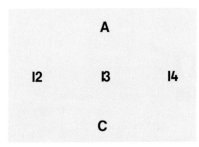

Fig. 23 *Burner and Minturn's study stimulus: an example*

AQA Examiner's tip

Note that the four factors discussed in this section are all named on the specification and there could be questions specifically naming these.

Link

See Gregory's theory of perception (p203) for an explanation of top-down processing.

Fig. 24 *Bugelski and Alampay's 'rat/man' figure*

Perceptual set is a tendency to notice particular features of the information that enters our sensory system, and ignore other features. Exactly what we do notice depends on a variety of influences such as our physiological state (for example, whether we are hungry), our past experiences (for example, whether we have perceived that stimulus before) and our emotional state (for example, whether we are anxious).

💡 Expectation

Expectation or anticipation is an important factor that influences how we perceive the world. This factor illustrates the active nature of perception and the importance of contextual or top-down processes.

Bruner and Minturn (1955) illustrated how expectation can influence set by showing participants an ambiguous figure '13' (that could be interpreted either as the letter B or as the number 13), which was set in the context of letters or numbers.

The physical stimulus '13' is the same in each case but it is perceived differently because of the influence of the context in which it appears. Participants shown letters perceived the figure as B, those shown the numbers reported it as the number 13. Furthermore, when they were later asked to draw the figure, their drawing was unambiguous indicating that they had stored the figure according to the context in which it had been perceived. Thus perception of an ambiguous object can be influenced by what one expects or anticipates.

We may also fail to notice printing errors because we read what we expect to find rather than what is actually there. For example, read the following sentences aloud:

Mary had a little lamp whose fleece was white as snow

Once

u p o n a

a t i m e

A study by Bugelski and Alampay in 1961 showed how expectations could influence perception using an ambiguous 'rat/man' figure (Figure 24). When participants were shown a series of animal pictures prior to seeing the ambiguous rat/man they were significantly more likely to perceive it as a rat than the control group who were shown a set of unrelated pictures. Simply being exposed to animal pictures beforehand had established an expectation to perceive an animal.

Evaluation of expectation

One implication of the findings of studies into expectation and set is that this concept can be used in professional training when individuals can be equipped with a system of **sets** to enhance performance. For example, police personnel are trained to notice and remember car registration numbers, or physical characteristics of people they meet.

There are also many examples of printing errors that have gone unnoticed because we read what we **expect** to find in that context.

These everyday examples of proof-reader errors indicate that the experimental findings are ecologically valid and do generalise to the real world.

■ Motivation

Hunger is a motivational state and can influence perception. There have been a number of experiments into the link between food deprivation and perception, which seem to show that when we are deprived of something our motivation (desire) is heightened. For example, studies have shown that the longer individuals are deprived of food, the more likely they are to perceive ambiguous pictures as food-related (Sanford, 1937).

In a study by Gilchrist and Nesberg (1952), food deprivation was associated with rating pictures of food as being visually brighter than non-food pictures. They asked two groups of participants to rate pictures according to how bright they were. One group had been deprived of food and the other group had not been deprived of food. Those who had gone without food for four hours reported that the pictures of food and drink were brighter than other non-food pictures. The findings indicate that when we are motivated by hunger and thirst we are more likely to have a **heightened sensitivity** to food images.

Much of the research on perception and set has been concerned with visual perception but other senses are also involved with perceptual set. For example, if you hear the words 'I Scream' and you are hungry, or in a place where you might expect to find 'Ice Cream' your interpretation of the words would be different according to the context and your motivation to eat.

Evaluation of motivation

Studies on food deprivation have been criticised on ethical grounds. In the Gilchrist and Nesberg study, participants were deprived of food and water for 4 hours. If the participants were healthy individuals this should not prove problematic. However, it would be important to ensure that participants have no medical condition, such as diabetes, prior to accepting them in the study. A further limitation of this study is that it lacks ecological validity due to the nature of the stimulus materials – the use of pictures rather than real food items. However, these studies do provide empirical evidence that motivational influences do affect how we perceive the world around us.

■ Emotion

There are two principles related to emotion and perception: **perceptual sensitisation** and **perceptual defence**.

Perceptual sensitisation

Perceptual sensitisation was demonstrated in a study by Lazarus and McCleary (1951) which illustrated the relationship between emotion and perception. Participants were given an electric shock when presented with certain nonsense syllables and their anxiety was measured. Later, participants were exposed to those and other syllables so fast that they could not consciously perceive them. The syllables to which they had been sensitised (i.e. which had been presented earlier with an electric shock) did raise their anxiety level, which was measured using the **galvanic skin response (GSR)**, even though they could not consciously distinguish them from any others.

> ■ Key terms
>
> **Perceptual sensitisation:** when the recognition threshold for a stimulus is lowered so that we are more likely to (unconsciously) recognise it.
>
> **Perceptual defence:** where the recognition threshold for a stimulus is raised making it more difficult to recognise.
>
> **Galvanic skin response (GSR):** a measure of the electrical response (conductivity) of the skin which increases with increasing perspiration, and may indicate emotional tension.

Perceptual defence

Perceptual defence is explained by Malim (1994) as a kind of 'anti-set'; this is because unlike 'sensitisation' where we are **more** likely to perceive a stimulus, with perceptual defence we are **less** likely to perceive a stimulus. Things that are anxiety provoking are more difficult to perceive at a conscious level. In a study by McGinnies (1949) on 'Emotionality and Perceptual Defence', participants were presented with a number of neutral words (for example, apple) and emotionally arousing 'taboo' words (for example, whore) and had to name the word as soon as it was recognised. The results showed that it took significantly longer for participants to name the taboo words, and higher anxiety levels were recorded on the GSR.

Evaluation of emotion

The experiments into the effect of emotion on perception can be criticised on ethical grounds. The use of 'taboo' words, for example, might be quite shocking to some people and may cause them embarrassment and discomfort.

The explanation that participants took longer to recognise taboo words than neutral words due to perceptual defence is only one interpretation of the findings from such studies. These findings could be due, for example, to social inhibition – the response is restrained (and therefore slower) because it is an unusual word to use in a social situation and may cause offence or violate social norms.

■ Culture

Culture refers to the ideas, information, code of behaviour, etc. that make up the environment in which we live. Psychologists have been interested in discovering whether the context and culture in which people have been raised affects the way they perceive the world. In other words, are there cultural differences in perception?

Early cross-cultural studies often consisted of presenting **visual illusions**, such as the **Muller-Lyer illusion** (see page 198), to different cultural groups and comparing the results to European findings. It was generally found that non-Europeans did not make the error on the Muller-Lyer illusion to which European adults and children were prone.

■ Key term

Visual illusion: when an image is misperceived.

■ Link

For more information on quasi-experiments, see Chapter 4 Research methods.

■ Research study: Deregowski (1972)

Aim: To investigate whether pictures are seen and understood in the same way in different cultures.

Method: This was a cross-cultural quasi-experiment where participants from different cultures, for example African and European (the independent variable), were shown two types of picture: either one with a top-view perspective or a 'split-type', as illustrated in Figure 25. They were asked to choose which drawing they preferred (the dependent variable).

Results: He found people from several cultures prefer drawings which do not show perspective, but instead are split so that both sides of an object can be seen. Split-type drawings show all the important features of an object whilst perspective drawings just give one view. Deregowski found a preference among African children

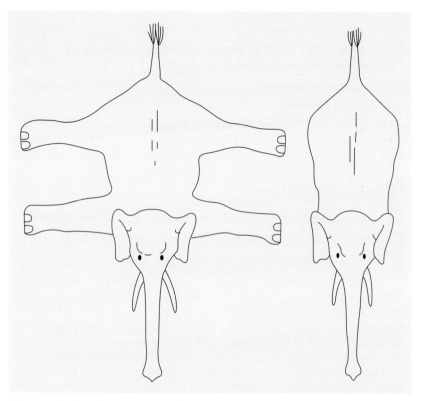

Fig. 25 *Elephant drawing from a split-view and a top-view perspective*

and adults for split-type drawings and argued that this split-style representation is universal and is found in European children too before they are taught perspective.

Conclusion: His findings suggest that perceiving 'perspective' in drawings is a specific cultural skill, which is learned. This means environment and culture must shape our perception of the world.

Evaluation: It might be that Deregowski's study was methodologically flawed because the remote tribe studied were not familiar with paper – and in fact rather than look at the drawing they were more interested in feeling and smelling the novel paper. When the study was made less culturally biased, by presenting the drawings on cloth (which the Me'en tribe were used to) then recognition of the drawings was much more accurate, even though the tribe would have never seen such a drawing before.

Evaluation of culture

Deregowski found that African people preferred split drawings to perspective drawings. Such findings can be interpreted in a culturally biased way by assuming perspective drawings are artistically superior (and thus a preference for them is culturally superior). However, as pointed out by some of the African participants, perspective drawings often hide important features of an object. It may simply be that some cultures have a 'stylistic preference' (Serpell, 1979) for split pictures.

AQA Examiner's tip

When asked about factors affecting perceptual set you should remember that many factors link together. So, for example, if you are asked about (or choose to discuss) motivation, then this factor may also be affected by expectation.

Key points:

- Perceptual set is a tendency to notice particular features of the information that enters our sensory system.

- The main factors affecting perceptual set are motivation, expectation, emotion and culture.

- Research has been carried out into the importance of each of these factors.

 Summary questions

18 Outline and give an example of how motivation influences perception.

19 What is meant by perceptual sensitisation and perceptual defence?

20 Outline two criticisms of studies into perceptual set.

Link

For more information on experimental design and ethical issues, see Chapter 4, Research methods.

 End-of-chapter activity

A practical activity that you could try is to design an experiment using the ambiguous rat/man figure. You will need to make a number of design and implementation decisions, for example whether to use a repeated measures or independent design. You will also need to operationalise your variables (the independent and dependent variable), and think carefully about how you can control potentially confounding variables, and about ethical issues.

To design the materials you could use four small cards each with pictures of a rat, and four with pictures of bald men with spectacles, and the ambiguous rat/man figure on a similar card. It is usually found that the presentation of pictures shown prior to the ambiguous picture will significantly influence the participant's response.

AQA Examination-style questions

1   (a)   Psychologists have found that motivation can influence visual perception. Name two other factors that can influence visual perception. *(2 marks)*

        (b)   Outline what is meant by a bottom-up theory of information processing. Give an example of one bottom-up theory. *(3 marks)*

        (c)   The illustration (Figure 1) shows a visual illusion.

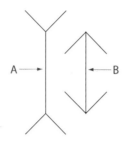

Fig. 1

            (i)   Name and briefly describe the illusion in Figure 1. *(2 marks)*

           (ii)   Give one explanation of why Figure 1 produces an illusion. *(3 marks)*

        (d)   Describe and evaluate Gibson's theory of visual perception. *(10 marks)*

AQA, 2006

2   (a)   Using an example, explain what is meant by an ambiguous figure. *(3 marks)*

        (b)   Outline what is meant by a top-down theory of information processing. Give one example of a top-down theory. *(3 marks)*

        (c)   (i)   Outline what is meant by the Gestalt principles. *(2 marks)*

           (ii)   Explain one criticism of the Gestalt school. *(2 marks)*

        (d)   Describe and evaluate the influence of two of the following factors on perception:

- motivation
- emotion
- expectation
- culture.

Refer to empirical evidence in your answer. *(10 marks)*

AQA, 2005

Individual differences

Introduction

As you go about your everyday life you meet all sorts of people – family, friends, acquaintances, strangers – and one thing you notice is that people are different. Some people are very friendly, others are quiet and reserved. Some people work hard and are keen to achieve their potential, others seem lazy and disinterested. Some people seem to worry excessively, others haven't a care in the world. Psychologists are interested in these individual differences, and those working in this field tend to look at either:

- individual differences in the 'normal' population – generally the study of personality and intelligence, or

- individual differences in people who are considered '**abnormal**'– sometimes known as 'psychopathology'.

The two topics studied at AS Psychology for Specification B are concerned with psychopathology, in particular those suffering from either anxiety disorders or autism. For each disorder, the symptoms necessary for a diagnosis of that disorder will be investigated. In addition, biological and psychological explanations will be discussed for both anxiety disorders and autism, together with an outline of the main treatments available.

Anxiety disorders

Anxiety is a negative emotion that makes an individual feel uneasy and tense. It is an unpleasant and persistent feeling of anticipation which is out of the person's control. It is not linked to anything specific but a general feeling of worry and suspense. This is different to a 'fear' which usually describes an emotional reaction to an identifiable threat, for example fear of a spider. The fear response might be rational (for example, fear of a red back Australian spider with lethal venom) or irrational (fear of a money spider in the UK). Anxiety disorders appear as a separate category on the **DSM-IV** classification system, and four anxiety disorders are identified:

- panic disorder
- phobias
- obsessive-compulsive disorder
- generalised anxiety disorder.

The AS Level Psychology Specification B course covers two of the named anxieties: phobias and obsessive-compulsive disorder.

Autism

The second topic under 'Individual differences' is autism. It appears on Axis 1 (Clinical Disorders) of the DSM-IV under 'Disorders usually first diagnosed in infancy, childhood and adolescence'.

Autism was first identified in 1943 as a separate childhood disorder categorised by 'autistic aloneness' (Kanner, 1943). This disorder differs from mental disorders that appear in adulthood, like schizophrenia, as it is evident in very early childhood, sometimes from birth. It is a particularly debilitating disorder which appears across all socio-economic and ethnic groups and is four times more prevalent in boys than girls. It is a lifelong condition and there has been a worrying increase in the number of children diagnosed as suffering from autism since the 1990s. Lots of theories have emerged about why this is the case and the media regularly investigates links between autism and the MMR (measles, mumps and rubella) triple vaccine.

Key terms

Abnormal: literally, 'away from the normal'.

DSM-IV: the *Diagnostic and Statistical Manual* (4th edition) widely used in defining and classifying mental disorders. It groups disorders according to common features. There are five axes, all of which are considered for a full diagnosis to be made.

AQA Examiner's tip

It is essential that you learn both these anxiety disorders. Examination questions can be on either one, or a combination of both phobias and obsessive-compulsive disorder.

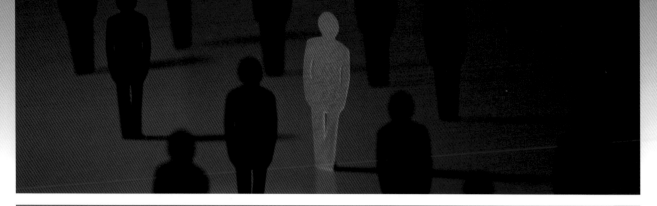

Specification	Topic content	Page
Phobias: definition and symptoms Agoraphobia, social phobias and specific phobias	Phobias: definition and symptoms	214
Obsessive-compulsive disorder: definition and symptoms; the distinction between obsession and compulsion	Obsessive-compulsive disorder: definition and symptoms	220
Explanations of phobias and obsessive-compulsive disorder, including biological, behavioural, cognitive and psychodynamic	Obsessive-compulsive disorder: definition and symptoms	220
Treatments, including systematic desensitisation, flooding, drug therapy, cognitive therapy; psychodynamic therapy	Treatments of anxiety disorders	225
Evaluation of these treatments	Treatments of anxiety disorders	225
Autism: definition and symptoms, including lack of joint attention; autism as a syndrome: the triad of impairments	Defining and diagnosing autism	231
An early explanation: cold-parenting	Explanations for autism	234
Biological explanations, including genetics and neurological correlates	Explanations for autism	234
Cognitive explanations, including theory of mind, central coherence deficit and failure of executive functioning	Explanations for autism	234
Studying autism: the Sally-Anne experiment; the 'Smartie tube' test; comic strip stories	Explanations for autism	234
Therapeutic programmes for autism, including behaviour modification, aversion therapy for self-injuring behaviour, language training, including the Lovaas technique, parental involvement	Therapeutic programmes for autism	244
Evaluation of these programmes	Therapeutic programmes for autism	244

Phobias: definition and symptoms

Learning objectives:

▨ Name and define the three main types of phobia.

▨ Outline the symptoms associated with each phobia.

▨ Describe and evaluate explanations of phobias.

▨ Key term

Fight or flight response: an automatic physiological response (of the sympathetic nervous system) in fearful situations that prepares the body to fight or flee. Physiological changes include accelerated heart rate, increased sweating and diversion of blood flow to the skeletal muscles.

▨ Links

▨ For more on the sympathetic and parasympathetic nervous system (the autonomic nervous system) and the fight or flight response, see Chapter 2 Biopsychology.

▨ The DSM-IV is explained on p212.

The word 'phobia' comes from the Greek god Phobos, who was fearless in battle and renowned for fighting and terrifying his enemies. A phobia is a persistent, disproportionate and irrational fear of a specific object or situation, which disrupts everyday life. The feared object or situation in fact presents little or no danger and the fear is even recognised by the individual as being groundless. However, this does not stop the person from reacting to the perceived threat with terror and panic, often accompanied by the **fight or flight response**. Not surprisingly, the phobic individual will try to avoid any stimulus that produces such a response.

The key characteristics of phobias are that they are **extreme** fears, which are **disproportionate** to the actual danger, and lead to **avoidance** of the object or situation. The DSM-IV identifies three categories of phobia:

▨ specific phobia – an intense and irrational fear of a particular item or situation

▨ social phobia – a persistent and irrational fear of social situations

▨ agoraphobia – a fear of having a panic attack in a public place.

🛈 Specific phobia

A specific phobia involves a strong fear and avoidance of a particular object or situation. When exposed to the feared object or situation, an individual will experience great anxiety, a panic reaction often occurs and the situation or object is usually avoided. Sometimes simply anticipating exposure to the feared object can bring on a panic attack. To be diagnosed as suffering from a specific phobia, the fear must:

▨ be excessive or unreasonable relative to the actual danger posed by the object or situation

▨ be triggered immediately on exposure to the object or situation

▨ interfere with everyday functioning, for example work, relationships.

A fear becomes a phobia when it begins to be maladaptive, that is when it begins to interfere with everyday life. Specific phobias are quite common, affecting approximately 10 per cent of the population, and are more prevalent in women than in men. There are five subtypes of specific phobias listed in the DSM-IV (see Table 1).

Table 1 *The five subtypes of specific phobia listed in the DSM-IV*

Subtype	Examples
Animal	Snakes, bats, rats, spiders, bees, dogs, etc. (zoophobia).
Natural environment	Heights (acrophobia), water (hydrophobia), thunder/lightning, etc.
Blood/injection/injury	Tend to faint rather than panic if exposed to blood/injections/injury.
Situational	Aeroplanes, lifts/elevators, enclosed places (claustrophobia), etc.
Atypical	Vomiting, choking, etc.

Social phobia

It is quite common to feel anxious in social situations or when we have to perform in front of other people, but a social phobia is much more debilitating than this. It is an **extreme** fear of embarrassment or humiliation in social situations. Often the anxiety is so strong that it causes avoidance of certain situations altogether. When the social anxiety interferes with work and social life it becomes a clinical condition. Social phobias can be either:

- **social phobias for specific situations**, for example, fear of using public toilets, fear of public speaking or fear of eating in public. Panic attacks usually accompany this type of social phobia and the panic begins to arise in connection with the particular type of social situation

- **generalised social phobia,** when the phobia is less specific and involves fear of many different types of social interactions. Examples include fear of initiating conversations, fear of speaking to authority figures, fear of attending parties, etc.

Social phobias tend to develop in late childhood/early adolescence and affect around 11 per cent of men and 15 per cent of women (Kessler *et al.*, 1994). This prevalence rate is much higher than previously acknowledged due to a change in the diagnostic criteria, which removed the necessity for the patient to have to avoid certain social situations in order to qualify for diagnosis.

Agoraphobia

Agora is the Greek word for 'public place of assembly' and agoraphobics have a particular fear of crowded public transport and public places like shopping centres. Approximately 2–3 per cent of the population suffer from agoraphobia, and the majority are women. There are two types of agoraphobia:

- **agoraphobia as a complication of panic attack.** Agoraphobics are anxious about having a panic attack in a public place and being unable to escape or find help. They begin to avoid situations for fear of panicking, and in the most severe cases they refuse to leave their home

- **agoraphobia without panic attacks.** This is less common than the above type, and is characterised by a spreading fear of the environment outside the safety of the individual's own home. This fear gradually increases in severity, until eventually the patient can become housebound.

Explanations of phobias

Biological explanation

Genetic explanation

Some people seem more susceptible to developing a phobia than others, and therefore a genetic explanation has been proposed to account for these individual differences. Studies have found some support for a genetic component:

- Fyer *et al.* (1995) found that those who had first degree relatives with a specific phobia were much more likely to have a specific phobia themselves. Although there was a high concordance (agreement) for specific phobias, there was no such concordance for social phobia.

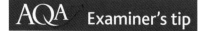

Examiner's tip

All three categories of phobia are named on the specification and you should know the symptoms and be able to give examples of each.

Fig. 1 *Many people have a specific fear of spiders*

Link

For more information on genetics, see Chapter 2, Biopsychology.

Individual differences

Torgesen (1983) investigated pairs of identical twins (100 per cent same genetic make-up) and fraternal twins (share only 50 per cent of the same genes), where at least one of the pair was agoraphobic. Findings showed that there was a much higher likelihood of the other twin also being agoraphobic in the identical twins than the fraternal twins, as the genetic explanation would predict.

Vulnerability

People vary in the extent to which they are vulnerable to experiencing anxiety and there may be a biological explanation for this. Eysenck (1967) proposed that some people are more easily frightened by fear-provoking stimuli. The autonomic nervous system controls emotional responses and according to Eysenck some people are born with high autonomic reactivity, which makes them more likely to develop a phobia.

Preparedness theory

Seligman (1971) proposed that we develop phobias to items and situations (for example, snakes, heights) that were potential sources of danger to us thousands of years ago. Furthermore, those individuals who developed such a phobia and therefore avoided a harmful item or situation would be favoured by evolution. He said there was a 'preparedness' (a physiological predisposition) to be sensitive to certain stimuli. It is not the fears themselves that are inborn, rather there is an **innate** (in-born) tendency to rapidly acquire a phobia to potentially harmful items – we are biologically prepared from birth.

Evaluation of biological explanations

▨ Research has shown that people with different anxiety disorders (for example, phobias, obsessive-compulsive disorder) have quite different reactions in the autonomic nervous system (ANS) and so the link between anxiety and the ANS is more complicated than Eysenck's theory proposed.

▨ The findings from the genetic studies could be alternatively explained by theories such as **social learning theory**. For example, close relatives might observe and imitate the behaviour displayed by their families. It is difficult to untangle the effects of environmental influences and genetic factors in family studies.

▨ Support for the preparedness theory comes from conditioning studies on humans and animals, in laboratory situations. Ohman (1996) found that humans are much more likely to be conditioned to particular stimuli such as snakes, which he termed 'fear-relevant', than stimuli such as flowers, which are 'fear-irrelevant'. Studies also show animals are biased to making particular associations, for example Cook and Mineka (1990) found monkeys readily acquired fears of toy snakes and toy crocodiles (even though they had no previous exposure to them) but could not be conditioned to fear a toy rabbit. Because the monkeys had never seen a snake or crocodile, this conditioned fear could not be accounted for by prior learning, and preparedness theory seems a plausible explanation.

▨ The studies on prepared fears have been criticised because there is evidence that the fears acquired under laboratory situations are easily removed simply by verbal instructions, and therefore these laboratory fears are unlike phobias that people acquire in the real world.

AQA Examiner's tip

Preparedness theory is both a biological theory as it relies on evolutionary ideas and innate tendencies, and also is part of the behaviourist approach, as the fears are acquired according to classical conditioning principles. In the examination you can discuss this theory under either approach.

▨ Key terms

Innate: in-born; present at birth.

Social learning theory: proposes that we learn through observing and imitating the behaviours of others.

▨ Links

▨ For more information on the behavioural approach, classical and operant conditioning, see Chapter 1, Key approaches.

▨ See Chapter 1, p8 for details of the Watson and Rayner study.

Behavioural explanation

Behaviourists would argue that phobic reactions are learned by classical conditioning. This is where a person can learn to fear a previously neutral stimulus (the conditioned stimulus or CS) if it is paired with a frightening event (the unconditioned stimulus or UCS). For example, a scream produces fear, so if someone screams when they see a spider you will associate the fearful response of the scream with the spider. According to the two-process theory (Mowrer, 1947), the learned fear is then maintained by operant conditioning because the person learns the fear is reduced by avoiding the stimulus. People avoid contact with spiders and therefore do not get the fearful response. This is a **two-factor theory** for the acquisition of phobias because the theory incorporates both classical and operant conditioning, and is generally known as **avoidance conditioning.** A classic study in 1920 by Watson and Rayner demonstrated how a fearful response can be conditioned through classical conditioning (see p8 for more details).

Fig. 2 *Little Albert and the white rat*

Table 2 *How Little Albert was classically conditioned to fear a white rat*

Before conditioning	During conditioning	After conditioning
The rat is a neutral stimulus (CS). Albert has no fear of rats. A loud bang (unconditioned stimulus, UCS) elicits fear (unconditioned response, UCR).	The rat (CS) is paired with the loud bang (UCS), and this naturally produces fear (UCR).	Albert shows fear (conditioned response, CR) of the rat (conditioned stimulus, CS).

According to the two-process theory, once this fear has become established it would continue due to operant conditioning. This is because once Albert had been conditioned to fear the white rat, he would then avoid rats which would in turn reduce his anxiety and strengthen his fear of them, making him more likely to avoid a rat in the future.

Classical conditioning is often shown as a diagram (see Figure 3).

Evaluation of the behavioural explanation

- There is empirical evidence to support the theory that fears can be acquired by a conditioning process. The early study on Little Albert demonstrated the human conditioning of a fearful response. In addition, there are numerous findings that fear reactions can be readily conditioned in animals in the laboratory. However, just because it can be demonstrated that some fears can be acquired this way, does not mean that all fears are acquired in the same way.

- In a study of people with a fear of dogs, Di Nardo *et al.* (1988) found that over 60 per cent could relate their fear to a frightening incident with a dog. This offers some support for conditioning theory, however this does not account for those who could not recall such an incident. Also, a similar number in the control group reported a painful incident with a dog but did not develop a fear.

- Although there is some evidence that fear can be induced in children (for example, Little Albert), the numbers are small and findings have been inconsistent. In addition, attempts to replicate the Watson and Rayner study have not been successful. Fears that develop gradually (for example, social phobias) and cannot be traced back to a specific incident, cannot be readily explained by the behaviourists. Also, fears sometimes occur when there has been no direct contact with the fear stimulus, which is difficult to explain using conditioning theory.

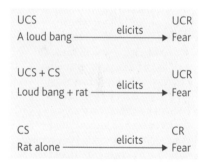

Fig. 3 *Arrow diagrams of pairing stimuli*

Individual differences

217

Cognitive explanation

Cognitive psychologists propose that a fearful emotional response is experienced due to the **interpretation** or **appraisal** of events. It is the interpretation of an event that triggers the emotion not the event itself. When a person has a phobia, their response to a situation/object is immediate and extreme, and the interpretation and appraisal distorted. Distorted appraisals include:

- automatic negative thoughts, for example 'There's a spider, there are probably hundreds of them here'
- over-generalising, that is the assumption that because you have had one bad experience in the past, then this will be repeated in similar situations in the future.

According to cognitive theorists, phobias generally develop and persist due to three main factors:

- **sensitisation** – anxiety becomes **associated** with a particular object/situation so that the presence of (or thinking about) a situation/object is enough to automatically trigger anxiety
- **avoidance** – after sensitisation occurs a person will **avoid** an item/situation and this becomes very rewarding because anxiety diminishes
- **negative self-talk/negative images** – these include three basic distortions:
  - over-estimating a negative outcome, for example 'What if the snake bites me and is poisonous?;
  - catastrophising, for example 'There would be no antidote and I would be disabled or die';
  - under-estimating ability to cope, for example 'I'd never be able to cope in a wheelchair.'

According to the cognitive theory, the **agoraphobic** person is hypersensitive to spatial layouts in the environment and also to being too far away from a caretaker. If access to home or the caretaker is blocked then fear is induced and the agoraphobic has an urgent need to return home. Beck *et al.* (1985) propose that agoraphobics possess latent fears of situations that might have been potentially dangerous to a child but are not dangerous for adults, for example crowded shops or open places.

The onset and maintenance of a **social phobia** has also been explained by cognitive psychologists. Social phobics have developed schemas (mental representations that serve as a plan or a guide to action) that include expectations that others will be negative and rejecting. Social phobics have become **hypersensitive** to picking up cues from others that they then interpret negatively. These schemas also include expectations that their own behaviour will be inept and unacceptable and that others will reject them because of this. The consequent focusing on their own bodily responses makes them less able to socially interact skilfully and a vicious cycle occurs.

Evaluation of the cognitive explanation

- The cognitive explanation is a coherent theory with practical therapeutic applications. The treatments have proved highly effective for anxiety disorders such as phobias.
- Cognitive theorists accept the acquisition of fear through learning, for example conditioning, but also emphasise the person's own interpretation of events.
- However, behaviour is not always driven by cognitions; evidence suggests that cognitions can be driven and/or maintained by inappropriate behaviour, such as avoidance.

Link

Notice that the cognitive approach draws on the behaviourist explanations of association and avoidance, but develops these to include cognitions, for example negative self-talk. Behaviourist principles such as classical and operant conditioning are also accepted by, and incorporated into, the cognitive approach. For example cognitive psychologists accept fear is a learned or acquired response, but they also focus on personal interpretations and cognitions.

Key term

Hypersensitive: excessively sensitive.

Psychodynamic explanation

💡 The psychodynamic explanation is that phobias occur when **id** impulses are repressed and the anxiety is displaced onto another object or situation. A detailed explanation for phobias was presented by Freud (1909) in his case study of Little Hans. In this case study, Freud illustrated his basic explanation that phobias develop due to an unresolved childhood conflict. One way the ego deals with a childhood conflict, such as the Oedipal complex which caused the young Hans to fear his father, is by displacing the fear onto another object. In the case of Hans, his fear of his father was displaced onto horses. In a similar fashion, other psychodynamic theorists have argued that a fear of spiders hides unconscious conflicts. For example, according to Sperling (1971), a fear of spiders is a defence against more threatening impulses of a sexual nature. Abraham (1927) proposed that the fear of spiders is symbolic of an unconscious fear of sexual genitalia.

Evaluation of the psychodynamic explanation

▨ The psychodynamic explanation for Hans's phobia for horses is complicated and the behaviourists provide a much simpler explanation. At age four, Hans had witnessed an accident when a horse collapsed in the street. This had greatly upset him and he could have been **classically conditioned** after the incident to fear horses.

▨ Freud's theory of anxiety lacks methodological rigour; for example, evidence for Freud's theory of phobias is drawn from clinical case studies, and these are limited in number and subjectively interpreted.

▨ Freud maintained that adult phobias only occurred in people with sexual problems. However, many people with anxiety and specific phobias have a normal sexual life, and Freud's assertion is almost certainly incorrect.

Key points:

■ There are three categories of phobias identified by the DSM-IV: specific phobia, social phobia and agoraphobia.

■ Biological explanations for phobias include: genetics, vulnerability in the autonomic nervous system, preparedness theory. The latter is both a biological and a conditioning (behavioural) explanation.

■ None of the biological explanations can yet offer a full account of phobia acquisition and several psychological theories have been proposed.

■ Psychological explanations for phobias include: behavioural, cognitive and psychodynamic explanations.

■ Key term

Id: an unconscious part of personality that is present at birth and demands instant gratification.

■ Links

■ The Oedipal complex and the study of Little Hans are discussed in Chapter 3, Gender development.

■ For more about case studies, see Chapter 4, Research methods.

💡 Summary questions

1. Outline the distinguishing features of three named categories of phobias.

2. Briefly describe one biological explanation for phobias.

3. Describe a study that illustrates a behavioural explanation for phobias.

4. Use an everyday example to explain how an inappropriate schema can explain a phobia.

5. Amy panics just thinking about needles and will not have an anaesthetic at the dentist, or a flu jab at the doctors, because she gets very panicky, has palpitations and runs away. She avoids any situation where needles might be present. Recently she has learnt that she may lose her job in the travel industry because she will not have the necessary injections for overseas travel. Assess whether Amy is suffering from a phobia. Use the information above to justify your answer.

Obsessive-compulsive disorder: definition and symptoms

Learning objectives:

■ Outline the major symptoms of obsessive-compulsive disorder.

■ Explain the distinction between an obsession and a compulsion.

■ Describe and evaluate explanations of obsessive-compulsive disorder.

Many of us have experienced obsessive thoughts. For example, as we set out on a trip we might think, 'Did I really lock that door?' Many of us have also experienced compulsions, for example feeling compelled to turn back to check that the front door is locked. As children we might have avoided the pavement cracks because we thought standing on a crack would bring bad luck. Obsessive-compulsive disorder (OCD), however, is much more distressing than this. It is a disabling mental disorder which often affects not just the individual but their family as well. According to the DSM-IV, to be diagnosed as suffering from this clinical disorder it has to be causing considerable distress and interfering with normal daily functioning. It occurs in approximately 2 per cent of the population and in men and women in equal numbers. The age of onset is often adolescence or early adulthood, but it can begin in childhood.

Obsessions

Obsessions are persistent and recurring thoughts, ideas, images or impulses that seem senseless but intrude into one's mind, such as images of violence or fears of leaving the door unlocked. A common obsessive thought concerns contamination, for example by germs. The obsessions occur automatically and are unwanted and disturbing to the individual. The thoughts and images are not just normal anxieties, but excessive worries that are usually unrelated to real-life problems.

Compulsions

Compulsions are repetitive behaviours and rituals that the individual feels compelled to perform in order to reduce the anxiety caused by the obsessive thought. For example, individuals obsessed with the thought of germ contamination might feel compelled to wash their hands up to 100 times a day, even sometimes scrubbing them with abrasive cleaners. The individual is aware that the rituals are unreasonable, yet feel compelled to perform them to ward off the anxiety associated with the obsessive thoughts of contamination. The conflict caused by the irresistible desire to carry out the senseless ritual is a source of anxiety and shame and sometimes despair. The most common compulsions include washing, checking and counting. 'Washers' are constantly concerned about avoiding contamination and avoid touching things such as door handles or shaking hands and spend hours and hours washing in order to reduce anxiety.

About 20 per cent of people suffering from obsessive-compulsive disorder only have the obsessions (which are not accompanied by the usual compulsion to carry out an act) and these obsessive thoughts are often concerned with causing harm to a loved one.

The **difference** between obsessions and compulsions is that an obsession is an unwanted and unbidden **thought**, whilst a compulsion is a repetitive **act** that one is driven to perform in order to dispel the anxiety associated with the obsessive thought.

Explanations of obsessive-compulsive disorder

Biological explanation

Genetic explanation

It has been proposed that there is a genetic component to OCD which predisposes some individuals to the illness. Evidence for this comes from family studies. Patients with OCD are more likely to have first degree relatives who suffer from an anxiety disorder (McKeon and Murray, 1987). In addition, Pauls *et al.* (1995) found a much higher percentage of OCD sufferers (10.3 per cent) in relatives of patients with OCD, than in a control group without OCD (1.9 per cent).

Biochemical explanation

Most anxiety disorders respond to a wide range of drugs but OCD seems only to respond effectively to those drugs that affect **serotonin**. This suggests that OCD is related to low levels of the neurotransmitter serotonin. Drugs which increase the amount of serotonin in the brain, such as the **SSRI** anti-depressants, also reduce obsessive-compulsive symptoms, providing support for the theory that low levels of the neurotransmitter serotonin may be responsible for OCD.

Neurophysiological explanation

Neuroimaging techniques have led researchers to implicate a part of the brain known as the basal ganglia in OCD. The basal ganglia system in the brain is responsible for innate psychomotor functions. Rapoport and Wise (1988) have proposed that hypersensitivity of the basal ganglia gives rise to repetitive motor behaviours, such as those found in OCD patients, for example repetitive hand washing.

Evaluation of biological explanations

- The findings from family studies which are used to support the genetic explanation could also be explained by environmental influences. For example close relatives of OCD sufferers might observe and imitate the behaviour displayed. As with other anxiety disorders, it is difficult to untangle the effects of environmental influences and genetic factors in family studies.

- Drugs such as the SSRIs, which interfere with the reuptake of serotonin in the brain, provide a partial remission for OCD, but most studies only report a 50 per cent improvement (Insel, 1991), thus suggesting there are other explanations for OCD.

- The therapeutic effect of SSRI drugs does not provide an adequate explanation for OCD. Just because administering SSRIs decreases OCD symptoms does not mean this was the cause in the first place. Taking a paracetamol relieves my headache but this does not mean my headache is caused by too little paracetamol!

- Another problem with the biochemical explanation is the time delay before any improvement in OCD is noticed. Taking SSRI medication increases serotonin levels in the brain within hours but the clinical response takes approximately 4–12 weeks.

- The evidence for the structural abnormality in the basal ganglia of OCD sufferers, found in neuroimaging studies, is inconsistent and a meta-analysis by Aylward *et al.* (1996) found no significant differences in the basal ganglia structures of OCD patients and controls. Even if the basal ganglia system is implicated in OCD it only explains some of the behavioural components of OCD, like the repetitive acts, but not the obsessional thoughts.

Key terms

Serotonin: a neurotransmitter in the brain.

SSRI: selective serotonin reuptake inhibitors.

Neuroimaging: a general term used for a number of non-invasive procedures that measure biological activity through the skull, for example PET scans.

Link

See Drug therapy, p225.

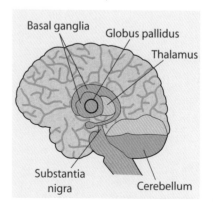

Fig. 4 *The basal ganglia system in the human brain*

Individual differences

Behavioural explanation

Operant conditioning would explain compulsive acts as learned behaviours reinforced by fear reduction. As with phobias, Mowrer's two-process theory of **avoidance learning** can be applied to OCD. This is where, first of all, two things become associated together – say, contamination by germs becomes associated with door handles. This association is known as classical conditioning. The worry about whether we have contaminated our hands can be reduced by washing. After thorough washing our anxiety reduces. The reduction in anxiety is reinforcing and this strengthens the response of hand washing so the next time anxiety arises further washing will occur. This continuation of the compulsive hand washing is maintained through the process of operant conditioning. Once learned these avoidance responses (like hand washing) are extremely difficult to remove (or extinguish).

One prediction from avoidance learning is that if clients were exposed to an object that caused anxious thoughts (for example, a toilet seat would cause worry of contamination), and then prevented from carrying out their normal ritual (for example, hand washing), anxiety levels should rise steeply. Once allowed to carry out the compulsive act (for example, hand washing), anxiety should drop quickly. Support for this prediction was found by Rachman and Hodgson (1980) who carried out a series of experiments and found that participants with OCD were distressed when exposed to a situation that elicited obsessive thoughts. If they were allowed to carry out the compulsive act anxiety levels dropped immediately. However, if prevented from their rituals, anxiety levels remained high for much longer, but did eventually subside.

In addition to supporting the behavioural explanation for OCD, this type of experiment also led to the development of a successful behavioural treatment. The patient could be shown how anxiety would eventually reduce naturally over time without the need to carry out the compulsive act.

Evaluation of the behavioural explanation

▨ Both the initial cause and maintenance of OCD can be explained by the two-process theory proposed by Mowrer (1947). It has shown how avoidance conditioning is successful in the short-term as it reduces the anxiety and provides temporary relief, and how in the long-term this avoidance behaviour is responsible for the continuation of the OCD.

▨ The avoidance conditioning theory has led to a successful behavioural treatment for OCD.

▨ The behaviourist explanation is not very helpful in explaining how the obsessions arise in the first place.

Cognitive explanation

People who suffer from OCD have obsessive **thoughts** and so clearly there is a cognitive link. When normal individuals have intrusive and obsessive thoughts, they can usually dismiss them, but for people with OCD these thoughts cause great anxiety. Cognitive theory proposes that people with OCD have a 'cognitive bias' when attending to environmental stimuli. For example, their attentional system might be **hypervigilant**. There is also evidence that memory processes in OCD sufferers is impaired. Sher *et al.* (1989) found that people with OCD had poor memories for their actions. For example, they really could not remember if they had switched the light off. In addition, Trivedi (1996) found people suffering from OCD had low confidence in their memory ability and also their non-verbal memory was impaired (although verbal memory was normal).

▨ **Key term**

Hypervigilant: excessively careful and watchful.

Some theorists argue that OCD sufferers have a cognitive vulnerability to anxiety (Williams *et al.*, 1997). One way that this vulnerability is manifested is through hypervigilance when entering a new environment, for example:

- using rapid eye movements to scan the environment
- attending selectively to threat-related stimuli rather than neutral stimuli.

Rachman (2004) outlines a case study of a patient with OCD that gives a good account of hypervigilance. A female patient had a severe fear of diseases, particularly the prospect of encountering other people's blood. She had catastrophic thoughts about the probability of harm (for example, contracting AIDS) coming from even a small plaster worn by someone. She over-estimated the seriousness of contact with anyone. When she went to a public place, she rapidly scanned the environment and the people she encountered, constantly on the lookout for evidence of blood, cuts, bandages, etc. She tended to misperceive as blood a wide range of dark-coloured spots and her hypervigilant scanning meant that she could recall in great detail the blood-related items that she had encountered over many years.

Evaluation of the cognitive explanation

- Cognitive bias (such as hypervigilance) seems to give a good account of individual differences in susceptibility to OCD.
- The treatment of patients with OCD by reducing hypervigilance has shown success, suggesting hypervigilance might be a contributory factor in OCD.
- The cognitive approach concentrates on internal cognitions as an explanation for OCD and tends to ignore the social factors that might be contributing to the condition.

Psychodynamic explanation

According to the psychosexual theory of development proposed by Freud, children aged approximately two to three years are in the anal stage, which is the toilet training phase. If children are not appropriately toilet trained (for example, if parents are too harsh when a child soils him/herself), then they can become fixated in the anal stage. Both obsessions and compulsions result from an unconscious conflict, which is essentially the conflict between the impulse of the id to let go and the ego to keep hold (of faeces). The id is the part of the personality that requires instant gratification and is driven by the instinctual forces of libido and aggression. If the id is dominant, aggressive instincts may lead to intrusive thoughts (obsessions) of, say, killing a loved one, or decorating the wall with faecal matter. Defence mechanisms are employed by the conscious mind to try to cope with the instincts of the id, and these can account for compulsions. For example, fixation in the anal stage may result in the use of the defence mechanism **reaction formation**, which is where the opposite of our desire may be employed, i.e. instead of spreading faeces we may act in an extremely clean and orderly manner.

According to Salzman (1995), OCD is the result of a trauma (possibly in childhood) which has been repressed into the unconscious. The anxiety is manifested via the intrusive thoughts. The obsessional thoughts, therefore, are the repressed memories of the trauma breaking through into consciousness, and the compulsive rituals are the conscious attempts to reduce anxiety caused by the thoughts. There is some evidence from case studies that OCD does follow a traumatic event.

> ### Key term
>
> **Reaction formation:** thinking and acting in a way that is the opposite to the actual impulse.

Individual differences

Evaluation of the psychodynamic explanation

- The link between childhood trauma and OCD relies on a limited number of case studies and therefore it is not possible to generalise to the larger population.

- There is no empirical research to support the psychodynamic theory of OCD.

- In a general sense, Freud did make some important contributions to our understanding of anxiety disorders. He proposed that our present behaviour is moulded by childhood experiences and that we have a number of defence mechanisms, such as repression and reaction formation, which we employ to defend ourselves against anxiety.

- Psychodynamic treatment that stems from this theory has not proved very effective in treating OCD.

Key points:

- Obsessive-compulsive disorder is a type of anxiety disorder where intrusive and worrying thoughts lead to the performance of certain rituals in order to reduce anxiety.

- Biological explanations include genetic, biochemical and neurophysiological causes.

- OCD can be explained by the two-process theory of conditioning proposed by Mowrer.

- There is some evidence that OCD is related to cognitive functions such as attention and memory.

- The psychodynamic theory suggests OCD can result from a repressed traumatic memory, or may be due to a failure to resolve a childhood crisis in psychosexual development.

---

i Summary questions

6 Distinguish between an obsession and a compulsion.

7 Outline one biological explanation for OCD.

8 Emma worries about contamination of food and is particularly frightened of cross-contamination between raw food and cooked food. Her cleaning ritual in the evening can take up to six hours. She never eats food prepared by anyone else and consequently cannot go on holiday or go out for meals, etc. At work Emma constantly thinks about germs and is very anxious. She is beginning to make mistakes and has had a formal warning. Emma could lose her job.

Discuss one psychological explanation for Emma's obsessive thoughts and compulsive behaviour.

Treatments of anxiety disorders

Learning objectives:

- Describe a biological treatment of anxiety disorders.

- Describe psychological treatments of anxiety disorders.

- Evaluate treatments of anxiety disorders.

Key term

MAOI: monoamine oxidase inhibitor.

Drug therapy

There are a number of drugs available for the treatment of phobias and obsessive-compulsive disorder. Selective serotonin reuptake inhibitor (SSRI) is a group of anti-depressant medications, for example Prozac, which have become the most widely prescribed drugs by doctors for the treatment of anxiety disorders. The SSRIs increase the levels of the neurotransmitter serotonin in the brain by preventing the reabsorption of serotonin at synapses (spaces between nerve cells). These drugs are particularly effective in the treatment of panic with agoraphobia and generalised social phobia. Because depression frequently accompanies OCD, SSRIs are particularly beneficial for this anxiety disorder.

MAO-Inhibitors (**MAOIs**) are an older class of anti-depressant medication which are sometimes used for those who gain no benefit from the SSRIs.

Evaluation of drug therapy

- SSRIs are easily tolerated and safe, even for older patients. They are not addictive and can be used long-term. Drug treatment is also much quicker and cheaper than psychological treatments.

- SSRIs can cause side effects including headaches, nausea and sexual dysfunction. In addition, there is a risk of relapse when coming off this medication.

- SSRIs also have the disadvantage that they take 4–12 weeks before any therapeutic benefit is noticed and this, together with the various side effects, can lead people to abandon their use.

- MAOIs have a strong panic-blocking effect and are most commonly used to treat agoraphobia (with panic attacks). There is also evidence that they can be effective with generalised social phobia.

- Although effective, MAOIs are usually the last in line to be tried because of the side effects (hypotension, weight gain, sexual dysfunction, etc.) and the requirement for dietary restrictions. A serious (even fatal) rise in blood pressure can occur when MAOIs are combined with foods that contain the amino acid tyramine (found in wine, cheese, ripe bananas, etc.), and certain medications.

Behaviour therapies

Systematic desensitisation

Wolpe (1958) developed an approach to the treatment of anxiety disorders known as systematic desensitisation. This therapy is based on the general premise that two competing emotions cannot occur at the same time. The fear response is therefore replaced with relaxation. The steps involved in this treatment are as follows:

1. The patient is trained in relaxation techniques, so that they can relax quickly.

2. The patient and therapist construct an 'anxiety hierarchy'; this is where the patient's feared situations are ranked from the least to

the most anxiety provoking. For example, a person with a phobia for snakes might rank 'a picture of a snake' the least frightening and 'holding a snake' the most frightening.

3   The patient relaxes and then imagines the least frightening case. When the patient can imagine this without feeling any anxiety, the next most frightening will be imagined, whilst again trying to remain as relaxed as possible. This continues until the patient reaches the top of the hierarchy.

This treatment can be carried out *in vivo*, that is actually being exposed to the phobic object/situation rather than simply imagining.

With those patients suffering from OCD who have observable compulsive behaviour, systematic desensitisation is very effective. However, some patients only have the obsessions without the compulsive rituals, and for these patients a cognitive analysis of the obsessive thoughts is necessary, rather than a desensitisation of the behaviour.

Virtual reality exposure therapy (VRET)

VRET is a new technique that is based on the principles of systematic desensitisation, but the therapy takes place in a virtual world. Although used largely to date with phobic patients, it is being trialled with other anxiety disorders too.

Patients are placed in a three-dimensional virtual world where they wear a head-mounted display which allows the individual to pick up sensory cues. A computer monitor shows the therapist what the patient sees. The steps involved in treatment for 'fear of flying' would include the following:

1   The patient is placed in the passenger cabin of a virtual aeroplane whilst wearing a head-mounted display that provides the same sensory cues that would be available on a real plane.

2   The patient is gradually exposed to a hierarchy of situations, similar to systematic desensitisation, for example sitting on the plane with the engine off, taxi-ing down the runway, taking-off, flying, landing.

3   Patients rate their anxiety periodically, using an anxiety scale.

Through this gradual exposure, patients find their anxiety levels decrease significantly, until they no longer have a fear of flying even in a real aeroplane.

Flooding

Flooding involves overwhelming the individual's senses with the item or situation that causes anxiety so that the person realises that no harm will occur and in fact there is no objective basis for the fear. The steps involved in this treatment are as follows:

1   A patient is exposed to the object or situation that causes anxiety (for example, a room full of snakes, or a public toilet seat).

2   The patient is initially overwhelmed and very fearful, but this subsides after a while.

3   The patient recognises that anxiety levels have dropped and that although such situations have been avoided in the past, there is in fact no reason for this.

Implosion therapy is similar to flooding but the individual is asked to **imagine** the situation.

Exposure and response prevention (ERP) is the name for a type of flooding used with OCD patients. The client is repeatedly exposed to a

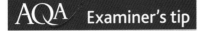

AQA Examiner's tip

VRET and ERP are contemporary behaviour therapies which could be used in appropriate examination answers. However they will not be specifically asked for as they are not named on the specification.

situation in which obsessive thoughts occur, for example a public toilet, and then prevented from carrying out their compulsive acts. These compulsive rituals are usually required to reduce the anxiety associated with the obsessive thoughts of contamination. As time passes, the client begins to realise that the anxiety reduces and nothing catastrophic has happened to them, even though the compulsion has not been acted on. Although largely behavioural, this treatment also requires a cognitive change and therapists usually engage in discussion with clients – so there is an element of cognitive therapy also.

Evaluation of behaviour therapies

▨ Systematic desensitisation can only be used when a particular phobic object or situation can be identified. Thus it would be suitable for, say, a phobia of snakes, but not for generalised social phobia. It is also of no value to patients with obsessions but no observable compulsive behaviours.

▨ Systematic desensitisation works well in the therapeutic situation and is a quick and cost-effective method. However the therapeutic effect does not always generalise to the patient's everyday life.

▨ Flooding produces high levels of fear and this can be very traumatic, and therefore has ethical implications.

▨ *In vivo* (real-life exposure) is more effective than *in vitro* (imagined exposure) for both flooding and systematic desensitisation.

▨ VRET has advantages over systematic desensitisation as it is much easier and cheaper and often more convenient, but still has a similar level of success.

▨ The equipment required for VRET is expensive and may not be suitable for all phobias. In addition patients do sometimes report negative side-effects, for example nausea.

▨ Exposure and response prevention (a type of flooding) for obsessive-compulsive disorder has been found to be more effective than medication (Foa *et al.*, 1998).

▨ Cognitive therapy

The aim of cognitive therapy is to replace unrealistic and fearful thinking about phobias with more realistic mental habits. It teaches patients to identify, challenge and replace counterproductive thoughts with more constructive thinking patterns.

Challenging distorted thinking involves using counterstatements (see Table 3).

Table 3 *Distorted thinking patterns challenged by counterstatements in cognitive therapy*

Distorted thinking	Counterstatement
Over-estimating thoughts	'Taking an objective view of the situation, how likely is it that the snake will be poisonous, given that there are no poisonous snakes in this area?' or 'How likely is it that if you do not wash your hands you will die?'
Catastrophic thoughts	'If the worst happened is it actually true that I would not be able to handle it?'
Under-estimating ability to cope	'If I did meet a snake then I could run, or if I was bitten I could immediately go to hospital' or 'If I did pick up a germ and became ill, there are medicines available that would quickly restore my health.'

Often cognitive treatment is used in conjunction with behaviour therapy and this is known as **cognitive behaviour therapy (CBT).** An illustration of the main features of a CBT approach to the treatment of 'a fear of the dark' in children is demonstrated by Graziano and Mooney (1980).

Research study: Graziano and Mooney (1980)

Aim: To demonstrate the superiority of cognitive behaviour therapy for the 'fear of dark' in young children, over a no-treatment condition.

Method: Seventeen children with a severe fear of the dark were taught to relax their muscles in bed, self-reinforce their efforts with praise, imagine a pleasant scene, recite brave self-statements. These children were compared to an untreated control group. Several measures of fear were taken by their parents, for example completing a behavioural scale.

Results: The treatment condition had significantly improved after treatment and this improvement was maintained at a three-year follow-up. The untreated control condition showed no such improvement.

Conclusion: CBT is an effective treatment for a phobia of the dark in children.

Evaluation: In this study, it is not clear which of the procedures were the active agent for change as both behavioural and cognitive components were involved in the therapy.

Links

Control groups are an important part of experimental psychology. For more on this see Chapter 4, Research methods.

The behavioural scale is a form of self-report measure. For others see Chapter 4, Research methods.

Evaluation of cognitive therapy

- There is a lot of empirical evidence to support cognitive therapy for anxiety disorders, particularly when combined with behavioural techniques.
- Marks (1987) reviewed 33 studies comparing behavioural and cognitive treatments for OCD and phobias. Very little difference was found in the effectiveness of these treatments.
- Although changes in patients' cognitions must take place during cognitive therapy, it is not clear what element of the therapy is most effective. It might be that any cognitive change is a consequence of some other factor (for example, medication or lifestyle change), and not the intervention by the therapist.

Psychodynamic treatment

Psychodynamic treatment aims to provide insight into what is unconsciously causing the symptoms of OCD and it ultimately requires clients to confront their fears. In order to do this, ego defence mechanisms have to be lifted to expose the unconscious fear. Techniques that can be used to access the unconscious include the following:

- **Free association** – The patient is encouraged to relax and say anything and everything that comes to their mind, no matter how absurd. The idea is that the ego will be unable to carry out its normal role of keeping check of the threatening unconscious impulses, and the conflict can be brought to consciousness. Once verbalised the therapist can interpret and explain the cause of the anxiety.

Dream analysis – According to Freud, the main purpose of dreams is wish fulfilment, and dreams are 'the royal road to the unconscious'. Repressed ideas in the unconscious (which cause us anxiety) are more likely to appear in dreams than when we are awake, and Freud referred to these ideas as the **latent content** of dreams. Analysing dreams to uncover the latent content allows the therapist to make sense of the patient's anxieties. Dream symbols are used to disguise unacceptable ideas, so, for example, a person who is anxious about sex might dream of horse riding. The horse would be the **manifest content** which according to the psychodynamic interpretation disguised the latent content, which is anxiety about sex.

Evaluation of psychodynamic treatment

- Psychoanalytic procedures have largely been ineffective in treating anxiety disorders and nowadays are rarely used.

- Anxiety can be reduced without undertaking a major analysis of a person's unconscious conflicts and childhood experiences by, for example, systematic desensitisation.

- Psychoanalysis is expensive and time-consuming – often taking years to complete.

- This treatment can also be very traumatic for patients. As the ego defences are broken down and all the anxiety that has been repressed comes into consciousness the guilt and fear associated with the repressed incident is also released. This is known as 'catharsis'.

Key points:

- The main drugs used for anxiety disorders are anti-depressants, such as Prozac.

- There are a number of drawbacks to the use of drugs for the treatment of anxiety disorders, including unwanted side-effects and the length of time before any benefit is derived from them.

- Systematic desensitisation and flooding are two behavioural techniques that have proved useful in the treatment of anxiety.

- Cognitive treatment aims to replace faulty thinking with more realistic and constructive thinking patterns.

- Psychodynamic treatment has proved the least effective of the treatments available for anxiety disorders, and is rarely used.

End-of-chapter activity

The preparedness theory states that we have an innate tendency to acquire a phobia to potentially harmful items. To test this theory, a scale could be drawn up which contains names or pictures of animals that are potentially harmful to humans, for example snake, bear, lion; and animals that are not usually considered harmful to humans, for example caterpillar, kitten, butterfly. Participants could then rate how frightened they are of the animals – perhaps on a scale: from not very frightening [1], quite frightening [2], frightening [3], very frightening [4]. It would be predicted that potentially harmful animals would have a higher 'fear rating' than animals considered less harmful.

Key terms

Latent content: what the dream really represents.

Manifest content: the dream as it appears to the dreamer.

Summary questions

9 Outline one drug treatment for anxiety disorders.

10 Outline how flooding (or ERP) would be used with one named anxiety disorder.

11 Give one strength and one weakness of systematic desensitisation.

12 Identify and outline one technique that could be used in psychodynamic treatment of anxiety disorders.

13 A cognitive behaviour therapist was interviewing Annie who had a phobia of spiders. The therapist asked, 'What do you think about when you see a spider?'

Annie replies, 'I think it is going to run very fast and crawl up my body and bite me. It will probably be followed by many other spiders, possibly hundreds of them, and the bite could be poisonous and I might die.'

Give an example of Annie's distorted thinking and a counterstatement that might be used in the cognitive treatment of her phobia.

AQA Examination-style questions

1   Jenny thinks constantly about germs and is afraid of touching door handles or any surfaces in case she picks up any germs. She showers up to 20 times a day and is constantly washing her hands. She has become so anxious about contamination that she spends hours washing and disinfecting her home and is no longer able to go to work. Jenny has been diagnosed as suffering from obsessive-compulsive disorder.

   (a) (i)   Identify three symptoms/behaviours that Jenny is displaying that might have led her doctor to diagnose obsessive-compulsive disorder.   *(3 marks)*

       (ii) With reference to Jenny's behaviour, explain the difference between obsessions and compulsions.   *(3 marks)*

   (b)   Briefly discuss one biological explanation for obsessive-compulsive disorder.   *(4 marks)*

   (c)   Describe and evaluate cognitive therapy for at **least one** anxiety disorder (for example, phobias and obsessive-compulsive disorder).   *(10 marks)*

2   (a) (i)   If Colin goes into the town centre, he begins to feel faint and sweaty. He is terrified that something awful is going to happen to him. State whether or not Colin has a phobia. Justify your answer.   *(2 marks)*

       (ii) Mandy is taking her pet dog for a walk, when a much larger dog runs towards her, growling. Mandy feels scared and her mouth goes dry. State whether or not Mandy has a phobia. Justify your answer.   *(2 marks)*

   (b)   With reference to a behaviourist explanation for phobias, suggest why someone might develop a phobia of trains.   *(4 marks)*

   (c)   Outline the process of flooding as used to treat phobias.   *(2 marks)*

   (d)   Describe and evaluate a psychodynamic explanation for obsessive-compulsive disorder.   *(10 marks)*

AQA, specimen question

10 Autism

Defining and diagnosing autism

Learning objectives:

- Outline the main symptoms that would lead to a diagnosis of autism.

- Explain what is meant by the term 'joint attention'.

- Understand why autism can be considered a syndrome.

Key terms

Pervasive developmental disorder: a severe impairment in several areas of development which starts early in childhood and becomes apparent as the child begins to develop.

Mental retardation: a disorder which is evident before age 18 and includes a number of deficits including low intelligence.

Savant: a person with an extraordinary ability in a particular field, for example someone who can calculate the day of the week on which any future date will fall.

Islets of ability: although children with autism are often poorer than their developmental equivalents on many tasks, on a particular task, such as rote learning names, they might have superior talent.

AQA Examiner's tip

Autism is generally defined by the characteristics or features that individuals present with.

Autism is a **pervasive developmental disorder** which covers all social classes and geographical areas and is approximately four times more likely to be diagnosed in boys than girls. Early population studies indicated a prevalence rate of approximately 4.5 per 10,000 (Lotter, 1966), but more recent research has suggested that the prevalence of autism is much higher. A review of 39 population studies by Wing and Potter (2002) produced an estimated figure of between 8 and 30 per 10,000 for the classic form of autism. ('Classic' in this respect means not including related disorders on the autistic spectrum, for example Asperger's syndrome.)

This huge increase probably does not reflect a real increase in cases (although this cannot be totally ruled out), but is probably partly due to a greater awareness of the disorder, which has led more people to come forward for diagnosis. Also, the diagnostic criteria have been widened, and it is likely that individuals may now be being classed as autistic when previously they had been diagnosed with some other form of **mental retardation**.

Autistic children appear to be physically healthy but differ from normal children in particular ways. For example, they are aloof and isolated and fail to interact with others normally, usually avoiding eye-contact. They often engage in repetitive behaviour such as rocking or spinning an object. They also usually display language difficulties – they could be mute or engage in echolalia, which is the repeating of words or phrases in a meaningless manner. Autistic children also have an obsessive need for sameness and would be panicked or outraged if a routine was altered. Occasionally autistic children have a superior talent in a particular area, for example drawing (sometimes such children are known as **savants**), but the majority of children have an IQ (Intelligent Quotient) below 70, which means they are intellectually retarded.

Autism was first described by Kanner (1943) who noticed a number of features in some of the children he saw, such as **autistic aloneness**, **a desire for sameness**, **islets of ability**.

The features first identified in children by Kanner in 1943 are still relevant to the diagnosis of this condition today. In order to be diagnosed with autism, behavioural criteria are set out in published manuals. The main publication is the *Diagnostic and Statistical Manual of Mental Disorders* (DSM-IV), which lists the essential criteria, which must have been present since early childhood. In order for autism to be diagnosed, there must be six or more items from the list of behaviours in the table.

Table 1 *The criteria required for a diagnosis of autistic disorder using the DSM-IV*

Impairment (relative to developmental level)	Behaviour	Number of impairments required in each category for diagnosis
Qualitative impairment in reciprocal social interaction	Poor use of eye gaze and of gestures; lack of personal relationships; lack of spontaneous sharing, for example joint attention; lack of social/emotional reciprocity.	At least two
Qualitative impairment in verbal and non-verbal communication	Delay in the acquisition of language, or lack of speech; stereotyped and repetitive use of language; failure to initiate or sustain conversation; lack of varied, spontaneous make-believe play.	At least one
Restricted repertoire of activities and interests	Repetitive or stereotyped movements, such as hand flapping; interests that are abnormally intense/narrow; adherence to specific, non-functional routines or rituals.	At least one

Key terms

Joint attention: where both infant and another person are attentive to the same object and to each other.

Syndrome: a set of symptoms that occur together and may have a common origin.

AQA Examiner's tip

In addition to the symptoms required for diagnosis outlined in the DSM-IV, the specification names 'lack of joint attention' and 'triad of impairment'. You could be asked about these terms specifically.

Autism and joint attention

Around the age of 9–15 months, most infants engage in a behaviour that results in a shared interaction between the infant and another person. The child's gaze will shift from an interesting event or object to another person in such a way that their own and another person's attention becomes focused on the same object. This is usually achieved by gazing or pointing and is known as **joint attention**. As the care-giver and child co-ordinate their gaze towards the same object, the infant is interested not just in the object but in the care-giver's attitude and feelings towards the object. This is a major developmental milestone because this pre-linguistic stage is important to the development of mutual understanding and sharing. This demonstrates an intention to socially interact with another person. Critically, this joint attention in pointing and sharing (and later in speech) is absent in children with autism (Sigman *et al.*, 1986).

Autism as a syndrome: the triad of impairments

The DSM-IV requires delays or abnormal functioning in at least one of the following areas, with onset prior to the age of three, for a diagnosis of autism to be given:

- social interaction
- language as used in social communication
- symbolic or imaginative play.

This has led researchers to look closely at whether these three domains occur together by chance or whether they form a triad of impairments that always occur together and therefore constitute a **syndrome**.

Research study: Wing and Gould (1970)

Aim: To discover how many children in a selected population showed symptoms of autism and whether these symptoms could be interpreted as a syndrome.

Method: A longitudinal study was carried out in Camberwell, London. A group of 914 handicapped children aged 0–14 years were screened for autistic symptoms and 173 were identified as displaying at least one of three behaviours typical of autism.

Children were observed and tested regularly and the parents/care-givers interviewed. A follow-up study was conducted when the participants were aged 16–30 years.

Results: When the children were tested on Kanner's main symptoms, for example aloofness and repetitive routines, 17 children (an incidence of 4.9 in 10,000) were found to be autistic.

However, an additional 62 children showed severe social impairment before the age of seven, a classic autistic symptom, and if these are included this equates to an incidence of 22.5 in every 10,000. Due to their very severe learning difficulties, the behaviours of these children were limited and they did not show elaborate routines, peculiar speech or islets of ability, and therefore did not fall into Kanner's autistic categorisation.

The socially impaired group of children were subdivided into a higher ability group (language comprehension age above 20 months) and lower ability group (language comprehension age below 20 months). Only in the high ability group was impaired communication and imagination clearly identifiable. Critically, all socially impaired children in this higher ability group showed impairment of all three features – social, communication and imagination.

Conclusion: The triad of impairments do not occur together by chance but can be considered a syndrome.

Evaluation: This was a longitudinal study carried out over a 16-year period. As with most longitudinal studies, it suffered from participant 'drop-out' and the final sample of socially impaired higher ability children was quite small, and specific to an area of London, making generalisation unreliable.

Evaluation of the triad of impairments

- Although too vague to be used reliably as a diagnostic tool, the three features of the triad do appear in the diagnostic manuals and further research into autism as a syndrome is ongoing.

- The triad of impairments does not tell us anything about other recognised symptoms that some autistic individuals display, for example islets of ability. It might be that such individuals who have the triad of impairments and one or more of these other symptoms may eventually form new sub-groups (which has already emerged with Asperger's syndrome).

Key points:

- Autism is a pervasive developmental disorder with an estimated incidence of between 8 and 30 per 10,000 of the population, and is four times more prevalent in boys than girls.

- Autism was defined by Kanner (1943), and the symptoms he first described are present in the criteria listed in the *Diagnostic and Statistical Manual* currently used to diagnose autism. Diagnosis requires impairment in social interaction and communication, and a restriction in activities/interests.

- Research has shown that autistic children fail to engage in joint attention.

- Some researchers propose that the triad of impairments present in autism can be considered a syndrome.

Link

Issues of generalisation and reliability are discussed further in Chapter 4, Research methods.

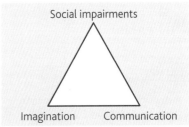

Fig. 1 *The triad of impairments*

Summary questions

1. Outline what clinicians mean by pervasive developmental disorder.

2. Use an example to explain what is meant by the term 'joint attention'.

3. James is 2½ years old and his parents are concerned because he does not seem to be talking yet. He goes to playgroup but his mother has noticed that he always seems to sit alone, sometimes under the table away from other children. She has had a word with the playgroup leader who agrees that James isolates himself most of the time and has also noticed that James repeats the same sound over and over again whilst rocking back and forth on the floor.

   Identify three behavioural signs or symptoms that James is displaying that might lead a clinician to suspect James has autistic disorder.

Individual differences

Explanations for autism

Learning objectives:

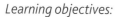 Outline the cold-parenting theory of autism.

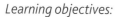 Describe and evaluate the main biological explanations of autism.

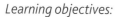 Describe and evaluate the main cognitive explanations of autism.

Key term

Autonomy: in this context, means the sense that you can have an effect on the environment.

An early psychological explanation: cold parenting

Kanner (1943) proposed that autism was caused by the personalities of the parents of the child, in particular cold, rigid parents. The notion that autism was caused by mothers who were cold and rejecting led to the label 'refrigerator mother'. The involvement of parents in the development of autism in their child, and the idea of 'cold parenting' were further developed by Bettleheim (1967), who proposed that the cause of autism is primarily due to the early interactions with parents/care-givers. According to Bettleheim, it is as a result of early parent–child interactions that children develop a sense of **autonomy** and a failure in the development of autonomy can lead to autism.

According to Bettleheim, autonomy develops in infancy when babies learn their actions make a difference. For example, when a baby cries an action often results and an adult brings comfort. The baby has a sense that they have initiated such action. Similarly, when a baby smiles, a smile is usually returned. Bettleheim believes that a sense of autonomy is central to the development of personality and the self. If, at an early stage, infants sense that key figures are not influenced by their efforts, but in fact attempts to get attention are met with indifference or anxiety, then autonomy can fail to develop. If, for example, breast feeding produces anxiety and irritation, the infant will sense this and give up trying to influence the environment by, for example, no longer searching for the nipple, or producing a smile.

According to Bettleheim, a child may fail to develop autonomy because:

the child feels unwanted, which leads to
↓
the child limiting behaviour to his/her own world, which leads to
↓
impaired social interaction and a diagnosis of autism.

Evaluation of cold parenting

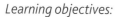 Although critics say that Bettleheim is blaming autism on the parents, Bettleheim himself says this is not his intention. The disorder is due to poor parent–child interactions, but Bettleheim thinks innate temperamental differences between parent and child may be the cause. Bettleheim has had some success with the treatment for autism provided in his school.

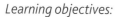 There is no real evidence that autism is caused by cold, rigid and rejecting parents (Roazen, 1992) and to discuss such a possibility is particularly hurtful to parents of autistic children, the majority of whom are usually loving and sensitive carers.

Biological explanations of autism

There are two biological explanations of autism:

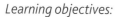 neurological correlates   genetics.

Neurological correlates

This biological theory proposes that autistic individuals have one or more abnormalities within the brain. The area of the brain damaged, or with structural abnormalities, in children diagnosed as autistic appears to correlate with those areas responsible for the development of normal communication, social functioning and play.

Post-mortem studies

Early research into structural abnormalities of the autistic brain included **post-mortem** studies. Such studies have revealed abnormalities in the frontal lobes (responsible for planning and control – see Link), limbic system (responsible for emotional regulation – see Figure 3), brain stem and cerebellum (responsible for motor coordination – see Link). From these studies no single abnormality has been found and it is uncertain which abnormalities are specific to autism. There are other problems with post-mortem studies in this area:

- Most post-mortems have been performed on adult autistic brains and therefore it cannot be concluded whether the observed brain abnormalities are a cause of the autism or whether the symptoms of autism, for example social impairment, bring about a physical change in the brain. It is not possible to determine cause and effect.

- Abnormalities in adult brains may also be due to other life injuries or traumas, for example a bang on the head.

Neuroimaging

Advances in technology have enabled researchers to examine the live brain. The major neuroimaging techniques used in autistic research are positron emission tomography (PET), single photon emission computed tomography (SPECT) and magnetic resonance imaging (MRI).

To obtain PET images, glucose containing a minute amount of radioactive isotopes is injected into the patient's arm. This compound then travels in the bloodstream and is carried to the brain. Sensors in the PET scanner detect the radioactivity as the compound accumulates in different regions of the brain. PET can provide images of blood flow which gives a reliable measure of brain activity either at rest or stimulation. Using such a technique, Zilbovicius *et al.* (2000) reported a functional abnormality in the temporal cortex in 75 per cent of the autistic children examined in his study. The autistic sample was selected from a children's psychiatric unit and were diagnosed according to the DSM-IV criteria. A mentally retarded comparison group showed no abnormality in this region.

PET presents a very sensitive analysis of the brain, but its use in children is limited because of the use of radiation and the requirement for numerous blood samples. It is for this reason that SPECT is preferred for use with children. SPECT is similar to PET but the procedure uses less radiation.

In a study using SPECT carried out by Ohnishi *et al.* (2000), various regions of abnormalities within the autistic brain were identified. A positive correlation was observed between:

- impairments in communication and social interaction, and blood flow in the frontal cortex;

- obsessive desire for sameness and blood flow in the right hippocampus and the amygdale (parts of the limbic system, see Figure 3).

The unusually high blood flow in the identified brain regions was interpreted as being a cause of the qualitative impairments in social interaction reported in the children.

The preferred method of neuroimaging in children is MRI mainly because there is no radiation effect. MRI uses magnetic fields and radio

Key term

Post-mortem: an investigation (for example, of the brain) carried out after the death of an individual.

Link

These sections of the brain are labelled in Chapter 2, Figure 6 (p25).

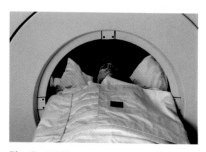

Fig. 2 *A PET scanner*

Link

For more information on post-mortem studies, neuroimaging and PET scans, see Chapter 2, Biopsychology.

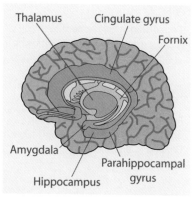

Fig. 3 *The limbic system of the human brain*

waves to produce high quality three-dimensional images of the brain structures. The most evident abnormalities in autistic brains from MRI scans have been found in the cerebellum. This area is thought to be implicated in the control of attention and an abnormality in this area would explain the attention deficit exhibited by many autistic individuals. Courschene *et al.* (1994) investigated 50 autistic patients and reported a significant reduction in the size of vermal lobules in the cerebellum of autistic people with or without mental retardation. Further studies have supported the findings that the cerebellum and brain stem are significantly smaller in autistic individuals.

Piven *et al.* (1995) measured the volume of the brain using MRI. Autistic individuals had significantly greater total brain volume compared to controls, a finding that has been replicated a number of times since. There is now converging evidence that there is brain enlargement in autism compared to normal and mentally deficient groups.

Evaluation of the neurological correlates explanation

▨ The advance in technology has enabled researchers to fully investigate the brain and its structures in more detail, and findings give more information on the nature of autism and its underlying biological cause.

▨ The different techniques each have their own merits but MRI is the most advanced neuroimaging technique and can obtain the most sensitive observations.

▨ Advances in technology have enabled us to identify possible regions of the brain which may be responsible for the autistic symptoms, for example social impairment, but none of the studies fully account for the range of autistic symptoms.

▨ Methodological factors can confound the comparison of studies because factors such as age, gender, IQ differ considerably between autistic samples and controls both within and between studies.

Genetics

▨ Research has shown that, if one member of the family is autistic, there is an increased chance of other members developing the disorder. If one child has autism then there is a 3–6 per cent chance of a second child developing it. This is up to 10 times higher than the risk in the normal population, which is approximately 0.6 per cent. Bolton *et al.* (1994) found that approximately 3 per cent of siblings of autistic children also had autism themselves, and a further 3 per cent had other pervasive developmental disorders. This was compared to a control group of siblings of children with Down's syndrome where no such concordance was found.

▨ Autism is more prevalent in boys than girls (approximate ratio 4:1) and this supports genetic influences.

▨ Research has found **concordance** rates for identical (MZ) twins to be as high as 90 per cent, but much less for non-identical (DZ) twins. As MZ twins share the same genetic make-up, these findings offer strong support for a genetic cause of autism. For example, Ritvo *et al.* (1985) investigated the concordance rates of 23 MZ and 17 DZ twin pairs and found 96 per cent concordance with MZ and only 23 per cent concordance with DZ twin pairs.

Key term

Concordance: 'agreement between'; the extent to which a pair of twins share similar traits or chacteristics.

Link

For more about monozygotic and dizygotic twins and concordance, see Chapter 2, Biopsychology.

Research study: Folstein and Rutter (1977)

Aim: A twin study to investigate the genetic cause of autism.

Method: Concordance rates for autism were investigated in 21 pairs of twin boys, 11 genetically identical (MZ) and 10 fraternal twins (DZ).

Results: Concordance rate for MZ twins was four out of the 11 pairs, and with DZ twins concordance was 0 out of 10.

In the non-concordant MZ group, many of the brothers did have a milder form of autistic disorder and their symptoms became more apparent with age. Concordance using wider criteria for the MZ twins was 90 per cent.

Conclusion: This study provides some evidence for a genetic cause of autism.

Evaluation: The milder symptoms experienced in the non-concordant MZ group suggest autism might be best explained with respect to a broader phenotype, which is consistent with the idea of an **autistic spectrum**.

Key term

Autistic spectrum: where there are different levels of impairment, not all people display the same symptoms with the same intensity.

A general conclusion drawn by Carson *et al.* (2000) from the family and twin studies reviewed was that 80–90 per cent of the variance in risk for autism is based on genetic factors, but the exact mode of genetic transmission is not yet understood.

Evaluation of the genetics explanation

Link

Phenotype and genotype are discussed in Chapter 2, Biopsychology.

- Both autism and MZ twins are relatively rare and therefore the number of twin pairs researched is low. This causes difficulty when analysing the results as the overall concordance rate in a study can be significantly affected by the addition of just one concordant or non-concordant twin pair.

- Studies conducted on relatives of autistic individuals show features of autism are present in other members of the family, for example aloofness, rigidity. However, these features may be a consequence of having to care for a child with autism.

- The search for genes responsible for autism is ongoing. Of particular interest is the study of large families with some autistic members where chromosomes of both affected and unaffected relations can be screened and compared. Although specific chromosomes that may be implicated in the development of autism (for example chromosome 7, Bailey *et al.*, 1998) have been located, how the genes influence the developing brain is currently an important question. Research on genetically modified mice is giving an insight into genetic influences on human brain development.

- Although the research findings from twin studies suggest a heritable component to autism, it is difficult to explain why DZ twin concordance (23 per cent, Ritvo *et al.*, 1985) is much higher than for ordinary siblings (approximately 2 per cent), as they each have the same proportion of genetic similarity (50 per cent). This points to an environmental influence, as twin pairs also share a more similar environment. It may be the case that children with a genetic predisposition for autism only develop the disorder under particular environmental conditions.

Cognitive explanations of autism

There are three cognitive explanations of autism:

 lack of theory of mind

central coherence deficit

impaired executive functioning.

Lack of theory of mind

From an early age, we automatically begin to think about mental states (both our own and the mental states of those around us), but this does not seem to be the case with autistic children. The ability to attribute mental states to others is necessary to predict their behaviour, and so if this mechanism is faulty or fails to develop then individuals would have problems. To investigate whether autistic children really do fail to develop a 'theory of mind' some intriguing studies have been carried out.

A theory of mind is an understanding of how the mind works; the acquisition of knowledge that other people can have a different belief than you. In 1983, Wimmer and Perner first studied the development of a theory of mind in normal children. They found that, by the age of four, children could understand that other people may have a different perception of a situation, and this could be a false belief – a belief about something that is not true. Baron-Cohen *et al.* (1985) decided to investigate this theory of mind in autistic children and found that autistic children were less able to see the world from another's point of view, and they used the term 'mind-blind'. Baron-Cohen *et al.* did a series of experiments and came to the conclusion that this 'mind-blindness' may explain many of the social and communication impairments found in autism.

Research study: Baron-Cohen *et al.* (1985)

Aim: To investigate whether children with autism would understand that someone else could have a belief that was different from their own.

Method: Three groups of participants were tested:

20 autistic children aged between 6 and 16 with a mean verbal age of 5½ years

14 children with Down's syndrome of similar age but with a mean verbal ability of 3 years

27 'normal' children with a mean chronological and verbal age of 4½ years.

Children were tested individually and were seated at a desk opposite an experimenter. Two dolls were introduced, Sally who had a basket and Anne who had a box. Sally places a marble in her basket and then goes for a walk. Whilst Sally is gone, Anne plays a trick and transfers the marble from the basket to the box. Sally returns. The child is then asked the 'belief' question: 'Where will Sally look for her marble?' The correct response is 'in Sally's basket', because the child will know that Sally is unaware of the switch to the box.

Three control questions were asked:

naming – asking which doll was which

reality – 'Where is the marble really?'

memory – 'Where was the marble in the beginning?'

Results: The percentage of correct responses to the belief question was: autistic 20 per cent, Down's syndrome 86 per cent, 'normal' 85 per cent. The results were signifiant at P>.001. There were no failures by any group on the naming, reality and memory questions.

Conclusion: Autistic children had a much higher mental age than the other two groups but still could not make the important inference that if Sally had not seen the marble moved she would think it was where she had left it, something the non-autistic groups had no trouble with. The researchers concluded that autistic children lack a theory of mind.

Evaluation:

- The experiment used dolls and the autistic children may not have seen them as representing real people; perhaps with real people findings would be different? In fact this does not seem to be the case, as Frith relates a study where she and Leslie played a game with an autistic child and hid a coin, which was then moved when Leslie left the room. The autistic child saw the researcher leave the room prior to the coin being moved and hidden in a new place. Still, autistic children erroneously thought the researcher would look for the coin in the secret new place rather than the place it was originally hidden.

- Perhaps there was something about the cognitive demands of the task, maybe the autistic children did not want to attribute a false belief to another person? Again, this would seem not to be the case, as illustrated in the 'Smarties' experiment.

Research study: Perner *et al.* (1989)

Aim: To investigate false belief in children.

Method: To operationalise false belief, a Smartie tube containing a pencil was shown to normal children and autistic children. Individually they were asked, 'What do you think is in this tube?' They answered 'Smarties' because they had no reason to believe otherwise. Then they were shown that the Smartie container actually held a pencil and were surprised. Then the Smartie lid was replaced and the children asked what their friend will think is in the box.

Results: Four-year-old children can correctly answer 'Smarties' although three-year-olds answer 'pencil'. However, the majority of autistic children reported that their friend who is new to the study would think there was a pencil in the Smarties box. Only approximately a third of autistic children are able to apply false belief to others.

Conclusion: 'Normal' children have an understanding of false belief and what might be in the minds of other people by age four. Autistic children do not seem to develop a theory of mind.

Evaluation: Some researchers have suggested that children may have difficulty with the wording of the question in the Smarties task. Lewis and Osborne (1990) found that if they asked children what their friend would think was in the box **before the lid was opened** they found that autistic children as young as three could succeed on the task.

> **Link**
>
> The importance of operationalising (deciding criteria with which to test something) is covered in more depth in Chapter 4, Research methods.

Individual differences

Comic strip stories

Studies have shown that children with autism have difficulty in a number of tasks that require an appreciation of another's false belief. Baron-Cohen *et al.* (1986) did a series of experiments with comic strip stories. Children with autism were shown sets of four pictures, each of which made a story. There were three types of story:

■ a mechanical story, so called because the action in the story did not involve any people

■ a behavioural story, which did include people but did not require any understanding of what the people were thinking

■ a mentalistic story that required an understanding of the beliefs about the characters in the pictures.

The children were given the pictures in a mixed up order, and were asked to place them in the correct order and explain what was happening in the story. The children with autism had no problem placing both the mechanical and behavioural stories in sequence and explaining the events, but they were very poor on the mentalistic stories – placing the pictures in the wrong order and only reporting what they themselves could see. They did not report anything about the mental state of the characters in the story.

Evaluation of theory of mind

■ A proportion of children with autism succeed on false belief tasks and this lack of universality weakens an explanation for autism based on a failure to understand minds (Charman, 2000). However, although it is true that a minority of autistic individuals can successfully complete theory of mind tasks, they do not have a profound understanding of other people's minds because they normally fail second order belief tasks. A first order belief task would be: 'I think that Sally thinks the marble is in the basket.' A second order belief is the understanding that a second person can have beliefs about a third person, for example 'I think that Sally thinks that Tom thinks the marble is in the basket.'

■ It is not clear whether a theory of mind is a cause or a symptom of autism.

■ A failure to understand that someone's belief differs from your own, and differs from reality, would make it difficult to interpret people and the environment. This could possibly lead to a social deficit and insistence on routine and 'sameness' – classic autistic symptoms.

■ The finding that people with autism have a deficit in understanding others' minds has stimulated a lot of new research but at present theory of mind can tell us very little about some of the specific deficits and abilities that some autistic individuals possess, for example echolalia and islets of ability.

Central coherence deficit

Central coherence is the tendency humans possess to process information for general meaning rather than focusing on individual elements. In normal cognitive systems, there is a need to form coherence over a wide range of stimuli and a wide range of contexts. For example, when we look at a picture we tend to make sense of the 'whole' by imposing meaning on it; similarly we remember the gist of a message rather than each individual word, and we tend to slot this meaning into a particular context. According to Frith (1989), it is this capacity for coherence that is diminished in the child with autism.

The theory of impaired central coherence can account for a number of findings:

▥ This theory would account for the way autistic individuals focus on details rather than global meaning. This is illustrated in the excellent ability of autistic individuals to carry out embedded figure tests. Such tasks prove difficult for normal individuals because they have a drive towards central coherence, what Frith calls 'a central cohesive force ... a natural and useful characteristic of the cognitive system'. It is this force which is weaker in autistic individuals and which can be debilitating in some situations (for example, social situations) but proves beneficial on some tasks (for example, embedded figures).

Research study: Shah and Frith (1993)

Aim: To investigate how well autistic children could locate hidden figures.

Method: Using a standardised test – the children's embedded figures test – a group of autistic and non-autistic children of the same mental age had to locate a small target shape which was located in a larger drawing.

Results: Autistic children were faster and more accurate at locating the embedded figure than normal children of the same age.

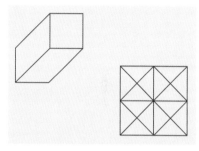

Fig. 4 *Example of an embedded figure*

Conclusion: Autistic children seem to have the ability to disregard context and do not succumb to the central coherence 'force' experienced by non-autistic children. Children with autism seem to have weak central coherence.

Evaluation: The superior performance of autistic children on the embedded figures test might be due to central coherence, however there are alternative explanations for such experimental findings, for example superior low-level processing.

▥ The superior rote memory often found in autistic individuals, which involves the learning of individual items without recourse to the overall deep processing of meaning, is consistent with weak central coherence. For example, in a study by Hermelin and O'Connor (1967) it was found that autistic individuals could recall lists of unconnected words equally as well as they could recall sentences, whereas non-autistic individuals perform much better with sentences.

▥ Research by Happe (1996) found that individuals with autism are more accurate in interpreting visual illusions than normal individuals as they do not process visual illusions in the holistic, top-down way that leads to the illusion. An example that she offers is the Ebbinghaus illusion (often referred to as the Titchener illusion) shown in Figure 5.

The middle circles in the two drawings are actually the same size but the one surrounded with smaller circles is often interpreted as being larger. For autistic individuals, this illusion is not as prevalent presumably because their visual perception is not as influenced by the surrounding context.

Central coherence is probably best seen as a continuum where some people have a strong force to process information as a whole (strong central coherence) whilst others are much more likely to engage with individual elements (weak central coherence), and weak central coherence

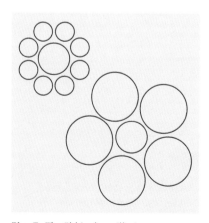

Fig. 5 *The Ebbinghaus illusion*

Individual differences

is particularly evident in autism. A study by Jarrold *et al.* (2000) investigated the relationship between two cognitive factors that have been implicated in autism – lack of theory of mind and weak central coherence – in both autistic and non-autistic school children. They were given the embedded figures test and false belief tasks. They found a positive correlation between poor theory of mind performance and weak central coherence, in children both with and without autism. They concluded that there is a relationship between theory of mind and weak central coherence. Such a finding supports the idea of central coherence as a continuum, where even within the non-autistic population there will be individual differences in this type of information processing.

Evaluation of central coherence deficit

▨ Weak central coherence may partially explain some of the exceptional abilities shown by **savants** who often show great attention to detail.

▨ Support for Happe's view has been found in studies of normal relatives of autistic boys, where 50 per cent of the fathers, although not autistic, showed weak coherence in processing both visual and verbal tasks, as indicated by their superior performance on such tasks.

▨ It is unclear whether the ability to discriminate fine detail, for example as shown in superior performance in embedded figures tests, is a consequence of weak central coherence or is better explained by some other theory, for example superior low-level processing. A number of recent studies have indicated autistic children have a particular difficulty in generalisation. For example, children with autism learned a particular pattern of dots very well but failed to generalise to another set of dots which had a slightly different layout. Such difficulties may be due to superior low-level processing, or inferior high-level processing.

Impaired executive functioning

The investigation of cognitive functions comes from cognitive neuroscience, which examines the control of actions through executive systems. Executive systems are needed for a number of higher level processes, for example multi-tasking, changing plan and over-riding automatic behaviour. All of these types of higher-order functions are particularly impaired in autistic individuals, who often spend their time engaging in routine and ritualised behaviours and have difficulty with change. To explain some of these difficulties, a theory of autism has emerged that proposes autistic individuals have **impaired executive functioning**.

An executive in business is a senior manager who makes and implements crucial decisions. One way to think about this executive function deficit is to consider what happens when the manager is not in work and no one is making the decisions. Individuals may not switch off repetitive actions or thoughts, and will have no executive manager or system to call on for the necessary higher level processing required when engaging with people and the environment.

Patients with frontal lobe damage also show impairments of executive functions but not in routine tasks, and this has led researchers to implicate the frontal lobes in these higher level cognitive functions. There is converging evidence that areas of the frontal lobes are responsible for some of the cognitive deficits found in autistic individuals who have executive functioning problems. Interestingly, recent studies using neuroimaging have implicated the frontal cortex with impairments in autistic patients, for example Ohnishi *et al.* (2000), and such biological findings complement the cognitive theories that are emerging.

■ Link

Ohnishi *et al.*'s study is discussed under biological explanations of autism – neurological correlates.

Experiments carried out to investigate the difficulties autistic individuals have with higher mental processing, such as switching from one task to another, include the Wisconsin card sorting task. This consists of a set of cards which can be sorted according to colour, shape or number, etc. The individual chooses a sorting task (say, colour) and is rewarded for this sorting; but then the sorting dimension is changed (unknown to the sorter) and rewards are for a different sorting task (for example, shape). People with good executive function will notice the change and switch very quickly to the new sorting dimension that is now being rewarded. Autistic individuals cannot switch task and persevere with the same old task. A critical control system of the brain (executive functioning) appears to be malfunctioning.

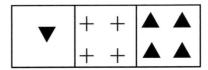

Fig. 6 *The Wisconsin card sorting task*

Evaluation of impaired executive functioning

- Executive functioning impairments can explain some features of autism not explained by theory of mind and therefore can complement other cognitive explanations.

- Frith (1996) has concluded that it is unlikely that one cognitive explanation would be found to explain all the cognitive deficits found with autistic individuals, and executive function can combine with other theories to give an overall picture.

- Additionally, Frith believes that cognitive and biological explanations will complement each other to give a better understanding of the cognitive deficits manifested in autistic individuals. This complementary evidence is now beginning to emerge.

Key points:

- An early explanation of autism was known as cold parenting. This theory proposed that cold and rigid parents caused autistic symptoms in their children; but this early theory has now been largely rejected.

- Two biological theories of autism – neurological correlates and genetics – suggest that autism is largely inherited and/or caused by abnormality of the brain.

- There is some evidence for biological explanations but brain abnormality could be an effect of autism rather than cause; and it is difficult to isolate the genetic component of autism from environmental influences.

- There are three main cognitive explanations of autism: lack of theory of mind; central coherence deficit; impaired executive functioning.

- There is a lot of empirical research into these cognitive areas, but neither deficit alone can account for the many symptoms often present in those with autism.

- Frith, a leading researcher in the field of autism, believes that cognitive and biological explanations combined will lead to a better understanding of this disorder.

Summary questions

4 Using an example, explain what Bettleheim meant when he said that the autistic child fails to develop autonomy.

5 Outline what is meant by neuroimaging and explain why this technique has been beneficial in the search for a biological cause of autism.

6 Describe a study into the genetic cause of autism. Refer to aim, method, results and conclusion in your answer.

7 Identify and outline one cognitive explanation of autism.

8 Kate is a five-year-old autistic child at school with her friend of the same age. Kate is shown a sponge in the shape of a duck and asked, 'What do you think this is?' She answers, 'A duck.' The sponge is placed in water and Kate is shown that it really is a sponge. She is then asked, 'What will your friend think this is?'

How is Kate likely to answer this question? Explain the theory of autism that this type of study is used to support.

Therapeutic programmes for autism

Learning objectives:

- Describe the main therapeutic programmes for autism.

- Understand strengths and weaknesses of therapeutic programmes for autism.

Treatments for autistic children usually involve trying to reduce their unusual behaviour and improve their communication and social skills. Because of the nature of the symptoms in children with this disorder, for example they often dislike change to routine, autistic children are a challenge and prove difficult to motivate. In fact treatment prognosis for autistic disorder is poor. In addition to the severity of the problems, response to treatment is typically poor and this is further compounded by the difficulty autistic children have when generalising across contexts. This means any learning that takes place may remain specific to that situation. So, for example, children may learn a particular word with the language therapist but not use it at home.

Behaviour modification

In behaviour modification, small increments of behaviour are modelled, shaped and positively reinforced. One popular behavioural approach to treatment for children with autism is **applied behavioural analysis** (ABA). ABA is a procedure that uses the principles of learning theory (for example, reinforcement and shaping) to improve selected behaviours in children. ABA is objective and improvement is measurable and such interventions often result in positive behavioural changes.

One type of ABA was pioneered by Lovaas (1987) and this was called **discrete trial training** (DTT). In DTT, skills are broken down into their most basic components and positive reinforcement is used to reward performance of each of the components. The tasks are broken down into short simple trials and a series of distinct, repeated lessons are taught one-to-one. Each trial consists of three parts (ABC):

- **a**ntecedent – a request for an individual to perform an action, for example 'Choose a crayon John'

- **b**ehaviour – a response from the person, for example John picks up a red crayon

- **c**onsequence – a reaction from the therapist, for example 'Well done John. Now let's draw a picture. What do you want to draw?'

Note that the consequence of the action is praise which is positively reinforcing (and may be accompanied with an extrinsic reward, such as a biscuit). Also note that John is given some choice in the crayon and what to draw; researchers have found choice to be important for a successful outcome (Koegal *et al.*, 1996).

Positive reinforcers are usually selected in response to the individual's own preference; some children respond well to praise whilst others may prefer an edible treat. DTT has proved to be one of the most effective long-term treatments for children with autism and has been used to effectively improve IQ, language and cognitive skills (McEachin *et al.*, 1993).

Research study: Lovaas (1987)

Aim: To investigate the effectiveness of intensive behavioural therapy technique for autism.

Method: Nineteen patients, younger than 46 months of age, received intensive behaviour therapy for at least 40 hours a week for a period of two years. The therapy was on a one-to-one basis. There were two control groups: one group were the non-intensive treatment group and only received 10 hours' one-to-one therapy each week, and a group who received no therapy.

Each child was given a task and their response resulted in a reinforcement or punishment. IQ and level of functioning at school were measured (the dependent variable).

Results: Forty-seven per cent of the treatment group achieved normal intellectual functioning and a further 40 per cent attained the mildly retarded level. Following treatment, most children joined mainstream school. When children were discharged to their parents, they continued to improve. However those who remained in an institution tended to regress.

In the control group of untreated children only 2 per cent achieved normal functioning, with 45 per cent at a mildly retarded functioning level.

Conclusion: The researchers concluded that a large proportion of the autistic children were 'transformed into normal children'.

Evaluation: Such intensive behaviour therapy is very expensive and is not available to all children. For improvement to be maintained the reinforcement has to be continued following the programme, and therefore only those parents/institutions with the finances, motivation and long-term commitment are able to benefit from such techniques.

In addition to DTT, other ABA approaches have proved successful such as **pivotal response training** (PRT). This is a naturalistic response intervention developed by Koegel *et al.* (1989). Two pivotal behaviours – motivation and responsivity to multiple cues – were identified that appeared to affect a wide range of behaviours. Changes in these pivotal behaviours would have an impact on a wide range of other behaviours. Unlike DTT, PRT is able to increase the generalisation of new skills and increases the motivation in children by allowing them to make their own choices, by encouraging turn-taking and reinforcement. PRT has been particularly effective in improving language skills, play skills and social behaviours in children with autism.

Evaluation of behaviour modification

There have been a number of methodological criticisms of the research by Lovaas and other similar studies, including:

▓ No random assignment to the two treatment groups took place in the Lovaas study. In fact the parents made this decision.

▓ The therapy provided at home was not observed and therefore this could have been a confounding variable, as households could have used different approaches to therapy.

▓ The Lovaas study compared different intensities of the same therapy rather than comparing different treatments.

▓ Sallows and Graupner (2005) have suggested that pre-treatment variables are the crucial predictor of treatment success, not the treatment itself. Prior to treatment if children are divided into 'rapid' and 'moderate' learners, rapid learners always improve more than moderate learners, irrespective of the type of treatment they receive. They concluded that if the pre-treatment skill of the child was poor then no amount of intensive training would benefit them.

Link

Classical conditioning is discussed under the Behaviourist approach on p7.

Aversion therapy for self-injuring behaviour

Aversion therapy is based on classical conditioning principles and is where an undesirable response is removed by associating the stimulus with another aversive stimulus. For example, an autistic boy may cause himself injury by banging his head against a wall. If this head-banging is paired with an electric shock then the boy will associate the pain of the electric shock with the head-banging behaviour, which should then cease.

Administering an electric shock has been effectively used with autistic children to remove self-harming behaviour. Lovaas (1977) found that self-harming behaviour could be extinguished almost immediately by using an electric shock as an aversive stimulus. However, there are some issues with the use of such methods:

- There are ethical implications of causing pain to another individual, particularly as a child is unable to give their own informed consent.
- Although this treatment does decrease the specific behaviour targeted, it does not easily generalise to other behaviours, which would therefore require further aversive stimuli.
- In extreme cases, where for example children might have to be restrained regularly and for long periods to avoid self-injury, then such extreme therapeutic measures might be considered appropriate.

Language training

Behaviour shaping has been used to train autistic children to communicate more effectively. The required behaviour would be first broken down into constituent parts and successive approximations towards the ultimate goal would be rewarded. For example, a child might be rewarded first for looking at the adult. After a while rewards would stop for this behaviour and the child would have to make eye contact to gain a reward. Then the child would have to utter a sound, then the sound would have to be identifiable as a word, finally a clearly discernible word would be required for a reward. Behaviour shaping is very time consuming but with perseverance and parental involvement it does bring success.

The **Picture Exchange Communication System** (PECS), first devised by Bondy (1998), uses visual supports for communication for children with autism. Individuals using PECS are required to give a picture of a preferred item to a partner in exchange for the item. The initial communicative behaviour targeted is 'requesting'. In the request, preferred items are presented as reinforcement of the response. The training is designed to take place in a social context, where initially there will be at least two therapists present. Teaching students to request is a communicative skill, and often leads to the teaching of other communicative intents. To begin 'request training' items or activities that are preferred by the individual have to be identified. Two therapists are required so that one sits behind the child and physically prompts the child to give a picture in exchange for a reinforcer. Physical prompts are quickly faded in order to ensure independent communication. Once the request with pictures is firmly established, the child is encouraged to verbalise the request.

Recently several studies have shown the efficacy of using computers to teach children with autism. For example, Bosseler and Massaro (2003) developed a **computer-animated tutor** to teach vocabulary and grammar to eight children with autism. Their programme included receptive and expressive language activities. The computer-animated programme was successful in teaching language to all participants and generalisation to the child's natural environment was reported. Other studies have shown that inappropriate

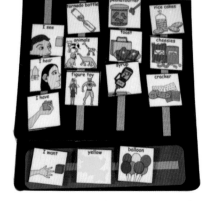

Fig. 7 *A Picture Exchange Communication System*

verbalisations can be decreased using a computerised intervention, and that skills used in this way can also generalise to a natural environment.

Medication

Many of the symptoms of autism such as aggressive behaviour, anxiety, hyperactivity, etc., can be treated with medication and there are a number of drug treatments that are used with autistic children. Table 2 lists the most common drugs currently used and their effects:

Table 2 *Drug treatments for autism*

Drug name and type	Effect of drug on autistic symptoms	Drawbacks of usage
Haloperidol (Haldol), an anti-psychotic drug	Can reduce social withdrawal, stereotyped motor behaviour and aggression	Many children do not respond to this drug and it has no effect on other symptoms. There are also potentially serious side-effects, for example one third of patients develop **dyskinesia**.
Fenfluramine, lowers serotonin levels	Some evidence of improvement in behaviour and thought processes	No consistent effect has been found on language or cognitive levels. Effects are often subtle.

Evaluation of medication

- No drug has yet been developed that reduces enough of the autistic symptoms to warrant long-term use.
- Medication would usually need to be combined with other interventions.
- Side-effects of the drugs often outweigh any gains.
- Many of the drugs have not been tested on children.
- Medication can provide relief from specific symptoms in the individual which in turn can relieve some of the stress experienced by carers.

Parental involvement

There is evidence that parents are central to educational improvement being maintained in autistic children, and that whenever possible parents should be involved in the programme. One of the reasons for this is that parents are present in many different situations and can help children to generalise behaviours they have recently acquired in one situation, to a range of contexts. Treatment contracts with parents are set up that specify the desired behaviour changes in their child and identify the techniques required to bring about change. Such techniques typically require parents to reinforce **adaptive** behaviour whilst withholding reinforcement for undesirable behaviour. Encouraging results have been found, particularly with parents who are able to commit themselves to a lengthy and time-consuming programme.

- Koegel *et al.* (1982) demonstrated that 30 hours of parent training was as effective as 200 hours of clinical treatment in improving the behaviour of autistic children.
- Koegal *et al.* (1996) found that most benefit was derived when parents concentrated on improving their autistic child's general motivation and responsiveness rather than targeting specific problem areas. For example, if natural reinforcers (like praise) were given for all attempts to respond, and the child was allowed to choose the teaching materials, then family interactions and positive communication improved significantly.
- Lovaas believed that one of the key elements in his ABA therapy was the involvement of the parents and he stated that 'the training only really works if you get the parents involved'. In a follow-up to his

AQA Examiner's tip

Although medication itself is not a therapeutic programme it is often used in combination with therapy to control some of the symptoms to enable the therapeutic programme (for example, ABA) to progress.

Key terms

Dyskinesia: involuntary, repetitive bodily movement.

Adaptive: behaviour that allows the child to fit into the environment, for example social interaction.

Individual differences

247

study he found that while the children had made strong gains during treatment, those sent back to mental institutions regressed to their earlier levels. Those who went back to their parents and continued the programme continued to progress.

▓ However, a risk of such intensive family involvement is that it puts families under a lot of pressure. Stress can result not just for the parents but also for the other siblings in the family, as the training takes up a lot of time, effort and expense.

▓ Not all autistic children can be treated at home. A small number of autistic children are severely disturbed, and are best cared for by mental health professionals, sometimes in a hospital or care home setting.

Key points:

■ Behaviour modification uses the principles of operant conditioning to change autistic behaviour into more desirable ones.

■ A key proponent of behaviour modification is Lovaas and ABA.

■ Aversion therapy has proved successful in extinguishing some self-injurious behaviours, but there are ethical implications involved with its use.

■ There are a number of drugs that can improve specific symptoms in some autistic individuals.

■ Both behaviour shaping and communication systems like PECS have improved lanj235

■ guage skills in autistic children.

■ Parental involvement in the therapeutic programme is important for continued progress in autistic children.

✓ **Summary questions**

9 Describe a study in which behaviour modification as a treatment for autism was investigated.

10 Outline one system for improving language in autistic children.

11 Outline one disadvantage of the use of drug treatment for autistic children.

12 John is a five-year-old autistic boy who does not interact with others normally, usually avoiding eye contact and isolating himself from social contact. He repeatedly hits his head against the wall, and his parents are worried that this will cause permanent brain damage.

Explain how aversion therapy could be used to treat John's head-banging behaviour.

💡 **End-of-chapter activity**

Make a set of 'loop cards'. Work in pairs and devise 12 questions and answers on 'Autism'. Place question 1 on a card with answer 12. All the other cards would have a separate question and an answer that is not to that question (see Figure 8).

Give out the cards you have devised (one to each student, or you can work in pairs if it is a large class) and whoever has number 1 starts by asking that question. The person with the answer to question 1 gives the answer aloud and asks their question, and so on until the last answer is back with the person who asked the first question. This is a particularly good practical because when you devise your own cards you are processing the material at a very deep level, and then you can enjoy testing the rest of the group on your questions.

Question 1	Answer	Question	Answer
True or false? Autism is more likely to be diagnosed in boys than in girls	Theory of mind	What is an embedded figure?	Aversion therapy

Fig. 8 *Examples of loop cards*

1 (a) Research has shown that autistic children do not engage in 'joint attention'. Use an example to explain what is meant by 'joint attention'. *(2 marks)*

(b) (i) Describe the Sally-Anne experiment used in the study of autism. *(4 marks)*

(ii) Outline either one strength or one weakness of the Sally-Anne experiment. *(2 marks)*

(c) One early explanation of autism was 'cold parenting'. Outline one criticism of this theory. *(2 marks)*

(d) Describe and evaluate behaviour modification as a therapeutic programme for autism. *(10 marks)*

2 (a) Three of the following are symptoms that commonly occur in cases of autism. In your answer book, write down the three that are symptoms of autism.

Persistent clinging to parents	Extreme sensitivity to pain
Restricted speech	Repetitive behaviours
Excessive pretend play	Lack of empathy

(3 marks)

(b) (i) Outline what is meant by aversion therapy. *(2 marks)*

(ii) Briefly explain how aversion therapy has been used in cases of autism. *(3 marks)*

(iii) Outline one criticism of the use of aversion therapy in cases of autism. *(2 marks)*

(c) Describe and evaluate the theory of mind explanation of autism. Refer to empirical evidence in your answer. *(10 marks)*

AQA, specimen question

References

Chapter 1 Key approaches

Anderson, J.R. (1995) *Learning and Memory*, New York: Wiley

Bock, G.R. and Goode, J.A. (eds) (1996) *Genetics of Criminal and Antisocial Behaviour*, Chichester: John Wiley & Sons

Cox, E. (2002) *AS Level Psychology for AQA Specification B*, Oxford

Gross, R.D. (2005) *Psychology: The Science of Mind and Behaviour*, 5th edition, Hodder Arnold

Heider, F. (1944) Social perception and phenomenal causality, *Psychological Review*, 51, 358–74

Neisser, U. (1967) *Cognitive Psychology*, New York: Appleton-Century-Crofts

Pennington, D. (2003) *Advanced Psychology: Child Development, Perspectives and Methods*, Hodder & Stoughton

http://en.wikipedia.org/wiki/Cognitive_psychology

Chapter 2 Biopsychology

Bailey, J.M. and Pillard, R.C. (1991) A genetic study of male sexual orientation, *Archives of General Psychiatry*, Dec; 48 (12), 1089–96

Bailey, J.M., Dunne, M.P. and Martin, N.G. (2000) Genetic and environmental influences on sexual orientation and its correlates in an Australian twin sample, *Journal of Personality and Social Psychology*, 78 (3)

Bearman, P.S. and Bruckner, H. (2002) Opposite-sex twins and adolescent same-sex attraction, *American Journal of Sociology*, 107, 1179–205

Bouchard, T.J. and McGue, M. (1981) Familial studies of intelligence: A review, *Science*, 212, 1055–9

Cooper, R.M. and Zubeck, J.P. (1958) Effects of enriched and restricted early environments on the learning ability of bright and dull rats, *Canadian Journal of Psychology*, 12: 159–64

Damasio, H., Grabowski, T., Frank. R., Galaburda, A.M. and Damasio, A.R. (1994) The return of Phineas Gage: Clues about the brain from the skull of a famous patient, *Science*, 264, 1102–5

Flanagan, C. (1997) *A-Level Psychology*, Letts

Gianoulakis, C., Krishnan, B. and Thavundayil, J. (1996). Enhanced sensitivity pituitary endorphin to ethanol in subjects at high risk of alcoholism, *Archives of General Psychiatry*, 53, 250–7

Hershberger, S.L. (1987) *The Journal of Sex Research*, Volume 34

Hubel, D.H. and Wiesel, T.N. (1963) Receptive fields of cells in striate cortex of very young visually inexperienced kittens, *Journal of Neurophysiology*, 26, 994–1002

Kirk, K.M., Bailey, J.M., Dunne, M.P. and Martin, N.G. (2000) Measurement models for sexual orientation in a community twin sample, *Behaviour Genetics*, 30 (4), 343–56

Pennington, D.C. (2002) *Introducing Psychology. Approaches, Topics and Methods*, Hodder & Stoughton

Plomin, R., Fulker, D.W., Corley, R. and DeFries, J.C. (1997) Nature, nurture, and cognitive development from 1 to 16 years: A parent-offspring adoption study, *Psychological Science*, 8, 442–7

Plomin, R. (1989) Environment and genes: Determinants of behaviour, *American Psychologist*, 44, 105–11

Scarr, S. and Weinberg, R.A. (1976) IQ test performance of Black children adopted by White families, *American Psychologist*, 31, 726–39

Smith, E., Nolen-Hoeksema, S., Fredrickson, B. and Loftus, G. (2003) *Atkinson and Hilgard's Introduction to Psychology*, 14th edition, Thomson Wadsworth

Tryon, R.C. (1940) Genetic differences in maze-learning ability in rats, *Yearbook of the National Society for the Study of Education*, 39, 111–19

Wickens, A. (2005) *Foundations of Biopsychology*, 2nd edition, Pearson Prentice Hall

Wilson, E.O. (1978) *On Human Nature*, Cambridge, MA: Harvard University Press

Zajonc, R.B. and Markus, G.B. (1975) Birth order and intellectual development, *Psychological Review*, 82 (1), 74–88

Chapter 3 Gender development

Bem, S.L. (1974) The measurement of psychological androgyny, *Journal of Consulting and Clinical Psychology*, 42, 155–62

Best, D.L., House, A.S., Barnard, A.E. and Spicker, B.S. (1994) Parent–child interactions in France, Germany, and Italy: the effects of gender and culture, *Journal of Cross-Cultural Psychology*, 1 June, 25 (2), 181–93

Bradbard, M.R., Martin, C.L., Endsley, R.C. and Halverson, C. F. (1986) Influence of sex stereotypes on children's exploration and memory: A competence versus performance distinction, *Development Psychology*, 22, pp. 481–6

Buss, D.M. (1994) Mate preferences in 37 cultures, in W.J. Lonner and R. Malpass (eds) *Psychology and Culture*, Boston: Allyn & Bacon, 197–202

Bussey, K. and Bandura, A. (1984) Influence of gender constancy and social power on sex-linked modelling,

Journal of Personality and Social Psychology, 47, 1292–1302

Connellan, J., Baron-Cohen, S., Wheelwright, S., Batki, A. and Ahluwalia, J. (2000) Sex differences in human neonatal social perception, *Infant Behavior and Development*, 23, 113–18

Damon, W. (1977) *The Social World of the Child*, San Francisco: Jossey-Bass

Diamond, M., Sigmundson, H.K. (1997) *Sex Reassignment at Birth: A Long Term Review and Clinical Implications*, Archives of Pediatrics and Adolescent Medicine

Eccles, J. (1987) Gender roles and women's achievement-related decisions, *Psychology of Women Quarterly*, 11, 135–72

Fagot, B.I. (1985) Beyond the reinforcement principle: Another step toward understanding sex role development, *Developmental Psychology*, 21, 1097–104

Fagot, B.I. (1978) The influences of sex of child on parental reactions to toddler children, *Child Development*, 49, 459–65

Freud, S. (1909) Analysis of a phobia of a five year old boy, in *The Pelican Freud Library* (1977), Vol. 8, Case Histories 1, 169–306

Furnham, A., and Farragher, E. (2000) A cross-cultural content analysis of sex-role stereotyping in television advertisements: a comparison between Great Britain and New Zealand, *Journal of Electronic and Broadcasting Media*, 44 (3), 415–36

Galligani, N., Renck, A. and Hansen, S. (1996) Personality profile of men using anabolic androgenic steroids, *Hormones and Behavior*, 30, 170–5

van Goozen, S.H., Cohen-Kettenis, P.T., Gooren, L.J., Frijda, N.H. and Van de Poll, N.E. (1995) Gender differences in behaviour: activating effects of cross-sex hormones, *Psychoneuroendocrinology*, 20, 343–63

Golombok, S., Spencer, A. and Rutter, M. (1983) Children in lesbian and single parent households: Psychosexual and psychiatric appraisal, *Journal of Child Psychology and Psychiatry*, 24 (4), 551–72

Hampson, E., Kimura, D. (1988) Reciprocal effects of hormonal fluctuations on human motor and perceptual–spatial skills, *Behavioral Neuroscience*, 102, 456–9

Idle, T., Wood, E. and Desmarais, S. (1993) Gender role socialization in toy play situations: Mothers and fathers with their sons and daughters, *Sex Roles*, 28 (11–12), 679–91

Imperato-McGinley, J., Peterson, R.E., Gautier, T. and Sturla, E. (1979) Androgens and the evolution of male-gender identity among male pseudohermaphrodites with 5-alpha reductase deficiency, *New England Journal of Medicine*, 300, 1233–7

Kohlberg, L. (1966) A cognitive-development analysis of children's sex role concepts and attitudes, in E.E. Maccoby (ed.) *The Development of Sex Differences*, Stanford, CA: Stanford University Press

Kortenhaus, C.M. and Demarest, J. (1993) Gender role stereotyping in children's literature: An update, *Sex Roles*, 28, 219–32

Maccoby, E.E. and Jacklin, C.N. (1974) *The Psychology of Sex Differences*, Stanford, CA: Stanford University Press

Malinowski, B. (1927) *Sex and Repression in Savage Society*, London: Routledge

Manstead, A.S.R. and McCulloch, C. (1981) Sex-role stereotyping in British television advertisements, *British Journal of Social Psychology*, 20, 171–80

Marcus, D. and Overton, W.F. (1978) The development of cognitive gender constancy and sex role preference, *Child Development*, 49, 434–44

Martin, C.L. and Halverson, C.F. (1983) The effects of sex-typing schemas on young children's memory, *Child Development*, 54, 563–74

McConaghy, M.J. (1979) Gender permanence and the genital basis of gender: Stages in the development of constancy of gender identity, *Child Development*, 50, 1223–6

McGhee, P.E. and Frueh, T. (1980) Television viewing and the learning of sex role stereotypes, *Sex Roles*, 6, 179–88

Mead, M. (1935) *Sex and Temperament in Three Primitive Societies*, London: George Routledge & Sons

Money, J. and Ehrhardt, A.A. (1973) *Man and Woman, Boy and Girl: The Differentiation and Dimorphism of Gender Identity from Conception to Maturity*, Baltimore: Johns Hopkins University Press

Munroe, R.H., Shimmin, H.S. and Munroe, R.L. (1984) Gender understanding and sex role preferences in four cultures, *Developmental Psychology*, 20, 673–82

Mussen, P.H. and Rutherford, E (1963) Parent–child relation and parental personality in relation to young children's sex-role preferences, *Child Development*, 34 (1963), 589–607

Pfost, K.S. and Fiore, M. (1990) Pursuit of nontraditional occupations: Fear of success or fear of not being chosen?, *Sex Roles*, 23, 15–24

Pierce, K. (1993) Socialization of teenage girls through teen-magazine fiction: The making of a new woman or an old lady? *Sex Roles*, 29 (1/2), 59–68

Pontius, A.A. (1997) No gender difference in spatial representation by schoolchildren in Northwest Pakistan, *Journal of Cross-Cultural Psychology*, 28 (6)

Rekers, G.A. and Lovaas, O.I. (1974) Behavioral treatment of deviant sex-role behaviors in a male child, *Journal of Applied Behavior Analysis*, 7, 173–90

Rekers, G.A. and Moray, S.M. (1989) Personality problems associated with childhood gender disturbance, *Italian Journal of Clinical and Cultural Psychology*, 1, 85–90

Roscoe, W. (1998) *Changing Ones: Third and Fourth Genders in Native North America*, New York: St. Martin's Press, p109

Slabbekoorn, D., van Goozen, S.H.M., Megens, J., Gooren, L.J.G. and Cohen-Kettenis, P.T. (1999) Activating effects of cross-sex hormones on cognitive functioning: a study of short-term and long-term hormone effects in transsexuals, *Psychoneuroendocrinology*, 24, 423–47

Slaby, R.G. and Frey, K.S. Development of gender constancy and selective attention to same-sex models, *Child Development*, 1975, 46, 849–56

Smith, C. and Lloyd, B. (1978) Maternal behavior and perceived sex of infant: Revisited, *Child Development*, 49, 1255–63

Sugihara, Y. and Katsurada, E. (1999) Masculinity and femininity in Japanese culture: A pilot study, *Sex Roles*, 40 (7/8), 635–46

Waber, D.P. (1976) Sex differences in cognition: A function of maturation rate? *Science*, 192 (4239), 572–4

Williams, J.E. and Best, D.L. (1982) *Measuring Sex Stereotypes: A Thirty Nation Study*, Berkeley, CA: Sage Publications

Chapter 5 Social influence

Adorno, T.W., Frenkel-Brunsik, E., Levinson, D.J. and Sanford, R.M. (1950) *The Authoritarian Personality*, New York: Harper

Allen, V.L. and Levine, J.M. (1971) Social pressure and personal influence, *Journal of Experimental Social Psychology*, 7, 122–4

Allport, F.H. (1920) The influence of the group upon association and thought, *Journal of Experimental Psychology*, 3, 19–82

Allport, F.H. (1924) *Social Psychology*, Boston, MA: Houghton Mifflin

Asch, S.E. (1951) Effects of group pressure upon the modification and distortion of judgements, in H. Guetzkow (ed.), *Groups, Leadership and Men*, Pittsburg, PA: Carnegie Press, 177–90

Asch, S.E. (1956) Studies of independence and conformity: A minority of one against a unanimous majority, *Psychological Monographs: General and Applied*, 70, 1–70

Baron, R.S. (1986) Distraction-conflict theory: Progress and problems, in L. Berkowitz (ed.), *Advances in Experimental and Social Psychology*, Vol. 20, New York: Academic Press, pp1–40

Baron, R.S., Vandello, J.A. and Brunsman, B. (1996) The forgotten variable in conformity research: Impact of task performance on social influence, *Journal of Personality and Social Psychology*, 71, 915–27

Bickman, L. (1974) The social power of a uniform, *Journal of Applied Social Psychology*, 1, 47–61

Bogdonoff, M.D., Klein, R.F., Estes, E.H., Shaw, D.M. and Back, K. (1961) The modifying effect of conforming behaviour upon lipid responses accompanying CNS arousal, *Clinical Research*, 9, 135

Chandra, S. (1973) The effects of group pressure in perception: A cross-cultural conformity study, *International Journal of Psychology*, 8, 37–9

Chen, S.C. (1937) Social modification of the activity of ants in nest-building, *Physiological Zoology*, 10, 420–36

Cottrell, N.B., Wack, D.L., Sekerak, G.J. and Rittle, R.H. (1968) Social facilitation of dominant responses by the presence of others, *Journal of Personality and Social Psychology*, 9, 245–50

Crutchfield, R.S. (1955) Conformity and character, *American Psychologist*, 10, 191–8

Dashiell, J.F. (1930) An experimental analysis of some group effects, *Journal of Abnormal and Social Psychology*, 25, 190–9

Deutsch, M. and Gerard, H.B. (1955) A study of normative and informational social influences upon individual judgement, *Journal of Abnormal and Social Psychology*, 51, 629–36

Doms, M. (1983) The minority influence effect: An alternative approach, in W. Doise and S. Moscovici (eds) *Current Issues in European Social Psycholog*, Vol. 1, Cambridge: Cambridge University Press, pp1–32

Gamson, W.B., Fireman, B. and Rytina, S. (1982) *Encounters with Unjust Authority*, Homewood, IL: Dorsey Press

Henchy, T. and Glass, D.C. (1968) Evaluation apprehension and the social facilitation of dominant and subordinate responses, *Journal of Personality and Social Psychology*, 10, 446–54

Hewstone, M., Stoebe, W. and Stephenson G.M. (1996) *Introduction to Social Psychology*, 2nd edition, Oxford: Blackwell

Hofling, K.C., Brotzman, E., Dalrymple, S., Graves, N. and Pierce, C.M. (1966) An experimental study in the nurse–physician relationships, *Journal of Nervous and Mental Disorders*, 143, 171–80

Hogg, M.A. and Vaughan, G.M. (2005) *Social Psychology*, 4th edition, Hemel Hempstead: Prentice Hall Europe

Larsen, K.S. (1974) Conformity in the Asch experiment, *Journal of Social Psychology*, 94, 303–4

Mandel, D.R. (1998) The obedience alibi: Milgram's account of the Holocaust reconsidered, *Analyse & Kritik: Zeitschrift für Social Wissenschaften*, Vol. 20

Meeus, W.H.J. and Raaijmakers, Q.A.W.(1986) Administrative obedience: Carrying out orders to use psychological-administrative violence, *European Journal of Social Psychology*, 16, 311–24

Michaels, J.W., Blommel, J.M., Brocato, R.M., Linkous, R.A. and Rowe, J.S. (1982) Social facilitation and inhibition in a natural setting, *Replications in Social Psychology*, 2, 21–4

Milgram, S. (1963) Behavioural study of obedience, *Journal of Abnormal and Social Psychology*, 67, 371–8

Neto, F. (1995) Conformity and independence revisited, *Social Behaviour and Personality*, 18, 7–12

Perrin, S. and Spencer, C.P. (1981) Independence or conformity in the Asch experiment, *British Journal of Social Psychology*, 20, 205–10

Sanders, G.S., Baron, R.S. and Moore, D.L. (1978) Distraction and social comparison as mediators of social facilitation, *Journal of Experimental Social Psychology*, 14, 291–303

Sherif, M. (1935) A study of some social factors in perception, *Archives of Psychology*, 27, 1–60

Sherif, M. (1936) *The Psychology of Social Norms*, New York: Harper

Sistrunk, F. and McDavid, J.W. (1971) Sex variable in conforming behaviour, *Journal of Personality and Social Psychology*, 2, 200–7

Smith, P.B. and Bond, M.H. (1993) *Social Psychology Across Cultures*, 2nd edition, London: Prentice Hall Europe

Triplett, N. (1898) The dynamogenic factors in pacemaking and competition, *American Journal of Psychology*, 9, 507–33

Watson, J.B. (1913) Psychology as a behaviourist views it, *Psychological Review*, 20, 158–77

Zajonc, R.B. (1965) Social facilitation, *Science*, 149, 269–74

Zajonc, R.B., Heingartner, A. and Herman, E.M.(1969) Social enhancement and impairment of performance in the cockroach, *Journal of Personality and Social Psychology*, 13, 83–92

Chapter 6 Social cognition

Abramson, L.Y., Seligman. M.E.P. and Teasdale, J.D. (1978) Learned helplessness in humans: Critique and reformulation, *Journal of Abnormal and Social Psychology*, 87, 49–74

Adorno, T.W., Frenkel-Brunsik, E., Levinson, D.J. and Sanford, R.M. (1950) *The Anthoritarian Personality*, New York; Harper

Asch, S.E. (1946) Forming impressions of personality, *Journal of Abnormal and Social Psychology*, 41, 258–90

Barrett, M. and Short, J. (1992) Images of European people in a group of 5–10-year-old English school children, *British Journal of Developmental Psychology*, 10, 339–63

Bartlett, F.C. (1932) *Remembering: A study in experimental and social psychology*, Cambridge University Press

Bower, G.H., Black J.B. and Turner, T.R. (1979) Scripts in memory for text, *Cognitive Psychology*, 11, 177–220

Brewer, M.B. and Campbell, D.T. (1976) *Ethnocentrism and Intergroup Attitudes: East African Evidence*, New York: Sage

Brown, R. (1986) *Social Psychology*, 2nd edition, New York: Free Press

Davison, G. and Neale, J. (1994) *Abnormal Psychology*, 6th edition, New York: Wiley.

Fiske, S.T. and Taylor, S.E. (1991) *Social Cognition*, 2nd edition, New York: McGraw-Hill

Gregory, R.L. (1966) *Eye and Brain*, London: Weidenfeld & Nicholson

Haire, M. and Grune, W.E. (1950) Perceptual defenses: Processes protecting an organised perception of another personality, *Human Relations*, 3, 403–12

Hamilton, D.L. (1979) A cognitive attributional analysis of stereotyping, in L. Berkowitz (ed.), *Advances in Experimental Social Psychology*, Vol. 12, New York: Academic Press, pp53–84

Han, S. and Shavitt, S. (1993) *Persuasion and Culture: Advertising Appeals in Individualistic and Collective Societies*, Unpublished Thesis, University of Illinois

Heider, F. (1958) *The Psychology of Interpersonal Relations*, New York: Wiley

Hendrick, C. and Constanini, A. (1970) Effects of varying trait inconsistency and response requirements on the primacy effect in impression formation, *Journal of Personality and Social Psychology*, 15, 158–64

Johnson, T.J., Feigenbaum, R. and Weibey, M. (1964) Some determinants and consequences of the teacher's perception of causality, *Journal of Educational Psychology*, 55, 237–46

Jones, E.E. and Harris, V.A. (1967) The attribution of attitudes, *Journal of Experimental Social Psychology*, 3, 1–24

Jones, E.E., Rock, L., Shaver, K.G., Goethals, G.R. and Ward, L.M. (1968) Patterns of performance and ability attribution: An unexpected primacy effect, *Journal of Personality and Social Psychology*, 10, 317–40

Katz, D. (1960) The functional approach to the study of attitudes, *Public Opinion Quarterly*, 24, 163–204

Kelley, H.H. (1950) The warm-cold variable in first impressions of persons, *Journal of Personality*, 18, 431–9

LaPierre, R.T. (1934) Attitudes vs actions, *Social Forces*, 13, 230–7

Lemaine, G. (1974) Social differentiation and social originality, *European Journal of Social Psychology*, 4, 17–52

Luchins, A.S. (1957) Primacy-recency in impression formation, in C. Hovland (ed.) *The Order of Presentation in Persuasio*, New Haven, CT: Yale University Press

Miller, R.S. and Schlenker, B.R. (1985) Egotism in group members: Public and private attributions of responsibility for group performance, *Social Psychology Quarterly*, 48, 85–9

Morris, M.W. and Peng, K.P. (1994) Culture and cause: American and Chinese attributions for social and physical events, *Journal of Experimental Social Psychology*, 67, 949–71

Pettigrew, T.F. (1958) Personality and sociocultural factors in intergroup attitudes: A cross-national comparison, *Journal of Conflict Resolution*, 2, 29–42

Rosenberg, M.J. and Hovland, C.I. (1960) Cognitive, affective and behavioural components of attitude, in M.J. Rosenberg, C.I. Hovland, W.J. McQuire, R.P. Abelson and J.W. Brehm (eds) *Attitude Organisation and*

Change: An Analysis of Consistency Among Attitude Components, New Haven, CT: Yale University Press

Schlenker, B.R., Weingold, M.F. and Hallam, J.R. (1990) Self-serving attributions in social context: Effects of self-esteem and social pressure, *Journal of Personality and Social Psychology*, 58, 855–63

Shavitt, S. (1989) Operationalizing functional theories of attitude, in A.R. Pratkanis, S.J. Breckler and A.G. Greenwald (eds) *Attitude Structure and Function*, Hillsdale, NJ: Erlbaum

Sherif, M., Harvey, O.J., White, B.J., Hood, W.R. and Sherif, C. (1961) *Intergroup conflict and cooperation: The robbers' cave experiment*, Norman, OK: University of Oklahoma Institute of Intergroup Relations

Storms, M.D. (1973) Videotape and the attribution process: Reversing actor's and observer's points of view, *Journal of Personality and Social Psychology*, 27, 765–75

Tajfel, H. (1982) Social psychology of intergroup relations, *Annual Review of Social Psychology*, 33, 1–39

Tajfel, H., Billig, M., Bundy, R.P. and Flament, C. (1971) Social categorisation and intergroup behaviour, *European Journal of Social Psychology*, 1, 149–77

Tak, J., Kaid, L.L. and Lee, S. (1997) A cross-cultural study of political advertising in the United States and Korea, *Communication Research*, 24, 413–30

Tyerman, A. and Spencer, C. (1983) A critical test of the Sherif's robbers' cave experiments: Intergroup competition and cooperation between groups of well acquainted individuals, *Small Group Behaviour*, 14, 515–31

Wetherell, M. (1982) Cross-cultural studies of minimal groups: implications for the social identity theory of intergroup relations, in H. Tajfel (ed.) *Social Identity and Intergroup Relations*, Cambridge: Cambridge University Press

Chapter 7 Remembering and forgetting

Atkinson, R. and Shiffrin, R. (1968) Human memory: A proposed system and its control processes, in K.W. Spence and J.T. Spence (eds) *The Psychology of Learning and Motivation*, Vol. 2, Academic Press

Baddeley, A. (1966) The influence of acoustic and semantic similarity on long-term memory for word sequences, *Quarterly Journal of Experimental Psychology*, 18, 302–9

Baddeley, A. (1990) *Human Memory*, Hove: LEA

Baddeley, A. (1995) Memory, in C. French and A. Colman (eds) *Cognitive Psychology*, Longman

Baddeley, A. (2000) The episodic buffer: a new component of working memory? *Trends in Cognitive Science*, 4, 417–23

Baddeley, A., Gathercole, S. and Papagno, C. (1998) The phonological loop as a language learning device, *Psychology Review*, 105

Baddeley, A. and Hitch, G. (1974) Working memory, in G.H. Bower (ed.) *The Psychology of Learning and Motivation*, Vol. 8, Academic Press

Baddeley, A. and Logie, R. (1992) Auditory imagery and working memory, in R.S. Nickerson (ed.), *Attention and Performance*, Vol. 8, Hillsdale, NJ: LEA

Bower, G. (1981) Mood and memory, *American Psychologist*, 36, 129–48

Bower, G., Clark, M., Lesgold, A. and Winzenz, D. (1969) Hierarchical retrieval schemes in recall of categorised lists, *Journal of Verbal Learning and Verbal Behaviour*, 8, 323–43

Bradley, B. and Baddeley, A. (1990) Emotional factors in forgetting, *Psychological Medicine*, 20, 351–5

Boring, E. (1930) A new ambiguous figure, *American Journal of Psychology*, 42, 444

Cohen, G. (1993) Everyday memory and memory systems: The experimental approach, in G. Cohen, G. Kiss and M. Levoi (eds) *Memory: Current Issues*, 2nd edition, Buckingham: OUP

Conway, M., Anderson, S., Larsen, S., Donnelly, C., McDaniel, M., McClelland, A. and Rawles, R. (1994) The formation of flashbulb memories, *Memory and Cognition*, 22, 326–43

Craik, F. (2002) in *Psychology: An International Perspective*, Academic Press, chapter 9

Craik, F. and Lockhart, R. (1972) Levels of processing, *Journal of Verbal Learning and Verbal Behaviour*, 11, 671–84

Craik, F. and Tulving, E. (1975) Depth of processing and the retention of words in episodic memory, *Journal of Experimental Psychology*, 104, 268–94

Eysenck, M. (1984) *A Handbook of Cognitive Psychology*, LEA

Freud, S. (1901) The psychopathology of everyday life, *Freud Library*, Vol. 5, Penguin

Glucksberg, S. and Lloyd, J.K. (1967) Motivated forgetting mediated by implicit verbal chaining: a laboratory analog of repression, *Science*, 158 (3800), 517–19

Godden, D. and Baddeley, A. (1975) Context-dependent memory in two natural environments on land and in water, *British Journal of Psychology*, 65, 325–31

Hebb, D. (1949) *The Organisation of Behaviour*, Wiley

Hunt, E. (1980) Intelligence as an information processing concept, *British Journal of Psychology*, 71, 449–77

Keppell, G. and Underwood, B. (1962) Proactive inhibition in short-term retention of single items, *Journal of Verbal Learning and Verbal Behaviour*, 1, 153–61

Levinger, G. and Clark, J. (1961) Emotional factors in the forgetting of word association, *Journal of Abnormal and Social Psychology*, 62, 99–105

McGeogh, J. (1942) *The Psychology of Learning*, New York: Spectrum

Miller, G. (1956) The magical number seven, plus or minus two: some limits on our capacity for processing information, *Psychological Review*, 63, 81–97

Morris, C., Branford, J. and Franks, J. (1977) Levels of processing versus transfer appropriate processing, *Journal of Verbal Learning and Verbal Behaviour*, 16, 519–33

Murdock, B. (1962) The serial position effect in free recall, *Journal of Experimental Psychology*, 64, 482–8

Parkin, A.J., Lewinson, J. and Folkard, S. (1982) The influence of emotion on immediate and delayed retention: Levinger and Clark reconsidered, *British Journal of Psychology*, 73, 389–93

Parkin, A. (1993) *Memory: Phenomena, Experiment and Theory*, Oxford: Blackwell

Peterson, L. and Peterson, M. (1959) Short-term retention of individual items, *Journal of Experimental Psychology*, 58, 193–8

Solso, R. (1995) *Cognitive Psychology*, 4th edition, Boston: Allyn & Bacon

Sperling, G. (1960) The information available in brief visual presentation, *Psychological Mongraphs*, 74

Tulving, E. (1972) Episodic and semantic memory, in E. Tulving and W. Donaldson (eds) *Organisation of Memory*, New York: Academic Press

Tulving, E. (1974) Cue-dependent forgetting, *American Scientist*, 62, 74–82

Waugh, N. and Norman, D. (1965) Primary memory, *Psychological Review*, 72, 89–104

Wright, E. (1992) The original of E.G. Boring's young girl/mother-in-law drawing and its relation to the pattern of a joke, *Perception*, 21, 273–5

Yarnell, P. and Lynch, S. (1970) Retrograde memory immediately after concussion, *Lancet*, 1, 863–5

Chapter 8 Perceptual processes

Bruner, J. and Minturn, A. (1955) Perceptual identification and perceptual organisation, *Journal of General Psychology*, 53, 21

Bugelski, B. and Alampay, D. (1962) The role of frequency in developing perceptual sets, *Canadian Journal of Psychology*, 15, 205–11

Deregowski, J. (1972) Pictorial perception and culture, *Scientific American*, 227, 82–8

Gibson, J. (1966) *The Senses Considered as Perceptual Systems*, Boston: Houghton & Mifflin

Gilchrist, J. and Nesberg, L. (1952) Need and perceptual change in need-related objects, *Journal of Experimental Psychology*, 44, 369

Gregory, R. (1972) Visual illusions, in B.M. Foss (ed.) *New Horizons in Psychology*, Vol. 1, Harmondsworth: Penguin

Helmholtz, H. (1910) *Treatise on Physiological Optics*, Vols 2 & 3, Rochester NY

Lazarus, R. and McCleary, R. (1951) Autonomic discrimination without awareness, *Psychological Review*, 58, 113

Lee, D. and Lishman, J. (1975) Visual proprioceptive control of stance, *Journal of Human Movement Studies*, 1, 87–95

Malim, T. (1994) *Cognitive Processes*, London: Macmillan

McGinnies, E. (1949) Emotionality and perceptual defence, *Psychological Review*, 56, 244

Navon, D. (1977) Forest before trees: the precedence of global features in visual perception, *Cognitive Psychology*, 9, 353–83

Sanford, R. (1937) The effects of abstinence from food upon imaginal processes: A further experiment, *Journal of Psychology*, 3, 145–59

Segall, M., Campbell, D. and Herskovits, M. (1963) Cultural differences in the perception of geometrical illusions, *Science*, 139, 769–71

Serpell, R. (1979) How specific are perceptual skills? A cross-cultural study of pattern reproduction, *British Journal of Psychology*, 70, 365–80

Chapter 9 Anxiety disorders

Abraham, K. (1927) *Selected Papers*, London: Hogarth Press

Aylward, E.H., Harris, G.J., Hoen-Saric, R., Barta, P.E., Machlin, S.R. and Pearlson, P.D. (1996) Normal caudate nucleus in obsessive-compulsive disorder assessed by quantitative neuroimaging, *Archives of General Psychiatry*, 53, 577–84

Beck, A.T., Emery, G. and Greenberg, R. (1985) *Anxiety Disorders and Phobias: A Cognitive Perspective*, New York: Basic Books

Cook, M. and Mineka, S. (1990) Selective associations in the observational conditioning of fear in monkeys, *Journal of Experimental Psychology: Animal Behaviour Processes*, 16, 372–89

Di Nardo, P.A., Guzy, L.T. and Bak, R.M. (1988) Anxiety response patterns and etiological factors in dog-fearful and non-fearful subjects, *Behaviour Research and Therapy*, 21, 245–52

Eysenck, H.J. (1967) *The Biological Basis of Personality*, Springfield, IL: Thomas

Foa, E., Franklin, M. and Kozak, M. (1998) Psychosocial treatments for obsessive-compulsive disorder: literature review, in R. Swinson, M. Antony, S. Rachman and M. Ritcher (eds) *Obsessive-Compulsive Disorder: Theory, Research and Treatment*, New York: Guilford, pp258–76

Freud, S. (1909) Analysis of a phobia in a 5 year old boy, in *Standard Edition*, Vol. 10, London: Hogarth Press (1955)

Fyer, A.J., Chapman, S. and Martin, L.Y. (1995) Specificity in familial aggregation of phobic, *Arch. Gen. Psychiatry*, 52, 564–73

Graziano, A.M. and Mooney, N.B. (1980) Family self-control instructions for children's night-time fear reduction, *Journal of Consulting and Clinical Psychology*, 48, 206–13

Insel, T.R. (1991) Has OCD research gone to the dogs? *Neuropsychopharmacology*, 5, 13–17

Kessler, R.C., McGonagle, K.A., Zhao, S., Nelson, C.B., Hughes, M., Eshleman, S., Wittchen, H.-U. and Kendler K.S. (1994) Lifetime and 12 month prevalence of DSMIIIR psychiatric disorders in the US: Results from the national comorbidity survey, *Archives of General Psychiatry,* 51, 8–19

Marks, M. (1987) *Fears, Phobias and Rituals: panic, anxiety and their disorders,* Oxford University Press

McKeon, P. and Murray, R. (1987) Familial aspects of obsessive-compulsive neurosis, *British Journal of Psychiatry,* 151, 528–34

Mowrer, O.H. (1947) On the dual nature of learning: A reinterpretation of conditioning and problem solving, *Harvard Educational Review,* 17, 102–48

Ohman, A. (1996) Preferential preattentive processing of threat in anxiety: Preparedness and attentional biases, in R.M. Rapee (ed.) *Current Controversies in the Anxiety Disorders,* New York: Guilford, 253–90

Pauls, D.L., Alsobrook, J.P., Goodman, W., Rasmussen, S. and Leckman, J.F. (1995) A family study of obsessive-compulsive disorder, *American Journal of Psychiatry,* 152, 76–84

Rachman, S. (2004) *Anxiety,* 2nd edition, Psychology Press

Rachman, S. and Hodgson, R. (1980) *Obsessions and Compulsions,* Englewood Cliffs, NJ: Prentice Hall

Rapoport, J. and Wise, S.P. (1988) Obsessive-compulsive disorder: Evidence for a basal Ganglia dysfunction, *Psychopharmacology,* 24, 380–4

Salzman, L. (1995) *Treatment of Obsessive and Compulsive Behaviours,* Northvale: Aronson

Seligman, M. (1971) Phobias and preparedness, *Behaviour Therapy,* 2, 307–20

Sher, K.J., Frost, R.O., Kushner, M., Crews, T.M. and Alexander, J.E. (1989) Memory deficits in compulsive checkers: A replication and extension in a clinical example, *Behaviour Research Therapy,* 27, 65–9

Sperling, M. (1971) Spider phobias and spider fantasies, *Journal of the American Psychoanalytic Association,* 19, 472–98

Torgesen, S. (1983) Genetic factors in anxiety disorders, *Archives of General Psychiatry,* 40, 1085–9

Trivedi, M.H. (1996) Functional neuroanatomy of obsessive-compulsive disorder, *Journal of Clinical Psychiatry,* 57 (8), 26–36

Watson, J. and Rayner, R. (1920) Conditioned emotional reactions, *Journal of Experimental Psychology,* 3, 1–22

Williams, J., Watts, F. and MacLeod, C. (1997) *Cognitive Psychology and Emotional Disorders,* Chichester: Wiley

Wolpe, J. (1958) *Psychotherapy by Reciprocal Inhibition,* Stanford, CA: Stanford University Press

Chapter 10 Autism

Bailey, A., Luthert, P., Dean, A. *et al.* (1998) A clinicopathological study of autism, *Brain,* 121, 889–905

Baron-Cohen, S., Leslie, A.M. and Frith, U. (1985) Does the autistic child have a theory of mind? *Cognition,* 21, 37–46

Baron-Cohen, S., Leslie, A.M. and Frith, U. (1986) Mechanical, behavioural and intentional understanding of picture stories in autistic children, *British Journal of Developmental Psychology,* 4, 113–25

Bettleheim, B. (1967) *The Empty Fortress,* New York: Free Press

Bolton, P., Mcdonald, H., Pickles, A., Rios, P., Goode, S., Crowson, M., Bailey, A. and Rutter, M. (1994) A case-control family history study of autism, *Journal of Child Psychology and Psychiatry,* 35, 877–900

Bondy, A. (1998) in Bondy, A. and Frost, L. (2001) *Behaviour Modification,* Sage

Bosseler, A. and Massaro, D.W. (2003) *Journal of Autism and Developmental Disorders,* December

Carson, R., Butcher, J. and Mineka, S. (2000) *Abnormal Psychology and Modern Life,* Allyn & Bacon

Charman, C.R. (2000) *Journal Child and Adolescent Psychiatry,* 39 (6), 694–702

Courchesne, E., Saitoh, O., Townsend, J.P. *et al.* (1994) Cerebellar hypoplasia and hyperplasia in infantile autism, *Lancet,* 343, 6–64

Folstein, S. and Rutter, M. (1977) Infantile autism: a genetic study of 21 twin pairs, *Journal of Child Psychology and Psychiatry,* 18, 297–321

Frith, U. (1989) *Autism: Explaining the Enigma,* Oxford: Blackwell

Frith, U. (1996) Cognitive explanations of autism. *Acta Paeadiatrics* supplement, 416

Happe, F. (1996) Studying weak central coherence at low levels: children with autism do not succumb to visual illusions, *Journal of Child Psychology and Psychiatry,* 37, 873–7

Hermelin, B. and O'Connor, N. (1967) Remembering of words by psychotic and sub-normal children, *British Journal of Psychology,* 58, 213–18

Kanner, L. (1943) Autistic disturbance of affective contact, *Nervous Child,* 12, 17–50

Koegel, R.L., Bimbela, A. and Schreibman, L. (1996) Collateral effects of parent training on family interactions, *Journal of Autism and Developmental Disorders,* 26, 347–59

Koegel, R.L., Schreibman, L., Britten, K.R., Burkey, J.C. and O'Neill, R.E. (1982) A comparison of parent training to direct child treatment, in R.L. Koegal, A. Rincover and A.L. Egel (eds) *Educating and Understanding Autistic Children,* San Diego CA: College Hill

Lotter, V. (1966) Epidemiology of autistic conditions in young children: I Prevalence, *Social Psychiatry,* 1, 124–37

Lovaas, O.I. (1977) *The Autistic Child: Language Development Through Behaviour Modification*, New York: Holsted Press

Lovaas, O.I. (1987) Behavioural treatment and normal educational and intellectual functioning in young autistic children, *Journal of Consulting and Clinical Psychology*, 55, 3–9

McEachin, J.J., Smith, T. and Lovaas, O.I. (1993) Long-term outcomes for children with autism who received early intensive behavioural treatment, *American Journal of Mental Retardation*, 97, 359–72

Ohnishi, T., Matsuda, H., Hashimoto, T., Kunhiro, T., Nishikawa, M., Uema, T. and Sasaki, M. (2000) Abnormal regional cerebral blood flow in childhood autism, *Brain*, 123, Part 9, 1838–44

Perner, J., Frith, U., Leslie, A.M. and Leekham, S.R. (1989) Exploration of the child's theory of mind: knowledge belief and communication, *Child Development*, 60, 689–700

Piver, J., Arndt, S., Bailey, J., Havercamp, S., Andreasen, N.C. and Palmer, P. (1995) An MRI study of brain size in autism, *American Journal of Psychiatry*, 152, 1145–9

Ritvo, E.R., Freeman, B.J., Mason-Brothers, A., Mo, A. and Ritvo, A.M. (1985) Concordance for the syndrome of autism in 40 pairs of afflicted twins, *American Journal of Psychiatry*, 142, 74–7

Roazen, P. (1992) The historiography of psychoanalysis, in Timms, E. and Robertson, R. (eds) *Psychoanalysis in its Cultural Context*, Austrian Studies III, 3–19

Sallows, G. and Gramper, T.D. (2005) Intensive behavioural treatment for children with autism: four year outcome and predictors, *Am. J. Ment. Retard.*, 110 (6), 417–38

Shah, A. and Frith, U. (1993) Why do autistic individuals show superior performance in the block design task? *Journal of Child Psychology and Psychiatry*, 34, 1351–64

Sigman, M., Munday, P., Sherman, T. and Ungerer, J. (1986) Social interactions of autistic, mentally retarded, and normal children and their caregivers, *Journal of Child Psychology and Psychiatry*, 27, 657–69

Wimmer, H. and Perner, J. (1983) Beliefs about beliefs: Representations and constraining function of wrong beliefs in young children's understanding of deception, *Cognition*, 13, 103–28

Wing, L. and Gould, J. (1979) Severe impairments of social interaction and associated abnormalities in children: epidemiology and classification, *Journal of Autism and Developmental Disorders*, 9, 11–29

Wing, L. and Potter, D. (2002) The epidemiology of autistic spectrum disorders: Is the prevalence rising? *Mental Retardation and Developmental Disabilities Research Reviews*, 8

Witkin, H., Oltman, P., Raskin, E. and Karp, S. (1971) *A Manual for the Group Embedded Figures Test*, Palo Alto, CA: Consulting Psychologists Press

Zilbovicius, M., Boddaert, N., Poline, J.B., Mangin, J.F., Barthelemy, C. and Samson, Y. (2000) Temporal lobe dysfunction in childhood autism: A PET study, *American Journal of Psychiatry*, 157, 1988–93

Index

A

ABA (applied behavioural analysis) 244–5, 247
ablation 27
abnormality 212–49, **212**
acquisition of gender roles 64–5
ACTH (adrenocorticotropic hormone) 32
actor–observer effect 156–7, **156**
adaptive factors 161, **247**
addictive states 8, 37
adoption studies 37–8
Adorno, T.W. 141
adrenal glands 32, **58**
adrenocorticotropic hormone (ACTH) 32
adrenogenital syndrome 57
affective component of attitudes 159
affordances 202, 203
age factors 38
see also children/childhood
agentic state 140
agents of socialisation 51
aggression 4
agoraphobia 214–16, 218, 225
aims of research 84
Alampay, D. 206
Allen, V.L. 135
Allport, F.H. 128
alternative hypotheses 86
ambiguous figures 199–200, 210
amnesia 172, 185
see also forgetting theories
anal stage of development 15, 74, 223
androgens 56, **57**
androgyny 44–5, **44**, 62
animal studies 113
anonymity 135, 136
ANS (autonomic nervous system) 31–2, 216
anterograde amnesia **172**
anxiety disorders 212, 214–30
applied behavioural analysis (ABA) 244–5, 247
appraisal of events 218
approaches to psychology 2–41
see also individual approaches
arousal theory 128–30, 188
articulatory suppression 176, 177

artificial intelligence 12
Asch, S.E. 133–6, 143–6, 150–2, 166
assimilation 71
Atkinson and Shiffrin's multi-store model 168, 170–3
attention 64
attitudes 159–62, **159**
attributions 154–8, **154**
atypical chromosome patterns 59–62
audience effect 128
auditory area of cerebrum 26
authoritarian personality 141, 165–6, **165**
authority 126, 138–42, 144, 165–6
autism 212, 231–49
autistic spectrum 237
autobiographical episodic memory 180
autokinetic effect 132
autonomic nervous system (ANS) 31–2, 216
autonomous state 140
autonomy 234
averages 117–21
aversion therapy 8, 246
avoidance conditioning 217, 218
avoidance learning 222
axons 21–2

B

Baddeley, A. 171, 175–8, 186
Bandura, Albert 10–11
bar graphs 114, 115
Baron, R.S. 130, 136–7
Baron-Cohen, S. 238–9, 240
basal ganglia system 221
behaviour modification 244–5
behaviour shaping 246
behaviour therapies 225–7, 228, 244–6
behavioural component of attitudes 159–60
behaviourist psychology 2, 6–9, 36–9, 89, 218, 222
beliefs 159, 238–40, 242
Bem Sex Role Inventory (BSRI) 45
Best, D.L. 50, 53
Bettleheim, B. 234
biased samples 107
biases 95, 154–8, 166, 222

Bickman, L. 140, 144–5
binocular depth cues 168, 194
biochemical approaches 221
biological approach 2, 4–5, 21–39
autism 234–7
gender development 48–9, 55–62, 66, 77
obsessive-compulsive disorder 221
phobias 215–16
biopsychology 2, 21–39
birth order genetic factor 37
Bock, G.R. 4
Bosseler, A. 246
bottom-up processing 201
Bower, G. 180, 186
brain 24–30, 57, 221, 235–6, 242–3
see also cognitive psychology
brain-damaged patients 173, 181
Brewer, M.B. 164
Broca, Paul 24, 28, 177
Broca's area 177
Bruner, J. 206
Brunsman, B. 136–7
BSRI (Bem Sex Role Inventory) 45
Bugelski, B. 206
Buss, D.M. 48–9

C

Campbell, D.T. 164
carpentered environment 198
case studies 94, **104**, 106
castration anxiety 74
CAT (computerised axial tomography) 28
catharsis 229
cause and effect 102–3
CBT (cognitive behaviour therapy) 228
central coherence deficit 240–2
central core of brain 25
central executive 175, **176**, 178
central nervous system (CNS) 21
central tendency measures 117–18
central traits 150–1, **150**
cerebellum 181
cerebral hemispheres 57
cerebrum 25–6
chemical stimulation methods 27–8, 29

children/childhood   19, 37–8, 63–4, 71–3, 231–49
   see also developmental psychology
chromosomes   **4**, 5, 56, 59–62
classical conditioning   7–8, **7**, 20, 217, 219, 222
closed questions   96
closure principle   192
CNS (central nervous system)   21
co-action   **128**
coding   **105**
cognition   **12**
cognitive behaviour therapy (CBT)   228
cognitive bias   222
cognitive component of attitudes   159
cognitive development   68–70, **68**, 77
cognitive psychology   12–13, 168–211
   autism   238–43
   forgetting   172, 182–9
   gender development   55, 61, 66, 68–73, 77
   obsessive-compulsive disorder   222–3
   perceptual processes   168, 191–210
   phobias   218
   remembering   168, 170–90
   social cognition   126, 148–66
cognitive therapy   227–8
Cohen, G.   180
coherence deficit   240–2
cold parenting   234
Cold War period   143
collectivist cultures   **143**, 156
comic strip stories   240
communication impairments   232–3
comparative methods   4
competence   112
competition for resources   163–4
compliance   **136**
compound histograms   **116**
compulsions   220
   see also obsessive-compulsive disorder
computational models   13
computer-animated tutors   246–7
computerised axial tomography (CAT)   28
concordance   **36**, 37, 215, 236–7
conditioned stimuli (CS)   217
conditioning theory   216–18
   see also **classical conditioning**
conditions of worth   **19**
confidentiality   **111**
conflict   130–1, 163, 165

conformity   126, 132–7, **132**, 143, 146, 161
confounding variables   **87**, 88
congruence   18–19, **18**
connectionist models   13
consent   **111**, 145
conserving   **69**
consolidation   **172**, 184–5, **185**
constancy   68–70, 73, **168**, 196–7, 204
construct validity   **63**, 93, 106
content analyses   94, **105**, 106
context-dependent forgetting   186
continuation principle   192
continuous data   **114**
control condition   **90**
controlling variables   87–9, 93–4
convergence   195–6
Conway, M.   180–1
Cooper, R.M.   39
correlation   **85**, 94, 101–3, 106
correlation analysis   **101**
correlation co-efficient   **101**
cortical function localisation   24–6
cortical specialisation   27–30
Cottrell, N.B.   130
counselling   18
counterbalancing   **88**
counterstatements   227
covert observation   **98**, 99
Craik, F.   173–5, 189
cross-cultural research   **49**, 51
Crutchfield, R.S.   141
CS (conditioned stimuli)   217
cue-dependent forgetting   186
cues   **182**, 185–6
   see also **depth cues**
cultural variations   49–51, 143, 155–6, 208–9

D

Damon, W.   70
Darwin, Charles   5
data
   collection methods   82, 101, 105
   production methods   106
   representing   114–21
debriefing   **112**, 145
de-centre   **69**
deception   **111**, 137, 144–5
defence mechanisms   16, **75**, 223
defiance of authority   141–2
demand characteristics   **88**, 89, 93, 134, 144
dendrites   21–2
denial   16
deoxyribonucleic acid (DNA)   4, 5
dependent variables (DV)   **86**, 87, 131
depth cues   168, 194–7, **194**, 204

depth perception   **194**
   see also levels of processing theory
Deregowski, J.   208–9
descriptive data   117–21
desensitisation   225–6, 227
   see also sensitisation
design *see* **experimental designs**
determinism   **61**, 154
developmental psychology   14–15, 219, 223
   see also gender development
Diagnostic and Statistical Manual of Mental Disorders   **212**, 214, 231–2
Diamond, M.   53
differences *see* individual differences
direct theories   201–2
discrete data   **114**
discrete trial training (DTT)   244–5
discrimination   163
dispersion measures   118–21
displacement   16, **172**, 183
dispositional attributions   **154**, 156
distorted thinking   218, 227
distortion illusions   198–9
distraction-conflict theory   130–1
distractor tasks   **183**
dizygotic (DZ) twins   34–6, **34**, 236–7
DNA (deoxyribonucleic acid)   4, 5
dominant response   **128**
dream analysis   229
drive theory *see* arousal theory
drug therapy   221, 225, 247
DSM-IV   **212**, 214, 231–2
DTT (discrete trial training)   244–5
dual-task experiments   177
duration of memory   171
DV (dependent variables)   **86**, 87, 131
dyskinesia   **247**
DZ (dizygotic) twins   34–6, **34**, 236–7

E

Ebbinghaus illusion   241
Eccles, J.   64
ecological relevance   **202**
ecological validity   **89**, 90, 93, 100, 143–4, **143**
ECT (electro-convulsive therapy)   185
EEG (electroencephalogram)   28, 29
ego   16
ego-expressive function   161
egocentric view   **69**
Ehrhardt, A.A.   54
Eichmann, Adolph   138
elaborative rehearsal   174

Electra complex 75
electrical stimulation methods 27–8, 29
electro-convulsive therapy (ECT) 185
electroencephalogram (EEG) 28, 29
embedded figure tests 241, 242
embryos 56
emotions 159, 207–8
empirical studies 175
encoding 71
endocrine system 32
engrams 182
environmental cues 185
environmental factors 37, 39, 185, 237
episodic buffer 177
episodic memory 179, 180–1
equality (gender) 42
ERP (exposure and response prevention) 226–7
ethical concerns 99, 111–13, 111, 137, 143–6
ethnography 49
evaluation apprehension theory 130
event schemas 149
evidence see data
evolutionary behaviour 5, 48–9
executive functioning impairments 242–3
expectation 206–7
experimental condition 90
experimental designs 90–2, 90, 133
experimental episodic memory 180
experimental hypotheses 85, 86
experiments 87–93, 87, 103
    arousal theory 129
    data production 106
    observational studies 98
    selective breeding 38–9
    social learning theory 67
    strengths/limitations 92–3
    types 89–90
    working memory model 177
exposure and response prevention (ERP) 226–7
external validity 143
extraneous variables 87, 88–9
'eye-blink' response 20
eyewitness testimony 13
Eysenck, H.J. 216

F
F-scale 165–6
facilitation (social) 128–31
Fagot, B.I. 52–3, 64
false belief tests 239–40, 242
family size genetic factor 37

family studies 37
Farragher, E. 51–2, 53
fatigue effect 88
fear see phobias
female sex 56, 59, 77
    see also sex determination
femininity 44–5, 60
    see also gender development
field experiments 89–90, 89
fight or flight response 31–2, 214
fine motor skills 57
Fiore, M. 64
fixations 15
flashbulb memory 180–1
flight or fight response 31–2, 214
flooding 226–7
foetuses 57
Folstein, S. 237
food deprivation study 207
forgetting theories 172, 182–9
form constancy 197
free association 14, 228
free will vs determinism 154
freedom loss 142
Freud, Sigmund 14–17, 74–8, 187, 219, 223–4, 229
Frey, K.S. 70
Frith, U. 240–1, 243
frontal lobe damage 242
Frueh, T. 64
functional imaging 177
functional separation 171, 172
functions of attitudes 161–2
fundamental attribution error 155–6, 155
Furnham, A. 51–2, 53

G
Gage, Phineas 24
Gall, Franz Joseph 27
Galligani, N. 59
Galton, Francis 37
galvanic skin response (GSR) 207
Gamson, W.B. 141–2, 144
Gazzaniga, Michael 26
gender constancy 68, 69, 70, 73
gender development 42–81
    biological approach 39, 48–9, 55–62, 66, 77
    cognitive approach 55, 61, 66, 68–73, 77
    psychodynamic approach 55, 61, 66, 72, 74–8
    sex distinction 44–7
    social learning theory 10–11, 55, 61, 63–7, 72, 77
gender identity 46, 54, 68–9, 69
gender roles 49, 50, 64–6
gender schema theory 71–2
gender stability 68, 69, 70

generalisation 95
genetics 4–5, 33
    autism 236–7
    behaviourist psychology 36–9
    obsessive-compulsive disorder 221
    phobias 215–16
    sex determination 46
genital stage of development 15
genotype 33
Gestalt principles 191–3, 191
Gibson, J. 201–3, 205
Gilchrist, J. 207
Glass, D.C. 130
Glucksberg, S. 187
Godden, D. 186
gonads 56, 57
Goode, J.A. 4
Gould, J. 232–3
graphs 114–16, 114, 130
Graupner, T.D. 245
Graziano, A.M. 228
Gregory, R. 150, 200, 203–5
groups 132, 133, 138, 165
Grune, W.E. 150
GSR (galvanic skin response) 207

H
haemophilia 33
Haire, M. 150
Halverson, C.F. 71
Hampson, E. 59
Han, S. 161–2
Happe, F. 241, 242
Harries, Lauren 46
Harris, V.A. 155
Heider, Fritz 154
height in plane cue 195
hemispheres of brain 24, 57
Henchy, T. 130
heritability 4
heterozygous genotype 33
hierarchy of needs 19–20
hippocampus 181
histograms 115–16
Hitch, G. 175–8
Hodgson, R. 222
Hofling, K.C. 145
homeostasis 25
homosexuality 37
homozygous genotype 33
hormones 56, 57–9
Hubel, David 27
humanistic approach 18–20
Hunt, E. 178
hypersensitivity 218
hypervigilance 222, 223
hypothalamus 57
hypotheses 84–6, 84, 203–4

I

iceberg analogy 14, 15
id 15, 16, **219**, 223
identification 64–6, **65**, 75–6, **75**
identity 46, 54, 68–9, 164–5
Idle, T. 63–4
illusions 198–200, 208, 241
imagination impairments 232–3
imitation 65–6, **65**
impaired executive functioning
    242–3
impairment triad 232–3
Imperato-McGinley, J. 46–7, 59
implosion therapy 226
impression formation 148–53,
    148, 161
independent groups design 63, **91**
independent variables (IV) 86, 87,
    152
individual differences 212–49
individualistic cultures **143**, 156
inference 149, 197
influence 126, 128–47, 161
information-processing approach
    12, 149
informational social influence
    136–7, **136**
informed consent **111**, 145
inhibitions 128
innate factors 48, 56, **216**
    see also biological approach
instincts 14–15
integrity 113
intelligence 36, 38
interactionist approach **54**, 181
interconnecting neurons 22–3
interference theory 183–4
internal validity **143**, 144
internalisation 66
interposition 195
interviewees/interviewers 96
interviews 95–6
invariants **202**, 203
invasive methods 27–8
inventories 45
islets of ability 231
IV (independent variables) 86, 87,
    152

J

Jarrold, C. 242
Johnson, T.J. 157–8
joint attention 232
Jones, E.E. 152–3, 155

K

Kanner, L. 231, 234
Katsurada, E. 50

Kelley, H.H. 151
Keppel, G. 184
Kimura, D. 59
Klinefelter's syndrome 60–1, **60**
knowledge function of attitudes
    161
Koegel, R.L. 245, 247
Kohlberg, L. 68–70
Korsakov syndrome 172

L

labelling graphs 116
laboratory experiments **89**, 98
language acquisition 177
language training 246–7
LaPierre, Richard 160
latent content **229**
latent stage of development 15
lateralisation **24**
Law of Effect **6**
Lazarus, R. 207
learning theory 10–11, 222
    see also **social learning theory**
Lee, D. 202
legitimate authority/orders 140
lesioning **27**
levels of processing theory 173–5,
    189
Levine, J.M. 135
limbic system 25, 235
line graphs 114–15
linear perspective 195, **198**
Lishman, J. 202
Lloyd, B. 63
Lloyd, J.K. 187
localisation 24–6, **24**
Lockhart, R. 173–5
long-term memory (LTM) 171–3,
    179–83, 185–6, 188
loop cards activity 248
Lovaas, O.I. 244–5, 246, 247–8
LTM see long-term memory
Luchins, A.S. 152
Lynch, S. 185

M

McCleary, R. 207
McConaghy, M.J. 70
McGeogh, J. 184
McGhee, P.E. 64
McGinnies, E. 208
magnetic resonance imaging (MRI)
    29, 235–6
maintenance rehearsal 174
majority influence 134, 135
    see also **conformity**
male sex 56, 59
    see also sex determination
Malim, T. 208

Malinowski, B. 77
manifest content **229**
**MAOIs (monoamine oxidase
    inhibitors)** **225**
Marcus, D. 70
Marks, M. 228
Martin, C.L. 71
masculinity 44–5, 59
    see also gender development
Maslow, Abraham 19–20
Massaro, D.W. 246
matched pairs design **91**, 92
Mead, M. 49–50
mean 118
measures of central tendency
    117–18, **117**
measures of dispersion 118–21,
    118
median 117, 118, 133
mediating cognitive factors **11**
medication 221, 225, 247
meditation 32
membership groups **132**
memory 179–81, 222
    loss 182–9
    models 168, 170–8
mental retardation **231**
meta-analysis 36–7
methodological issues see research
    methods
metrosexual men 44
Michaels, J.W. 129
Milgram, S. 138–42, 143–5
Milner, Peter 27
'mind-blindness' 238–40, 242
minimal group **165**
Minturn, A. 206
modality **170**
mode 117, 118
modelling behaviour 64–6, **65**
models **64**
    computational/connectionist 13
    memory 168, 170–8
    people as 10, **64**
Money, J. 54
**monoamine oxidase inhibitors
    (MAOIs)** **225**
monocular depth cues **168**, 194
monozygotic (MZ) twins 34–6,
    34, 236–7
moon illusion 199
Mooney, N.B. 228
Moray, S.M. 76
Morris, C. 175
motion parallax **194**
motivated forgetting theory 187–8
motivation 10, **65**, 142, 187–8,
    207, 245
motor area of cerebrum 25
motor neurons 21–2, 23

motor skills 57
Mowrer, O.H. 222
MRI (magnetic resonance imaging) 29, 235–6
Muller-Lyer illusion 198, 199, 204, 208
multi-store model 168, 170–3
Munroe, R.H. 70
MZ (monozygotic) twins 34–6, **34**, 236–7

N

natural sciences 2
naturalistic observation 98
nature–nurture debate 48–54, 55, 163
Navon, D. 192
Necker cube 199
negative correlation 102
negative reinforcement 7
negative self-talk/images 218
nervous system 21, 31–2
Nesberg, L. 207
networks 13
neuroimaging 221, 235–6
neurological correlates 234–5, 236
neurons 21–3
neurophysiological approaches 221
neuroses 14
neurosurgery 27, 29
neurotransmitters 23
non-experimental methods 94–105
non-human animals 113
non-invasive methods 28–9
non-participant observations 99
Norman, D. 182–3
normative social influence 136–7, **136**, 161
norms 51, 140
null hypothesis 85
nurture argument 51
    see also nature–nurture debate

O

obedience to authority 126, 138–42, **138**, 144
objectivity 2, 93
observational learning 10
observational studies 94, 98–100, 106
observer effect 99
obsessions 220
obsessive-compulsive disorder (OCD) 16–17, 212, 220–4, 226–9
Oedipus complex 74, 75–6, 77
oestrogens 56, **57**
old/young woman ambiguous figure 199

Olds, James 27
open questions 96
operant conditioning 6–8, **6**, 10, 217, 222
operationalising variables **84**, 131
opportunity sampling 110
optic array 201
optic chiasm 26
optic flow patterns 201
oral stage of development 15, 74
order effect 88
ovaries 56, **57**
overt observation **98**, 99
Overton, W.F. 70

P

panic attacks 214, 215
parasympathetic nervous system 31–2
parenting factors 234, 247–8
participant observation 98, 99
participant variables 91
Pavlov, Ivan Petrovich 7–8
PCT (person-centred therapy) 18
PECS (Picture Exchange Communication System) 246
peer factors 140
penis envy 75
percentage error 134
perception 168, 191–210
    depth cues 168, 194–7, 204
    Gestalt principles 191–3
    theories 201–5
    visual illusions 198–200
perceptual defence 207
perceptual organisation 191–3, **191**
perceptual sensitisation 207
perceptual set 206–10, **206**
performance–arousal relationship 129–30
performance of gender roles 65–6
peripheral nervous system (PNS) 21, 31–2
peripheral traits 150
Perner, J. 238, 239
Perrin, S. 135
person-centred therapy (PCT) 18
person schemas 149
personal responsibility 140
personality factors 15–17, 141, 165
pervasive developmental disorder 231
PET (positron emission tomography) 29, 235
Peterson, L. and M. 171
Pettigrew, T.F. 166
Pfost, K.S. 64
phallic stage of development 15, **74**

phenotype 33
phenylketonuria (PKU) 33
phobias 8, 212, 214–19, 225, 227, 229
phonological loop 175, 176–7
phrenology 27
physiology 4
pictorial depth cues 194–5
Picture Exchange Communication System (PECS) 246
pilot studies 97
pivotal response training (PRT) 245
PKU (phenylketonuria) 33
planning research 82, 84–6, 122
Plomin, R. 36, 38
PNS (peripheral nervous system) 21, 31–2
Pontius, A.A. 50
Ponzo illusion 198, 199
Popper, Karl 14
population sampling 107–8
positive correlation 101, 102
positive reinforcement 7
positron emission tomography (PET) 29, 235
post-mortem studies 28, 29, **235**
power of uniforms 140
practice effect 88
Pragnanz 191
pre-natal development **57**
prejudice 141, 150, 163–6, **163**
preparedness theory 216, 229
pressure to conform 132
presumptive consent 145
primacy effect 151–3, **151**, 166, 172
privacy 145
proactive interference 183
procedural memory 179
progesterone 59
protection of participants 112, 145
proximity factors 139, 192
PRT (pivotal response training) 245
psychoanalytic theory 74–8
psychodynamic approach 14–17
    gender development 55, 61, 66, 72, 74–8
    obsessive-compulsive disorder 223–4, 228–9
    phobias 219
    treatments 228–9
psychological effects of hormones 57–9
psychopathology 212–49
psychosexual development 14–15, 219, 223
punishment 66

Q

qualitative data **105**, 106, 114
quantitative data **101**, 106, 114, 117–21
quasi-experiments **89**, 90, 129
questioning methods 96
questionnaires 45, **95**, 166

R

Rachman, S. 222, 223
random allocation **89**
random sampling 108
randomisation 88–9, **88**, 108
range **119**
rationalisation 16
raw scores **114**
Rayner, R. 8, 217
reaction formation **223**
realistic conflict theory **163**, 165
rebellion 142
recency effect 151–3, **152**, 172
reductionism **61**
reference groups **132**
rehearsal **170**, 172, 173–4
Reimer, David 58
reinforcement 7, 10, 65–7, **65**
Rekers, G.A. 47, 76
related measures design **91**
relative size cue 195
relaxation techniques 225–6
relay neurons 22–3
reliability **82**
remembering 168, 170–90
repeated measures design **91**, 133
report-writing 122
representative samples 107
repressed memories **187**
reproduction **65**
'request' training 246
research hypotheses **85**
research methods 82–125
  data presentation 114–21
  ethics 99, 111–13
  experimental methods 87–93
  non-experimental methods 94–105
  planning 82, 84–6, 122
  qualitative vs quantitative methods 106
  sampling 91, 107–10
  social influence 143–6
respect 111–12, 145
respondents **95**
response bias **95**, 166
responsibility 112–13, 140
retention **64**
reticular formation **27**
retina/retinal disparity **196**
retrieval failure theory 185–6

retroactive interference 184
retrograde amnesia 185
retrospective accounts **47**
right to withdraw **112**
Rogers, Carl 18–19
role models **65**, 142
role schemas 149
roles (gender) 49–50, 64–6
rooting reflex 5
Roscoe, W. 50
Rubin's vase 199
Rutter, M. 237

S

Sallows, G. 245
Salzman, L. 223
sampling **91**, 107–10
sampling frame **108**, 109
Sanders, G.S. 131
savants **231**, **242**
scanning methods 28–9
  see also functional imaging;
    neuroimaging
Scarr, S. 38
scattergrams **101**, 102, 116
schema 71–2, **71**, 148–53
schizophrenia 23
schools of psychology 2
scripts **71**
s.d. (standard deviation) 119–21, **119**
selective breeding **4**, 38–9
selective serotonin reuptake inhibitors (SSRIs) **221**, 225
self (concept of) 18–19
self-actualisation 19–20, **19**
self-efficacy **65**
self-esteem 136, 165
self-injuring behaviour 246
self-report methods 94, 95–7, 106
self schema 149
self-serving bias 157–8, **157**
Seligman, M. 216
semantic memory 179–80, **179**
sensations 168, 191
sensitisation 207, 218
  see also desensitisation
sensory neurons 22, 23
sensory register 170
serial position effect 172
serotonin **221**, 225
sets 206–10
sex determination 42, 44–7
sex-role stereotyping 51–3, **51**, 78
sexual development 14–15, 219, 223
sexual orientation 37
shadow cue 195
Shah, A. 241
shape constancy 197

Shavitt, S. 161–2
Sherif, M. 132–3, 144–5, 163–4
Shiffrin, R. 168, 170–3
shock generator study 138–40
short-term memory (STM) 170–3, 182–5, 188
  see also working memory model
Sigmundson, H.K. 53
significance of hypotheses 85
similarity factor 176, 192
single photon emission computed tomography (SPECT) 235
situational attributions **154**, 156
situational factors, obedience 139–40
size constancy 196–7, 204
size of majority 135
Skinner, Burrhus Frederic 6–7, 8
Slabbekoorn, D. 58
Slaby, R.G. 70
SLT *see* social learning theory
Smith, C. 63
social cognition 126, 148–66
social constructs **66**
social facilitation 128–31, **128**
social identity theory 164–5, **164**
social impairments 232–3
social influence 126, 128–47, 161
social inhibition **128**
social learning theory (SLT) 10–11, 55, 61, 63–7, 72, 77, **216**
social norms 51, 140
social phobias 214, 215, 218, 225
social psychology 42, 126–67
social schemas 148–53, **148**
social support 139, 142
socialisation **51**, 55
socially desirable responses **97**
somatic nervous system 31
somatosensory area of cerebrum 25–6
sorting tasks 243
specialisation (cortical) 27–30
specific phobias 214
SPECT (single photon emission computed tomography) 235
Spencer, C.P. 135
Sperry, Roger 26
spiders, fear of 212, 215, 219
split-brain research 26
split-type drawings 208–9
SSRIs (selective serotonin reuptake inhibitors) **221**, 225
stability (gender) 68, 69–70
standard deviation (s.d.) 119–21, **119**
standardisation **88**
state-dependent forgetting 186
stereotypes 51–3, 67, 78, **150**, 163
steroids **59**

STM *see* short-term memory
Storms, M.D.   156–7
stratified sampling   109–10
stress response   32, 129, 145
structural approaches   159–60
structured interviews   95, 96
subjectivity   2
subjects   104
sublimation   16
Sugihara, Y.   50
superego   15, 16, **75**
symbolic modelling   10
sympathetic nervous system   31–2
synapses   22, **23**
syndromes   232–3, **232**
systematic desensitisation   225–6, 227
systematic sampling   108–9

Tajfel, H.   164–5
target population   107, 108
task difficulty factor   135, 137
tautological exam answers   107
temporal validity   63
testes   56, **57**
testosterone   58
texture gradient   195, **201**
theory of mind lack   238–40, 242
therapeutic programmes *see* treatments
Thorndike, Edward   6
three-component model of attitudes   159–60
three-dimensional images   191, 193
Titchener illusion   241
top-down processing   149–50, **203**, 204–5
trace decay   182–3, **182**
traits   150–1

transcripts   114
transsexuals   46
traumatic event effects   223–4
treatments   18, 221, 225–9, 244–8
triad of impairments   232–3
Triplett, Norman   126, 128
Tryon, R.C.   38–9
Tulving, E.   174, 185–6, 189
Turner's syndrome   60
twin studies   34–5, 36–7, 236–7
two-dimensional images   191, 193
two-factor theories   217

UCS (unconditioned stimuli)   217
unanimity   135
unconditioned stimuli (UCS)   217
unconscious forces   74–5
unconscious inference   197
unconscious mind   14, 74–5, 197, 228–9
Underwood, B.   184
unethical research   113
uniforms, power of   140
universal behaviour   **49**, 68
unstructured interviews   95, 96

validity   82
   experiments   89–90, 93
   observational studies   100
   qualitative data   106
   social influence research   143–4
   social learning theory   63
values   159
Van Goozen, S.M.H.   58
Vandello, J.A.   136–7
variables   84, 86–9, 91, 93–4, 101–3, 131
vicarious reinforcement   10

virtual reality exposure therapy (VRET)   226, 227
visual area of cerebrum   26
visual constancies   196–7
visual illusions   198–200, **208**, 241
visual perception   150, 191–3, 201–5
visuo-spatial scratchpad   175, 176
VRET (virtual reality exposure therapy)   226, 227
vulnerability factor   216, 223

Wada test   27–8
Watson, John Broadus   6, 8, 217
Waugh, N.   182–3
Weinberg, R.A.   38
Wernicke, Karl   24, 26, 177
Wernicke's area   177
Wertheimer, Max   191
Western society   49, 50
Wiesel, Torsten   27
Williams, J.E.   53
Wimmer, H.   238
Wing, L.   232–3
Wisconsin card sorting task   243
withdrawal from research   112
word-length effect   176
working memory model   175–8

Yarnell, P.   185
Yerkes-Dodson law   129

Zajonc, R.B.   128–9
zero correlation   102
Zubeck, J.P   39
zygotes   34